GIVING IT AWAY

ALSO BY CHARLES OSBORNE

The Gentle Planet (poems)
Platonov (play; adapted from Chekhov)
Australian Stories of Today (ed.)
Opera 66 (ed.)
Fifty Works of English Literature We Could Do Without (with Brigid Brophy and Michael Levey)
Kafka
Swansong (poems; illustrated by Sidney Nolan)
The Complete Operas of Verdi
Ned Kelly
Australia, New Zealand and the South Pacific (ed.)
Letters of Giuseppe Verdi (trans. and ed.)
The Bram Stoker Bedside Companion (ed.)
Stories and Essays by Richard Wagner (trans. and ed.)
The Concert Song Companion
Masterpieces of Nolan
Masterpieces of Drysdale
Masterpieces of Dobell
Wagner and his World
Verdi
Dictionary of Composers (ed.)
The Complete Operas of Mozart
Rigoletto ('Masterworks of Opera' series)
The Opera House Album
W. H. Auden: the Life of a Poet
Klemperer Stories (with Kenneth Thomson)
The Complete Operas of Puccini
The Life and Crimes of Agatha Christie
The Round Dance and Other Plays by Arthur Schnitzler (trans.)
The World Theatre of Wagner
How to Enjoy Opera
The Dictionary of Opera
Letter to W. H. Auden and Other Poems
Schubert and his Vienna

GIVING IT AWAY

□ □ □

The Memoirs of an Uncivil Servant

CHARLES OSBORNE

SECKER & WARBURG
LONDON

First published in England 1986 by
Martin Secker & Warburg Limited
54 Poland Street, London W1V 3DF

British Library Cataloguing in Publication Data

Osborne, Charles, 1927–
Giving it away.
1. Osborne, Charles, 1927– 2. Arts
administrators——Great Britain——Biography
3. Authors, English——20th Century——
Biography
I. Title
700′.92′4 PN149.9.08

ISBN 0–436–35401–2

Typeset, printed and bound in Great Britain
by Richard Clay (The Chaucer Press) Ltd,
Bungay, Suffolk

to the memory of my parents,
Vincent Lloyd Osborne (1896–1978)
and
Elsa Louise Osborne (1896–1978)

CONTENTS

LIST OF ILLUSTRATIONS

□ □ □

Photographs 11, 14, 15, 18 and 19 are by Ken Thomson

ACKNOWLEDGEMENTS

Some of the material in this book has appeared, not necessarily in precisely the same form, in the *London Review of Books*, the *Observer*, *The Times* and *The Times Higher Education Supplement*. I am grateful to Michèle Brandreth, whose suggestion for a title I have adopted, and to Ken Thomson, who read the typescript and from whose editorial advice I have profited.

Du musst dein Leben ändern
(You must change your life)
Rilke

Du bist am Ende was du bist
(You are, to the end, what you are)
Goethe

1

LIVING IN THE NEW WORLD

□ □ □

THE MOST DIFFICULT PART of writing one's memoirs, or writing anything else, is the beginning. One could say, quite simply, 'I was born in Brisbane on 24 November 1927,' or one could go back a century or two and talk about one's ancestors, or one could skip the date of one's birth and start somewhere around puberty, which is when one begins to have something to write about. If, as I am, one is a somewhat reclusive and secretive creature, only occasionally and imperfectly disguised as a thick-skinned self-publicist, there is an additional problem: does one want to tell anything about one's early years at all? For that matter, does one want to tell anything about any period of one's personal life?

Clearly I want to tell something, or I would not be writing these lines. But what? Is it the truth, or is it some kind of imaginative idealization of what once was true? And what, as some Biblical jester is reported to have asked, is truth? Leave that. Walk away, and start again somewhere else.

Start, then, with a different problem. Age. Timing. 'Aren't you rather young, or at least not quite old enough, to be writing your memoirs?', more than one friend or acquaintance has asked. I have a kind of answer to that. Yes, I am too young to be writing my autobiography, but not too young for a volume of memoirs. Autobiography is a summing-up of one's life, but memoirs are allowed to reflect upon simply one period or one aspect of a life. Anyway, what is young? About to enter my sixtieth year, I am young for a politician, senile for a pop singer, and fortunately ageless for a writer, even a writer who has been impersonating an arts administrator for the past twenty years.

Writing is selection. Select something and start.

I select the fact that I was an only child, and that growing up must have been a somewhat lonely process. Brisbane in the nineteen-twenties and thirties had the aspect of an overgrown country town. Its population was around three hundred thousand, its sub-tropical climate brought pleasant, mild winters which were all too short, and long, sweltering summers whose relentless sunshine was punctuated by thunderstorms which people always said would 'bring a little relief' but which never did. Or perhaps I did not recognize the kind of relief they brought. In the north of the state lay the tropical part of Queensland, the rain forests, the coral reefs, the crocodile-infested rivers, the aborigine settlements. We never dreamed of going up there. 'It isn't white man's country,' my father used to say. I found it easy to believe him, for I didn't think that even Brisbane was white man's country.

The suburb in which we lived consisted of several hills, a regular little Rome though with a different kind of architecture. The wooden houses were built on stilts. We lived in one of the bigger houses, but when I was twelve we moved a few hundred yards to a smaller one. The streets were wide, unpaved and dusty, and the only shade-giving trees were in people's back yards.

My parents, who seemed to me while they lived to be amiable but ordinary, I now perceive to have been (my mother especially) rather extraordinary, and I plan to write about them in another volume. This, meanwhile, is a book about me.

I spent my first twelve years in a house on top of a hill, with large grounds. The earth was stony. I remember no grass, only a grape vine and some ferns. I could feel the curve of the land as I pedalled across it in my red toy motor-car, and I believed that what I could feel was the earth's curvature – one of those absent-minded lies my father told me. I remember, too, my father's kisses, which tasted of what I identified years later as claret. There were roses in the front garden, but the roses I remember most clearly are those which formed the pattern on the linoleum in the kitchen. As a two-year-old I would sniff at them, intrigued by their lack of perfume. When I was four I already experienced a kind of nostalgia for the innocence of childhood, for I knew by then the difference between reality and its representation.

Shortly after my fourth birthday I began to attend the kindergarten in our suburb of Paddington. My mother took me every morning and came to bring me home again at midday. What on earth did we *Kinder* do there? Sang terrible songs, I suppose, and, oh yes, were made to eat apples. I was continually hiding apples with one reluctant bite taken out of them. To this day the apple is a fruit I do not willingly eat.

A year of this was preparation for the Petrie Terrace Girls' and Infants' School, which I began attending at the age of five. I cannot now remember at what age I ceased to be an infant and graduated to the Petrie Terrace

Boys' School, where I remained until I was fourteen, when I passed what were called the Scholarship Exams (with, I seem to recall, the highest marks for that year in the State of Queensland), and chose the Queensland State High School for my secondary education.

State High was not too bad. It was those years leading up to Seventh Grade at my primary school that were so awful. Boys whose names and faces I can still conjure up: Ronnie Johnson, Jackie Green, Frank O'Neill, Noel Kemp, Colin McIntosh, Geoffrey Pike (very fat), Norman and Edward Angel (twins). I never saw any of them again. Some were friends, some were 'enemies'. My close friend for a time was Ronnie Johnson, but how well did I know him? I've no idea whether he is now a captain of industry or a bus conductor. We all shared in the boredom of childhood, the aimless discipline of school, but our knowledge of each other was purely superficial. Children are extraordinarily self-centred.

There must, I suppose, have been a certain amount of furtive sex, but in comparison with an English public school we were disastrously chaste. Lots of talk but not much action. Smutty talk and, I suddenly remember, smutty song. Our school choir had a large repertoire of classical melodies with new words by God knows whom. *'La donna è mobile'* from *Rigoletto*, for instance, became 'Fair shines the moon tonight . . .' But a sophisticate amongst the boy sopranos taught the rest of us even newer words. *'La donna è mobile'* became 'Little boys are half-a-crown,/Standing up or lying down./Bigger boys are seven-and-six,/They take the larger pricks . . .' And, as we paraded to the tune of the Colonel Bogey March, several of the bolder spirits amongst us were singing 'Hitler – has only got one ball;/ Goering – has two, but very small./ Himmler – has something sim'lar,/And Doctor Goebbels has no balls at all.'

Was it not Mark Twain who said that truth was so precious a commodity it should be used only sparingly? Enough of these childhood truths, then. They have, in any case, a limited appeal to other people unless they are used fictionally and imaginatively. The essential truth of my childhood is that it was lonely. Perhaps it would have been, in any case, but I think that my loneliness was exacerbated by my mother's fierce determination to keep me away from every other child in the neighbourhood. She regarded them all, no doubt rightly, as ghastly urchins who would contaminate her little angel.

Her little angel consoled himself by learning certain skills on his own, away from school. I taught myself to read, way beyond the childish pap we were fed at school, by studying my father's newspaper every morning and asking him the meaning and pronunciation of unfamiliar words. From this I progressed to books, and before long I was able to astonish my eight-year-old contemporaries by reading quickly and fluently to them paragraphs from some 'grown-up' book (I remember using Ruskin's *Sesame and Lilies* for this shameful purpose) while they were floundering in *Rumpelstiltskin* or whatever. Of course, I had no real understanding of what I was rattling off, but it infuriated the other little buggers, which was the object of the exercise.

When I was not showing off, I made a more respectable use of my reading skill. There was a complete set of Dickens in the house, and I methodically ploughed through it. There were a number of 'popular classics' in cheap editions, and these too I devoured. Later, the first Penguin paperbacks began to appear, pink covers for straight fiction and green for murder mysteries, and I bought as many as I could afford. I do not remember ever reading a children's book – I saw no point in them – but my choice of adult novels was wide and undiscriminating. I loved going to the cinema, usually with my mother; but, if a film I had enjoyed was based on a novel, I insisted on the book being procured for me: *Dr Jekyll and Mr Hyde*, *Goodbye, Mr Chips*, *The Thin Man*, *The Last Days of Pompeii*, *The Count of Monte Cristo*, *Anthony Adverse* – no 'book of the film' escaped me.

I also taught myself to play the piano. I must have been four or five when I clambered onto the piano stool and began, so the family story went, to pick out with one finger the melody of 'God Save the King' in C major. A patriotic beginning, but after I had discovered the delights of chords it was the popular tunes of the day that I preferred. Shirley Temple numbers played a prominent part in my repertoire. But I would also listen to 'serious' music on the radio, or on the gramophone, and then produce my own version, usually in C, F or G, on the piano. Strauss waltzes, the 'Moonlight' Sonata, Chopin preludes and *études*, all were grist to my pianistic mill. I could not read any of the music stacked away in the piano stool, nor was I at all interested when my parents sat at the piano. Stupidly, they chose to regard the facility I soon acquired as merely a party trick. They did not send me to a piano teacher, and it did not occur to me to ask them to do so until I was twelve. By then, of course, I had been playing 'by ear', as my parents used proudly to say, for some years and had acquired very bad habits. I found it immensely difficult to unlearn all I had been doing and to start again with tedious exercises.

However, I persevered throughout my teens, exhausting a number of teachers in the process. There are three whom I remember with affection and gratitude: Ken Best, who had ears like Dumbo and patience to match; Archie Day, who played the organ at the principal Methodist Church in Brisbane; and Rosa Horwitz, who had once taught Eileen Joyce. I learned most about music, as distinct from piano technique, from Archie, who knew that I would never become a concert pianist but recognized my feeling for music. He lent me scores, books, gramophone records, encouraged me to go to concerts and recitals, and pointed me in all the right directions.

There was a fourth piano teacher, whom I remember with affection but not much gratitude. She was Irene Fletcher, who was in her eighties and who had been a pupil of Clara Schumann. I went to her because I liked the idea of a link with Schumann, but Irene was a dedicated member of the local branch of the Communist Party and no longer much interested in the past. She didn't care how badly I played Schumann's *Kinderszenen*: all she wanted to do was talk of the revolution which she was convinced was imminent.

For a time, during the war years, I played the harmonium at the local Methodist Church and Sunday school. (My mother, who was friendly with the preacher, had sold me into this slavery.) I now have a wide repertoire of Moody and Sankey gospel hymns which I tend to play or sing at the drop of a surplice – 'The Old Rugged Cross', 'Shall We Gather at the River?', 'What a Friend We Have in Jesus' – and I can still hear those shrill little Aussie kids' voices, screeching out the depressing message of

Jesus bids us shine with a clear, pure light,
Like a little candle, burning in the night.
In this world of darkness, so we must shine,
You in your small corner, and I in mine.

It was from records played on a wind-up gramophone that I learned much of the standard orchestral repertoire. Concerts were few and far between in the Brisbane of those days, probably no more than five or six a year, given in the Town Hall by the local symphony orchestra. There were also recitals by visiting 'celebrity artists', again perhaps a half-dozen a year, but it was from the gramophone that I first heard Mahler's *Das Lied von der Erde*, played by the Vienna Philharmonic under Bruno Walter; Beethoven sonatas played by Schnabel and Gieseking, of whom I preferred the latter; the Schubert E flat Trio (Op. 100 we called it, before we knew Otto Erich Deutsch and his Schubert catalogue) played by Rudolf Serkin and the Busch brothers; and opera.

There were no live performances of opera in Brisbane. But on the gramophone there were Lotte Lehmann, Elisabeth Schumann, Maria Olczewska and Richard Mayr in *Der Rosenkavalier*; Helge Roswaenge, Erna Berger, Tiana Lemnitz and Gerhard Hüsch in *Die Zauberflöte*, conducted by

Beecham; Act I of *Die Walküre* with Lehmann and Melchior under Bruno Walter. And there were arias from the Verdi and Puccini operas, sung by Björling, Schipa, Caruso, Melba, Lawrence Tibbett and scores of other wonderful singers. Georges Thill sang Wagner in French, Tauber sang Verdi and Puccini in German, Gigli sang Bizet and Massenet in Italian. To this day I can still sing, or croak, most of those arias in their wrong languages (and transposed down a third): *'Mon cygne aimé'* from *Lohengrin*, *'Freundlich blick' ich'* from *Rigoletto*, *'Salve dimora casta e pura'* from *Faust.*

The world of the German Lied opened up to me, too: Hüsch in Schumann's *Dichterliebe* and the Schubert cycles; Kipnis in the *Vier Ernste Gesänge* of Brahms; the erotic voice and poetic artistry of Richard Tauber in Schubert, Schumann, Brahms and Strauss, and for that matter in everything else from Handel's *'Ombra mai fu'* to Haydn Wood's 'A Brown Bird Singing'.

If my hands were too small for me to become a concert pianist, perhaps I could be a singer. Heavens above, I already was a singer. I'd sung solos with the wretched school choir as a boy soprano, and in 1938, at the age of eleven, I had turned myself into a boy tenor, and won the Bobby Breen Singing Competition by singing that child star's hit song, 'Rainbow on the River', from the film of that name, at the Tivoli Roof Garden in Brisbane. (Bobby Breen was a Hollywood child star, a kind of male Shirley Temple, and my exact contemporary. Where are you now, Bobby Breen?)

Sitting at the piano, I used to sing Lieder and Mozart arias in the gravelly bass-baritone (range F to F) I was left with after puberty. At the age of eighteen I found my first singing teacher. His name was Vido Luppi, and he was an Italian baritone in, I suppose, his late fifties. (On the screen he would have been played by Fortunio Bonanova.) For months I persevered with Vaccai exercises until one day Vido allowed me to attempt Pergolesi's 'Nina'. I sang it well enough to progress to other *arie antiche.* But 'Avoid opera,' Vido instructed me. 'Your voice is not big enough.'

As singing teachers go, Vido could have been worse. He knew about the placement of the voice, but he was really very unmusical. He played the piano atrociously and he had no sense of rhythm whatsoever. I came to the conclusion that he was something of a fraud, mainly because he was continually reminiscing to me and his other pupils about his dear colleague, the world-famous Italian tenor, Tito Schipa. He and Schipa, he said, had as young men shared the same teacher, and they were still close friends. Schipa, a most elegant and musical tenor, was one of my idols, and I wanted to believe that my singing teacher was his friend. However, what made this difficult was a photograph, proudly displayed in the studio, of Vido Luppi and Tito Schipa together. It was so obviously faked. Two separate studio portraits had been placed side by side and re-photographed.

I had been Vido's pupil for some months when an announcement appeared in the local morning newspaper, the *Courier-Mail*, to the effect that Tito Schipa was engaged upon a tour of Australia and that he would give a recital in Brisbane. The delight I anticipated at hearing the great tenor in person was tempered with acute embarrassment on Vido's behalf. How would he explain that he was not able to introduce any of us to his 'great friend', who, I was now convinced, had never heard of him?

As the date of Schipa's arrival approached, Vido seemed unperturbed. And, finally, one day Schipa actually turned up at the studio to hear one of Vido's sopranos. He and Vido greeted each other like long-lost brothers. Schipa promised to return to Brisbane at the end of his tour, and participate in a recital of Vido's most promising pupils. I was not considered good enough to be included, and sat in the audience listening to Vido and his favourite soprano in *'La cì darem la mano'*, and Vido (solo) in a terrible performance of Giordani's *'Caro mio ben'*, in which he sang through all the rests, to the consternation of his pianist. The great Schipa sang Scarlatti arias like an angel, and then shouted his way through Neapolitan songs.

Vido Luppi was only the first of many teachers who attempted to make a singer of me. There was a contralto, Bessie Dougall; an elderly, ex-Sydney Conservatorium professor called Hugh Neville Smith; later, in Melbourne, a lyric baritone, Frank Laslett; and, the only really distinguished singer amongst them, Browning Mummery, a tenor who had retired after a respectable career in England and America. He had sung Rodolfo to Melba's Mimi at her Covent Garden farewell in 1926. Browning Mummery, a kindly man, persevered with me for two or three terms before advising me to, so to speak, diversify. I had already revealed some talent for the stage, so he suggested I should look to operetta and musical comedy rather than to opera or concert song. He had heard me play the piano: perhaps I should concentrate on that. I would certainly make a good teacher, in due course, and had I considered a career in music criticism? Mr Mummery was clearly desperate.

I remain grateful to Browning Mummery for having stopped me from wasting my money on any more singing lessons. I still have the twelve-inch 78 rpm record he made, around 1930, with the superb dramatic soprano Florence Austral, of duets from *Il trovatore*. Was it true, I asked him, that Florence Austral had undertaken to sing the mezzo-soprano part of Azucena in *'Ai nostri monti'* at a few minutes' notice because the mezzo had failed to arrive? It was not true. Austral, he said, could sing virtually anything, and they had planned to record both duets. (Years later, in the 1960s, I helped raise money for Florence Austral when she was terminally ill and in straitened circumstances. It was through those records with Mummery that I had first come to know and love her rich, warm voice.)

What was I really interested in as a child? As a teenager I became a singer *manqué*, a poet and critic and, in due course, an actor. But had any of these activities, or the possibility of them, even occurred to me as a child? I think not. It is not easy to remember what did occupy my thoughts in pre-pubertal years. Messing about at the piano was fun, showing off my reading skills was almost equally enjoyable. But if my parents, observing me from their adult distance, had been asked, 'What does your little boy want to do when he grows up?', would they have known how to answer?

I remember quite clearly how I answered when the question was put to me at school, during an art class. (I was never any good at 'art': my landscapes always looked like fried eggs.) 'I want you all,' Mr Lawson said to the class, 'to draw for me what you see yourselves doing at the age of forty.' What a thing to ask twelve-year-olds to do. Most of them produced crayon drawings of various kinds of worthy activity, driving a locomotive, sitting behind a desk or flying an aeroplane. I drew a tombstone in pastel shades, with the inscription: 'Here lies Charles Osborne, 1927–1967.' 'Unnecessarily morbid, Osborne,' Mr Lawson commented, 'but no doubt prophetic.'

It suddenly occurs to me that the cinema was my only real interest during my years at school. Very early in life I became a Hollywood addict, introduced to the drug by my mother, who used to take me to see the most unsuitable films. She was fond of murder mysteries, especially if they were frightening. Murder-cum-horror, I suppose, would be the category. One of the earliest films I can remember was a spooky murder mystery, *While the Patient Slept*, based, I think, on a novel by Mignon G. Eberhart. Another was the Fredric March version of *Dr Jekyll and Mr Hyde*, during which I hid under the seat whenever Hyde was struggling to emerge from Jekyll.

By the time I was old enough to take myself to the Saturday *matinée* at the Paddington Theatre (cinemas are still called theatres in Australia), I was a fan of the cowboys: Tom Mix, William Boyd ('Hopalong Cassidy') and Buck Jones; the adventure heroes: Tarzan (Johnny Weissmuller), Flash Gordon (Larry 'Buster' Crabbe), Mandrake the Magician (but who played Mandrake, could it have been Warren William?); and, somewhat improbably, the suave romantic leads such as William Powell, Cary Grant, Carole Lombard, Irene Dunne and Kay Francis. I even liked the villains, particularly Charles Middleton, who played most of them and who was especially memorable as Ming the Merciless in the Flash Gordon serials. I also became fond of Asta, the wire-haired terrier who appeared with William Powell and Myrna Loy in the 'Thin Man' films. (This is why one of the two people I now live with is a wire-haired terrier named Asta.)

Most of all, though, I loved Laurel and Hardy. And I still do. They received no adult critical attention until their careers were over and one of them, Oliver Hardy, was dead. Then, slowly, they were admitted to the hall of comic fame where Chaplin reigned supreme. It became respectable for grown-ups to enjoy Laurel and Hardy when I was approaching the age of thirty. But I had never ceased to enjoy them. On my first visit to California, some time in the late 1950s, I walked up and down outside Stan Laurel's apartment block in Santa Monica, hoping he would appear so that I could stage a casual encounter.

By then I had actually seen him and Ollie on stage. It must have been in 1953 or 1954, on their last visit to Britain. They were top of the bill at the Finsbury Park Empire, and they appeared in two sketches, one in each half of the variety programme. The first sketch was a Feydeau-like affair involving much split-second timing with the doors in a hotel suite, and the second was a version of one of their two-reel films, *County Hospital*, in which Ollie is the patient, his leg gigantic in plaster, and Stan comes to visit him bringing a gift of – to Oliver's disgust – hard-boiled eggs and nuts. They were both old and tired, Stan in particular looked terribly lined and ill, and they were only intermittently funny. But they received a rapturous reception from the audience, because we were there not to be amused but to be reminded of our childhood, and to salute the two lovable clowns who had helped us to endure the growing-up process. We sat there, smiles of affectionate reminiscence on our faces.

Joe E. Brown was another comedian who whiled away those Saturday afternoons in the thirties with me. And Wheeler and Wolsey, a team whose films are never revived. There was Shirley Temple, of course, a great tragic actress whatever Graham Greene may have written. 'Oh please, don't take me away from Grandpa, *please*,' she was continually pleading, whenever she was not being plumply cute in song and dance. What was her attraction for me, her exact contemporary? Did I think, 'When I grow up I want to be a child molester, and I'll begin with *her*?' I certainly did not want to emulate her: in my fantasies I was usually the misunderstood friend of the hero, falsely accused of something or other but finally vindicated and thus becoming the hero.

Shirley Temple was pretty. But I was equally fond of her plain rival,

Jane Withers. The male child stars were of less interest to me. Freddie Bartholomew, two or three years my senior, I considered a frightful sissy, which was odd and unfair of me. Unfair because he was no sissy, he was merely an English boy in American films; odd because my schoolmates' perception of me was as an affected pseudo-Freddie Bartholomew with a pommy accent. (I had nothing of the kind: I simply never learned to pick up that lazy nasal drawl which Australians go in for.)

Judy Garland was something else. I fell in love with her in *The Wizard of Oz* and remained faithful through to the last, sad years, three decades later. But she essentially belongs to my teenage years, years which she shared with Bette Davis and Katharine Hepburn, Fredric March and Henry Fonda. In her particular *Fach*, she was as remarkable and as affecting a singer as Gerhard Hüsch. As for Mae West, I think I realized from the age of seven that she was George Raft in drag.

I went off the cowboys and Indians quite early. By the time those terrible people like Gene Autry and Roy Rogers began to make movies at the end of the thirties, usually for tatty companies such as Republic or Monogram, I had ceased gracing the Western with my presence. I had become a snob about Hollywood studios, too. MGM, Paramount, Twentieth Century-Fox, Warner Brothers and United Artists, they were the really classy producers of films. Universal and RKO-Radio were runners up, and Columbia was in there, somewhere, as well. When Nelson Eddy moved from MGM to Universal for *The Phantom of the Opera*, I thought it was the beginning of the end. When, subsequently, he appeared in a film for Republic, *End of the Rainbow*, I knew he was on the skids ('down the tube', as a friend in Las Vegas much later taught me to say). It was then that he began to tour night clubs, his film career a thing of the past.

I bitterly regretted the passing of the old studio system. Now, whenever I am in Los Angeles, I make a point of walking past Paramount and what used to be RKO next door, and Warners, and Twentieth Century-Fox (though multi-storied office blocks have sprouted up on what used to be their back lot), and Universal, and of course MGM, though it is a bit off the beaten track, and I usually just drive past it on my way to visit my good friend the novelist Joseph Hansen.

I could, as they say, write a book about the cinema and my childhood. But it had better not be this book.

The reality of my childhood, then, was a reality of the imagination. Just as real to me as the dusty streets I walked to school were those parts of suburban Los Angeles where they shot the Laurel and Hardy two-reelers, or those few well-worn acres of Arizona over which Buck Jones was continually chasing cattle rustlers, or the Gothic castle behind whose walls Dr Frankenstein was forever experimenting. The poetry I had to read aloud in class at school, all that Lars Porsena stuff, and the ranks of Tuscany (who cared whether they could scarce forbear to cheer or not?), and that Dame Mary bloody Gilmour, even worse, what was all that compared to Maria Ouspenskaya's incantation: 'Even the man who is pure at heart/And who says his prayers at night/May become a wolf when the wolfbane blooms/And the autumn moon is bright'? Forty years later, my friend Ken Thomson said casually to me over supper, 'I had lunch with an old guy from Hollywood today, a writer-director called Curt Siodmak. He made a lot of those horror films for Universal. Says he once wrote a piece of doggerel for one of them, "Even the man who is . . ."' I finished the quotation for him, and gazed at my friend as I would at someone who had once seen Shelley plain.

Childhood was also a time of being constantly lied to by adults, not only one's parents and teachers but virtually every adult whom one encountered. Why do they do it? If I had ever had children, would I have done it too? I have in front of me a certificate, issued by the Queensland Band of Hope. A Temperance Pledge it purports to be, but the pledge that I appear to have signed reads: 'I promise, God helping me, to abstain from all intoxicating liquors as beverages.' Not temperance but abstinence. I am, as it happens, a temperate drinker, but I began to drink wine at the age of twelve, only four years after signing that pledge at the age of eight. How, I wonder, was I bullied or cajoled into signing it? And who can have imagined that a pledge extracted from an eight-year-old child could possibly have any effect upon his adult behaviour? What was in it for the adult who contrived to get my neat, round signature on that piece of paper? The adult in question seems to have been one A. V. Webb, Secretary of the Queensland Band of Hope, who has appended his own signature to the statement that 'the person who has signed this pledge has also signed the pledge register'. You were at best a misguided fellow, A. V. Webb, and at worst a miserable old wowser. But you were only one of a vast army of adults who knew best, who only did things for one's own good, who in fact remembered how miserable their own childhoods had been made by adults and were determined to perpetuate the process.

I think, though I cannot be certain, that I got the better of you, you adult ogres of my first twelve years of existence. If I did, it may well be because my parents never really aided or abetted you. The sins of my parents towards me were those of omission rather than commission, and thus they avoided pushing me in any particular direction. I think my father would have liked me to become a solicitor, and I know my mother would have been overjoyed to see me comfortably settled as a professor (of anything) at Queensland University. But they were averse to coercion.

Partly as a consequence of their attitude and partly because of my own temperament, which was introverted though not too distressingly so, I went through childhood in my own private way, hardly noticing what went on above my head. I look now at newspaper clippings which I salvaged from my parents' house after they died eight years ago, clippings which fail to conjure up any mental image. The absurd social column of the *Telegraph* of 4 April 1942 tells me that 'Mr and Mrs Osborne (Paddington) are staying in Sydenham'. Where was Sydenham? Somewhere on the coast, I suppose. I was in my fifteenth year, I must have been with them. But the family holidays I do remember were all at Southport or Surfers' Paradise.

Another clipping, undated but perhaps from the late twenties, when I was a baby, is perplexing to me. Did my parents really indulge in these dreadful pursuits? I am embarrassed enough at being reminded that the house was called 'Bon Vue' (not even Bonne Vue):

> A pleasant evening was spent on Saturday evening last at the residence of Mr and Mrs V. Osborne, Bon Vue. Mr & Miss Eaton played several choice selections on the pianoforte and violin respectively, and was [*sic*] well appreciated. Messrs Hargraves and Jackson caused great fun and merriment in their various recitations. Songs were rendered by the Misses Smith and Eaton. A dainty supper was then served in the dining-room, after which games and music were again indulged in, when the merry party dispersed. The guests included Misses Jackson, Treger, Eaton, Harrison, Cootes and Haysom, and Messrs Eaton, Smith, Jackson, Hargraves, Harrison and others.

I remember no such awful musical evenings. I do remember, after a fashion, some fairly dreadful things from my childhood, but my truthful recollection of them is now spoiled by my having romanticized them in a novel I wrote recently, and then put aside: *The Pink Danube*. They are now set in my mind in their fictionalized form, and I am either unable or unwilling to retrace my steps and peer behind that safety curtain of fiction. I shall, instead, resort to the habit of self-borrowing which was indulged in so creatively by, among others, Bach, Handel, Rossini, Donizetti and Schubert, and lift, for instance, my next few paragraphs from *The Pink Danube*, a book which, after all, I may decide to suppress.

Most teen-age crises are caused either by sex or by religion or, more frequently, by one masquerading as the other. And it is when experiences present themselves in disguise that life can appear to be puzzlingly, idiotically cruel. By the time one has become an adult, the unwanted and hateful confidence imposed by the process of enduring does at least enable one to smile tolerantly at the sight of friends posing as enemies or (again, more frequently) *vice versa.* At fourteen, however, one is terrified of masks.

I never had any trouble with religion, for I could never understand, except imaginatively (and then only with the greatest effort) and momentarily, the need for it. But, hating to feel I was missing out on a dramatic experience, since so many of my schoolfriends were indulging in emotional crises in which they claimed they were losing their faith, I really did try very hard to acquire a faith, in order that I too might, in a blinding flash, undergo an anti-Pauline conversion and lose it again. However, it was not to be. I had been conducted through childhood by my parents in the belief that one should try to make life as pleasant as possible for oneself and, therefore, for others; that selfishness was self-defeating; and that, as Dr Johnson had claimed, the arts helped one, depending on one's temperament, either to enjoy life more intensely or to endure it more easily. When I reached my fourteenth birthday, my father said to me: 'You are of an age now to reason for yourself. Many people lean on a religion to help them through life. You should begin to read about the various religions, and perhaps sample at first hand those which have churches or temples in Brisbane.'

So I put away such childish things as Jane Austen, Thomas Mann, Dostoevsky, Goethe, Heine, Stendhal and Shakespeare, and turned to the holy books about Jehovah, Christ, Mohammed, the Buddha and others. And I was taken by my father to a succession of church services, some of them very strange indeed. None appealed to me as having any relevance to my life, or to life in general, and the saddest of them all, I thought, were the various Protestant meetings, which put me in mind of the rude mechanicals in *A Midsummer Night's Dream.* 'What hempen homespuns have we swaggering here?' I would murmur as some mindless Methodist intoned his meaningless illiteracies.

I realized, much later in life when I came to know Vienna, that if I had been brought up in that infuriating and so greatly loved city, and taken my religion at Fischer von Erlach's *Karlskirche* with large doses of Haydn, Mozart and Schubert masses, I might have been hooked. But there were no orchestras in Brisbane's architecturally undistinguished churches, only organs. Today I can hardly bear to listen to that most vulgar, imprecise and unmusical of instruments.

For months, however, despite the nonsense which I used dutifully to contemplate week after week in the places of worship of Catholics, Jews, Anglicans, Methodists, Baptists, Presbyterians, Congregationalists, Seventh Day Adventists, Rosicrucians, Spiritualists, Buddhists, yes, and even the Rationalists, I continued to pray to be given a faith which I could discover no reason to acquire. The ear of God remained deaf. 'Bugger off, then,' I shouted to the Almighty at last, 'I don't need you.' And failed even to give myself the slightest *frisson* in so doing. No, I was never in any serious danger from religion, for which the Gods be thanked. My teenage crisis was a sexual one (and there, at least, is a real problem), and my first two experiences, in which I was messed about with by adults, came near to turning me off sex for life. Well, perhaps I exaggerate.

Mr Ross (I am not using real names for these adults) I remember now as an attractive twenty-two-year-old. But to me at fourteen he was simply one of my teachers at school and an adult male of indeterminate age. He conducted the school choir of which I was a member and for which, when Mr Wentworth was too drunk to perform, I occasionally played the piano. Mr Ross used also to be in charge of a group which met after school hours, called the Crusaders. He tried, unsuccessfully, to persuade me to join his Crusaders. I wonder now what they used to get up to: ostensibly they were some kind of pious religious group.

One sticky summer's day, Mr Ross turned up for choir practice wearing shorts. He was a tall, slim, fair young man, amiable of countenance and with a good figure. Some of us sniggered conventionally as he entered the music room that day in his khaki shorts, for we were not used to seeing our teachers wear, even in the hottest weather, anything but three-piece suits. It was I alone whom Mr Ross picked on. 'What's the matter, Osborne?' he asked. 'Don't you like my legs?'

I didn't think he expected an answer. I smiled primly and looked at the floor.

'Well?'

'Yes, sir.'

'Oh, you do. I'm flattered.'

The choir laughed, I blushed, and a few moments later we all launched into Mr Ross's own dreadful arrangement of the first movement of the 'Moonlight' Sonata, which we sang to limp verses provided by a Queensland poet.

It so happened that Mr Ross had arranged for me to stay behind after choir practice that day, not for a meeting of his mouldy old Crusaders, but to profit from his private voice coaching. I had entered for another singing competition, and he had offered to help me, as my voice had been for some weeks uneasily poised between silvery boy tenor and croaky adolescent baritone.

In due course the rest of the choir was dismissed and I remained behind with Mr Ross, who hitched his short shorts higher, sat at the upright piano, which was badly in need of tuning, and showed me how to render 'Oh, Promise Me'. School was over for the day, and we were probably the only people in that wing of the building.

After fifteen minutes or so of my pathetic fourteen-year-old's imitation of Nelson Eddy, Mr Ross stopped playing. 'You've quite a pleasant voice, Osborne,' he said. 'And you're a very attractive boy.' From the way he had been looking at me as I sang, I guessed what was on his mind. Though I had not experimented sexually with other boys, my theoretical knowledge was considerable. (We talked a lot, and the more daring of us smoked Capstans.) 'This is it,' I thought. I felt curious, frightened, powerful: the possibility of simply saying 'No' never occurred to me.

Mr Ross, still seated at the piano, had swivelled round on his seat. Taking my arm, he gently pulled me towards him. He placed his hands on my hips and smiled at me. I was surprised that he was not being more circumspect, and I worried momentarily that perhaps it was obvious to all, boys and masters alike, that this was the kind of lad I potentially was. But he looked so pleasant and friendly that I smiled back. I knew I was rushing towards something, but I wondered in that same moment what his first name was. I knew only an initial. H. Harold? Hector? He pressed his head against my chest, and involuntarily I put my right hand on his shoulder, and slowly stroked his blondish, curly hair with my left hand. It was, I suppose, a gesture of despairing tenderness. I did not feel sexually aroused. I was by now in a state of excited terror, and my ears were ringing. But to have stood passively, my hands by my side, would have seemed inadequate. Harold-Hector Ross's arms were around my waist now. He squeezed, and his head stayed pressed to my chest. 'It's up to me,' I knew in a flash. 'He's as frightened as I am.' And I wanted to comfort him. 'It's all right,' I whispered hoarsely.

I closed my eyes and imagined it was Vivien Leigh whose hair I was stroking. No. No, Hedy Lamarr. Yes, Hedy Lamarr. She was beautiful and she needed me. Though she was perhaps ten years older than I, we loved each other deeply, and I wanted nothing more than to protect her from the cruelties life had inflicted upon her. She breathed heavily, and I could feel that with one hand she appeared to be adjusting her dress. 'It's all right,' I murmured again. She took my left arm and guided my hand downwards, rising from her piano stool as she did so. I opened my eyes and found I was grasping her large, uncircumcised cock. 'Sir!' I squawked indignantly, involuntarily. It was the first erect prick, other than my own, that I had seen. I quickly let go, but it continued to menace me like a none too steadily aimed revolver.

Mr Ross immediately realized he had made a wrong move. Pulling me closer, he sat again, looking into my face yearningly, stretching upward and drawing me down to him. I closed my eyes again, our cheeks brushed, and then Hedy's lips found mine. We kissed. Awkwardly, tremblingly at first. Her tongue forced my lips apart; her mouth tasted neither of claret like my father's, nor of lipstick and tobacco like my mother's, but of peppermint. While her right arm held me close, her left hand was fumbling at the flies of my trousers. The buzzing in my ears returned, intensified. I kept my eyes shut. But when her hand closed on my cock, I felt strangely relaxed. She drew it out. 'Is she looking at it?' I wondered. 'I hope she likes it.' She began to play gently with it, and slowly it blossomed and rose under her touch. Our mouths gulped for air and came together again. Farewell, 'Oh, Promise Me'. Instead, the music my mother used to sing at the piano pulsated in my ears, in my throbbing prick. *'O sink hernieder, Nacht der Liebe.'*

Hedy's fingers continued to manipulate me rhythmically. Her face left mine and slowly moved down towards my thighs. Loosening my belt, she tugged at my trousers till they fell to my ankles. She knelt before me. Her lips formed into a circle and wrapped themselves around my cock. Her head now took up the rhythm abandoned by her fingers. She paused occasionally when her lips reached my pubic hair; my cock must have been tickling the top of her throat. Then she took up the rhythm again. I too, began to move, in and out, as I felt the sperm rising within me. I exploded into her mouth as the music in my ears swelled, *'in des Welt-Atems wehendem Allertrinken, versinken – unbewusst – höchste Lust'*, and I groaned, 'He – dy.'

There was a sound as of gulping. Then, 'Pardon?' said the voice of Mr Ross.

I cannot pretend that I did not find that episode of furtive sex exciting and, yes, enjoyable. But, unsurprisingly, it left me feeling not only dissatisfied but also curiously guilty. I say 'curiously' because I could not then, and cannot now, discover any reason for guilt. Still, although my feeling of guilt may have been curious, it was not entirely inexplicable. Even though I personally had escaped being brought up to accept the conventional Christian sense of original sin which blights so many lives, I was, after all, part of a society which, certainly in Australia in the nineteen-thirties and -forties, still superstitiously accepted original sin and various other taboos. And this common consciousness had tainted me slightly, though fortunately I possessed an intelligence sufficiently independent to resist, if not entirely to overcome, its influence.

I state this glibly now, but of course it took me months to arrive, at the age of fourteen, at such self-knowledge. At first I lived with my guilt without understanding it. Mr Ross appeared to assume that, having failed to repulse that first onslaught, I would be available to him from time to time for similar, perhaps more adventurous encounters. In this assumption he was mistaken. I did, after the first shock had subsided, occasionally experiment, but only with other boys at school. With Mr Ross my manner became increasingly formal, even, dare I say it?, priggish. After I had refused two further invitations to stay behind after school for private coaching, he got the message and stopped asking me.

It is not my intention to record here the details of my pragmatic sex education. For one thing, a natural reticence inhibits me; for another, I find few descriptions more tedious than those of sex. There is, after all, a limited number of acts one can perform, however inventive one may be; and to go on recounting them over and over, merely altering the names of the other people, would quickly induce boredom both in oneself and one's readers. I shall, however, have to mention one more sexual experience which, together with the Mr Ross incident, contributed to my adolescent crisis. I have already mentioned that I came near to having a permanent distaste for sex inculcated in me by my being made the plaything of two adults. The twenty-two-year-old H. Ross was the first of these. About fifteen months later, at the age of fifteen, I succumbed to the somewhat more mature advances of my second adult and my first female, Anna Kunz.

Frau Kunz, a widow whose husband had last been heard of in the concentration camp of Theresienstadt, was a Viennese Jewess in her late thirties. She was a close friend of my mother, and came frequently to our house. In Vienna she had studied piano. Brisbane, however, was unable to support her as pianist or music teacher, so she had gone into the rag trade. During the war years she owned and personally managed three boutiques, two in Brisbane and one in Surfers' Paradise on the Pacific coast, some sixty miles south of the city. Sometimes my parents and I, more often only my mother and I, went to stay with Anna at her beach house just outside Surfers' Paradise. Once, when my parents were holidaying in the Blue Mountains in New South Wales, Anna invited me alone to spend a long weekend with her at the beach. I accepted without a qualm. She was a close friend of my mother.

There had always existed between Anna and me a degree of flirtation, a kind of silly family joke which arose from her Viennese love of *'Küss' die Hand, gnädige Frau'* and all that stuff – polite *galanterie* at symphony concerts, formal greetings when my mother and I met her at Basil's, Brisbane's one coffee house, run by another European refugee, *'Spanische Tuerei'.*

Anna was an elegant woman, with black hair which she wore short, and brown eyes which she wore big, using them to great expressive effect. Now her eyes were tender, now playful, now mocking, now bigger than ever in pretended surprise, bigger even than Luise Rainer's. Sometimes, when she thought she was unobserved, they could be narrowed to calculation point, or left half-open as she listlessly contemplated a past too tragic for deep feeling.

She was known to have lovers, and they were usually men younger than she. Her affairs tended to last for a few months before, on her part, boredom set in. I knew all this because Anna made a confidante of my mother, who revealed most of her friend's secrets to me. The current lover was Brian Tatley, a radio announcer and one of the earliest of that breed, at least in Australia, to refer to himself, *à l'Américaine*, as a disc jockey: a squat, round-faced young man. Brian used often to come to Anna's beach house for an overnight visit while my mother and I were there. But, during the four days I was to spend with Anna in my parents' absence, it was understood that Brian would not be putting in an appearance. He was broadcasting during the entire weekend.

I caught a train on the Friday afternoon, immediately after leaving school, and by early evening I was in Surfers' Paradise, where Anna was waiting outside the station in her little red Renault. We drove eight miles south along the coast to the eccentric yet rather cosy house she had designed for herself, only a few yards from the white sandy beach and the blue Pacific ocean. The house itself, a good half-mile distant from its nearest neighbour, was made partly of brick, partly of wood, and painted white. It was a fort-like structure, a hollow rectangle whose eastern side, consisting of a long living-*cum*-dining room and kitchen, faced onto the ocean, of which it offered an uninterrupted view through the plate-glass window which ran the entire length of the house. Four bedrooms, two of them with bathrooms *en suite*, a library, and another bathroom occupied the other three sides, while the interior of the rectangle was simply a private sunning beach, open to the sky. A wooden verandah ran round this courtyard of sand, onto which all of the rooms directly opened.

It was getting dark as we arrived. Anna put her car away in the garage, which she had deliberately sited about a hundred yards away in a hollow, so that it was hidden from the house by sand dunes. I went inside, dumped my suitcase in my corner bedroom, and walked along the verandah into the big east room to look at the ocean. I loved the sky and the sea here. On summer nights the dark blue heavens would mysteriously lower themselves almost to within touching distance, and the sky, Damoclean with stars, would hover in what I felt to be an exquisite menace. I loved those oppressive nights when my parents, Anna and Brian (or whoever the lover of the month happened to be) would sit talking and drinking after dinner in the room with its long, uncurtained window, while I lay out on the beach in the darkness, listening to the sea, looking up at the surely tangible richness of the sky, only vaguely conscious of the lighted warmth of the room and the occasional friendly sound of laughter.

I had always been at home in this house and, although I had never stayed in it alone with Anna before, I felt at home now. She was so much a part of our family circle that I, an only child, almost thought of her as a much older sister. In fact she was, though she certainly didn't look it, quite old enough to have been my mother.

Anna joined me in the living room. *'Etwas zu trinken, Lieberl?'* ('Something to drink, darling?'), she asked. At fifteen I drank only wine. 'The usual, please.' The usual was a white wine from Gumpoldskirchen which Anna contrived to get cheaply from a warehouse which had imported far too much of it just before the war, and now dared not advertise it. Anna always claimed she could not accustom her palate to Australian wine. It was a harmless snobbery: really it was not even that, but nostalgia for Vienna, for the *spritzig* Austrian wine kept her in touch, or in taste, with the old days before the *Anschluss* when life meant Schubert, Mahler, the State Opera, and a *Stammtisch* (regular table) at the tiny Café Hawelka in the Dorotheergasse; not sun and sand and nasal Aussie accents.

I opened the bottle Anna had taken from the refrigerator. She poured the wine, and we sat in armchairs looking out at the white surf playing on the darkening beach, and at the first stars to pierce the approach of night.

That first evening was relaxed and uneventful. After supper, which consisted of a *Kalte Platte* followed by Anna's version of *Linzertorte*, we took a walk along the beach for nearly a mile. When we returned to the house, we decided to have a gentle splash in the surf. Afterwards we lay on the still warm beach until we were dry, came back to the house, showered in our respective bathrooms and drank a final glass of wine while we listened to a Mozart Divertimento on the gramophone. Then, pleasantly drowsy, we said goodnight.

For most of the next day, Saturday, Anna left me to my own devices. She drove off to do some shopping in Surfers' Paradise, and to lunch with people who lived in a villa three or four miles away. I spent the day on the beach, in the ocean, in the house sleeping, back to the beach again, swimming, dozing, reading, eating, swimming, reading. Some time during the afternoon, Anna returned for a late siesta. We were to drive further down the coast into New South Wales that evening, to a cocktail party, and dine on our way back at a rather good seafood restaurant not far from the state border. And, indeed, we did both these things. The party was full of expectedly dull people, the fish supper at the restaurant was excellent. I drank my first gin at the party, did not much like it, so stuck thereafter to tomato juice until our supper *à deux*, when I helped Anna polish off a bottle of the splendid local, somewhat Rieslingish wine which she still affected not to like. By the time we drove home after supper, Anna was, well, by no means drunk, but certainly in a state of euphoria. I was a trifle high, too. She allowed me to garage the car. When I had done this and walked to the house, I found her in the living room pouring two glasses of her Gumpoldskirchner. 'A nightcap, *Lieberl*,' she said.

We sat together on a sofa, and at first our talk was the aimless chatter in which we usually indulged. We would talk of books, people, music, and Anna would deplore my lack of desire to take up music as a profession. That night we talked also of some of the people who had been at the party. Over supper we had discussed at some length a married couple who had been present. She was an amiable, feather-brained actress, he an Air Force officer and in civilian life a local government administrator. She was known to be completely devoted to him, while he was known to be almost equally devoted to the sexual pursuit of boys. Anna and I had argued about the morality of this situation, and we had speculated as to whether Sandra knew of Gordon's proclivities. Now, at home, Anna returned to the subject. Women, she asserted, never had the slightest idea what went on in their husbands' minds. 'Maybe,' I replied, 'but surely they sense what goes on in their husbands' bodies. I can't believe Sandra hasn't at least some intuitive knowledge of just what Gordon's infidelities are.'

'Why should she, darling? Presumably he satisfies her physically. And she's quite a stupid woman, you know. And vain. Why would it enter her pretty head that he might look at another woman, to say nothing of a young man?'

'P'raps you're right.' (This was my arrogant, teenage way of saying, 'I'm sure you're wrong, but it's of no consquence.') 'But he must be mad. She's delicious.'

'Let me refill your glass, *Liebling*? Here.' And Anna refilled my glass. 'So you fancy her, do you? She's twice your age.'

'Twice my age, Anna, is still young.' And I added, gallantly, 'For that matter, so is three times my age.'

I do not remember how much more of this banter we engaged in. But I do remember Anna in pink slacks and a white shirt, one leg tucked under her, an arm extended towards me along the back of the sofa. Myself inclined towards her, my head resting against the sofa back. And I remember her saying, '*Carlchen*, you do look uncomfortable. Stretch out. Tired, darling?'

'Not in the slightest.' And now I lay on my back, my head resting against her thigh. She smiled, and stroked my hair back from my forehead. There was some more desultory talk, then I remember she moved and lay beside me. Now her arm was around me, and my head nestled against her shoulder. In my condition of somewhat less than absolute sobriety, I appreciated the intimacy of the position without being properly conscious of the danger. I enjoyed the perfumed smell of her body, just as I used, when younger, to enjoy snuggling close to my mother.

For some time Anna and I remained thus, talking, falling silent. I began to feel drowsy. I think I must actually have dozed off when she took my left hand, moving it from around her waist and placing it on her right breast. But I awakened suddenly and felt immediately tense. The enemy had taken me unawares: that was the odd thought in my mind. I tried to relax again. I knew I could not possibly behave so churlishly as to remove my hand, and so I nervously squeezed her breast in a manner that I hoped would communicate affection rather than passion, then made a contented noise and pretended to be still almost asleep.

It was not a pretence I was able to keep up for long. Anna's right hand was unbuttoning her shirt, half removing it. As the material slipped away, my hand was left limply poised over a small, firm, naked breast. 'Cocks, tits,' I thought behind my closed eyes, 'what am I going to get a handful of next? I wish they'd pick on someone their own size.' But, involuntarily, my flesh was responding, was betraying me. I felt myself becoming erect. Without quite meaning to, I fondled the breast in my hand. I sensed that the other one, also now bare, and close to my face, was steering itself towards my mouth. With my eyes still closed, like a newly born kitten with its mother, I sought the nipple and caressed it with my lips. Opening my mouth wide, I let the determined breast plunge in. Anna was now lying on top of me. When I came up for air, opening my eyes and looking at her, or perhaps for her, she slithered down until our faces were level. In those big, usually sad, brown eyes there was now a look of wonder, and a dancing light. Taking my head in her hands, she kissed me. Then she got up, took me by the hand, and led me to her bedroom. We both undressed completely and in silence. When we were in bed, Anna spoke. 'Did you expect this, little Carl?'

At fifteen, one does not care to be called little. We were, after all, the same height. 'No,' I answered. And, deciding that a degree of sophistication was called for, I added, 'It's a bonus.' We lay on our sides, facing each other. The frankness with which she explored my body, by look and by touch, somehow both increased and reduced my nervousness. I had confidence in my neat, slim figure, but I felt silly with an erection. She took it seriously, however, handling it with a frown of intense concentration, bending to examine it more closely while my heart beat faster. ('Gosh, do girls do that, too? Terrific.') But she moved her face away from it again, brushing my chest lightly with her lips, then gently pushed my shoulders until I lay supine. 'I'll give you bonus,' she promised as she straddled me, guiding me into her. I gave a gasp of surprised pleasure which made her laugh. 'Lie still,' she said, 'I'll do all the moving.' And she did, writhing above me and looking down at me to observe my reactions. I felt weak, helpless, and in a state of bliss. I came far too quickly, of course, but she was not at all disconcerted. 'Stay in there,' she ordered, and rested quietly on top of me for some minutes until I felt myself rising to the occasion again. The second time we reached a climax simultaneously. 'Anna, I love you, I love you,' I heard my voice whispering.

'Silly, of course you don't,' said Anna.

Her voice sounded quite sharp, and not even faintly affectionate. Immediately, I began to cry. Tears of self-pity, I suppose, but also of sadness at the sudden, momentary intimation of aching loneliness that I had experienced.

Anna was quickly contrite and tender, perhaps only at that moment remembering how young I was. And my fit of weeping passed. As she murmured reassuringly to me, I felt quite miserable still, but I fell asleep in her arms.

I cannot bring myself to describe the rest of the weekend. It was awful. We spent much of it in bed, but we can hardly be said to have made love. We made, instead, rather joyless sex. I learned to do many things: the foundations of my sexual technique were as well and truly laid that weekend as I was. Anna was an aggressive sex partner, but also an ingenious one. My body responded to her with alacrity, and I tried to match my mood to her beautifully pure hedonism. My mind, however, continued to be distracted by what I now realize was the sound of Time's wingèd chariot, though I imagined it then to be simply an uneasy conscience. I think Anna would have liked me to continue to be a kind of *cavaliere servente* to her, but that one weekend of quasi-cicisbeism was enough for me.

I fear I may have failed to convey the effect those first two sexual encounters had upon me. As I write of them now, it is impossible for me not to make them appear enjoyable in some way. Indeed, it is not easy for me now to understand how desolating, momentary physical pleasure apart, they both were.

It was not until I was an adult that I discovered love and sex to be not the same thing at all. Then I learned that love lifts the sex act onto a different plane of experience; that sex without love can be immensely enjoyable; that love without some element of sex is very rare; and that the situation to be avoided when having sex for the first time with someone is that in which your partner is heaving with romantic love while you simply want a quick screw. It was not until I was an adult that I learned to be honest and not to say 'I love you' when all I meant was 'I want to fuck you.' I had been unlucky enough to be introduced to sex by two adults, both of whom treated me merely as an object. I brooded on this for a year or more, during which time I even seriously contemplated renouncing sex altogether. The natural outcome of this was that, at the age of seventeen, I became sex-mad, and leaped in and out of bed with whomever I found attractive and could attract, of either sex. I just wished there were more sexes. I was an exhausted nineteen before I matured sufficiently to embark upon my first real love affair, and to forgive both Anna Kunz and H. Ross.

The Second World War came to an end several weeks before my eighteenth birthday, which was extremely considerate of it, for I was thus spared from having to decide whether or not to register as a conscientious objector. I am not sure what I would have done. I certainly would not have wanted to place myself in the way of danger; but, although at my secondary school I was the only boy wearing a blazer and grey flannels on Friday afternoons when everyone else was prancing about on parade in the uniforms of the Officers' Training Corps or whatever it was called, I could not conscientiously have called myself an objector to killing in wartime on either religious or moral grounds.

On rational grounds, yes, for I do not see how international differences can intelligently be settled, and complex arguments decided, by killing masses of people innocent of any involvement in those differences. To the extent that I worship at the shrine of human reason, with George Bernard Shaw as my only saint, I am, I suppose, a pacifist. But, as those who know me will have observed, though not aggressive I do tend to defend myself when attacked. *Très méchant.* I can, therefore, imagine myself killing in self-defence. But organized war, like organized religion or organized sport, is abhorrent to me. Though I used to run and swim well, I always refused to compete for my school. (This, I must admit, was mainly because I derived pleasure from seeing the sports master, a beast called Lockie, frothing at the mouth.)

Brisbane State High School, where I spent the war years, is on the south side of town. I used to travel to it daily by tram from Paddington to the corner of George and Adelaide Streets in the centre of town; then a walk of one block to Queen Street, where, at Circular Quay, I would catch another tram to South Brisbane, across the river. As the tram swung round to the left on the south side of town, it passed a slum area with, on the first corner, a sordid-looking pub around which drunken aborigines swarmed like flies. (With the exception of a singer, Harold Blair, who had a brief career on the concert platform, I never spoke to an Australian aborigine until I visited the tropical north of Queensland in 1985. Don't let anyone say we are ignorant of apartheid in Australia.)

In a recent book on Commonwealth literature, I was surprised to read of myself that 'Charles Osborne (b. 1927), an expatriate, burnished a more polished surface' than some other Australian poet, while Peter Porter, 'another expatriate, projects a wry reaction to the stresses and absurdities of the present'. Peter Porter, in my view one of the best English-language poets of our time, is a Brisbaner too. A couple of years younger than I, he used as a teenager to frequent the bookshop which, between 1947 and 1949, a friend and I owned and ran. Peter wrote about what he called the 'intellectual Brisbane' of those post-war years in the Australian literary magazine *Quadrant* nearly thirty years later:

> Brisbane has produced a surprisingly large number of writers and literary movements. *Meanjin* [a literary magazine], of course, began there. But the *Barjai* movement interests me more. I was just the right age to have partaken of this strangely anachronistic literary ganging-up, but years in Toowoomba and my own diffidence kept me from joining Barrie Reid, Charles Osborne, Barbara Patterson, Laurie Collinson, Laurie Hope, Cecil Knopke and the rest. I did meet Louis Green at my South Brisbane boarding-house, but I doubt that he knew that I wrote poetry. Louis (now a historian at Monash) was very exotic, and the once or twice I met Charles Osborne I found him dauntingly sophisticated. Charles ran the Ballad Bookshop in the city, where I often bought books – I still have my first copies of Auden stamped with the shop's markings. Charles was a musician and actor, as well

as a poet. I recall him in a play about Oscar Wilde in which he played alongside a visiting star (rather threadbare) named Ross Buchanan, and also a performance of *Candida* he put on, with himself as Marchbanks, to retrieve the failing fortunes of the bookshop. Charles was always a man of great courage, and he led the way in defying Brisbane's puritanism and philistinism. He cultivated a sort of cheerful decadence, but he was grounding himself well in his favourite art, music, so that very little of the dissipated time was wasted.

All this group dared to practise a mixture of left-wing politics and high camp at a time when such notions were dangerous. They had an *F6* period: I think the Group Theatre and the Auden of the thirties were their chief talismans. I admired them from a distance, though I found much of their poetry derivative. They believed not only in art but in the calling of the artist. I have always preferred to practise art behind a front of bourgeois respectability – it's less time-wasting – but I never forgot the example of the *Barjai* group. Now that several of them are my friends, most especially Charles Osborne, who is also a colleague with whom I have worked closely in London, I am sorry that I was too shy to seek them out in the late forties. It might have made my life in Brisbane less lonely.

Peter is not entirely accurate. Courage I have never possessed to any significant degree, as far as I know, but I am willing to confess to cheerful decadence. One had to wear some kind of protective covering to survive in the Brisbane of those years, and the juvenile desire to *épater les bourgeois* which most of us go through was all too easy to gratify in the steamy capital of Australia's Deep North.

During the war, Brisbane had something of the atmosphere of a wild frontier town. Inundated with American servicemen, it venally set about catering for their needs, which were several and remarkably various. The Australian soldiers, puritanical scroungers that they were, used to stand early in the queues for the town's two heavily overworked brothels, and then sell their places to sex-hungry, dollar-packed Yanks. My barber, a mindless and by no means compensatingly pretty queen whose name (I swear) was Percy Bottome, confided to me that he earned quite large sums several nights a week by working part-time in one of the two establishments. 'When they get so busy that the girls can't cope, the Madam rings me up and I go across the river and put on me drag and me Ginger Rogers wig. I can do about a dozen blow-jobs an evening, at thirty bob a time.'

I entertained the troops more decorously by joining a concert party which toured the Australian and American camps in Brisbane and elsewhere in Queensland. I had, by this time, discovered in myself a dramatic as well as a musical talent. It was not much of a dramatic talent, but it (plus musical journalism) supported me throughout my twenties. It first emerged when I found myself, at short notice, having to step in front of a radio microphone and perform a role in a script I had written, the juvenile actor who was supposed to play the role having succumbed to a sudden onslaught of puberty or laryngitis and lost his voice. Unlike many actors, including some really first-rate ones, I had the ability to sight-read fluently and intelligently. I neither stumbled over nor mispronounced words, and I was able to convey the dramatic sense of what I was reading, immediately and easily. I became a radio actor.

Radio actors, at least in Australia, are the dregs of the profession. I progressed to the stage. Marchbanks in Shaw's *Candida* was a natural role for me, and I played it in two different productions, once at the Guild Café Theatre, in my own production, and once for a co-operative group, Globe Theatre, when the producer was Arthur Davies, an eccentric and endearing Australian Broadcasting Commission staff producer who had studied in London under Michel Saint-Denis.

From Shaw, it was downhill all the way. There was not much professional theatre in Brisbane, so one could not entirely forsake radio. But on the stage I played a succession of silly juveniles in sillier plays, with an occasional Shakespeare thrown in, directed two or three plays, and was a member of the company which reopened the nineteenth-century Theatre Royal in Elizabeth Street. Derelict for years, the theatre had recently been taken over by Will Mahoney, an American vaudeville comedian who, with his wife Evie Hayes ('the Californian songbird'), had improbably come to roost in Brisbane. I liked working for Mahoney. He told fascinating stories about the great days of American vaudeville, and I loved watching his act, in which he tap-danced on a xylophone, though he sometimes fell off it unintentionally. He ran the Cremorne Theatre as a vaudeville house, and started a legitimate company at the Theatre Royal.

I was a regular visitor to the Cremorne, where there was a weekly change of bill. One could see the great Australian comedians, 'Mo' and George Wallace, there, and a host of acts past their best days in American vaudeville or British variety or music-hall, among them Jenny Howard, Tommy Fields (Gracie's brother) and the marvellous Ella Shields, the original Burlington Bertie. I had a weak spot for the really tatty comedians, the kind whom John Osborne was to sum up in Archie Rice. My favourite was Morrie Barling, closely followed by Syd Beck, who one day was found dead on the railway line not far from the Cremorne Theatre. I remember, in 1948, taking Sidney Nolan to see 'Mo', who was to Australian vaudeville what Max Miller was to English variety.

At the Theatre Royal we opened in 1947 with *Peter Pan,* in which I played one of the pirates – Smee, I think. Another pirate was Leo McKern, who was also Assistant Stage Manager. Leo wore his glass eye on stage, but used occasionally to take it out when he was on duty in the prompt corner. On at least one occasion he forgot to put it in again when he came on stage. In the scene in which the pirates are searching for the boys, he startled me by thrusting his face, with one empty eye socket, into mine.

Leo was married to a fine actress, Jane Holland. When they decided to seek their fortune in England, we were all certain that Jane would become a star, and we hoped that, when she did, she would not leave Leo in the lurch. But it was Leo who became famous. Jane is still Mrs McKern.

It must have been earlier than this, during the war years, that for a few awful weeks I was a cadet announcer at one of Brisbane's three commercial radio stations, 4BH (owned by Alderman Chandler, our Lord Mayor and a friend of the family, who gave me the job). I had to encourage the housewives at the community singing broadcast, and also produce instant doggerel for a drunkard called Les Daley, who had a programme in which he would appear to improvise songs on themes sent in by his listeners. The programme began with Les sitting at the piano and singing

Oh, the sun will soon be shining in the sky,
Pack away your troubles and never say die,
Let 4BH make your troubles fly,
And the sun will soon be shining in the sky.

That was his own, unaided work, and that, presumably, was why I had to write some of his material for him. Another young announcer at the station was an agreeable youth with a bad skin, named Ray Barrett. He is now often to be seen in Australian films.

I scored one of my biggest successes on the Brisbane stage in a play which shocked audiences not only there but in most towns to which it toured. This was *Oscar Wilde,* by Leslie and Sewell Stokes. It was first performed in London with Robert Morley as Wilde. In the Australian production, Wilde was played by a fading star, Ross Buchanan, and my role was that of Charlie Parker, a tough Cockney stable-boy whom Wilde picks up. In one scene, set in the Café Royal, Oscar and Charlie are seen dining together, and at the end of the scene they dance, clasping each other tightly, to the tune of 'You should see me dance the polka'. It was completely innocuous stuff, but after we danced our polka and had got off stage the curtain used to descend every evening to icy silence.

I enjoyed being an actor. I kept in work and, if much of the time I was playing small parts, that was fine because it meant that I had more time in my dressing-room to get on with my writing. My poems began to be published in Australian magazines, but I was writing prose as well, and I even attempted plays. I also started to write musical and literary criticism. At school I had edited a magazine pretentiously called *Intelligentsia*. The literary group to which I later belonged published the magazine *Barjai* (an aboriginal word meaning 'today'). Our rival was *Meanjin* (an aboriginal word meaning 'meeting place', or perhaps I've got the meanings the wrong way round). The leading poet of the *Barjai* group was Barrie Reid, who later became a librarian. I was considered to be our prose stylist. We took ourselves more seriously as a group than I was ever able personally to take myself.

I am not a modest person. As I have written on more than one other occasion in the hope that my phrase will find a place in someone's dictionary of quotations, 'Modesty is the fig-leaf of mediocrity'; and my detestation of mediocrity is the natural obverse of my admiration of excellence. So when I say I was a poor actor, I am not being modest but am merely appraising myself as accurately as I can. When I auditioned for parts by having a script thrust at me to read a scene at sight, I usually got the job, for I read much better than the other applicants. But if I was sent a script in advance, and asked to learn and play a scene at the audition, as often as not I failed to land the part, for there were almost certain to be better actors auditioning for it. Sometimes, after I had been rehearsing in a play for a week or so, the director would take me aside and say, 'It's still rather superficial, Charles, rather like your first reading of the part at the audition. But when it develops, it'll be fine.' 'Little do you know,' I would think smugly, 'that this is it. It doesn't develop.'

At the age of seventeen, encouraged by having had poems published in Australian and New Zealand magazines, among them *The Bulletin*, the only Australian political-literary weekly, I had sent a batch of poems to *Penguin New Writing*, which was edited from London by John Lehmann. Mr Lehmann had written back, accepting three of the poems and asking me to send a photograph and a paragraph of curriculum vitae. I was overjoyed to think that I was about to be published in England by a famous literary editor, and excitedly sent off a photograph. My *vita* had not accumulated much of a *curriculum*, so I was able to accompany the photograph with no more than one sentence, which read: 'Charles Osborne is a seventeen-year-old Australian who writes poetry.'

I then waited to receive the issue of *Penguin New Writing* in which my poems appeared. What I received, however, about a year later, was a letter from a Miss Barbara Cooper, John Lehmann's secretary, regretting to inform me that the magazine was about to cease publication, and that they had not got round to using my poems, which she now returned to me. Alas!

Music was a consolation in the war years and immediate post-war years in Brisbane. There was no opera, but a number of fine musicians managed to find their way to Australia's northernmost capital, and I met most of them: the eccentric genius Klemperer, the exciting Rafael Kubelik, the suave Alceo Galliera. There were Australian singers such as Peter Dawson, Harold Williams, Essie Ackland (accompanied by the *very* young Geoffrey Parsons) and, confined by polio to a wheel-chair, Marjorie Lawrence, a great Wagnerian soprano. There were the pianists Solomon, Moiseiwitch, Friedman, and three young pianists (two Australians and one American), whom I knew and who were friends of one another, all of whom died tragically while still young men: William Kapell, Richard Farrell and Noel Mewton-Wood. There was also Gracie Fields, who sang 'The Lord's Prayer' and did a complete cartwheel at the end of it.

Except for most of 1946, when I worked in radio and plays in Melbourne, including a stint with J. Beresford Fowler's company in Shakespeare and Ibsen (Fowler was a gallant survivor, an actor-manager of the old days and a dreadful ham), I remained in Brisbane until 1951, when I decided to move to Melbourne as the first stage in my plan to leave Australia. My parents seemed not to mind. I had, in any case, not been living at home for a year or two, and was sharing a maisonette with Barrie Reid in South Brisbane. By this time, I cordially loathed my native town and hoped never to see it again. I did see it again, of course, for even after I had begun to live in London I returned occasionally to see my ageing parents. But I did not really come to terms with the city of my birth until my 1979 visit, after the death of my parents, when somehow the burden of my past was lifted from my shoulders.

I chose Melbourne rather than Sydney when I moved away from Brisbane because, although Melbourne was a thousand miles away, while Sydney was a mere six hundred, I had enjoyed my year in Melbourne in 1946, whereas I had not enjoyed my week or two in Sydney in 1945. Admittedly, the only section of Sydney that I knew was King's Cross, a kind of Soho-plus-Chelsea area with its own shoddy 'Latin Quarter' type of glamour during the forties.

A strange world was King's Cross, a world of layabouts, artists, crooks, students, male and female prostitutes, American servicemen, and those incredible bodgies and widgies, our equivalents of the British Teddy-boys and girls: the bodgies, the Aussie-type junior spivs (in pre-war years known as larrikins) with their Harlem zoot-suits and Cornel Wilde haircuts; the widgies, their girl-friends, petulant imitations of Betty Grable.

But what gave the Cross its unique flavour was that it was then the favourite residential area of Sydney's theatrical profession. 'Show biz' is perhaps a more fitting term, for professional theatre usually meant revivals of *Rio Rita* or *Maid of the Mountains*, and by far the greater number of those engaged in the entertainment industry were employed by Sydney's many commercial radio stations. Pop singers (occasionally of some talent, unlike today's ghastly international crew), dance-band musicians, musical comedy tenors, radio actors, disc jockeys, lady journalists who broadcast women's fashion programmes, interviewers: these were among the fiercest denizens of the King's Cross jungle. The friendly promiscuity, the sentimentality of this time and place belong to youth in turmoil anywhere, but the air of hectic, subconsciously forced gaiety which characterized the European twenties had, like most things, found its way to Australia twenty years later, and permeated life in King's Cross, Sydney.

It took me only a week or so to see through King's Cross at the age of eighteen. Staid Melbourne, where I supported myself for most of the following year, was more to my liking. It was in Melbourne that, for five minutes one day, I had been completely happy and at peace: my one and only mystical experience (I discount a later experience in London, which was drug-induced).

I had got on a tram at its terminus at Flinders Bridge, by the Yarra river. I was out of work and short of money, and had been considering approaching my parents in Brisbane for help. As I sat in the tram, waiting for it to move off and gazing out of a window at the bridge, the river and the passers-by, an almost indescribable feeling of pure bliss came upon me. It lasted for only a few moments, but such extraordinary moments that they seemed, in retrospect, an age. They have remained in my memory ever since.

During those moments, which seemed an eternity, I was filled not only with sheer happiness but also with complete serenity. I knew then that all was as it should be, that the pattern of the universe was not only logical but also supremely satisfying, that life itself was of the utmost beauty, and that I was an integral, planned and significant part of it all. Like Saul on the way to Damascus, I suddenly, in a flash of complete and absolute revelation, understood the meaning of existence. As the tram began to move, the sensation faded, and I turned my head to look back at Flinders Bridge, fearing I was leaving my happiness behind.

The moment of revelation is, of course, no more than a moment, and one does have to leave it behind. Nor can one ever really describe it adequately. But the memory of it persists, and I have more than once been able to draw comfort and sustenance from recalling and contemplating my sense of supra-rational ecstasy in a tram leaving Flinders Bridge for the depressing Melbourne suburb of Prahran.

Some Australian expatriates find it easier to cope with their Antipodean past by completely rejecting it, and affecting to despise the country in which they were born. I do not feel that way: if Australia were not geographically so remote from the more interesting parts of the world, I would be happy to live there – if, for instance, it were moored somewhere off the Isle of Wight, or in the middle of the Mediterranean. When I was able to view Brisbane without the weight of my parents and my past on my shoulders, I thought it a rather charming place. On my most recent visit, in the early part of 1985, I was not so charmed by it, for in its demolition plans the city seems deliberately to be obliterating all traces of me. The theatres where I acted in *Peter Pan* (Theatre Royal), in *Candida* and *Junior Miss* (Guild Café Theatre), and in *Outward Bound*, *Red Sky at Morning*, *A Midsummer Night's Dream* and *Henry V* (Albert Hall), are no longer there. The Pink Elephant Coffee Lounge, where I held my twenty-first birthday party (several members of the Ballet Rambert came, and it all ended in tears with Johnny Gilpin nearly arrested for letting off fireworks in the street outside), has disappeared. The church organ I played has been destroyed, and even the Victoria Bridge, on which a carful of thuggish detectives once accosted me because they thought my hair was too long and my shirt the wrong colour, is no longer the same bridge but a more recently constructed anonymity. The Tivoli Roof Garden where I won the Bobby Breen singing contest has been demolished.

On one of my recent visits to Brisbane, Barry Humphries was performing there as Dame Edna. He was also launching his latest book with a press conference at the University, and asked me to come along and introduce him. To a bunch of Aussie journalists and TV cameramen, I delivered a speech in which I equated the image of Australia projected abroad by Dame Edna with Dickens's picture of Victorian England or Dostoevsky's of Tsarist Russia. (Received intellectual opinion in Australia has it that Dame Edna gives a False Impression of the country to the poms.) As a reward, Barry gave me lunch in a seafood restaurant in Petrie Terrace, only a few hundred yards from my old primary school. After lunch, I walked around the school and its playground. Changed, changed utterly. Worst of all, my parents' house in Cochrane Street, Paddington, where I lived until I was fourteen, has been torn down, and three or four houses now stand in the grounds which it occupied. The hilly slope in our garden, which I used to think was the very top of the round world as I rolled down it in my red toy automobile, is now the darkness underneath an ugly brick bungalow.

When I reached adulthood, although I found I could earn some kind of a living by writing and by acting, I still did not really know, had certainly not decided, what I would do when I grew up. I no longer pictured myself as pushing up daisies at the age of forty, but I used to wonder exactly what I would be doing at that age, and how. I was a dropout before that became the fashion, trained to do nothing, not even to think properly, and my only assets were my musical and literary talents, in the use of which I had no idea of discipline, no conception of the ways in which I should attempt to deploy those talents to best effect. I wrote poems when I felt like it, and occasionally a short story. Before I was out of my teens, I had completed a couple of rhapsodical, Rimbaud-like prose poems of book length, *Anger at the Moon* and *All Clouds to Heaven*. I made no attempt to have them published, nor would I have succeeded had I tried. Instead, I circulated them among my friends. Sidney Nolan told me recently that he still has his copies.

I tried, somewhat half-heartedly, to compose music. I began a number of highly derivative (from the Viennese classics) piano pieces, but the only composition I ever completed to my satisfaction was a set of five songs to poems by Shelley. When I looked at them many years later, I thought that two, 'I fear thy kisses, gentle maiden' and 'Goodnight, ah no, the hour is ill', had quite pleasant sub-Schubertian melodies. They were performed at least once in public by a tenor friend of mine, Max Oldaker, an Australian operetta favourite of the forties (who, as a Royal Academy student in the thirties, had sung Walther in *Die Meistersinger* under Barbirolli).

Always able to improvise at the piano in the style of the great composers, and to produce instant, and instantly forgettable, tunes, I once played a cruel trick on one of my Brisbane mentors, Dr Robert Dalley-Scarlett, an elderly composer, conductor and specialist in eighteenth-century music, who claimed to be descended from the Scarlatti family. I told him that I had read, in a European magazine, of a newly discovered early Mozart piano sonata, that the first movement had been reproduced in the magazine, and that I had learned it. 'Play it for me, dear boy,' he exclaimed. I immediately improvised a simple, early Mozart sonata movement, to his great delight. He thought it a particularly fine example of the young Mozart, but when he asked me to learn the entire sonata and broadcast it for the Australian Broadcasting Commission, I had to own up.

Dalley-Scarlett liked no music written after the death of Mozart. Even his own compositions were pastiche eighteenth-century. One evening he attended a chamber music recital given by the Musica Viva players, with whom Hephzibah Menuhin played Beethoven's 'Archduke' Trio and the César Franck Quintet. (I turned the pages for her.) After the recital (which had begun with a Haydn quartet, the reason for Dalley-Scarlett's presence) I heard him say to Hephzibah: 'Why does so fine a musician as yourself play all that nineteenth-century stuff?'

A shocked Hephzibah replied, 'The Beethoven is a work of great depth.'

'Beethoven has depth, yes,' said Dalley-Scarlett, 'but you should devote yourself to Haydn. Haydn has *style*.' The purr that came into his voice as he breathed the word 'style' made it clear to us that for him this was the most valuable attribute of all. But he must have had a very superficial idea of style to have said that.

I was twenty-three when I moved to Melbourne. I had already decided that it was essential for me to leave Australia because, with the exception of books, most of the things I cared about were not to be found there. There was a certain amount of music making, it is true, but how much more of it there was in London. When I left Brisbane, I had not heard a live performance of a Mahler or a Bruckner symphony. The local orchestra was mediocre: visiting conductors occasionally succeeded in making it play well, and Otto Klemperer made it sound like the Vienna Philharmonic. But Klemperer was Klemperer. There was, as I have said, no opera to be heard in Brisbane. Now, of course, there are opera companies in all the major cities, though the locals say there is only one real opera house; its stage is in Melbourne, its auditorium in Sydney, and its orchestra pit in Brisbane. When I recently suggested to a senior officer of Australian Opera that the various waves of post-war European immigration must have made a great difference to the size of their audiences, he replied: 'My dear, nothing has changed. Without the poufs and the Jews we'd be lost.'

In theatre in the 1940s, the situation was hardly better: a steady diet of recent West End or Broadway comedies (I was the juvenile lead in one of them, *Junior Miss*, a peculiarly mindless affair), and a few revivals of old musical comedies, on tour from Sydney or Melbourne. I wanted to see operas, real plays, real operettas for that matter, and to look at paintings and baroque churches, and even see some real modern architecture. Modern architecture had passed Australia by: our leading architect, Robin Boyd, had, in despair, written a book called *The Australian Ugliness.*

Melbourne was merely the first stop. Having worked there for most of 1946, I knew the Melbourne radio and theatre scene better than its Sydney equivalent, and in any case I rather disliked Sydney. It seemed too Americanized, whereas Melbourne was, I thought, probably similar to Manchester. I was right about that. (Years later, Jonathan Miller described Melbourne as Manchester with the central heating on too high.)

My plan was to work for a year or two, save as much money as possible, and then bugger off to Europe. And this, in fact, is what I did, although it took me a full two years to achieve my aim. During those two years I continued to write, but I also accepted every theatre engagement that was offered to me. I played Morris or Henry (I cannot remember which: they are both ciphers) in the first Australian production of Coward's *Present Laughter* at the Arrow Theatre; I stage-managed a production of Mozart's *Così fan tutte*; I acted in innumerable radio plays and serials, and commercials; and when 'resting' between engagements I worked in a bookshop (Angus & Robertson's) or the gramophone record department of a music shop (Allan's in Collins Street). I played Edwin Drood in a completion and adaptation for the stage of *The Mystery of Edwin Drood*, and I understudied two roles which, fortunately, I was never called upon to play, for I did not have the *physique du rôle* in either instance: Joe Bonaparte in Clifford Odett's *Golden Boy*, and Stanley Kowalski in *A Streetcar Named Desire.*

The only engagement of those two years that I look back upon with any pleasure was a tour of Victorian country towns in 1952 for the Council of Adult Education's Travelling Theatre. The CAE in Victoria (and, I suppose, in the other states) regularly sent out tours of plays and groups of musicians to perform in the outback. (A few years later, Barry Humphries began his career in one of these companies.) In 1951 they had toured J. B. Priestley's *An Inspector Calls*, Wilde's *The Importance of Being Earnest* and Molière's *The Miser.* I had successfully auditioned for the role of John Worthing in *The Importance*, but at the last moment had got cold feet about disappearing for months into the bush. All those one-night stands, and what would the accommodation be like? I could not, and still cannot, face the prospect of beginning my day without a shower or, preferably, a bath in which I can lie back and psychoanalyse myself before going out into the world. Visions of outside loos (dunnies in Australese) and of putting one's head under a pump had risen before my eyes. Also I could not see Wilde's wittily decadent *aperçus* bringing a chuckle to the throats of Aussie farmers' wives. I elected to remain in town, such as it was. However, a friend who went on one of those tours came back entranced and panting for more. When I was invited to join the first of the 1952 tours, and play the hero, Kung, in *Enduring as the Camphor Tree*, 'a Chinese Play Written and Produced as Through Western Eyes' by one Russell J. Oakes, I accepted.

The play was a load of old codswallop, but the company was fun and the country through which we toured was fascinating. We opened in Melbourne, and I remember that, on the day of our opening, news had just been received of the death of George VI. Standing on stage at the Melbourne Little Theatre waiting for the curtain to go up, I heard the usual gramophone record of the National Anthem begin to play, and the noise of the audience rising to its feet. Suddenly our director, Irene Mitchell, rushed to the prompt corner and lifted the pick-up arm from the turntable, abruptly stopping the record. 'We can't play "God Save the King",' she hissed to the stage manager. 'He's dead. There's a Queen now.'

'You bloody fool, Irene,' I yelled at her, 'it's the same tune,' and I dashed over to the prompt corner and put it on again.

We played in large country towns and small townships, which in England would be called villages. We made an occasional foray across the state borders into New South Wales and South Australia, travelling in a huge pantechnicon which stored our scenery and costumes, with a small cabin up front for the actors. Everywhere we played, we were treated as though we were the Oliviers heading an Old Vic company. In the more remote areas perhaps they thought we were. From the book of press clippings I have kept, I select names of towns we played, many of which I have completely forgotten: Boort, Colac, Charlton, Euroa, Myrtleford, Bordertown, Kyabram, Nagambie, Warrnambool, Ararat, Port Fairy, as well as larger places such as Shepperton, Ballarat and Albury.

For the most part we played in Mechanics' Halls, 'School of Arts' halls, the occasional cinema, and even some charmingly dilapidated nineteenth-century theatres. In one of these, a theatre left over from the gold rush days, we found a caretaker-stage doorman who had come to the town years earlier with a Shakespeare company which had got stranded there. The company had dispersed, but he had stayed on, an old man with an old actor-laddie's wide-brimmed hat and a flowery manner.

We played in forty-one towns over a period of eight weeks. In some places we were put up by local bigwigs, in others there were quaint old country pubs. Usually the food in the pubs was atrocious. 'I have not been able to eat any of the three sick-making meals served to us today,' is a typical entry in my diary. Often we bought bread, cheese and sausage. After the performances, we resorted to séances, Scotch and sex. While travelling, we played games which we invented, or sang songs. I taught the others a number of German folksongs which we gave forth lustily in the pantechnicon (which we called 'The Monster') as we made our way from Bordertown to Narracoorte, or from Warracknabeal to Nhill.

One of our diversions was to see who could invent the most obscene variation on a well-known phrase. Most of the entries must have been pretty innocuous, since I won with 'Absinthe makes the arse grow fonder' and 'There are fairies at the bottom of my guardsmen'.

At Penola, I was entertained by a Viennese named George Kaufmann, a nephew of Elisabeth Schumann. He showed me a first edition of Schubert's *Müller Lieder*, published in Vienna in 1832 (four years after Schubert's death), and we sang and played a number of songs from it. He also gave me my first decent cup of coffee in four weeks.

We played in the Ned Kelly country – Euroa, Benalla, Tungarrah – and in the pub at Euroa I met an old man who was supposed to be Ned's young brother, Jim. One had to be careful what one said about Ned Kelly in those places, for feelings ran high, even though Ned had been dead for seventy-one years. There was a certain amount of in-breeding in some of the smaller townships. I think it was Tungarrah that boasted a population of 225, of whom 150 bore the family name of Saunders.

As we travelled along a dusty road one morning, I saw an eagle sweep down only a few yards in front of our vehicle, and carry off in its claws a rabbit which had been scuttling across the road. (I thought of Goethe's *Ganymed.*) We frequently saw emus, kangaroos, wallabies and koalas. One day I had a rifle thrust into my hands by a farmer and was invited to shoot at a pack of kangaroos. I deliberately aimed very high and frightened them off. When I refused, on another occasion, to shoot a rabbit, even my fellow-actors were thoroughly disgusted with me.

Reviews of *Enduring as the Camphor Tree* were uniformly favourable, if sometimes rather oddly written. One critic was astonished that we could be heard clearly 'in every part of the hall, even when the actors turned away from the audience'. The reviewer in Port Fairy was especially impressed by our sound effects: 'For instance, during the performance there were frequent peals of thunder, and it would have been very hard to distinguish it from the real. The effect was produced from a gramophone record, but whether the record was made in a real storm or not it would have been hard to say.' In Myrtleford, the local paper said that our 'costumes were delightful and provided excellent support'.

We played matinées for schoolchildren, who made surprisingly attentive and quiet audiences, and who mobbed us for autographs afterwards. Maureen Stott (the young English actress who played opposite me) and I being the prettiest members of the company, we received the most attention. I was continually being screamed at by hordes of pubescent girls. I suppose they thought that an Osborne in the hand was better than a Brando in the bush.

Once or twice, our reception was less flattering. At a place called Wycheproof, during a scene involving Maureen (heroine), myself (hero) and Grant MacIntyre (villain), someone in the audience called out to Grant, 'Get stuffed!' I muttered between clenched teeth to Maureen: 'The sooner we get back to the Old Vic, Vivien darling, the better.' And at Warracknabeal, when I and two other actors walked past the local shirt factory, the factory girls leaning out of the window chanted at us: 'What does the train say? Pouf, pouf!' I consoled my fellow actors with Othello's 'I swear 'tis better to be much abused/Than but to know't a little.'

Grant MacIntyre, who played the villainous Lord Ku, had been in the chorus of the London production of Cole Porter's *Anything Goes* in 1935. During our tour, he taught the rest of us the tap-dancing routine to which that show's title number had been performed. 'In olden days a glimpse of stocking/Was looked on as something shocking./Now, Heaven knows,/ Anything goes.' I can still, more than thirty years after having been taught it by Grant, remember the routine, but as a party piece I must admit it is second in unpopularity only to my kookaburra imitation.

At the end of the tour, I returned to Melbourne, where I picked up some radio work again and also, emboldened by having won a competition on tour for having the most shapely legs in the company, earned a little extra cash by posing nude for the life class at the National Art Gallery. Early the following year, 1953, I accepted an engagement with a new drama company which had taken over the Plaza Theatre at Northcote, a Melbourne suburb. The Globe Theatre Players billed themselves, inaccurately, as 'Australia's First Professional Repertory Company'. The company was owned by its leading lady, a big blonde of indeterminate age named Margaret Clarke, and their plays were to be directed by Jay Ross, who looked like a slightly younger Groucho Marx. When I joined them, their opening production, *Touch of the Sun* by Hugh Hastings, was already in rehearsal, with Margaret Clarke and a talented young Australian-Jewish actor, John Bluthal (now successful in English TV), in the leading roles. I understudied the role of Manners. After it opened, we began to rehearse what was to have been the Australian première of Christopher Fry's *The Lady's Not for Burning*, with Margaret and John in the roles created in London by Pamela Brown and John Gielgud, and me in the role created by Richard Burton.

'First read-through of *The Lady* today,' I noted in my diary. 'No kidding, they're all bloody awful, except for John Bluthal, who can act, and who looks like a young Emlyn Williams. The others are bad even by the most relaxed standards . . . I was driven home afterwards by the producer, Jay Ross – also quite unsuitable, I'm afraid. What a fucking company.'

The end was easily foreseeable. *Touch of the Sun* played three weeks to poor houses, and when pay-day came round Margaret had difficulty in paying all the salaries and attempted to borrow a few hundred pounds from me. But I was saving it to get out of Australia ('Don't leave,' said Jay Ross, 'you could have a big future with this company'), so I responded by threatening Margaret with Equity proceedings. She scraped up the money elsewhere, and paid us all. Next day I informed her that, unless she sacked the man I regarded as incapable of playing his role, Peter Fairaine, I would leave. She sacked Fairaine. Next pay day, not only was Margaret unable to produce our salaries, she was not even able to pay the rent for the theatre. The owner chucked us out, the others assembled on the pavement and discussed where to carry on rehearsing while Margaret found another theatre, while I simply snorted derisively and walked off into the sunset.

I had first met Sidney Nolan, a young Melbourne painter (not even painters called themselves artists in those days: now, of course, '*nous sommes tous des artistes*'), in 1946, when I was nineteen and he was twenty-nine. I had heard from him much about his benefactors, the Reeds, who lived in a charming house with fields running down to the Yarra river at Heidelberg, an outer suburb of Melbourne, virtually in the country. The Reeds were patrons of modern art, and helped a number of painters, writers and musicians. Consequently they attracted a large circle of talentless hangers-on, as well as the impecunious talented. Nolan, when he came up to Queensland to paint, made our Ballad Bookshop his headquarters, and from there made forays further north and into the outback. One day, in a back room of the shop, he painted in a few hours a huge portrait of me in shiny ripolin paint. Barrie Reid arrived at the end of the day, looked at it briefly and pronounced it a failure. Nolan immediately painted over it. By the next afternoon I had become a landscape.

In Melbourne I met Sidney Nolan's benefactors (not related to Barrie Reid). I liked them, though I had reservations both about the nature of their involvement with their protégés and about their incredibly fey outlook on life. Their world was both precious and claustrophobic, it seemed to me, and I took care never to become fully an inhabitant of it as my friends, particularly Barrie, did. The official party line was that John and Sunday Reed were virtually angels. They were certainly very generous with their money, their time and their interest, but they seemed to want one's soul in return. Survivors of that period still remind me of the occasion when I told the gentle Sunday that I thought she was the most evil woman I had ever met. Evil she may not have been, but she was a sad, unfulfilled woman and, perhaps in spite of herself, extraordinarily destructive. People around her tended to die. Perhaps she attracted mostly those who, for one reason or another, were about to die. Some died of disease. At least two killed themselves. She enticed Sidney Nolan to her bed, the successful Kundry to his too-weak Parsifal. But Sidney eventually found the strength to leave Heidelberg, and married someone whom the Reeds had always assured him was a dreadful woman: John Reed's sister, Cynthia. (A few months ago, Sidney and I reminisced, over lunch, about the Reeds. We decided that they had created a fictitious world – there are always plenty of fictitious characters about, waiting to be used – and lived in it to the end. 'Patrick White should have written about them,' I suggested. 'A novel called *I Chose Madness*.' '*Madness for Two* would be a better title,' said Sidney.)

Now, forty years on, John and Sunday are dead, and my old friend Barrie Reid lives in their house. I spent a night there in 1985, expecting to encounter ghosts of the past. I think they were present, but they chose to ignore me. I was always too worldly for that enclosed little world. Even in the early fifties, in the two years when I was based in Melbourne, my relationship with Heidelberg was weakening while Barrie's was being strengthened. We were looking in different directions from dissimilar positions.

I was by now nearly twenty-five. Unless I were to get out fairly soon, it would be too late. There comes a time in the lives of Australians after which they have become so completely brainwashed and sun-maddened that they are unable to observe anything in the rest of the world beyond such mundane facts as that Venice smells, Paris is overcrowded, London dirty, Munich noisy, New York corrupt, and the weather everywhere pretty crook. Already I imagined I could feel my intellectual and aesthetic arteries beginning to harden. I intensified my efforts to escape.

In July 1953, accompanied by Peter Kerr, a young actor who had been on the *Camphor Tree* tour, I left Melbourne on an Italian ocean liner, the *Oceania*, bound for Genoa. Our ports of call were Fremantle, Jakarta, Colombo, Bombay, Aden, Suez, Port Said and Naples. I loved my first long sea voyage: prior to this, I had done no more than cruise around the coast from Brisbane to Melbourne, once on a coastal steamer, the *Orungal*, and once on an overseas liner, the *Maloya*. I think I could stay at sea forever, sailing around the world, if the ship had a sufficiently extensive library, and the Captain agreed to put in at ports where there was an opera house to be found. A reasonable itinerary might take one from Tilbury (after a nostalgic farewell to the Royal Opera House, Covent Garden) to Oslo, Leningrad, Stockholm, Copenhagen, Hamburg, across the Atlantic to Boston, New York, Buenos Aires, San Diego, San Francisco, Vancouver, then across the Pacific to Sydney and across the Indian Ocean to where? (Cape Town, I suppose), up to Lisbon, Barcelona, Nice, Monte Carlo, Rome, Naples, Venice and Trieste. I should be sorry to lose contact with Vienna, Berlin, Chicago and Santa Fe (I think I could do without Paris), but one must make the occasional sacrifice in this life, must one not?

I spent most of my time on the voyage from Australia to Europe thinking about the future and the past. The future meant making a living, supporting myself. I wondered what on earth I was good at. I could earn enough to live on, for the time being, by acting and writing, but sooner or later I was sure to be found out, and then what? I made an annotated list of my abilities:

> *Acting:* mediocre, but able to get work.
> *Writing:* can earn tiny amounts with my poems, tidier sums from literary and musical journalism. In due course may be able to write books. Any money in this? Haven't tried my hand yet at novel-length fiction.
> *Singing:* Not worth persevering. Would never get beyond the chorus of a not very good opera house.
> *Piano:* Will never be up to concert standard. Forget it.
> *Composition:* Might be able to write the kind of music that would get by in musicals, or for film sound-tracks. Anything serious I attempt turns out to be pastiche.
> *Other skills, abilities or assets:* Precious few. Can probably impress a prospective employer as being well-educated, well-read, and an absolute (if occasionally abrasive) charmer. But what kind of employer? What kind of job? Should I have loitered in the groves of academe and become, as Mum still hopes I will, a Professor of Eng. Lit.? Surely not, for I lack the one essential prerequisite: I'm not sufficiently boring. I suppose I should note that I have directed plays quite successfully, but then surely anyone can do that.

So that is what I was approaching: an uncertain future. What was I leaving? What had I gained from living for nearly a quarter of a century on the nervous edge of that strange continent with its delightful fauna (kangaroos, wallabies, koalas, emus, wombats, crocodiles) and its somewhat forbidding flora? The more I thought about this as I sailed across the Indian Ocean, the less it seemed to me I had derived from being an Australian. I began to realize that I had always felt myself to be, if not *un citoyen du monde*, then at least a European. Even the 'Australian literature' that was taught in our schools seemed sheer muck to me, whereas official opinion in Australia was that we had our local geniuses, the counterparts of Michelangelo, Dante, Goethe, Shakespeare, Tolstoy, Dickens, Shaw.

'What have you enjoyed most in Australia?' I asked myself. It was an easy question to answer. I had enjoyed hearing great musicians playing European music: Lili Kraus and Schumann's *Carnaval*; Klemperer conducting Beethoven; Ignaz Friedman in Chopin; my childhood memories of Tauber breathing Schubert's secrets; of Lehmann's exultant Brahms; and, more recently, of Todd Duncan, Gershwin's first Porgy, singing Schubert's *Winterreise* so beautifully; of Joan Hammond in Hugo Wolf; of Ninon Vallin in Fauré; of the superb Marjorie Lawrence; the warm voice of Essie Ackland; even the delightfully absurd Erna Sack; and of course my friend Max Oldaker in Johann Strauss and Lehár and Romberg and Friml. All of this, I thought, had been a preview of life. I am travelling to Europe to be born. Australia had been a sort of womb.

But there must have been something else. What about the outback? The centre of Australia? What is there at the centre? For an Australian, that is still an unanswerable question. Everything is there, and nothing. The tales the aborigines tell one another are there, and perhaps some of our unremembered dreams are there, too. Most of us have never seen the interior of the country. We just know that it exists, remote, inaccessible, but waiting on the other side of the bush country, which we sentimentalize about more easily. And when civilization does encroach upon it, it moves elsewhere.

Not, as they say, a painter's country (despite the existence of the Aussie school of painting). Well, not a country for any old painter, perhaps; but obviously, in this empty space, where history has managed to scrawl only a few calligraphic lines across geography, there lay the landscape for which Sidney Nolan had been searching, the landscape which he might almost have been created to paint.

The first of Nolan's works to be seen in Europe, at about this time, were his outback paintings, his landscapes of the central interior. Birds walked upside-down on the unseen air watched by lonely men, J. Sheehan's Agricultural Hotel sat firmly in the middle of beyond nowhere, and the elegant great heron on the riverbank fixed the artist with its disbelieving eye. Most startling, ominous and inevitable were Nolan's desert paintings, panoramas of a giant, mythical Never-Never Land dreamed into existence by the aborigines. These, even as the *Oceania* cautiously entered the Mediterranean, were mixed up in my mind with Rethberg and Pinza singing Mozart, with Eugene Ormandy and Tchaikovsky, with Isaac Stern and Brahms.

Australia, I decided as we sailed between Scilla and Charybdis with Etna belching forth fire into the midnight sky, is not a country, merely a state of mind. By the time I took my first steps on European soil in Naples, I had ceased to be an Australian. Or so I thought. Later I was to find it useful, on certain occasions, to retain an Antipodean perspective. And, over the years, I was even able to relax sufficiently as a European to be able to, so to speak, turn up my Australian volume. Living in a country, one can explore facets of it closely; but to see it, as to see any object, in the round, one has to move away from it. A country requires to be examined from a distance in space and in time. In Australia I had no other experience against which to measure the country. I had only picture books and travellers' tales. It was not until I came to England and saw four distinct seasons appearing and disappearing, for example, that I really began to understand the English nature poets whose verses I had been made to rattle off so glibly at school.

In the last thirty years, I have visited Australia many times, but never for more than a few weeks on each occasion. I cannot claim, in any sense, that I live in two hemispheres, but I do by now realize that I would never want to be permanently deprived of either. I want the silence of Australia and the dialogue of Europe; the cold wind tearing through my bones in Bourke Street, Melbourne, and the not too fierce sun of a Mediterranean summer. I want to see crocodiles in the rivers of northern Queensland and squirrels in New York's Central Park. (It makes me happy when, occasionally, I see one in Green Park, London.) I want to listen to Geminiani in Sydney because there is no baroque visual experience to be had in Australia (with the exception of that neo-baroque misnamed Opera House) and to read Patrick White by the banks of the Danube because there is no solitude in Europe to equal his. I want English theatre and Australian intellectual laziness. I want Delphi, its sky darkened with eagles and history; and the beach at Moreton Island off the coast near Brisbane, its modern sky excitingly oppressive. I want that constant renewal of my childhood feelings that wandering around the streets of Brisbane can still give me, and the continued stimulus of new experience that I can find in so many places from O'Connell Street, Dublin, to Ulitsa Gorkova, Moscow.

But this is not how I felt when I first arrived in Europe. Stepping off the ship, I experienced a sense of exhilaration with, at its edge, a certain trepidation. 'Off with the new, on with the old,' I told myself as I gazed at Naples, at Santa Lucia, at Vesuvius. Perhaps for the first time in my life, I knew what it was like to feel completely free. Freedom, I suddenly realized, was mostly joy, and partly fear.

2

MOVING TO THE OLD WORLD

□ □ □

I HAD ESCAPED AT last to liberal, decadent, civilized Europe, a refugee from Australian culture. Disembarking at Genoa, Peter and I made our way slowly by train through Italy, Switzerland and France, getting off and staying here and there for a few days. In Milan I saw my first open-air opera at the Castello Szedesco (*Madama Butterfly* with Rina Gigli) and went to a students' concert at which I noted on my programme that one Renata Scotto, a plump little number who sang '*Un bel dì*' most beautifully, was likely to have a successful career. It was not until later that I began to study Italian seriously, but my French and German were respectable, if a trifle rusty, so in Lausanne I spent most of my time at the movies, seeing films in both French (a dubbed Laurel and Hardy, amongst others) and German (I remember a delightfully kitsch Martha Eggerth–Jan Kiepura movie, the kind of film that did not get exported to Australian film festivals). It was in a Lausanne cinema that I was, as I thought, sexually accosted for the first and only time. In the darkness, the man beside me placed a hand on my knee. I moved slightly, and he removed his hand. A few minutes later, he did it again. This time I dug him in the ribs with my elbow, and he said, 'Woof!' When the lights came on, he revealed himself to be a large St Bernard dog.

In Paris, we stayed on the left bank at a cheap hotel in the rue du Bac, took in plays by Sartre (*Huis Clos* and *La Putain Respectueuse*), Gide and Montherlant, and walked all over the city. We went to the Opéra and the Opéra Comique, of course. Verdi in French at the Opéra was decidedly lacklustre, but I serendipitously caught, at the Opéra Comique, what I only years later realized was the farewell performance of Georges Thill. It was a double-bill of *Cav.* and *Pag.* in which Thill sang Canio in *Pagliacci.* He began not too well. The wobble which I had heard seven years earlier in Melbourne was still in evidence, and his voice had lost some of its former quality. But by '*Vesti la giubba*' he was singing with his old ease and splendour. It was a big voice, and his wide open B flats brought the house down. In the last scene he was even better, excitingly dramatic, and he received the most tremendous ovation at the end of the opera, taking at least twenty curtain calls and finally indicating by mime that he wanted to go home to bed.

At the Opéra Comique I also heard the golden-voiced Léopold Simoneau as Almaviva in what was performed, with Beaumarchais's dialogue instead of Rossini's recitative, as *Le Barbier de Séville.* The tenor's wife, Pierette Alarie, sang Rosina. Simoneau was also an elegant Alfred in *La Traviata* at the Opéra. His career faded away disappointingly, due, I gather, to personal problems.

The programme booklets at the Opéra and the Opéra Comique contained synopses of the plots in, I think, four languages. The English was often comical: we were inaccurately informed that, in *Pagliacci*, 'Canio arrives in time to see the lovers parts.'

Finding ourselves caught in Paris by a transport strike which affected the railways, we had to borrow money from the Australian Embassy. After a few days, we managed to get to Dieppe by car and thence to Newhaven, and arrived in London in mid-August. A week later I was in Edinburgh for the Festival, having procured tickets for many of the performances before leaving Australia. I enjoyed much of what I saw, was enthralled by Alicia Alonso's dancing with the American National Ballet Theatre, and discovered a superb *Lieder* singer, the Canadian baritone Bruce Boyce. 'No voice to speak of,' I noted in the diary I continued to keep, on and off, for the next fifteen years or so, 'but a fine actor-singer, excelling in Wolf.'

I was sorely disappointed by the Old Vic's Hamlet, Mr Richard Burton. 'Surely,' I wrote, 'the actor playing Hamlet must be able to convince us that he is capable of discussing philosophy, poetry, art – Bernard Shaw has a comment on this – but the image which Burton presents is of a young Welsh extrovert whose main interests are football and floozies. This can no doubt be sublimated into the patriotic and warlike Harry, but not to Hamlet's intellectual and critical self-consciousness. So Burton started with all the natural disadvantages imaginable. And I'm afraid he did nothing to overcome them. He has three methods of talking his way through the script (he has, alas, but one way of walking through it, and that is a splay-legged stroll). First, he shouts in a very menacing fashion. Then, in the interchanges with Marcello, Bernardo etc, he quickly drains his words of all meaning and fires them out in a rapid monotone. Thirdly, for the greatest passages in the play, for the poetry and the thought, he adopts the intonation of a Nonconformist preacher. Smug, ranting balderdash is all he can make of it. What difference is there between this Hamlet and Fortinbras? Hamlet is a hypocrite, that is all.'

I was sceptical of Eleanor Steber as a *Lieder* singer. She seemed to me to be signalling to us, 'This is kids' stuff. You should have heard me as Elsa at Bayreuth.' But a performance of the Beethoven Violin Concerto by Menuhin with the Philharmonia Orchestra under Karajan was an overwhelming experience. Menuhin had the sad task of announcing to the audience the death of Jacques Thibaud, the great French violinist who had been killed the previous day in an air crash. The performance of the concerto that followed was of such serenity, nobility, and a kind of tenderness that somehow penetrated beyond sorrow, that it was almost a relief to be reminded by some faulty intonation in the final movement that Menuhin was not inhumanly perfect.

It was at the Edinburgh Festival that I heard Dietrich Fischer-Dieskau in person for the first time. In Australia I had admired his recording of the Schubert cycle, *Die schöne Müllerin*, without finding it as compelling as the old Gerhard Hüsch pre-war recording. I wanted to prefer Dieskau, because Hüsch, so my German-Jewish refugee friends in Australia told me, was a Nazi. And I certainly enjoyed Dieskau's all-Beethoven recital with Gerald Moore, especially the delightful *An die ferne Geliebte* (though Hüsch had my allegiance there, too). I concluded that what set limits to my admiration for Dieskau was his failure to communicate with the broad emotional sweep of Hüsch. Instead, he substituted a certain pedagogic approach. He seemed as often as not to be lecturing me on the songs rather than interpreting them directly to me. It was, in fact, not until I saw Fischer-Dieskau at the Vienna Staatsoper as Mandryka in *Arabella* (with the incomparably lovely Lisa Della Casa in the title-role) that I completely succumbed to him. I think it was Desmond Shawe-Taylor who wrote somewhere that Fischer-Dieskau might have been created by an opera-loving deity purely in order to portray Mandryka.

I renewed acquaintance in Edinburgh with the entrancing art of Irmgard Seefried, whom I had first heard in recitals in Melbourne. 'Here,' I wrote, 'is a singer I can love.' How marvellously simple and direct her Schubert was, as opposed to the mannered over-interpretation of Elisabeth Schwarzkopf. (Years later, when I talked to Seefried about Schubert interpretation, and mentioned Fischer-Dieskau's way with the composer, she said, 'The difference is that I live in Vienna, and Mr Dieskau lives in Berlin.')

But I was a stern critic, in my diary, even of my favourites. Of Irmgard Seefried's performance in Edinburgh of Brahms's *Die Mainacht*, I wrote: 'Miss Seefried must either drop *Die Mainacht* from her repertoire, or else sing it properly. It is a lovely song, and I don't really mind her not being able to phrase it, and resorting to a breath between adjective and noun in "*dunklere*

Schatten" and "*einsame Träne*". (I remember Kipnis's huge intake of breath before the verb at "... *und die einsame Träne rinnt*".) But she must not continue to produce four different vowel sounds on the four notes of "*Träne*". No, no, no.'

The Glyndebourne company was in Edinburgh that year, and they introduced me to *Idomeneo*. (The only Mozart operas I had been able to see in Australia were *Die Zauberflöte, Don Giovanni, Le nozze di Figaro* and, of course, *Così fan tutte*, which I had stage-managed.) I thought Sena Jurinac a very fine Ilia, and admired Richard Lewis as Idomeneo although both his Italian and his acting left much to be desired. I heard the Vienna Philharmonic Orchestra for the first time (though their recordings of Mozart, Schubert and Mahler under Bruno Walter were among my most treasured possessions). Their performances of Beethoven's Third ('Eroica') and Fourth Symphonies, conducted by Furtwängler, were tremendous experiences, the orchestra truly worthy of the music. When I heard them again, a few days later, conducted this time by Bruno Walter, it was as though I had been transported to Heaven. Mozart's 'Jupiter' and Beethoven's 'Pastoral': such warm, all-embracing, lovable re-creations of the symphonies.

By the middle of September I was in London, looking for work and accommodation. My bank had found me somewhere to stay temporarily, a bed-sitter in Lady Margaret Road, Kentish Town, but I found the area squalid and my landlady inappropriately genteel. When an Australian friend rang and left his Brixton telephone number for me to ring back, the Lady Bracknell-like inflection Mrs Drury gave to 'Brixton' when she delivered the message quite alarmed me.

I had met the music critic Felix Aprahamian, who had visited Australia, was inexplicably fond of Australians, and indeed had a houseful of them. Felix lived with his mother in Muswell Hill, and rented rooms cheaply to Australian musicians. When Peter Kerr and I moved in, the other inmates of this agreeable madhouse included Douglas Whitaker, at that time principal flautist of the BBC Symphony Orchestra; Peter Andry, another flautist who is now the Director of the International Classical Division of EMI Records; and Peter's brother, Dr Robert Andry, an eccentric but amiable psychologist. Mrs Aprahamian, Felix's mother, was a sweet little Armenian lady who cooked marvellous meals and was terrorized by the wicked Felix. (Felix had a brother, Francis, who did not live at home. Francis, who visited his mother occasionally, was a pleasant man who happened to be a member of the Communist Party. 'The Queen is very annoyed with Francis,' Felix told his mother one day. 'In fact, she may have him hanged if he doesn't see the error of his politics.' A frightened Mrs Aprahamian came to me for comfort, and I had to assure her that Felix was only teasing.)

The Aprahamian household provided for me a wonderful ambiance in which to spend my first year in London. Musicians were frequent visitors to the house: Monique Haas, Louis Kaufmann, Manoug Parikian, Henry Krips, Gérard Souzay. The atmosphere was delightful. Felix's wit and erudition kept me on my toes, for he could speak of Proust as knowledgeably as of Poulenc, and Felix himself was extremely helpful to me, introducing me to those people in broadcasting, journalism and the gramophone record industry whom he thought it would be useful for me to know.

I had decided to continue earning my living in the same way that I had done in Australia, combining acting with literary and musical journalism, and I soon began, with Felix's help, to build up a core of free-lance contacts from whom I received enough commissions to be able to keep my head above water. I wrote sleeve-notes for long-playing records, mostly for EMI but also for other companies, among them Deutsche Grammophon, RCA Victor, CBS, Decca and Philips. If you bought an LP of a Mendelssohn symphony, or a Schubert quartet, or Fischer-Dieskau's recording of *Die Winterreise* (or Gérard Souzay's, for that matter), or recital records by Kirsten Flagstad or Jussi Björling or Hermann Prey, or a complete opera – *Aida* with Leontyne Price, or the Karajan *Otello* – you were in danger of getting with it a thousand or more golden words on the subject by me.

I also began to broadcast on BBC musical programmes, the Sunday morning *Music Magazine* and the Saturday *Record Review* as well as individual programmes of my own devising. I continued to broadcast frequently for the next twenty-five years, until I found I needed more time for the books I was commissioned to write when I became comparatively successful as an author. Something had to give, and I decided it would have to be the more ephemeral radio and TV. But for a quarter of a century, the BBC and the record companies between them helped to keep the dingo from my door.

I had no immediate intention of giving up my acting career. If I could fool people in Australia into giving me jobs as an actor, presumably I could do it in England. I passed an audition for the BBC as an actor, but got very little work from them either in radio or TV, and not much more from commercial TV when it arrived: a few small parts in plays whose names I and the public have consigned to oblivion. I was a little more successful in the theatre. Having been given the names of several agents by British actors whom I had worked with in Australia, I dutifully did the rounds. If you were not an attractive enough proposition for an agent to want to represent you exclusively, you could get yourself 'put on the books' of several agents, the theory being that they would bring you to the attention of managements if none of their real clients were available. Of course, you had to be potentially marketable to get onto their books. I was taken on, in this way, by at least six agencies. If you had not heard anything from them for some time, you could always call at the office, usually to be told, 'Sorry, nothing for you at the moment.' Among the agents who at least from time to time sent me along to audition for this or that role were Fraser and Dunlop, Gordon Harbord, John Penrose Productions, and Denton and Warner.

Denton and Warner's offices were in that big building on the south-east side of Cambridge Circus, opposite the Palace Theatre. Either MI6 lived in the same building, or one of the spy novelists pretended they did. Denton and Warner's suite was indescribably dingy. Denton was, I imagine, long since dead, and the show was run by Miriam Warner, the doyenne of tatty agents. If you could not get a job in some ghastly twice-nightly rep. company through Miriam Warner, you would have to be completely unemployable as an actor. I got plenty of job offers through Miriam Warner, but the agency I preferred to deal with was just one rung higher up the theatrical ladder – John Penrose Productions, in Rupert Street. John Penrose was also an actor, a plumpish, porcine individual who looked like an understudy for Charles Laughton's Captain Bligh. Although I had not previously known his name, I recognized him when I first entered his office, for he had played a Nazi officer in the Robert Donat movie, *The Adventures of Tartu*, during the war, and had also been very effective in *Kind Hearts and Coronets* with Alec Guinness and Dennis Price.

John Penrose's cynicism amused me, and something about me, my lack of ambition, perhaps, appealed to him. We got on well. Eventually, he agreed to take me on as one of the twelve clients he wanted to limit himself to, and I in turn agreed that he could represent me exclusively. No more messing about with Miriam Warner. Under my photograph in *Spotlight*, the Actors' Directory in which we all exaggerated our past achievements and lied about our height, I was able to announce that 'All enquiries should be directed to John Penrose Productions'. I felt that I was on the way.

What I was on the way to was an agreeable four or five years in which, subsidized by my earnings from free-lance journalism and broadcasting, I could audition for stage and film jobs, hang out with other out-of-work actors either in the coffee bar downstairs at the Arts Theatre or a theatrical café in Gerrard Street the name of which I have forgotten, and occasionally manage to work. Work included the provincial reps (and there were hundreds in those days before television and the Arts Council killed most of them off), tours of West End successes with non-West End casts, small roles (Australian characters) in films, and commentaries for documentaries. All things considered, the auditions were more interesting than the other activities. I can truthfully say that I have appeared on the stages of most existing West End theatres, as well as several no longer standing. The latter include the St James's Theatre in King Street, where *The Importance of Being Earnest* had its première; the Scala in Charlotte Street, where I gave representatives of the Royal Shakespeare Theatre a taste of my Iago; the Stoll in the Kingsway, where I did actually sing in opera, in the chorus. For the most part I appeared, however, not before large and paying audiences but before select groups of bored producers, directors and casting managers.

Offers of 'special week' engagements with repertory companies were, I found, relatively easy to come by. To do a special week meant that one was engaged by the management for one play, because their resident company was too small or contained no one suitable for a particular role. A special week involved one in two weeks' employment, one week rehearsing and one week playing. As often as not one would be kept on for the following play as well, since that was cheaper for the management than paying a couple of additional train fares to and from London.

To begin with I refused these special weeks, thinking it better to hold out for a permanent engagement with a repertory company. Of course, what I really wanted was to act in the West End of London, though I realized this was not likely to happen until I had amassed some experience in the provinces. Managements, understandably, were not impressed with what one had done in Australia. They had no idea what Antipodean standards might be like, and no easy way of telling whether or not one was exaggerating or inventing.

Peter Kerr, the young actor who had travelled from Australia with me, had joined the repertory company at Morecambe, a seaside resort in Lancashire. 'I know I'm as good as anyone in the company, having now seen their work,' he wrote to me a few days after his arrival there, 'and you, my dear, would be considered a second Laurence Olivier.' The second Laurence Olivier continued to audition two or three times a week. Unfortunately, when I was offered jobs out of London I kept refusing them. I auditioned successfully for Joan Littlewood at the Theatre Royal, Stratford, in the East End, and was offered the role of Bolingbroke in *Richard II* at Stratford and on a European tour. I was tempted by this, as the tour was to include Eastern Europe, but the pay was meagre, and when I was given the chance to appear in the West End of London, for no pay at all, I jumped at it and said no to Joan Littlewood.

In the fifties there were still a number of theatre clubs in London where professional actors were willing to appear either at salaries below the Equity minimum or for no salary at all, while they were waiting for more prestigious engagements. These clubs performed the function of 'shop windows', where agents and managements could look at new talent without the formality of an audition. One such club, in the East End, asked me to play Romeo and Benedick in a season of Shakespeare (they must have been hard up for actors), but I chose to accept another offer, from the Hovenden Theatre Club, which at least had the advantage to me that its performances took place on Shaftesbury Avenue, albeit in the crypt of St Anne's Church.

The Hovenden Theatre Club, whose director was Valery Hovenden, was mounting a revival of an eighteenth-century comedy, *The Natural Son*, by Richard Cumberland, a playwright who is perhaps better known as a critic of the drama. (He was pilloried by Sheridan as 'Sir Fretful Plagiary' in revenge for an unfavourable notice.) *The Natural Son* was first produced at Drury Lane in 1742, and not revived until this production, in which I played one of the leading roles, that of Jack Hustings, a somewhat blustery country gentleman. *The Stage* said of this, my first appearance on any European stage, 'Charles Osborne brings with him a tang of the countryside as the good-hearted but unpolished squire.' Is that a favourable notice? I was not sure. Anyway, a number of people praised what they described as my naturalness or relaxation on-stage. We ran for two-and-a-half weeks, and I felt, naively, at the end of it that I had made a satisfactory English début.

Through Roy Wilson, an actor who had just returned from some years in America and who had played Blushenly ('a virtuous young man') in *The Natural Son*, I met the delightful Athene Seyler, who charmed me into appearing in a Christmas play, *Second Eden* by John Ormerod, which she and her husband, Nicholas Hannen, were presenting at Christ Church, Chelsea. Working with Athene was fun, but the three performances of *Second Eden* did not lead to anything else, for theatrical managements were not in the habit of sending their talent scouts to religious plays performed in churches.

Roy Wilson seemed to have a number of churchy connections. He later cajoled me into playing a leading role in a play he had written pseudonymously as 'Mark Haywood', called *Happier Still*, which was given a few performances in another church crypt (I began to feel like 'the cat i' the adage'), this time that of St Martin-in-the-Fields. 'Roy Wilson acted extremely well as the undergraduate who, learning that he is soon to die, marries his friend's discarded mistress to provide for her coming child. Charles Osborne was pleasing as the erring friend.' (I was beginning to learn that one could always rely on *The Stage* for at least a not unkind notice.) The most talented member of the cast of *Happier Still* was Jeremy Cadell, an eighteen-year-old who had just emerged from the Bristol Old Vic Theatre School, and who I was convinced would have a highly successful career. Alas, Jeremy killed himself because of an unhappy love affair, while he was still in his early twenties.

I lost touch with Roy Wilson nearly thirty years ago. In April 1986, however, reading an article about those two brothers in Worthing who went on a fast to save their local theatre, I noticed that their names were Roy and Michael Wilson: behind the emaciated features of the older-looking brother in the accompanying photograph I eventually recognized 'my' Roy Wilson.

My first months in London were enjoyable enough to convince me that I wanted to stay indefinitely. It seemed to me that I would be able to support myself with a judicious admixture of theatre, writing and part-time jobs, though I was so fascinated by the rich variety of plays, operas and concerts on offer that I was not as assiduous in the pursuit of professional engagements as I should have been in my first year. I spent far too much time attending performances. I saw as much as I possibly could, dashing off to matinées of dreadful plays which today I would cross several streets to avoid, simply because I wanted to see what this or that famous actor or actress was like.

Nevertheless, I was critically quite discriminating. My diary for that period is full of scathing comments on actors, singers, directors, playwrights and composers. Not even my idol, Laurence Olivier, was exempt. One Saturday evening in November 1953, I took myself to the Phoenix to see the Oliviers in *The Sleeping Prince*, a new play by Terence Rattigan:

> A very dull play, saved mainly by the gorgeous presence of Martita Hunt. Vivien just did not have a role to play. She was adequate, but any of fifty chorus girls would have done as well. Olivier's problem was that he came across as the imaginative actor being too imaginative about this particular role. It was such unsatisfactory material that he obviously felt the need to remould it, and play a feasible and realistic character of his own inventing. But in doing so, he came close to exposing the flimsiness of the rest of the play. He also directed and, I suppose, did as much as he could with so boring a 'comedy'. At least, I suppose it's a comedy, because Rattigan says it is. But, although one doesn't expect of him the verbal felicities of a Coward, that brittle poet of light and elegant comedy, surely even in a play which relies so heavily on situation there must be some verbal delight, must there not?

Before the end of the year I had made my first visits to London's two opera houses where, over the years, I was to experience so many magnificent, excellent, adequate, mediocre and atrocious performances. At Sadler's Wells Theatre, where the Sadler's Wells Opera Company played before it moved to the West End to become English National Opera, the first opera I saw was an English translation of Mozart's *Die Entführung aus dem Serail*, which was billed not as *The Abduction from the Harem* but as *Il Seraglio*: a reminder of the days when all foreign-language opera had to be Italian, when even Covent Garden referred to *Il flauto magico* and *I maestri cantori*. *Il Seraglio* retained its Italian title in England long after companies had ceased to perform it in Italian, even when, as at Sadler's Wells, it was being sung in English. A splendid production by Clive Carey, good orchestral playing, but 'singing not so hot,' I noted, 'except for Jennifer Vyvyan, a fine Constanze, and Owen Brannigan, though he lacked the bottom D that Osmin must have.'

At Covent Garden, 'a real Opera House, unlike Sadler's Wells', my first visit was to *Die Walküre*. 'Good orchestra under Stiedry, bad production, Hans Hotter a wonderful Wotan, Margaret Harshaw a fine Brünnhilde, Sylvia Fisher an even more impressive Sieglinde, and Ramon Vinay, perhaps not *quite* up to her level, as Siegmund.' I regretted that I would now never have an opportunity to see the great Kirsten Flagstad as Brünnhilde, for some weeks earlier I had attended her farewell appearance. This was at a concert in the Royal Festival Hall. In the first half the BBC Symphony Orchestra, conducted by Sir Malcolm Sargent (complete with carnation, as always), had played the Fourth Symphony of Sibelius. Then, after the interval, Flagstad appeared and sang Wagner's *Wesendonk Lieder*. The programme was to have concluded with Ravel's *La Valse* but, after Flagstad had returned to the platform several times to acknowledge applause, Sargent turned to the audience and announced, 'Madame Flagstad has said that, if we will play the Prelude to *Tristan*, she will sing the *Liebestod*.' Hysterical applause and shouting. She did sing it beautifully, and her voice did not sound like that of a woman approaching sixty. 'I suppose,' I wrote, 'I'd admire her more if she were less stolid an interpreter, but the voice itself is so radiant it almost persuades you. Isolde is surely not her role; what a glorious Brünnhilde she must have been.'

I had left Australia armed with letters of introduction, mostly to ex-Viennese musicians living in Great Britain. I used very few of these, but I did make myself known to Mrs Katharine ('Käthe') Breuer, matriarch of a distinguished Viennese Jewish family. Käthe Breuer entertained me at her house in Holland Park, a very *gemütlich* dwelling, its furnishings and atmosphere redolent of 'old Vienna'. She also gave a party for me, inviting a number of people whom she thought might be helpful to me. Through her I met Bruno Walter and also, somewhat unexpectedly, a young actor named Denholm Elliott, whom I had admired at the Edinburgh Festival in T. S. Eliot's new play, *The Confidential Clerk*, which was now playing in London. I visited Denholm in his dressing-room at the Lyric Theatre in Shaftesbury Avenue, and he gave me much useful and friendly advice concerning managements and agents.

Always something of a lone wolf, I did not want to become too involved with other Antipodeans in London, but inevitably I encountered several of them: the actors Lloyd Lamble, Alan Cuthbertson, Peter Finch, Diane Cilento (whom I had first met, years earlier, in Brisbane when her mother brought her to my bookshop); the composers Arthur Benjamin, Edwin Carr, Malcolm Williamson (now Master of the Queen's Musick but then working at Boosey and Hawkes); the pianists Gordon Watson, superb Lisztian whom I had met in Brisbane during the war (when we attended an Ignaz Friedman recital together), and Geoffrey Parsons, who was at the beginning of his international career and busily accompanying singers of every kind. I was delighted to meet Anne Ziegler and Webster Booth at a party given by Geoffrey in Balham, and I think Webster Booth was delighted, and surprised, when I spoke appreciatively of his recordings of Handel and Italian opera. Most people thought of him simply as the male half of the duet team with a repertoire stretching from Rudolf Friml to Hans May.

Geoffrey Parsons and I shared a love of the German *Lied*, and we talked frequently of the *Lieder* singers of the past, of Tauber, Lehmann, Schumann, Karl Erb. Our great favourite was Gerhard Hüsch, the distinguished German baritone of the years between the wars. We talked of Hüsch's Wolf performances on record, of the two Schubert cycles, of the *Dichterliebe*. How absurdly delighted and proud I felt, two or three years later, when I heard Gerhard Hüsch sing Schubert's *Winterreise* and *Die schöne Müllerin* in the Cartoon Gallery at the Victoria and Albert Museum, with Geoffrey Parsons at the piano. For many years now, Geoffrey has been at the pinnacle of his profession: not, I think, because he is necessarily a better pianist than his three or four most serious rivals, but because of his encyclopaedic knowledge of the song repertoire and, especially, his love of song and of the voice.

My first months in London were encouraging. I had made a number of contacts and some new friends. I had auditioned at so many theatres that I was able mendaciously to assure my parents that I was doing well: 'I've already appeared on some of London's leading stages: the St James's Theatre, the Whitehall, the Theatre Royal, Drury Lane, the Scala, the Lyric, and lots of others. Don't *worry*, Mum.' Actually, I received many more offers from provincial repertory companies than, at this stage, I accepted, for I wanted, if at all possible, to remain in London. I had not fled from Melbourne in order to end up in Manchester, or somewhere even worse. I said no to Leatherhead, no to Kidderminster, no to several tatty tours. I can see clearly now that I was never really very serious about this theatre business. When I discovered that an old friend from Brisbane, Val Vallis, was in London doing postgraduate work at London University, I decided that going to concerts and operas with Val was much more enjoyable than rushing up north somewhere for a couple of weeks to play in a Vernon Sylvaine farce, or down to some coastal resort to be the young man who turns out to be the murderer in an Agatha Christie whodunnit. Anyway, most of these 'special week' jobs offered a salary of no more than £8 a week, whereas I could earn twice as much by writing one or two sleeve-notes for LP records, which I could polish off in a couple of afternoons.

Occasionally, I would get sidetracked. For instance, to earn some extra cash over Christmas in 1953, I took a job at Imhof's in New Oxford Street, selling gramophone records. I stayed on for a few weeks into the new year at their request. I knew a little more about the music on the records than the average sales assistant, and I was asked to write reviews for the monthly newsletter. But it was bound to end in tears, for I became bored with the customers. I detested snide shop assistants, and here I was turning myself into a prime example of the type. When some shrill-voiced Knightsbridge matron bore down upon me with the words, 'I'd like *A Night with Harry Belafonte*,' I would reply, 'You'll be lucky' or 'Wouldn't we all?', or something equally unacceptable.

I didn't last all that long at Imhof's, but long enough to strike up an acquaintance with one of my customers, the elegant Anton Walbrook, who for years had been one of my screen heroes. And long enough to have, one day, a delightful conversation with Dame Myra Hess, who was about to record Schumann's *Symphonic Studies* but was worried about the opposition. 'What other recordings of it are available?' she asked me.

'Only Moura Lympany.'

'Not Cortot?'

'No, his recording has been deleted.'

'That's all right, then.' And she breathed a sigh of relief.

One day, in the post-Christmas lull when the shop was almost empty, I attempted an experiment. Arming each of my fellow-workers with a different 78 rpm record of Schubert's *Heidenröslein*, I sent them into the six listening-booths on the mezzanine floor. On the ground floor, like some maniac Malcolm Sargent, I gave a decisive down-beat, and Richard Tauber, Elisabeth Schumann, Alexander Kipnis and three other singers all began *Heidenröslein* together. They did not stay together for long, of course, for they sang at different tempi, and indeed in different keys. I continued to conduct, attempting to hold back by gesture the far-too-impulsive Schumann, or to speed up the sluggish Kipnis. The resulting cacophony brought an enraged manager racing out of her office, threatening dismissal.

At this stage (it was in April, 1954), the Argo Record Company momentarily entered my life. My friend Gordon Watson, who recorded for Argo, persuaded the company that, as I seemed able to sell his records at Imhof's when no one else in London was moving them, they should engage me as their Sales Manager. They did. It was probably the worst move they ever made. 'They' were Harley Usill and Cyril Clarke. With money provided by Ian Dalrymple, a film producer whom they were taking for a ride, they were busily recording twentieth-century English music, much of it by composers I did not admire. While I was with Argo, I persuaded them to branch out into other fields, and I think I had something to do with their acquiring the BBC radio production of Dylan Thomas's *Under Milk Wood* starring Richard Burton. (I remember Burton coming to our premises in George Street, off Baker Street, accompanied by his agent to haggle over terms.) *Under Milk Wood* was not Thomas at his best, by any means. But it was very 'poetic' in the Third Programme sense of the word, and Argo did very well out of it.

After a few months, Harley and Cyril realized that I was not increasing the sales of Argo records, mainly because I couldn't bring myself to walk into a record shop and start behaving like a salesman, which was what being Argo's Sales Manager meant. There was no sales force: I was the Chief and all the Indians too. Argo and I parted company by mutual agreement. All they got out of me during my period of employment were a few sleeve-notes on John Ireland piano pieces and French folk songs. When they thought I was out and about flogging their records, I was as often as not auditioning.

I think it was when I auditioned for the American director of a successful Broadway comedy, *The Teahouse of the August Moon*, which was to be staged in London, that I most spectacularly talked myself out of a job. He had asked me to learn a scene from the play, and come back the following day to perform it for him. I duly appeared the next day and did my piece. 'Wonderful,' he said. 'So wonderful to be shown an actor thinking. The way you hesitate, search for the words, you show me the thought processes so clearly. You are giving me *intellectual* acting. Wonderful.' I couldn't stand it. 'I'm not giving you intellectual acting,' I told him. 'I'm giving you not being able to remember the wretched stuff properly. It's such bilge I can hardly bring myself to utter the words I do remember.' I did not appear in the West End production of *The Teahouse of the August Moon.*

When Athene Seyler rang me to ask if I would act in her Easter production at Christ Church, Chelsea ('No salary, but it's a wonderful shop window') I accepted, though I feared I might spend my entire life in British theatre as a star of shop-window productions at no salary. Fortunately, before rehearsals got under way I was rescued by Associated British Films. My agent rang me to say he had got me an interview with someone there who was casting a World War II epic, *The Dam Busters,* about the exploits of an RAF Squadron which had contained a few Australians. I was being considered for the role of Pilot Officer Foxlee because I was Australian and I did not look too disastrously unlike the real Foxlee.

My interviewers satisfied themselves that, in person, I did not look any less like Foxlee than my photographs did, and then began to ask me about my film experience. I tried to tell them about my stunningly successful stage appearances as Marchbanks in *Candida,* but they wanted film. I had to improvise, and indulge in a little reality-enhancing. Knowing that the average Australian film of the forties and early fifties was rarely shown outside the state in which it was made, let alone the country, I described film tests as films, documentaries for the Queensland Education Department as lavish epics, and an amateur film of *Henry V,* made as an offshoot of a stage production for schools, as the Antipodean answer to Olivier's version. The Associated British casting people were impressed, or perhaps they saw through me and did not care. I was invited to do a screen test for Foxlee.

The test was satisfactory and I got the part. When the contract arrived, I felt quietly and smugly pleased. I read it over and over: '. . . under contract to Associated British Picture Corporation Ltd . . . minimum of twenty days' filming at £24 per day . . .' This was as much as I had expected to earn that entire year. A week or two later, my part of the script arrived, with a covering letter, signed by G. L. T. Scott, Production Manager. The letter was almost as long as the extract from the script which it accompanied. But I memorized Foxlee's two or three lines, and waited to be called. Another week or two passed, and then I received a phone call. My scenes would be shot over the next three weeks, and I would probably be needed on the set on certain specified days. I noted the dates and times. I was about to ask what was the most convenient way to get to Elstree from Muswell Hill, when the voice continued. 'We'll send a car for you at six am.'

They'd send a car! I began to feel like Clark Gable. And indeed the studio limousine which, for the next few weeks, picked me up from the Aprahamian house in Methuen Park impressed the neighbours and Mrs Aprahamian mightily, but not Felix, for he was never up at six am.

The daily Call Sheet for *The Dam Busters* for Friday, 18 June 1954 reveals that on that day, on Stage 2 at Elstree Studios, we were shooting four scenes set in the Briefing Room at Scampton RAF base in Lincolnshire. Thirty-three actors were involved, as well as four stand-ins (to relieve the tedium for Richard Todd, Michael Redgrave, Derek Farr and Ernest Clark) and one hundred and three extras (a hundred aircrew and three Station Officers). The actors were listed on the Call Sheet in order of the importance of their roles, and after the four leads came a number of other well-known names: Frank Duncan, Robert Shaw, Nigel Stock, Brewster Mason (whom I thought then nearly as boring an actor as I do now), John Fraser, Bill Kerr. My name appeared below these but above George Baker, Alun Owen (later to make his name as a playwright) and a dozen others. I shared what, in comparison with cramped theatre back-stage accommodation, one could only describe as a large and sumptuously appointed dressing-room with two other actors, David Morell and Denys Graham. My make-up call on that day was for seven-thirty am, and I was required to be on the set by nine.

The director of the film was Michael Anderson, but the lighting cameraman, I discovered, was of almost equal importance, and Anderson frequently deferred to his judgment when setting up shots. He was Erwin Hillier, a Berliner who had worked in British cinema since 1929. Films for which he had been lighting cameraman included *I Know Where I'm Going*, *Private Angelo* and *Castle in the Air*. He clearly knew his job, his approach to which was much more professional than that of several of the actors, and when my one and only close-up was being shot he was more helpful to me than Michael Anderson, who opened his mouth only when it was finished to say, 'Thank you, Charles.'

Most days on the set were long ones: a good twelve hours. Sometimes I stayed on to look at the previous day's rushes, but more often I got away as quickly as possible. Twelve hours of the company of other actors is far too much of a not-so-good thing.

During the filming of *The Dam Busters* I wandered onto a nearby set to watch Alan Ladd making *The Black Knight*, and witnessed the following scene:

Ladd (in character, as a mysterious knight at the court of King Arthur): Say, King, I got noos for ya. The Saracens are comin'.
Director: Cut. That was fine.
Ladd (relaxing out of character, and addressing the company at large): Say, what the heck are Saracens, anyway?

Deciding that I needed a rest after my strenuous exertions on *The Dam Busters*, most of which finished up on the cutting-room floor, I enrolled in the Dartington Summer School of Music, and travelled down to Devon at the end of July. 'I find,' I noted on arrival, 'that most of the other students are either pimply youths or dowdily breastless middle-aged ladies,' but I enjoyed my time at Dartington and made some new friends and acquaintances, though not in the aforementioned categories. John Amis and William Glock were running the Summer School at the College of Arts, which provided a quite beautiful setting and background for both study and socializing. John, a Billy Bunterish figure of a man a few years my senior, was someone I had already met *chez* Aprahamian. (Reading his pleasant volume of memoirs recently, I realized that John and I had done many of the same things throughout our careers, and even been helped on our way by the same people: for most of the time John was five or ten years ahead of me, though I at least discovered I was not going to be a great star of opera somewhat earlier in my career than John in his.)

I attended the master classes in piano and singing at Dartington in that summer of 1954, derived both pleasure and instruction from the performances and lectures of Rosalyn Tureck, became friendly with the attractive, though slightly *maladif* French baritone, Gérard Souzay, and delighted in the company and the eccentric personality of the Swiss tenor, Hugues Cuénod. I went with Gérard to a recital by the Vegh Quartet, whose second violinist had arrived from Nice with only a few minutes to spare. The four players rushed onto the platform before the other three noticed that, although they were in lounge suits, he was wearing white tie and tails. Bitter recriminations in Hungarian preceded their somewhat rough performance of Beethoven's op.74, after which they recovered to give a wonderful account of that nervous, thrilling work, the Fifth Quartet of Bartok.

Gérard Souzay was not very pleased with the pupils who had been selected for his master classes. When he asked me what I thought of them, and I gave my opinion, he agreed with me. 'They are not very exciting,' he said, 'and one of them, the almost tenor, is the bottom.' Gérard was equally displeased with Ibbs and Tillett, his English agents, and with Decca, for whom he made gramophone records. I agreed to act as his manager in England and also specifically to re-activate the question of an Australian tour, the negotiations for which had been mishandled by Ibbs and Tillett. But this arrangement did not endure: I had not the time to deal responsibly with Gérard's affairs, and in any case I eventually came to realize that virtually all performing artists are dissatisfied with their managements.

When I look back now at that Dartington summer, I consider that its greatest value to me was in leading me to a love of the Fauré *Requiem*, a work for which I had previously felt no more than a cool appreciation of its lack of bombast. A choir formed from the students (I was among the basses) rehearsed under John Clements, with George Malcolm as organist substituting for the orchestra, and we performed the *Requiem* in the parish church at Totnes, with Elsie Morison and Gérard Souzay as soloists. I practised the *'Hostias'* and *'Libera me'* movements on my own, in the unworthy hope that Gérard's slight cold might worsen and I would be plucked out of the chorus to stand in for him. That did not happen, and his voice of rich velvet graced the performance along with Elsie Morison's beautifully poised account of the *'Pie Jesu'*.

The pattern, or rather lack of pattern, of my first year in England was to be repeated for the following three or four years, with the difference that, having in 1953 and 1954 refused so many theatre jobs rather than leave London (no to Swindon rep, no to Colchester, no to a tour of Agatha Christie's *The Hollow* with Jeanne de Casalis), I subsequently relented and accepted engagements on tour and in rep. There was, I was forced to concede, no point in hanging about the West End, failing to pass audition after audition. On the day that I was refused a role in *Can-Can* at the Coliseum and offered 'The bleeding sergeant' in *Macbeth* somewhere else, I thought I had reached my nadir. I was tempted by the suggestion that I should teach a class in *Lieder* interpretation at the Royal College of Music. No, not tempted, really, just flattered, for I did not want to teach. I could have gone on forever, keeping my head above water by writing musical and literary journalism, enjoying my midday plate of spaghetti and glass of chianti for five shillings at Bianchi's in Soho, where Elena Salvoni was so friendly and welcoming for so many years, and my evening meals *chez* Felix, reviewing the occasional Festival Hall concert or Wigmore Hall recital, meeting my more successful colleagues in theatre and music and enjoying their in-jokes and occasionally writing a poem at the request of some little magazine in Australia.

If I had really been serious about a career in the theatre, I would surely have accepted more of those dreary offers I received to work in the provinces, or indeed to tour Australia with John McCallum and Googie Withers in *Simon and Laura*. Within a couple of years I found myself accepting the kind of offers I at first snootily rejected, but in those first two years I was determined to hold out for something in London.

Picking at random a day from my 1954 engagement diary, I find that I modelled in the morning, lunched with Eric Portman, auditioned in the afternoon (twice), and translated an Éluard poem, *Bonne Justice*, between auditions. In the early evening I drove to Basingstoke with Geoffrey Parsons 'and two lasses from the Arts Council' to see the Council's Opera Group perform Rossini's *Cenerentola* with piano accompaniment. That must have been my first contact of any kind with the organization which was eventually to employ me for twenty years.

By the spring of 1955 I had also begun to work, on and off, for Adolf Borsdorf, a concert agent, and I had played a one-line role, of a photographer, in a boring film called *Geordie*, directed at Ealing by Frank Launder (with, to rub salt in the wound, Olivier directing his *Richard III* on the set next door). I had directed readings of plays by the Spanish dramatist, Jacinto Benavente, at the Spanish Institute, with a cast including Marie Ney, Robert Eddison, Anita Sharp-Bolster (an Irish-born Hollywood character actress), Brian Cobby (whose plummy voice now tells you the time when you dial 123), and Oriel Ross.

Oriel Ross was a beauty *d'un certain age*, a glamour-puss of the thirties who had been sculpted by Epstein (it is in the Fitzwilliam at Cambridge), had married into and subsequently out of the aristocracy (she had been the Countess Poulett and still rather liked to use the title), and now lived in a house in Ebury Street (number 22). I think she owned the house: she lived on the upper floors of one side of it, letting out the ground floor as a TV studio. Oriel agreed to rent to me the top floor of her maisonette, and in November 1954 I moved from the Aprahamian household in Muswell Hill to take up residence in Ebury Street SW1, where before me had lived Mozart, George Moore and Patrick White (no, not simultaneously). Geoffrey Parsons helped me move in.

Number 22, the most imposing house in the street, had at some time in the nineteenth century been a school for the children (of the staff, I suppose) from nearby Buckingham Palace. In the twentieth century it was, for a time, Mosley's headquarters, the American Embassy and, until Oriel moved in, the residence of the revue star, Henry Kendall. Eric Portman swore the place had also been a morgue, but I think that was just Eric's idea of humour.

It was at 22 Ebury Street that I experienced my, so far, only poltergeist.

Oriel had warned me that I might, as she put it, 'occasionally undergo a certain *frisson* on the stairs', but that I was not to worry. She had, she assured me, lived with this psychic phenomenon for some time. I did not take her seriously, but one night, after I had been living in the house for several weeks, I arrived home around midnight, went to bed and read a book for about half an hour before going to sleep. I awoke suddenly an hour or two later with the feeling that there was someone else in my bedroom. I lay still and listened, rather frightened. As far as I can remember now, I thought there might be some*one*, not some*thing*, there. I became aware that the room was very cold (though the house's central heating was thermostatically controlled). At some point the feeling came to me that what I was experiencing was not rational, that no one could have got into the room, and that this must be a psychic experience. This did nothing to diminish my fear, but I decided that – or perhaps I remembered reading something to the effect that – electric light was a reliable dispeller of ghosts, so I plucked up the courage to push my hand out from under the blanket and switch on my bedside lamp.

Nothing there. I sat up and listened again. Suddenly, from my kitchen next door I heard a series of loud sounds, as of smashing crockery. Immediate fright: there was someone in the kitchen. Then silence. I may have waited another minute before venturing to explore. I got out of bed, walked across the room, opened my bedroom door, walked out into the passage, opened the kitchen door a mere two or three steps away, and switched on the light. My kitchen was small, with one window opening onto the roof. Two cups and saucers, at least four wine glasses, two or three plates and a milk jug were lying on the floor. My first thought was that Oriel's cat had got in and out again through the roof window. But it had not, and the window was shut as the door had been. And the objects were lying, not in pieces as though they had fallen from the shelves on which they had reposed, but in fragments as though they had been hurled with tremendous force. I remember being particularly impressed with the number of pieces into which the milk jug had splintered.

Oriel was not surprised when I reported to her the following morning. She had, of course, not heard a thing, but then she was tipsy by the end of most evenings. She replaced the broken items and told me it would probably happen again. But it did not, for the remainder of my stay. I had to make do with more mundane excitements, like the appearance of our neighbour from Gerald Road, Noël Coward, at Oriel's parties. Or my introduction to celebrities of an even older generation: Oriel took me with her to tea with the poet and dramatist Clifford Bax in his rooms in Albany, where we were joined by the famous cricketer, C. B. Fry. Clifford Bax was charming, and encouraged me to send him some of my poems. I did not expect him to like them, and was not surprised when he wrote to me: 'In my view verse is based on Repeated Rhythm, whereas in prose that is precisely what we have to avoid. I believe you would do well to make your poems more architectural – to give them a firmer form.' By today's lack of standards, of course, my poetry is far too formal.

Bax singled out one poem which had appealed to him. When, in 1955, Oxford University Press approached me for permission to use a poem in *The Oxford Book of Australian Verse*, which Judith Wright had edited for them, I was interested to see that Judith had chosen the same poem, 'So fly by night':

So fly by night,
my phrase will not pursue you
through darkness and the
evil that men do.
Your flirting breath may dance
on time and passion,
or hide from sorrow
in a word or two.

But don't be sad,
for gentleness surrounds you,
and though I move without
your gay deceit,
I know that you with time
and love will find me,
and bless, promiscuous truth,
the day we meet.

I spent the New Year's weekend in Paris as Gérard Souzay's guest at his apartment in the Avenue de la Motte-Picquet, near the *Ecole Militaire*. Gérard's mother was a charming old lady, like Proust's grandma. His sister, Geneviève Touraine ('she is crazy'), an excellent soprano, was good company, and I met a number of interesting people at a party at Pierre Bernac's flat, a few floors higher in the same building as Gérard's.

Gérard and I tried to plan a number of things together: Victoria de los Angeles wanted to record duets with him, Yehudi Menuhin had expressed a desire to perform Bach cantatas with him, Wilhelm Kempff had asked him to perform the Schubert cycles, and I was determined to get him an engagement at the 1955 Proms. None of these things came to pass, for several reasons. Mainly, I was too inexperienced as a negotiator, and Gérard's official but inactive British agent, Emmie Tillett, proved more adept at putting spokes in wheels than in advancing his career. Although Gérard and I discussed several projects, our weekend was more productive socially than professionally. We visited the composer Jacques Leguerney in his apartment in the rue de Madrid, and took him off to dinner at the Boule d'Or. And we talked much about singers of the past. Gérard greatly admired Ninon Vallin, and he loved the art of Lotte Lehmann (I later discovered from Lehmann that she reciprocated his admiration.) It was in his apartment that I first heard the very moving record of her farewell recital in New York. Of Georges Thill, whose Fauré and Duparc recordings I had praised, Gérard said, 'He is a good singer, but he fucks too much.'

I rather wasted the year 1955 in London. I still thought of myself as basically earning my living from acting, with journalism as a useful sideline, but I continued to refuse offers from provincial reps, such as Shrewsbury and Leicester. It is a wonder to me now that my various agents bothered to persevere with me. Oriel Ross decided to make one of her periodic comebacks to the theatre, and went off to Salisbury for two weeks of *King's Rhapsody*. I had the entire maisonette to myself, and took the opportunity to do a little tactical entertaining, giving one or two small parties to which I invited people who were in a position to offer me engagements, theatrical or journalistic.

When Oriel was in residence, entertaining of any kind was rather difficult. When, as I occasionally did, I brought a male friend home, she was able to place her objection on what appeared to her to be firm ground. 'You must remember, dear,' she admonished me one morning-after, 'that we are living on the Duke of Westminster's estate, and very close to Buckingham Palace. The Queen is really against that sort of thing. Because of the Duke, you know.' (I did not know, and still do not.) 'Of course, I have no personal feeling against it.'

For some months I had been increasing my experience as a concert agent by working regularly for Adolf Borsdorf. Adolf, who came from a well-known musical family, was a delightful man, if not a wildly successful agent, who operated from his flat at 104 Baker Street, above Pelling and Cross's camera shop. Adolf's father, Friedrich Borsdorf, was a famous German horn player who had settled in London, and Adolf's three brothers were all horn players. One, Oskar, had emigrated to the United States; another, Francis, had become principal horn in the London Philharmonic

Orchestra; and the third, Emil, who turned up frequently at Adolf's flat, was a free-lance who was useful in recruiting other free-lance musicians.

Adolf seemed to have a direct line to the musical powers-that-be in the Soviet Union. It was he who handled the first London appearances of such famous Soviet musicians as Khatchaturian, Oistrakh, Rostropovich and Vishnevskaya, and it was through working with Adolf that I met these fascinating creatures. When Khatchaturian wanted to hear Moura Lympany play his piano concerto before rehearsing it with the orchestra, I was able to engage Geoffrey Parsons to play second piano. Geoffrey and I occasionally dined together at an excellent Polish restaurant, the Polonia, in Grosvenor Gardens, which was only a few yards from my Ebury Street abode. I remember asking Geoffrey, one evening over Veal Porjarsky, if he thought I should concentrate on concert management as a career. I could see myself signing him up to play sonatas with Menuhin, engaging Douglas Gamley to conduct an opera (probably one by Malcolm Williamson) at Covent Garden, getting Peter Andry an engagement to play a Mozart flute concerto at the Royal Festival Hall, and sending June Bronhill off to appear in *La Fille du Régiment* at the Opéra Comique. I would specialize in Australian artists. Fortunately, Geoffrey was not enthusiastic. 'There are plenty of agents and managements,' he said. 'Stay with what you do best: writing about music.'

Dealing with Adolf's Soviet artists was an education in itself. When David Oistrakh and Aram Khatchaturian agreed to record Khatchaturian's Violin Concerto for EMI, they revealed a certain difference in their attitudes to the question of a fee. 'Most of our earnings,' said Oistrakh, 'we pay to the Soviet Government, and that is why I must ask a large sum, to make as much as possible for my government. I shall require £5000.' 'Yes,' agreed Khatchaturian. 'Most of our fees go to the government, and that is why I shall insist on a fee of £50 for conducting the concerto. Why should they have any more than that?'

We were expecting Ivan Petrov, one of the Bolshoi Opera's leading basses, to arrive at Heathrow. For some bureaucratic reason he was delayed in Russia, and when I turned up at the airport to meet his flight, he was not on it. The next day in Adolf's office I answered the phone to hear a heavily accented voice saying, 'Here is Petrov. I am at airport, and no one is meeting me. What should I do?' I began to burble apologies and directions over the phone, which Petrov seemed not to understand. Eventually he began to giggle, and I realized I had been tricked. It was Felix Aprahamian enjoying himself. We talked for a few minutes, and Felix hung up. About a quarter of an hour later the phone rang again, and a voice said, 'Here is Ivan Petrov. I am at airport. There is no one to meet me, and –'

It was a busy afternoon, and Felix's joke had been only mildly funny the first time. 'Fuck off, you silly Armenian prick,' I shouted, and slammed the receiver down. Unfortunately, this time it was the real Petrov, as I discovered when an aggrieved Soviet Embassy official rang back on his behalf a minute or two later.

Rostropovich was the most engaging of the Russians. When Adolf took him for a walk in Windsor Great Park, the distinguished cellist kept removing his hat, and bowing in the direction of Windsor Castle. 'Just in case your Queen is at home and is watching us from a window,' he explained.

Adolf invited me to join his firm on a permanent basis. I said I would think about it overnight. That evening, as I turned the pages of the Brahms D minor Violin Sonata at the Chelsea Town Hall for Geoffrey Parsons, who was giving a recital with the violinist Carl Pini, I thought carefully about Adolf's offer. Despite Geoffrey's advice, I was tempted. And I was certainly not getting very far in the theatre. I had auditioned, a week or two earlier, for the Old Vic company which was to tour Australia, headed by Katharine Hepburn and Robert Helpmann, and had just been informed that they would not be requiring my services. I was relieved, in a way, for I did not want to return to Australia, though the chance of doing so with Katharine Hepburn and the Old Vic had been worth considering. But they did not want me, and Adolf did. It was all very well for Geoffrey and other friends to say they thought I had more to offer as a critic, but the only magazine which at that time was engaging me to review concerts regularly was *Music and Musicians*, which had recently been begun by an Australian, Evan Senior, who was its Editor. And my relationship with *Music and Musicians* was soon to founder. I had given an unfavourable review to Sir Malcolm Sargent, who complained to Evan. They were friends, and Evan did not want to offend Sargent. When the irate conductor said, 'I hope I never see that Osborne person's name in your magazine again,' Evan assured him that he would not. But he did not want to sack me. Instead, he asked me if I would continue reviewing, but under a pseudonym. So I became Karl Raumer. And then the inevitable occurred. Karl Raumer wrote something which annoyed Malcolm Sargent. 'I hope I never see that Raumer person's name in your magazine again,' said Sargent. Evan asked me to choose another name, but I'd had enough and I quit.

My life had become absurdly complicated – for no good reason. Consulting my diary for one day in 1955, I find that in the morning I was summoned to the Whitehall Theatre to audition for Brian Rix, who was casting a play called *Reluctant Heroes*. I was punctual, Mr Rix was late, and I surprised his stage manager by deciding, after thirty minutes, not to wait any longer. I visited my agent and said no to an offer from Felixstowe Rep. I returned home to Ebury Street, made some phone calls, found both hotel accommodation and a rehearsal studio for Gérard Souzay and his pianist Dalton Baldwin, wrote a publicity release for Webster Booth, read Auden's *The Enchaféd Sea* and finished writing an essay on Schubert's *Winterreise* for Fischer-Dieskau's EMI recording of the cycle.

After some months I decided it was time to move on from Ebury Street. I went out and looked for a room. I was not very good at this, and made two false starts, in Radnor Walk, Chelsea, and Kensington Park Gardens, before finding sanctuary in a flat in Richmond Mansions, Old Brompton Road. The owner, an eighty-year-old retired actor named Theo Tresize, was prepared to let his two spare rooms to anyone who would listen to his theatrical reminiscences. I was a good listener, and he a pleasant enough old number. We got on well, and I kept Richmond Mansions as my London address for the next year or two, even though I spent much of that time away from London. Theo already had another lodger, the Maltese tenor Paul Asciak. Paul was often abroad, singing in opera: usually Theo and I had the flat to ourselves.

It was clear that, if I was going to take seriously the acting profession which was providing the major part of my income, I would have to relax my unwritten but hitherto firmly adhered-to rule that I would not accept engagements outside London. I informed my agent, John Penrose, accordingly. At the same time I made another pact with myself. I was now in my twenty-eighth year. Unless I had made an enormous breakthrough and been discovered as the new Olivier or Donat or Redgrave by the time I was thirty, I would quit the profession. Acting did not seem to me to be a job for adults, and I had extended my adolescence about as far as it would stretch. If one had the genius and dedication of a great actor, that was another matter. Acting then became something entirely different. But to go on doing it simply because you weren't much good at anything else no longer satisfied me. I did not want to become one of those tatty forty-year-old 'leading men' in weekly repertory, dreaming of eventually making it in the West End.

I agreed to play in *Branwell Brontë*, a new play about the Brontë brother which was being staged at the Gateway Theatre Club, but thought it a load of rubbish when I began to rehearse. After a few days, I walked out. I played the Chorus, or rather one-third of it, in the Watling translation of Sophocles's *Philoctetes* at the Theatre Centre in St John's Wood. Stephen Spender lived a few yards from the Theatre Centre. More than once I began the evening with drinks at his house, then walked across Loudon Road to do justice to Sophocles, and then back to Stephen for a nightcap. He was then still co-editor of *Encounter.* 'There are no more than twenty poets in this country good enough to publish,' he said to me one evening, 'but I have to print more in *Encounter.*'

Peter Kerr, the young actor who had accompanied me to England from Australia, rang to ask my help. Now twenty-one, he was shortly to audition for the role of the sixteen-year-old Troilus in Jean Giraudoux's play, *La guerre de Troie n'aura pas lieu*, which, translated by Christopher Fry as *Tiger at the Gates*, was to be staged in the West End with Michael Redgrave as Hector, Diane Cilento as Helen, Leueen MacGrath (Mrs George Kaufmann) as Cassandra, Barbara Jefford as Andromache, and a distinguished supporting cast which included Nicholas Hannen, John Laurie, Catherine Lacey, Walter Fitzgerald and Robert Shaw. The play was to be directed by Harold Clurman, co-founder of the famous Group Theatre in New York in the thirties.

Peter asked me to coach him in the role of Troilus. I spent several hours with him, giving him what help I could, after which he auditioned, and got the role. A few days later, my agent arranged for me an interview with Stephen Mitchell, who was presenting the play in London and subsequently on Broadway. Mr Mitchell did not ask me to audition, but immediately suggested that I should join the company as Assistant Stage Manager and understudy. The prospect of working in what was clearly going to be a highly prestigious show was tempting, even in the lowly position of a.s.m. 'What role would I understudy?' I asked. 'Troilus,' Mr Mitchell replied. 'It's a sixteen-year-old character, but I think you could get away with it.' 'I'm afraid that, for personal reasons, I shall have to say no,' I told him.

Short of cash, I took another day-time job. I had run into Roy Wilson (he of *The Natural Son* and *Happier Still*) at the Arts Theatre coffee bar. Roy had been working as a commissionaire at the Academy Cinema in Oxford Street, but was about to leave his job precipitately, having landed a part in a film which was about to begin shooting. Would I like to replace him at the Academy? Indeed yes, so he took me along to the cinema and introduced me to the manager, a friendly, middle-aged man named Francis Howard, who had worked in the cinema industry all his life. I could have the job, the manager said, if one of the three uniforms would fit me. Roy was taller than I, but one of the other uniforms was an excellent fit. 'Fine, you can begin tomorrow,' said Mr Howard.

I stayed at the Academy for some weeks. In those days it was, I suppose, London's only 'art' cinema, owned by a Hungarian film director,

George Hoellering, who looked not unlike George Zucco, a Hollywood-British 'heavy' of the thirties. The assistant manager, an attractive ex-trapeze artist, thought I looked 'Madly Continental – very Anton Walbrook' in my uniform, and this encouraged me to act the role. I wore my peaked cap at what I considered a suitably insouciant angle as I sauntered along the waiting queue in Oxford Street, warning people that there were few seats left in the three-and-sixpennies, or walking up the side aisles of the auditorium to discourage patrons from amorous exploration of one another in the back stalls.

For the entire period of my employment at the Academy, the film being shown was a very popular Japanese movie, directed by that bloody Kurosawa, called *Seven Samurai.* I never managed to see it from beginning to end (for which the Gods be thanked): whenever I was on duty inside the cinema the images on the screen were of ugly Japs squatting in huts while the rain pelted down. God, how I came to loathe *Seven Samurai.*

Mr Hoellering visited his cinema once or twice a week. On the first occasion that he encountered me doing my best to attract people into sampling the Japanese rainy season, he merely said, 'Straighten your cap.' I did so, but reverted to my usual style as soon as he had left. The next time, some days later, he passed me without a word and proceeded upstairs to the manager's office. My cap was at its usual rakish angle, and I was surprised that he had not reprimanded me again. When he left an hour later, he merely smiled at me politely and said, 'Good evening.' Shortly afterwards, the manager came down to the foyer. 'I'm sorry, my dear,' he told me, 'but he says I have to sack you. He says you refuse to *look* like a commissionaire.'

A week or so later, John Penrose phoned me. He could arrange for me to audition for a repertory company in Northern Ireland, but he would not do so if I was going to be my usual temperamental self and refuse any offer they might make. 'Oh, all right,' I said. 'But only for a few weeks, during which time you'll find me something in London, won't you?'

I auditioned for the management of the New Theatre, Bangor, in John's office, by telling them that I had nothing prepared, grabbing a script from John's desk, and launching into the first speech that leapt to my eye. I got the job. And this time I accepted it. I had been rehearsing at the Theatre Centre, St John's Wood, for another of those 'shop-window' productions (this one was *The Man Born to be King* by Dorothy L. Sayers), from which I cheerfully withdrew to catch a train the following day to Heysham and thence by ferry to Belfast.

I travelled with Tony Beckley, an actor a year or two younger than I, whom I had met in Penrose's office, and who was also going to work for the New Theatre, not at their home base in Bangor but on tour throughout Ulster in J. B. Priestley's *Eden End.* Tony and I got on well, and became close friends. His career progressed more rapidly than mine. He played supporting roles in a number of films. I have a card from Spain, whither he had gone to play Poins in Orson Welles's Shakespearian movie, *Chimes at Midnight*, in which Welles was Falstaff: 'Still I languish here amongst the Orsonic chaos. I have had enough now and want to finish and come home,' Tony wrote. Though, after I stopped being an actor, we saw each other less frequently than before, we remained friends until the day he died in Hollywood in 1979, as the result of a brain tumour, shortly after being acclaimed for his performance as a mad killer in an American movie, *When a Stranger Calls.*

Bangor, in County Down, is a seedy coastal resort about twelve miles from Belfast. Margery Mason, who is now occasionally to be seen playing old ladies on TV, managed a weekly repertory company there at the New Theatre, where she staged, for the most part, mindless comedies which had been successful in the West End of London in previous seasons. The plays in which I appeared were *Is Your Honeymoon Really Necessary?*, *To Dorothy, a Son*, and two others whose titles I have forgotten. Though it was all very exhausting, and totally unrewarding aesthetically, I enjoyed my time at Bangor. But I resigned after a month, and travelled back to London with Tony Beckley, this time via Liverpool. In the taxi from Euston to the Old Brompton Road, as we drove down Park Lane in the pale spring sunshine, I thought I had never seen London looking lovelier. The sun had just burst through a shower, the air was light, the light was air, and I almost burst into song.

I rang John Penrose, who was frothing at the mouth because I had not stuck it out at Bangor. Would I go to Kidderminster? I looked it up on the map and thought not. 'Really! There's no pleasing some people,' John exclaimed unoriginally but, under the circumstances, mildly. I took a job, instead, at the Battersea Park Festival Pleasure Gardens, where I (shades of the Academy Cinema) stopped people having sex on the tree walk and in the showboat. Was this to be my niche in life? To be an old spoilsport like Jesus? There were a lot of resting 'artistes' working at the Pleasure Gardens: I especially enjoyed the company of one old music-hall performer. We would hide behind the mechanical organ in the showboat and sing some of the old Victorian and Edwardian numbers. He was impressed that I knew songs like 'For Old Time's Sake' and 'Boys of England', and even more so when I told him that their words and music had been written by one Charles Osborne, my grandfather's cousin.

Why John Penrose persevered with me, I cannot imagine. Perhaps he did not have very many actors on his books. I could be the leading juvenile at Ventnor, on the Isle of Wight, for £8 a week, or at Tunbridge Wells for £10. The choice was not difficult for me to make: Tunbridge Wells was, after all, close to Glyndebourne, and I envisaged myself sneaking off to the occasional Sunday performance, as the Tunbridge Wells company was not to perform on Mondays and so would not have to dress-rehearse on Sundays.

The Tunbridge Wells summer season was several weeks away. I now found myself juggling with two agents, for Diane Cilento had introduced me to Fraser & Dunlop, who handled her career. Jimmy Fraser, a very theatrical Scotsman, looked after films while his partner, Peter Dunlop, an RAF-type complete with regulation moustache, dealt with theatre. They now were lining up interviews and auditions for me and asked me to consider a four-week stint as guest artist with the Harry Hanson Court Players in Crewe (twice nightly).

Harry Hanson, something of a legend in the world of tatty rep, ran an entire network of companies in theatres up and down the country, managing his business from his flat in Brighton. Four weeks as guest artist fitted in nicely with my plans, tiding me over until the beginning of the Penguin Players' summer season at Tunbridge Wells. I took the train to Brighton to meet Harry Hanson. Due to the fact that, from anxiety, I arrived at his flat a half-hour earlier than the time of my appointment, I think I may have become the only actor ever to see Mr Hanson without his ill-fitting wig, which had been a source of innocent merriment to the theatrical profession for years. A bald-headed little fellow answered my ring at the door. When I gave him my name, he shut the door in my face, and reappeared a minute later with a full head of the most improbable hair I had seen. He did not want me to audition for him, he merely wanted to tell me how fortunate I was to be working for him, and how wonderful I would find the company, the theatre and the working conditions in Crewe.

Though I imagined that twice-nightly rep would be absolute hell (and it was), my engagement was for only four weeks, so I looked forward to it with interest. It would certainly add to my experience. I accepted Mr Hanson's offer, after some very quick and, it seemed, purely formal haggling over terms. 'I can give you ten pounds a week.' 'I never work for less than twenty,' I lied. 'I'll stretch to fifteen.' 'I accept.'

Two weeks later, on Whit Monday, the Crewe Theatre's expensive guest artist hitch-hiked from London to Crewe, it being the first day of a nation-wide rail strike. At Crewe I found a lovely though somewhat run-down Edwardian theatre, with a decent-sized auditorium consisting of stalls, circle and gallery, and a quite large and well-equipped stage.

I opened in *No Trees in the Street*, a play by Ted Willis (now Lord Willis), in which I played the leading role, Tommy Gold, an East End Jewish teenager precipitated by social conditions (of course) into a life of crime. When the curtain went up on Act I, I was discovered lying on a bed, wearing only a pair of Y-fronts. On the first night, when I got up and walked downstage, I heard a woman in the front stalls exclaim to her neighbour, 'Eh, 'e's nobbut a lad!' I chose to consider it a compliment.

Twice-nightly weekly rep was pretty exhausting. One had little enough spare time in once-nightly rep, but none at all when one was performing every evening at six-thirty and eight-forty. The play opened on the Monday evening. On Tuesday morning one had a first rehearsal of the following week's play. On Tuesday afternoon one learned Act I of that play, and rehearsed it on Wednesday morning. On Wednesday afternoon one learned Act II for rehearsal on Thursday morning. Thursday afternoon was spent learning Act III, which was rehearsed on Friday morning. I suppose Friday afternoon was theoretically free, if one felt so confident of one's lines that one saw no need to study. On Saturday one rehearsed the entire play, and there was a dress rehearsal on either Sunday evening or Monday morning.

I was still coping with a number of regular writing chores – dashing off a 'London Letter' for an Australian newspaper from the wilds of Northern Ireland or Cheshire in order to catch the air mail was the most surrealistic of these – and would have to find time to visit the local library where, more frequently than not, I would fail to find the reference books I needed in order to check the facts or the dates in my sleeve-notes for EMI on Schumann's *Carnaval* or Schubert's 'Death and the Maiden' Quartet, or whatever songs were being sung by Jussi Björling or Kirsten Flagstad on an LP. At the same time, I was determined to keep up with my reading. My diary tells me that, in my five weeks' sojourn in Crewe, as well as learning pages of theatrical bilge and writing for Australian magazines and English record companies, I managed to read books by Jules Supervielle, Virginia Woolf, Ezra Pound (the volume of *Translations*), Julian Green, Scott Fitzgerald and Eric Bentley. The heading of the news item in *The Stage* which I proudly cut out to send to my mother in Brisbane was an apt one:

Busy Life

> CHARLES OSBORNE has just returned from Northern Ireland and is appearing with Harry Hanson's company at Crewe Theatre as guest artist for four weeks. This week he plays as Tommy Gold in *No Trees in*

the Street, to be followed by *It's Never Too Late*, *Wuthering Heights* and *The Chinese Bungalow*. Finishing at Crewe on July 2nd, he begins rehearsals on July 4th for a summer season at Tunbridge Wells, where he will play with Richard Burnett's company. Since his arrival in England from Australia, Mr Osborne has had two film roles, and is currently under consideration for another.

The film role for which I was then under consideration was something in *A Town Like Alice*, in which Peter Finch was to play the lead. I had tested for it, and I think Peter had spoken up for me. I was, in due course, offered the role but was unable to extricate myself from whatever stage commitment I had at the time. Meanwhile, I got myself from Crewe to Tunbridge Wells. 'Gay Nights for Royal Tunbridge Wells' was the innocent headline *The Stage* gave to its news item announcing our summer season.

The contrast between Crewe and Tunbridge Wells was quite startling. In Crewe I had stayed in old-style theatrical 'digs', with a landlady who was straight out of a north-country comedy of working-class life. A friendly woman in her sixties, with a dying eighty-four-year-old mother, she had treated me as a son. I tried to emulate her warmth, though I could not stand being fussed over. Her husband, a butcher who looked like W. C. Fields, had a friend who spent most of his time at the house. He was one of the striking railwaymen, trying to exist on two pounds a week strike money, and he wanted nothing more than to go back to work. 'Bluddy union worn't let me,' he said.

In the elegant residential resort of Tunbridge Wells I rented for the thirteen-week season a pleasantly furnished flat in an attractive quarter of the town, a short walk from the theatre. Audiences were middle-class and knowledgeable, unlike those in Crewe, and if people didn't slap one on the back in the street and say, 'Ee, that were a right good show last night,' they were certainly friendly and hospitable in their more restrained way.

The company consisted, not surprisingly, of rather better actors than those who had graced the boards in Harry Hanson's Court Players, and I felt I had taken a step up in the theatrical world. (But anything had to be a step up after twice-nightly in Crewe.) Repertory companies in those days were made up of stock types: leading man, leading lady, character man, character woman, male juvenile-character (that was my category), female equivalent, male and female juveniles, and a stage manager and assistant stage manager, both of whom also played small roles. For our first two weeks we had an additional male juvenile in the company, Gordon Gardner, with whom I soon became friends.

The summer of 1955 was one of those gloriously sunny, long summers which we keep saying have gone forever (until the next one comes along), and the Tunbridge Wells company was a successful and reasonably happy one. The plays were safe, conventional stuff, but with one or two exceptions they were not the absolute dregs. Tunbridge Wells boasted two newspapers, and I was surprised and delighted to find myself getting favourable notices in both.

In *Johnny Belinda* I was the villainous Locky McCormick, who rapes poor deaf-and-dumb Belinda – on stage. One evening, as Sheelagh Tiffany and I lay panting in each other's arms waiting to get our breath back after the curtain had fallen on that scene, we heard an indignant female 'county' voice from the stalls: 'It's just as well the curtain came down when it did, Mother!'

Emlyn Williams's *Someone Waiting* was the cause of a certain degree of tension between the younger juvenile, Brian Charteris, and me. Which of us would be cast as Martin, a splendid role for a young actor? I wrote in my diary:

> I want it, of course, and in my opinion Brian hasn't the experience to cope with so sustained a role. But the little bastard has already told John [Ingram, the director] he knows the role and has played it – which of course he hasn't, he doesn't even know the play and was questioning me about it last week. He is about six years younger than I (but also about six inches shorter – a tall midget, really), so he may get it, although in theory it should go to me. I am certainly not going to start intriguing about it. Will maintain me dignity. *On verra!*

He got it. A slight *Schadenfreude* is discernible in a later diary entry:

> Everyone distressed at Brian C's handling of the role of Martin. John Ingram tearing what hair he possesses, Peter Thorpe telling me every evening he wishes I were playing it. [He played the Emlyn Williams role.] I told 'em so.

However, I later had one of my best roles of the season as Henry (created in the West End by David Tomlinson) in *The Little Hut*, the Nancy Mitford adaptation of André Roussin's play, in which Brian Charteris came on at the end as a monkey. There *is* justice in the world.

Later in the season I played a crooner, a Johnny Ray caricature, in Vernon Sylvaine's farce, *As Long As They're Happy*. In this, I was required to play the piano and sing two or three numbers, one of which was *High Noon*. 'Congratulations first,' wrote one of the local critics, 'to Charles Osborne who, as the sobbing crooner, Bobby Denver, did not have an easy part. He did extremely well with it and, although his crooning was abominable, nobody really cared.' Fair enough.

I enjoyed my Tunbridge Wells summer. I basked in the adulation of teenagers who wrote sloppy fan letters, and the hospitality of local families, among them the Thesigers. (Judge Thesiger was a brother of the actor, Ernest Thesiger, whose company and friendship I also appreciated. I seem to remember that, one Saturday afternoon, I assisted Ernest in opening a fête.) I even enjoyed the dotty curtain speeches I was occasionally called upon to make. What I did not enjoy was being tied up for the entire summer, unable to consider other offers. I had to forgo an engagement with H. M. Tennent, the leading West End management, because of Tunbridge Wells. They never asked me again. If only actors could save up their job offers, I thought, and spread them evenly throughout the working year, how much more agreeable a profession it would be.

Returning to London, I began to look around for the next job. I auditioned for George Devine, who was looking for actors for his new English Stage Company, which, at that time, it was thought would begin operations at the old Royalty Theatre in Dean Street, Soho. (Something went wrong with the arrangements, the Royalty was demolished, and the company went to the Royal Court Theatre in Sloane Square, Chelsea, where, thirty years later, it is still in residence, although it lost its artistic impetus a good many years ago, some would say on the death of George Devine.)

Devine was polite and sympathetic at my audition, but I could tell he didn't think much of me. Some weeks later, J. C. Williamson Theatres Ltd. invited me to go to Australia with *The Reluctant Débutante*, but I was reluctant to return to my native land so soon, even though I was more than usually short of cash. For several weeks, I had been giving three pounds a week to an actor friend who was out of work, and desperate, and I had also, foolishly, responded to an appeal by wire from Australia: someone from my past had got someone else from my past pregnant, and urgently needed fifty pounds towards an abortion.

On the afternoon that, instead of studying Act III of whatever at Tunbridge Wells, I raced up to London to visit my agent, I also dashed into the Wimpy Bar in Coventry Street a half-hour late for an appointment with Tony Beckley. As I approached from the other side of the street, I could see Tony sitting just inside the entrance. Not wearing my spectacles, I failed to notice the plate-glass door, through which I crashed at alarming speed, the point of contact being my forehead. 'Must have an astonishingly thick skull,' I admitted to my diary in the train back to Tunbridge Wells for my evening performance, as I didn't even bruise myself, though I'd splintered the entire door to smithereens. Pandemonium – except for Tony, who greeted me with 'Well, really!' as he spooned glass out of his coffee. I was afraid I'd be presented with a bill for £150, but instead I was treated considerately, indeed with great deference, by manager and waiters, and we were not even asked to pay for our coffee. While we were there, Greta Garbo turned up, in dark glasses and beret, with a middle-aged man who looked like Cecil Beaton.

I could no longer afford to stay at Theo Tresize's flat, so I moved to a room in Courtfield Gardens which I described in my diary as 'very similar to the one in which Raskolnikov murdered Elizavieta'. I now cannot remember this room at all. (I have, readers will by now have realized, an extremely selective memory which, I am told, quickly discards what it will not enjoy remembering. In this regard I am not unlike Hazlitt's sundial: '*Horas non numero nisi serenas*'.)

I took stock of my situation. I was becoming increasingly bored with acting, but could not earn enough to live on from my writing. Miron Grindea, who edited a literary magazine, *Adam* (years later, at the Arts Council, I would find myself offering it subsidy), had accepted some poems of mine, but he was a year or so behind with his ostensibly quarterly issues, and, in any case, it would be a long time, I realized, before I made any real money from my writing. Continuing to publish the occasional poem in an Australian or British magazine was necessary to my sense of identity. I never expected it to be profitable as well, and indeed I think there is something intrinsically sordid in adopting poetry as a profession. That leads to the churning out of poems in order to keep up an output and, worse, leads also to the poetry-reading circuit, to the writing of disposable verse to perform for small audiences and large Arts Council grants. Poetry is either a way of life or a part-time activity. Or both.

I was already beginning to wonder if I should break away from acting. Work was scarce in the autumn of 1955, and I decided to cheer myself up by going to Stratford-on-Avon with Tony Beckley, to see Olivier's Macbeth. That was an experience I shall never forget. It was quite simply the most exciting evening I have ever spent in the dramatic theatre. (The second most exciting was two years later, watching Olivier as Archie Rice in John Osborne's *The Entertainer* at the Royal Court.) At Stratford we were given two seats in the centre of the front row of the stalls, and by the end of the play, I, for one, felt that I had been part of the performance, though I was not sure whether Macbeth had been played by Olivier or by Edmund Kean. I was certainly reminded constantly of Kean, in Hazlitt's phrase, 'illuminating Shakespeare by flashes of lightning', for that is what Olivier did. From his first brooding entrance, and his Mahlerian 'So foul and fair a day I have not seen', to his final ecstasy of despair, it was a remarkable display of great acting. It was dramatic poetry come to life. I saw the dagger when Macbeth saw it, I was almost blasted out of my seat by his scene with Banquo's ghost, I was excited by the risks he took with so many lines in injecting electric new life into them, terrified by the epileptic fit with which he greeted the information about Birnham wood, filled with pity at his inflection on '*troops* of friends', and moved to tears by his glimpse of the void in 'Tomorrow and tomorrow and tomorrow'. When I read the play now, it is Olivier's voice I hear still, it is his face I see, his nervously flickering glance, his almost somnambulistic walk.

If one could not even hope to aspire to be an actor of that calibre, was there any point in remaining in the profession? I think my firm decision to quit must have had its beginnings in the train back to London, though it took me another two years to find the will-power to implement it.

As a result of my reading Aldous Huxley's *The Doors of Perception*, which had just been published, I decided to experiment with mescalin. This was the first time in my life that I had messed about with drugs, and there will never be a second: the experience, on the night of 21 November 1955, was terrifying to me. I wrote several pages of overwrought, sentimental and self-pitying rubbish. Some months later, I attempted to recollect the emotions of that night in relative tranquillity:

> After ingesting the mescalin, I took myself off to the Golders Green Hippodrome to see an American play called *The Anniversary Waltz*, a comedy about an American couple and their two children, their interfering in-laws, and their feelings about television, education and love. In my normal condition I should probably have been bored by it. On this occasion, however, I reacted to the play as at other times I have reacted to *King Lear*. I felt I was witnessing a great tragedy, in which the entire contemporary situation was being dispassionately examined. The things that the people in the play said and did to one another appeared to me to be shocking, brutal and horrifying. And I felt that those actions which were supposed to be the important and climactic points of the domestic comedy (the infuriated destruction of a TV set, the parting of the young couple) were as nothing compared to the extraordinary acts of betrayal which took place every few

moments among the various characters, and which were apparently intended as good clean fun. My sentiments were those of Prince Mishkin towards judicial murder: 'You can't treat people like that.'

By the time we had reached the third act (and I had spent the intervals sitting still and silent, trying to concentrate on the advertisements in the programme) I was overcome by tears of compassion for the human condition. I was aware that my reactions to the play were not those of the rest of the audience, who had laughed immoderately throughout the performance. And I was aware that, under normal circumstances, although I might not have been laughing with them, I would certainly not feel so strongly, would not be moved to so great a pity for the characters. (At this time I both felt, and observed my feelings, as I frequently do. There is within me a consciousness, an awareness which is always functioning and which it seems I can never escape. There have been occasions when this ever-watchful consciousness has become for me a kind of guardian angel. This single identity which I cannot describe, this 'I' which is me when I am absent – '"Je" est un autre' – certainly saved me from the abyss later that night.)

I left the theatre, intending to walk home. It was a cool autumn night, and clear. I walked all the way into the West End, and then along Piccadilly to Knightsbridge and South Kensington. As I walked on the south side of Piccadilly, there came to me an extraordinarily strong sense of well-being. I felt at peace with the metropolis, the buildings of Mayfair, the stars above Green Park, the clubs and bars of Knightsbridge.

'For a few moments before the fit, I experience a feeling of happiness such as it is quite impossible to imagine in a normal state, and which other people have no idea of. I feel entirely in harmony with myself and with the whole world, and this feeling is so strong and so delightful that for a few seconds of such bliss one would gladly give up ten years of one's life, if not one's whole life.'

I have just looked up that passage: it is Dostoevsky in a letter to the critic Nicolai Strakhov. That was it. Unlike Dostoevsky, I am not an epileptic, but on this autumn night I looked up at the stars, and for an instant I *knew*, and all was well. I saw the pattern completed. God's purpose, perhaps. I knew. And all power was given unto me. I forgave my enemies, joyously repented of my misdeeds, and my heart shouted a great yes to the world.

And then the chaos. I had only to walk along Knightsbridge and into Brompton Road, but at two hours after midnight I stood outside my apartment block, wondering where I had been for the previous two hours. I am writing this four months later, and I can now recollect my intention to walk home, my glorious moment when the doors of perception swung open in Piccadilly at about 11.30 pm, and then – nothing, until I found myself sweating on the front steps, inserting a key, entering the hall, taking the lift to the second floor, and opening my own front door.

I have had occasional bouts of anxiety-neurosis, but on that night I felt I was being dragged to the precipice of Hell, after I arrived home. If the perception of bliss is transitory, then so too is the vision of perdition. I do not now remember what terrified me. I do remember the state I was in when I first got home. My last conscious sensation had been of some two hours past. 'His sensation of being alive, and his awareness increased tenfold . . . all his agitations, all his doubts and worries seemed composed in a twinkling, culminating in a great calm, full of serene and harmonious joy and hope, full of understanding and the knowledge of the final cause.' (*The Idiot*). I re-read *The Idiot* last week, and was struck not only by the resemblance that my experience bore to Mishkin's seizures, but also by the parallel between Ippolit's confession and a document I wrote that night. The same high pitch of fever, the side-tracking from one subject to another even in mid-sentence, the mad emphases, the lack of any but the grimmest humour, the superb egocentricity. My world was thronged with monsters that night, and tranquillity was but a distant and beloved memory on which I attempted, in vain, to focus.

I sat down to write, addressing myself to my oldest friend in Australia. I never sent the document to him, for when I read it over the next day it seemed to me to be the ravings of a madman. Its thought was incoherent, its language and style embarrassingly awful, its tone that of a frightened self-pity. It would have been of interest only to a psychiatrist. I cannot bring myself to reproduce it here, but towards the end there is a passage whose meaning seems to be that I feel as though I have either just committed, or wish to commit, an act of violence: 'I have the feeling that I have just completed a task before returning to my flat, and I fear to think what it may have been. Should anyone come in now, I would kill him. For no *reason*.' (This involvement with *'l'acte gratuit'* has never been part of my undrugged life.) After two or three more paragraphs, the letter or whatever it is trails off. It is signed four times in four different ways.

I awakened next day at noon. I felt fine. No hangover, a perfectly clear recollection of my excitement, but no idea whatsoever of the missing hours.

I turn to the final paragraph in Huxley's book, and I am made to feel foolish and inadequate, as though I had turned a unique spiritual experience into a psychopathic orgy. 'The man who comes back through the Door in the Wall will never be quite the same as the man who went out. He will be wiser, but less cocksure, happier but less self-satisfied, humbler in acknowledging his ignorance.' Oh, yes? Perhaps I'll give it another go, sometime.

I never did give it another go, nor shall I. The thought of messing about with one's mind now appals me.

The new year, 1956, began for me with a resolution: 'I shall take whatever acting jobs are offered this year, whatever or wherever they may be.' I adhered to my resolution, as a consequence of which I spent almost the entire year away from London, missing a number of concerts and opera performances I would have preferred to attend, and missing, too, the opportunity Stephen Spender offered me to meet Christopher Isherwood, who was about to descend upon London from Santa Monica. (I was not to meet Christopher until two years later.)

I toured in three shows, between which I returned to London only long enough to appear in TV plays (three in all, throughout the year). My first tour was the most arduous. It was also, I suppose, my most ignominious engagement, yet I enjoyed it enormously, for it took me to towns and villages which no first-class touring company would ever have condescended to visit. We were the Caryl Jenner Mobile Theatre, and our inaptly named Spring Tour (January to May, and more like a *Winterreise*, with the country covered in snow for most of the time) took a programme of three one-act plays, under the title *Trio for 1956*, to more than seventy theatres, halls, prisons, and two mental asylums.

There were seven of us. Sally Latimer and I played in Noël Coward's *Red Peppers* and a new play, *The Pen of My Aunt* by Gordon Daviot, directed by Caryl Jenner, a very butch number who dressed like a sea-captain at rehearsals. Everyone in our company had a responsibility in addition to his or her roles: mine was for the lighting, an aspect of theatre about which I knew considerably less than the average road-sweeper. But by the end of the tour I was shouting, 'Take out number two, bring up the amber,' quite authoritatively to some local electrician during our set-up of the show, to the great amusement of my colleagues.

Most of our dates were one-night stands. We played in medieval guildhalls (King's Lynn, for instance, where Shakespeare and Burbage acted sometime between 1585 and 1595), in school halls, cinemas, municipal halls, and very occasionally theatres, in virtually every county of England. In Stamford we were in a school hall, but I made my way to the derelict eighteenth-century theatre and sniffed Edmund Kean's dank and gloomy dressing room. At the Haymarket Theatre in Basingstoke, on the coldest day of my life (eight degrees, or twenty-four below freezing), I shivered my way through both my roles to an audience of twenty-four (I counted them during one of Sally's speeches in *The Pen of My Aunt*). We usually got full houses, especially in the more God-forsaken places. At Falfield Prison, we had a discussion afterwards with our captive audience. Over supper, I said to the Governor that they all seemed such nice people with pleasant accents, unlike the kids at a Borstal in which we had recently performed. 'Oh, yes,' replied the Governor, 'we usually get the better class of offender here, you know. Fraud, mostly, and the occasional sex offence.'

Driving around Devon released in me certain atavistic stirrings, much more strongly than when I had visited the county two years earlier to attend the Summer School of Music at Dartington. My father's family came from Barnstaple in North Devon, and could trace themselves back, or so I was always told, 'to the time of the Armada'. What precise significance, if any, the Spanish Armada held for us I never bothered to ask my father. When I first visited Spain, I did discover a popular Spanish brandy called Osborne (pronounced in three syllables), but that does not help. Anyway, there are still Osbornes in Barnstaple, distant cousins of mine whom I have never felt the urge to know, and there is even an Osborne Hotel. And when I, last of my branch of the family, was whizzing about the county with a one-night-stand fit-up tatty tour, I felt very Devonian indeed.

Cornwall, too, was fascinating. I loved St Ives, and the Arthurian coast around Tintagel. The hall in which we played at Tintagel provided the tiniest stage I have ever stood upon: I played the whole of my role in *The Pen of My Aunt* without moving my feet. In Newquay we played at the Cosy Nook Theatre on the beach, but in Bodmin we performed to the inmates of the grim-looking Victorian asylum. I met the two oldest inmates, who had been admitted as children when Queen Victoria was on the throne. Poor lost darlings, they seemed gentle enough, and contented. Perhaps they were too gentle for the outside world. They had, it seems, spent their lives in the asylum because there was no one prepared to look after them. I asked them if they were related, if they were perhaps brother and sister. They did not know, and neither did the member of staff who introduced them to me.

Our performance for the inmates was unnerving. Playing our first scene, Sally and I found it difficult to make ourselves heard above the restless chatter in the auditorium. Instinctively we began to slow down the tempo of our speech, and eventually, when we were speaking very slowly indeed, we won their attention. At the end, they cheered and screamed as though we were the greatest performers they had ever seen. 'Satirical bastards,' I muttered to Sally, rather than admit that I was moved.

Our assistant stage manager told me that she was fascinated by the warm and friendly grin I always flashed to the audience at curtain calls, even when they had been a dismally small or unresponsive lot. How did I manage it? 'I learned it from a friend, Max Oldaker,' I told her, 'who had been taught it by Noël Coward during the run of Coward's *Operette* in the thirties. You simply murmur to yourself, "Silly cunts", and it gives you the right expression.'

I used to find that, after I had given, say, the ninetieth performance of whatever I was touring in, not only twaddle like *Enduring as the Camphor Tree* and *The Pen of My Aunt*, but even Shaw's *Candida*, I would become so bored with it all that my mind would switch off in mid-scene, and I would begin to think about something else: something I was trying to write, or what to have for supper after the show, or who done it in the Agatha Christie novel I was reading. Several times, I suddenly came to, to find myself on-stage and in mid-sentence, with no idea of what I had been saying for some minutes. I had been going through the moves and the dialogue automatically. It happened to me in *Red Peppers* on this tour, in Cromer on the Norfolk coast (where the next land to the north, apparently, is the Pole, and it felt like it). I suddenly snapped out of a dream to find that I was in a theatre dressing room. My first thought was, 'Shit! I must get back on stage.' Then I realized I *was* on stage: the scene was a theatre dressing room, and I managed to respond to the cue Sally Latimer was giving me without an appreciable pause.

Sally, an ex-girl-friend of Caryl's, was a seasoned rep actress, having founded a company at the Amersham Playhouse which she ran from 1936 to 1949. She and I did not get on all that well. She thought me a supercilious little prick (or so she said to another member of the company), and I thought she epitomized the dizzy rep actress. I remember she was furious when anyone said of me that I bore a certain facial resemblance to Marlon Brando. (It is not so. Some photographs pointed up a likeness, but in any case the days when Mr Brando could kid himself he looked like me are, for him, long past.) Sally kept referring to this. I cannot think why it irked her so much. When I played one performance in pain from an abscess on a tooth, which caused me to speak with less than my usual perfect articulation, she muttered to me as we took our calls, 'Not so Marlon Brando tonight, was it, dear? More like Clive Brook.'

One never knew, from night to night on that tour, what one's accommodation would be like. First-class hotels, dumps and theatrical digs alternated with private hospitality, usually in ordinary, middle-class homes, but occasionally somewhat better. When we played several towns and villages in the vicinity of Middlesborough, Yorkshire, I stayed for a few nights as the guest of Colonel and Mrs Pennyman at Ormesby Hall. The Pennymans used one wing of their beautiful eighteenth-century country house as a luxury hotel, but we stayed in their part of the house. I was given a huge room with four-poster bed, open fireplace and superb English furniture, on the first floor. At night from my room I had a view of the moonlit lawn and fields. In the mornings I participated in an English breakfast scene straight out of Coward. Squirrels cavorted on the lawn. This, I thought, is what England is supposed to be like. And then I went off to play in another mental institution.

The tour finished towards the end of April. Back to London. After turning down a number of minor parts, I was eventually offered, through John Penrose, the juvenile role in a tour of *Small Hotel*, a comedy by Rex Frost which had been successful in the West End with Gordon Harker in the lead. His role was to be played on tour by Leslie Henson. Penrose reminded me forcibly that I had assured him I would not keep turning jobs down this year, so, after being assured by one of my other agents, Peter Dunlop, that Leslie Henson was fun to work with and that there was nothing much happening in town, I accepted.

We opened our tour at the Harrow Coliseum at the end of May, though we actually closed the theatre there, by which I mean we were the last show to play at the Coliseum. At the end of our week they began to tear the place down in order to create a shopping complex. Our Saturday night performance, therefore, was an emotional affair, with a full house (for the first time in years at the Coliseum, apparently), a speech by Leslie, and a heartfelt account of *Auld Lang Syne* by actors and audience. The curtain came down very slowly. Leslie remarked that it was the curtain from the old Gaiety Theatre in the Strand, where he had experienced some of his greatest successes in the twenties and thirties, and where he had made a similar farewell speech when the Gaiety closed for the last time in 1939.

Peter Dunlop was right. Leslie *was* fun to work with, and so was our leading lady, Iris Hoey. Iris, already over seventy but still able to play middle-aged parts, was an adorable survivor from the Edwardian theatre. I loved listening to them both reminisce: Leslie recalling what George Grossmith said to him, or Iris recounting what happened in New York when 'Diamond Jim' Brady took her to supper. Iris had a wonderfully feline walk, like an amiable panther. When, one evening, I apologized to her for having introduced an unrehearsed bit of business which got a laugh at her expense, she said to me: 'Don't apologize, dear. Keep it in. Beerbohm Tree once told me that every additional laugh was worth another guinea at the box office.' I had heard that one before – Beerbohm Tree must have said it to everyone he knew – but at least Iris had appeared in Shakespeare with him at Her Majesty's Theatre. She played Ariel in his production of *The Tempest*. Iris and I took to each other, and often lunched together during the tour. She was a creature of great self-possession and unfailing charm. Well, almost unfailing: a dangerous glint came into her eye on one occasion in a Lyons Corner House, when a woman came up to her and asked, 'Aren't you Olga Lindo?'

After Harrow and a week in Cardiff, we played Brighton – the lovely old Theatre Royal, built in 1806 and haunted by Prinny himself. The following week, in Margate, where there is an exquisite little eighteenth-century Theatre Royal, we played the Winter Gardens, a horrid, huge rectangular hall whose stage lurks in the middle of one of the long sides of the rectangle. I spent most of my spare time on the beach with *The Brothers Karamazov*. 'Although it was brilliantly sunny,' I wrote after one such day, 'and the beach was crowded, I was the only person stripped for sun-bathing or swimming. All around me were working-class families of mum, dad and the kids, or else teddy-boys and their girls. But all fully dressed. Some of the men were daring enough to expose their white torsos, or roll their trousers up to the knee, but most sat on the sand in their navy blue suits. Some of the women tucked their dresses up and paddled, the shameless hussies. Funny people.'

A diary entry at the end of the Margate week reads: 'Disgust at self. Indecision. Inability to concentrate on packing a suitcase – or even to raise the physical energy to start doing it.' Why this, now? Too much Dostoevsky and Cyril Connolly [I had been reading *The Unquiet Grave*]? Or too much *Small Hotel*?' Probably I was unsettled and indecisive because I had, during our Brighton week, popped up to London to talk to Hugh Hunt at his request. Hugh, a distinguished director, had gone to Australia to run the newly set-up national theatre company there, the Elizabethan Theatre Trust, and he had written to me about the possibility of my returning to join the company. Hugh was now in London to sign up actors, and when we met there he offered me the role of one of the Kelly gang in Douglas Stewart's play, *Ned Kelly*, which was to open in Melbourne in November, during the Olympic Games. I tentatively agreed, and had now been informed that passages for

Leo McKern (who was to play Ned Kelly), Kevin Miles and myself had been booked on the *Otranto*, sailing on 24 July. It was already 23 June. I was still by no means certain I wanted to return to Australia, and in any case I had not yet approached the *Small Hotel* management to see if they would release me from my run-of-the-play contract.

I think I was depressed, too, about Mary Clare, an actress I had greatly admired in films, but who, when I saw her at a matinée performance of *Ladies in Retirement* in Margate, merely stood about and spoke her lines without much conviction, when she could remember them. The poor woman was broke, an actor in her company told me, and had been making lampshades for a living before her pathetic attempt at a return to the stage in the role she had initially created back in the thirties. She could not have been much over sixty. I felt sorry for her – which, I suppose, was a way of feeling sorry for myself. I did not want to be making lampshades or failing to remember lines at sixty, probably without even the bitter comfort of a successful career behind me. What the hell did I want?

On the Sunday between Margate and Cambridge, I stopped off in town, changed into a dinner jacket and caught the train to Glyndebourne to see *Idomeneo*, clutching a copy of Sartre's *Baudelaire* to read in the dinner interval. Later, at home, I wrote: 'I think one must look at things with what I call "the third temper". Tonight, for instance: being quasi-schizoid as I am, it is easy for me to be in a good and a bad temper, almost simultaneously. In a good temper, I would describe my trip to Glyndebourne as enchanting, the locale sheer delight, the performance first-rate, and the general ambience highly enjoyable. In a bad temper I would dismiss it all as snobbery, as something catering to an audience of well-to-do louts who have no taste or feeling for music but pay their five guineas [!] and dress up because it's the thing to do. I would denounce the very idea of such an opera house, inaccessibly located miles from nowhere. But one must combine these two approaches. This is the only way to approximate to an objectivity which of course one can never attain. And this blending of the two, the good and the bad, I call "the third temper".'

On Monday morning, I went to see Hugh Hunt again, and told him I did not want to break my *Small Hotel* contract with Charles Killick (who had just become Chairman of the Society of West End Theatre Managers). Hunt was sympathetic, and agreed to my withdrawing from *Ned Kelly*. I then called at Charles Killick's office to inform him, and rushed up to Cambridge to join my colleagues at the Arts Theatre. Killick later rang our company manager to tell him how delighted he was that I was remaining with the show and how impressed he was with the 'gentlemanly' way I had handled the affair ('whad-I-do?); he instructed him to increase my weekly salary.

During the Cambridge week, I had permission to skip the curtain call on Thursday evening and rush to London to participate in the *Night of a Hundred Stars* gala at the Palladium, in aid of the Actors' Orphanage. I was not, I need hardly say, one of the hundred stars, but one of the 'lesser breeds without the law' who contributed by being ushers and programme sellers. On the bill that night we had, amongst others, Robert Morley, Margaret Rutherford, Paul Scofield, Peter Ustinov, Laurence Harvey, Hermione Baddeley, Edith Evans, Peggy Ashcroft, Jack Benny, Bob Hope, Laurence Olivier, Tony Martin, Billy Daniels, Van Johnson, Robert Cummings, Tyrone Power, Jean-Pierre Aumont, Lloyd Nolan, Luise Rainer and Vivien Leigh.

After Cambridge, Bradford (the Alhambra Theatre), where I found amongst my mail a letter from my old friend Judith Wright, the leading Australian poet of her generation. I had asked Judith if she would write a Foreword to my small collection of poems, *The Gentle Planet*, and this was her immediate response. Out of diffidence I did not use what she wrote then, but I make amends now by doing so thirty years later:

> This is a book about a country upon a gentle planet – the strange, sad star of love. Its poems are brief and tender. They move to the rhythms of folksong, nursery rhyme, and the muted speech of lovers, and in them the old tale of youthful love is renewed, and moves through its known course of joy, doubt and loss with a serious grace. In the situation of love, even the poem is 'too many words'; yet afterwards the poems remain, small, beautiful forms assumed and left behind by feeling as it moves on its way; and it is Charles Osborne's gift that he neither over-decorates these forms nor tortures them into verbalism, but leaves the shape of his experience true and simple. No book of poems needs an introduction, this one because of its completeness less than any.

On we trudged with *Small Hotel*, to Edinburgh, then by plane to Dublin and back to Leeds, then up to Glasgow, playing those huge, Matcham-designed Edwardian theatres which in those days we treasured less than we do now. With nothing to do between the end of Act I and the beginning of Act III each evening, I began, encouraged at a distance by Tony Beckley, to write a play, *Actor by Moonlight*. Diffidently put it away in a bottom drawer, from which I extracted it only some years later to show to a friend, the Australian poet and playwright, Ray Mathew. Ray thought the play had great potential but needed more work done on it. My usual laziness led me to tell him that, if he felt like tinkering with it, he could share the by-line and any eventual proceeds. He did tinker, and he substantially improved the play. Eventually he went off to New York, taking *Actor by Moonlight* with him. I think it's now in another bottom drawer, somewhere in the East Seventies.

Back in London after *Small Hotel*, I reverted to type and said no to various offers whilst being turned down for others. When I was eventually offered a role in *The Trial of Mary Dugan*, an old American court-room thriller which was being sent out on tour with Joan Rice and John Stuart in the leads, I dejectedly accepted. Joan Rice was a pretty J. Arthur Rank starlet whose chief claim to fame was that she had been Burt Lancaster's leading lady in a South Seas buccaneer romp, *His Majesty O'Keefe*. John Stuart's career was more respectable: he had been a star of silent films and a character actor in sound films in the thirties and forties. Now, he was a charmer and could remember hardly a line of his dialogue. Joan was a charmer, too, remembered all of her dialogue, which she delivered to the best of her ability, and seemed to me alarmingly flirtatious off-stage. By the second week of the tour she was offering to do my laundry for me.

At the request of Tony Beckley, I had helped a young friend of his, a pleasant young West Indian named Loxley Russell, to secure a role in the play. Loxley was a dancer and had never spoken dialogue, but after intensive coaching from me he passed the audition. On our first week out of London, he found difficulty in getting accommodation. 'Sorry, I don't take coloured people,' a Brighton landlady astonishingly informed him. For the remainder of the tour, Loxley and I roomed together, and I wrote off in advance for accommodation, making it clear that one of us was black and one white. There were no further direct rebuffs, though two landladies had 'no vacancies', which may or may not have been genuine.

After the tour ended, I went to the Queen's Theatre, Hornchurch, to play in one of J. B. Priestley's less successful plays, *Mr Kettle and Mrs Moon*, with an agreeable young actor named Dinsdale Landen. Before the end of the year I had also been seen in *Othello* at the Theatre Royal, Lincoln (in the doublet worn by Olivier when he played Malvolio at Stratford), and, according to *The Stage*, in a revue at the New Lindsay Theatre, though this must have been an absolute stinker for I have repressed all memory of it.

J. Nevin Tait, the Tait brother who ran the London office of J. C. Williamson's, asked me if I would be interested in playing, in Australia, the role which George Rose had created in Enid Bagnold's *The Chalk Garden* in London. But I was already regretting having promised to join the Elizabethan

Theatre company in Sydney the following year. The thought of being trapped in Australia terrified me. Over Christmas, which I spent with Beverley Nichols and Cyril Butcher at their house in Ashstead, I gave serious consideration to my future. A month previously I had become twenty-nine. I made a firm decision, once again, to give myself no more than one more year in the theatre. If, by the time I reached thirty, I had not achieved real success, then I would give up and seek, for the first time in my life, gainful employment. I had already told myself this, but I had to keep reaffirming it until I convinced myself.

A few days into the new year, 1957, I auditioned for the role of Ham in André Obey's *Noah*, which was being toured around schools by Nottingham Rep. The director, Roy Hope, liked my reading sufficiently to offer me the role immediately, and also asked me to join the permanent company at Nottingham. I said yes to the tour, but could not bring myself to agree to staying away from London for an indefinite period.

When I look back now on my years in the theatre, it seems to me that I could never have taken acting at all seriously, for I was continually finding reasons not to accept engagements. But apparently I was occasionally serious in my approach to my work, the occasions being those rare ones when the work in hand was of a quality worth taking seriously. Here are two excerpts from the diary I kept at Nottingham:

> *January 22nd 1957* We began to rehearse *Noah* yesterday. It is a long time since I have been interested in and excited by my work. One finds oneself for so much of the time rehearsing and playing muck. Amiable muck sometimes, rather nasty muck at other times. Obey's *Noah* I had never seen, and although of course I knew something about the play, and St Denis's *Compagnie des Quinze* who first presented it, I had never even read it. It came to me at our first read-through yesterday as something new and fresh, direct, simple and generous. One of those minor masterpieces that can change one's world ever so slightly.
>
> Interesting, incidentally, to read the cast list of the St Denis production of twenty-one years ago, and to find out who played what. The only member of that original cast whom I know at all well is Harold Young, who was in *Kettle and Moon* with me recently. He must have been thirty-seven when he played the twenty-one-year-old Shem – so I don't feel quite so bad at attempting, in my thirtieth year, the nineteen-year-old Ham. Gielgud was Noah, and this I can't easily imagine. I hope he didn't play the role with that beautifully English, small, quivering voice. Noah should be richer and bigger. I can visu-

alize the young Marius Goring as Japheth, and Jessica Tandy as one of the girls. The animals included Harry Andrews and Alec Guinness. And even simply by reading the lines of the man at the end of Scene i, I can see how George Devine must have revelled in playing him.

Thursday 24th We've now been rehearsing four days, and we all feel happy and excited about the play and the production – a rare feeling for an entire company to have. I shall love playing Ham. I see him as the first rebel, the first 'outsider', and I shall play him rather like a medieval Brando. Medieval because, in Roy Hope's production, which is along somewhat Brechtian lines, we are medieval players presenting *Noah* as a Biblical mystery play. We have a chorus which chants, we have dances and songs – songs which Roy has written. The one at the end of the first Act, as we enter the ark, is quite beautiful. It seems to derive both from the Negro spiritual and from Italian monody. Roy looked surprised when I told him this: he'd just plucked it out of the air, the way I do. (The world may be full of us embryonic composers!) Obey's conception of the animals has a St-Exupéry *Petit Prince* quality that appeals to me.

Notes on Ham: Scene i (our Act I). His first entrance singles him out from his brothers. He enters alone, refuses to conform, to participate in the group feeling. He obviously admires the ark, but has to be grudging in his admiration to Noah, and then sarcastic. He is worse when with the crowd, his individuality (but almost an impersonal thing) *must* assert itself. He is really the first rationalist (his speech about building houses in the middle of the forest). The speech which begins, 'But, my dear father, here we are in the middle of a great drought', must be sarcastic rather than angry. Then, when the others all exit gossiping about the ark, he turns to the audience. Three distinct things here: (1) a gesture of exasperated rebellion; (2) his line, 'Crazy', to audience; (3) he slouches off, but in the direction the others have taken. He is curious in spite of himself.

I enjoyed the *Noah* tour. Our company was a pleasant one, and audiences liked me. Our Assistant Stage Manager, a cheerful seventeen-year-old named Ray Brooks (whom I recommended to my agent), later achieved some success as an actor on TV. Back in London I divided my time between refusing more jobs in the provinces and assembling material from my diaries for a book about acting. I gave it a title, *Actor's Ego*, and sent it off, first to Max Reinhardt, who thought it 'stimulating' but would prefer me to try my hand at a novel, and then to John Calder, who seemed to me the liveliest and intellectually most interesting of the younger publishers. For many months I heard nothing. It was only later, when I got to know him, that I came to realize that John was also the most accomplished procrastinator since Elizabeth I.

Actually, I am by no means sure that John ever read *Actor's Ego*. It was rejected eventually and, it seemed, reluctantly, by his editor, Pamela Lyon, who wrote to me that she dipped into my typescript whenever she felt the need for communication with real people, after exasperating periods with authors and their agents. Into that bottom drawer it went. I also determined at that time that I would never again write anything 'on spec'. I would write only if commissioned by a publisher, and would not set fingers to typewriter before my palm had been crossed with suitably large amounts of silver. With one exception (a novel which I wrote in order to get it out of my mind), I have adhered to this self-imposed ordinance.

Rejected by John Calder Ltd, I fought back my tears and plunged again into a round of auditions. I was called by the Royal Shakespeare company to re-audition for them. (Apparently they couldn't remember how bad they had thought me last time.) The Oliviers were taking their Stratford *Titus Andronicus* on a European tour, and a number of the smaller roles were being re-cast. I failed that one, of course. My particular ambition, to act in a play or film with the greatest actor since Kean, was not to be realized so easily. Was not to be realized at all. But on one incredible day in 1957, I accompanied Diane Cilento to the dress rehearsal of *Titus* (at the Stoll, before they set out on their tour), experienced Olivier making wonderful bricks without much straw, and in the evening of the same day saw him play Archie Rice in John Osborne's *The Entertainer*, a considerably better play than *Titus*. There are actors who can stagger you with technique, and there are actors who can move you by the intensity of their feeling and the immediacy of their ability to communicate it. I know of no other than Olivier who, at his best, was able to do both, overwhelmingly and simultaneously.

(It was when I was reading the reviews of Olivier's Archie Rice that I first came across that absurd misuse of the word 'committed' – it is used frequently when 'convincing' would do perfectly well – which in recent years has been taken up by opera critics. They use it often when they mean that the singer performed with conviction. 'Miss Barstow was a committed Leonore,' one will read, or 'Fischer-Dieskau was a specially committed Mandryka.' Committed to what, for Christ's sake? I read recently of a tenor in *Parsifal* who was said to be 'deeply committed, almost to a fault'!)

My decision that, if my career had not taken a spectacular leap forward by my thirtieth birthday in November, I would leave the profession and the British theatre could take the consequences, was reinforced by the phone conversation I had with a TV producer, who asked me if I could play some role or other in a play he was casting. Alas, I was not free, I said. I had agreed to appear at York in E. Martin Browne's production of the York Mystery Plays, and the dates clashed. 'Well,' continued the TV producer, 'can you recommend someone else for this role? I need to cast it in a hurry, and I've already scraped the bottom of the barrel.'

That is it, I thought. I am not hanging around at the bottom of the barrel; I am going to crawl out.

We performed the Mystery Plays in the gardens of the eleventh-century St Mary's Abbey, as part of the York Festival. We were twelve professional actors and about two hundred local amateurs (who played small parts and crowds) under Martin Browne's direction. I suffered from severe hay fever throughout the entire series of performances, which I got through each evening only with the help of one of the amateurs, a local doctor, Reginald Dench, who played Abraham, and whose twenty-two-year-old daughter Judi was making her professional début as the Virgin Mary. Rain stopped play the night the Queen and Prince Philip came, but the principals were presented to the royal couple, who were probably relieved to have been spared two or three hours of medieval doggerel.

I enjoyed living in York for two or three weeks, though the town was full of tourists with cameras which they clicked in one's face when they recognized one as an actor they had seen the previous evening. 'Wow, it's the devil,' said a Mid-Westerner as he stopped at my table at a restaurant, his camera and flash attachment at the ready. I am not normally averse to being photographed, but that kind of thing made me feel uncomfortably like an object. I suppose the policemen outside Buckingham Palace get used to it.

At a service in York Minster for the opening of the Festival, I found myself being blessed by the Archbishop of York. In Moscow three weeks later, at a reception in the Kremlin, I shook hands with both Bulganin and Kruschev. Is this a record? I had gone to Moscow to participate in something called a World Festival of Youth and Students. Although I was no student I was still, in the eyes of the organizers, a youth, since I was a few months on the right side of their age limit, thirty. I reviewed performances for *Opera*, *The Stage*, and a couple of Australian magazines, which meant that virtually every night I was in Moscow I attended a concert or theatre or an opera performance. For several months before I went, I attempted to study Russian, but progressed no further than mastering the Cyrillic alphabet and acquiring a grammarless vocabulary of a few hundred basic words.

I was by no means the only British actor in Moscow. At the Art Theatre, London's Theatre Workshop was performing its modern-dress *Macbeth* to full and wildly enthusiastic houses, and *Look Back in Anger* was enjoying a more modest success at the Art Filial. But as one of the representatives of British theatre I was greeted everywhere with open arms. The Muscovites seemed to be a warm, friendly and spontaneous people, and there was very little evidence of that traditional Russian suspicion of the foreigner which one might have expected to be exacerbated under Communist rule. Wherever I walked in Moscow, I was mobbed. If I stopped to talk to anyone, a crowd gathered. Flowers, autograph books were thrust at me, photos were taken, and I found myself continually answering questions in English, French, German, operatically flavoured Italian, and (towards the end of my stay) the few words of Russian I had mastered.

At the Maly Theatre, I saw a play by the contemporary Icelandic author, Halldor Laxness, called *The Betrayed Lullaby*. It appeared to be a rather simple story about a young wife who deserts her husband and child to join a variety company run by a charming rogue. She does not find happiness in the theatre, and while she is touring her child falls ill and dies. Moral: a woman's place is in the home. But my interest lay in seeing the terrific resources of acting and production that were lavished on this trifle. The performances were all in one style, all directed to one purpose. Most of the roles were alternated, and, as in all the Moscow theatres, the plays were done in repertoire so that there was little chance of an artist becoming stale through wearisome repetition of a part. I saw Khorkeva (a Russian Ashcroft) as the wife, and Mezhinsky as the director of the variety theatre. His was a superb performance, rich, human, understanding and brilliantly funny. Mezhinsky was also responsible for the production, which was realistic to an extraordinary degree. One scene took place in a sports car being driven at night along country roads at a great speed. This was the production's *tour de force*, and remarkably effective it was, too. Their visual and sound effects were astonishing. We, the audience, whizzed along with the car, *à la* Cinerama. 'It's foolish but it's fun.'

Perhaps my most stimulating theatrical experience in Moscow was at the Mayakovsky Theatre, where I saw Oklopkov's much-talked-about production of *Hamlet*. The play was staged in heavy, sumptuous sets, with all the magical stage effects one could imagine. I suppose this is the kind of production that Beerbohm Tree continually strove towards. It is, in a sense, a more honest way of presenting Shakespeare in a picture-frame stage than our attempts at compromise, and our pretence that the proscenium arch is not there. One huge, massive, heavy scene followed another, and the action of the play was accompanied in the pit by a symphony orchestra playing a score pieced together from Tchaikovsky's *Manfred* and *Hamlet* as well as a number of original themes composed for the production. The first scene was played down-stage against a great pair of iron gates which covered the entire area of the proscenium frame. Later (for the play scene in particular), these divided into many squares on different levels. They also swung open to reveal the big sets: the throne room with its huge stained-glass windows; the 'To be or not to be' soliloquy with Hamlet on a high rock above the sea, an angry sky racing past him, and waves dashing against the cliffs. All much more realistic than the corresponding scene in Sir Laurence's film. Hamlet himself was alternated by their beloved Samoilov and the younger Kozakov, whom I saw: a beautiful, dark, Georgian countenance, a virile and poetic delivery. I thought him closer in spirit to Hamlet than any English actor I had seen. (I had not then seen Redgrave's Hamlet.)

All this and the Bolshoi too. The Bolshoi Theatre is very beautiful, with its six tiers of gold and crimson, and its magnificent central chandelier. The stage is immense, both extraordinarily wide and deep. Of the ballet repertoire, I saw *Swan Lake* twice, with the young Karelskaya a brilliant Odette-Odile, and *Fountain of Bakhchisarai*, in which they indulge in the favourite Bolshoi trick of burning a huge mansion on stage. Members of the company told me that they were not able to do this effectively at Covent Garden. It was certainly an astonishing sight at the Bolshoi. And then there was the wonderful *Romeo and Juliet* with Ulanova and Zhdanov. A superb production, a magnificent spectacle, and at the heart of it all Ulanova, fourteen years old, remote as a child, gay, tender and loving.

I tried to see as many Russian operas as possible. The most magnificent was *Boris Godunov* with Petrov as Boris, a great performance in the Chaliapin manner. Since there were a number of foreign companies performing in Moscow during the Festival, I attempted to fit in as many as possible. The result was aesthetic indigestion, and I found that when I was interviewed on Moscow TV I had so much to say about their theatres and their city that I was almost incoherent. I was escorted over the Mosfilm Studios and met many of their actors and actresses, but that was one of the days when at lunch the toasts were too many and the vodka flowed too freely. I cannot remember much about it.

Was it all incredibly sunny? Well, no. The shoddiest of Western goods seemed like luxuries to the ordinary Soviet citizen. There was nothing in the shops, except in the special shops which accepted only Western currency and which most Russians cannot enter. There was no unemployment, officially, but they did not keep records of those who were unemployed because they were forbidden to work and were then (*Catch 22*) branded as parasites. There was, of course, no freedom of discussion.

If Moscow, in that summer of 1957, seemed a strange and exotic place to us, the thousands of westerners who poured in, how much more exotic must we have seemed to the citizens of that city, most of whom had never before laid eyes on capitalist devils. Many intense and, inevitably, short-lived relationships blossomed. (It was no surprise to me to read in an article in the *Observer* in July 1985 that 'For some middle-aged Muscovites, 1957 is remembered as the erotic highlight of their lives. Popular wisdom has it that Russia's first coloured babies were born a prompt nine months after the Festival had ended.') I can still remember the feverish intensity of the Festival's last night. When I returned to my hotel, some time after midnight, the lift was out of action (as usual) and I had to walk up several flights to my floor. On every landing, and all along the corridors, couples were making love, to use the polite euphemism, on the floor. In my room, both beds were already occupied: I threw a Russian actress and an American pianist out of my bed. In the other bed, my legitimate room-mate, a British journalist (male), was wrapped around a dancer (also male) from the Bolshoi.

The next morning there was a general exodus from Moscow. Many of us left for Western Europe by train, and several of our newly and briefly found friends or lovers came to the station to see us off. The scenes of parting were both heart-rending and comical, spurious sentiment abounded, and I found myself enacting an absurd little scene which was considered most affecting by the journalists who shared my compartment on the train.

I had taken with me to Moscow a number of small gifts to distribute to people, rather in the manner of a missionary offering beads to natives. I had also taken with me a King James Bible which my grandmother had given me when I was a child. Though I had no use for religion, I valued the Bible, of course, for its prose. I had not intended to give it away in Moscow: I merely thought that, as Bibles were scarce in Moscow, someone might find it interesting. And indeed one of the friends I had made, an intelligent young Armenian architect named Yuri, who had a religious temperament, did find it fascinating.

Yuri came to the station to see me off. Acting on an impulse, I gave him my Bible. He was overwhelmed. He sat in the compartment with me, a few minutes before the train was due to leave, reverently turning the pages. 'Read me your favourite part,' he asked. I was not sure that I had a favourite part, but I took the volume from him, found the First Epistle of St Paul to the Corinthians, and looked through it until I came to the chapter I was seeking. I began to read. 'Though I speak with the tongues of men and of angels, and have not charity, I am become as sounding brass, or a tinkling cymbal . . .' As I read, I was aware that not only Yuri but also my cynical British colleagues were moved by my reading. I was almost moved, myself. 'For we know in part and we prophesy in part . . .' Oh dear, people were brushing away tears. I continued to the end of the chapter. '. . . For now we see through a glass darkly . . .' I had never liked the translation of 'agape' as charity, so I substituted the Revised Version's 'love'. 'And now abideth faith, hope, love, these three; but the greatest of these is love.'

Whistles blew, Yuri embraced me quickly and leaped out onto the platform. The train began slowly to move. In the carriage we all waved. Yuri was soon lost to our view, but we continued to wave at the scores of Muscovites standing on the platform, all of whom looked as though they wanted nothing more in the world than to come with us. One Russian, in fact, tried to come with us. Some French musicians hid him in their compartment, up on the luggage rack behind the suitcases. Of course there was a thorough search at the Polish border. Very thorough. Soldiers climbed onto the roofs and peered underneath the carriages as well. The poor lad was found and dragged off.

One of the dissident writers who made himself known to me in Moscow was a thirty-year-old poet, Valentin Sokolov. Although he had spent nine years in a labour camp for having, at the age of twenty, been a member of a youth group said to be 'anti-Soviet', he impressed me as being remarkably unembittered, and even light-hearted. He was an amusing companion with a rich fund of stories, some fascinating, some hilarious, some chilling. I never heard from or of him again after my return from Moscow. In 1985 he died, and it was from his obituary notice in *The Times* that I discovered he had been arrested again a few months after I had met him, and sentenced to a further ten years' imprisonment, again for 'anti-Soviet propaganda'. He had been released for a brief period in 1967, had continued to write poetry, which he was not allowed to publish, was arrested for the third time, and was eventually committed to a clinic at Chernyakhovsk, in the north-west of the Soviet Union, where he died. The gentlest and least rancorous of souls, he had spent two-thirds of his life, and virtually all of his adult life, unjustly imprisoned.

When I returned to London from Moscow, I spent my first ten days writing an English adaptation of an early Chekhov play, *Platonov*, which I based on a literal translation given to me by a Russian actor I had met in Moscow. I decided to adapt rather than to produce a straight translation because I thought that the play, as it stood, was flawed, and also because it seemed to me that Platonov himself was rather thin as a character. I fattened him up with some long, world-weary soliloquies, deleted a few minor characters, and made one or two other changes. Two years later I sent my version to Bernard Miles at the Mermaid Theatre. Bernard liked it, and accepted it for production.

I went to the Mermaid to talk to Bernard and his gaily coloured macaw about casting. Bernard began to enthuse again over my version of the play. He knew another translation by Basil Ashmore. In fact, he said, Ashmore, who was a friend of his, had often tried to persuade Bernard to stage his version. But Bernard had not cared for the play until he encountered my adaptation. While we were discussing business the phone rang. It was a call for Bernard from George Devine at the Royal Court. George had heard that Bernard was in the process of casting my *Platonov*. He thought we should know that he had acquired a new translation, that his casting was complete, and that his Platonov (a character whom Chekhov and I described as being twenty-seven years old) would be Rex Harrison (who was then in his early fifties!).

Bernard and I gave up, and my *Platonov* went into that metaphorical bottom drawer. In due course I saw the Royal Court production, through which Rex Harrison inappropriately sauntered as his usual self. It was one of those performances that could have been phoned down to the stage from the actor's dressing room. For it, naturally, he won the *Evening Standard* Award as the Best Actor of 1960. More than twenty years later, the National Theatre commissioned yet another version of *Platonov*, which they called *Wild Honey*. In it Ian McKellen had a deservedly huge success.

I was by now earning just about enough to live on from my musical and literary journalism. I broadcast for the BBC on the Sunday morning *Music Magazine* regularly for about twenty years until its amiable and eccentric producers, Anna Instone and Julian Herbage, known to their colleagues as 'the poppets', left to retire. I survived for a time in the successor programme, *Music Weekly*, but the new producers had their own favourites and wanted to be seen not to depend on the old reliables: after I had declined two or three offers of engagement, because the dates were not convenient, they stopped asking me. Another of my regular programmes was the Saturday morning *Record Review*, on which I enjoyed working with John Lade, head of the BBC's Gramophone Department, until his retirement not all that long ago. My regular radio years were from the mid-fifties until the beginning of the eighties, a long enough stint for anyone.

What was especially satisfying to me about broadcasting was the voluminous correspondence it engendered, particularly after my individual programmes for Radio Three or Four, and also for the World Service. I used to write and broadcast programmes about composers, conductors and singers, and would receive dozens of (usually though not invariably) appreciative and flattering letters after each one. When I broadcast about Richard Tauber or Franz Lehár, my correspondents would always include a few old survivors from pre-war Vienna, some of whose letters contained fascinating information about music and musicians of those fondly remembered days. People wanted an excuse to share their memories with someone who appeared to care about the past that they remembered, and I provided them with that excuse. In the Viennese programmes I usually tried to include interviews with musicians of those days, who had been colleagues of Lehmann or Tauber or Lehár: people like Josef Krips, Mischa Spoliansky, Evelyn Laye, Lea Seidl.

I enjoyed broadcasting, and fortunately many of my listeners seemed to enjoy my broadcasts. One who did not was a correspondent who wrote me such foul letters that I could not bring myself to admit to anyone else that I had received such devastating and insultingly expressed criticism, until one day in a BBC studio another broadcaster mentioned having received a letter from the same man, George Richards of Poole. I discovered that he wrote regularly, and in the same scathing terms, to virtually everyone who broadcast about music. Here is a sample of his style from one of the many letters I received from him:

> Figure of fun as a music critic, exposed and excoriated as callow cretinous tyro apropos of The Hundred Books (joint Brophy effort), possessor of the most pansy and unradiogenic voice of any broadcaster. One thought it was hardly possible for you to cut a more ludicrous figure. You achieved this, however, last night in that excruciating session of cosy giggling, cackling merriment by exposing a degree of insentience regarding what is anatomically (if no other way) the most highly organized living creature (the cat), a self-exposure as gross, complete and gratuitous as it was indecent. Pitiable imbecile!

As my thirtieth birthday approached, my theatrical career appeared to be really in the doldrums. A semi-professional London opera group asked me to produce Gounod's *Roméo et Juliette* for a derisory fee; I failed an audition for a series of TV films about the Australian 'Flying Doctor'; and I auditioned for, and nearly succeeded in getting, the small role of a Brando-type Method actor in the musical, *The Bells Are Ringing*, starring Janet Blair at the Coliseum. ('Nearly succeeded' merely means they dithered for a time before saying no.) To add a final insult to all this injury, my ludicrous agent John Penrose rang to ask me if I would consider modelling Meridian underwear.

It was time to quit. On 25 November, the day after my birthday, I informed John and the few other agents with whom I had been free-lancing that I was no longer available. Given the state of my career at the time, this hardly sounds now like the most momentous of decisions. But for some months afterwards, the phone continued occasionally to ring, and it took a certain degree of will-power not to accept the more attractive offers. Surely there could be no harm in my agreeing to appear in Arthur Miller's *All My Sons* for this repertory company, or to play Jimmy Porter in *Look Back in Anger* for that one? No, it was important to make a clean break. Feeling terribly strong and determined, I rejected all offers. Well, almost all: I simply could not resist the temptation of participating, as an extra again, in another Italian opera season, this time at Drury Lane early in 1958. I appeared in a few performances of *La forza del destino* and *Turandot*, both under the bad-tempered baton of the grand old man of Italian opera, Tullio Serafin.

Memory does tend to tidy up one's act for one, does it not? On consulting diaries and press cuttings which I had not looked at for more than twenty-five years, I find that it was in April, 1958, five months after my 'retirement', that I appeared as the villain, Captain Levison, in a new musical, *Lady Isobel's Lover*, for the Hovenden Theatre Club, which had moved from Shaftesbury Avenue to St Martin's Lane. I had two songs to sing. 'A musical *East Lynne* – Ivor Novello style,' said Alan Dent in the *News Chronicle*, noting that I made 'an oily though moustache-less dastard' of Captain Levison. 'But is there ever to be an end to the turning of famous plays into operettas?' he asked. There was an end to this one very quickly: to be exact, after nine performances.

To supplement my earnings from journalism after my withdrawal from the theatre, I took a job in Ian Norrie's High Hill Bookshop in Hampstead. Ian and I got on well, and when he asked me to set up and manage a gramophone record department within the bookshop, I agreed. It was at this time that, through Ian, I met his friend Martyn Goff. Martyn, a novelist who was knowledgeable about music and records, was then running his own bookshop in Banstead. Years later, he became Director of the National Book League (at about the same time that I became Literature Director of the Arts Council). Our jobs have required us to keep in touch over the years, and this in turn has made our friendship easy to maintain. Like myself, Martyn is a survivor. Despite attempts made by the ungodly to remove him from the position he has filled with such distinction for so long, he is still today the Director of the National Book League.

Agreeable though it was to work with Ian Norrie in Hampstead, I had not given up the theatre in order to turn myself into a shop assistant. I was a writer, and therefore had to accept the fact that I would need to supplement my income through some activity ancillary to writing; but bookselling was, surely, too ancillary. What, then, should I do? Suddenly, the serendipity which has usurped divinity in shaping my end decided to assert itself: John Lehmann, to whose *Penguin New Writing* I had sent my poems all those years ago, now entered my life. Jeremy Kingston, a young playwright (later to become drama critic of *Punch*, and now an occasional reviewer for *The Times*), who was acting as part-time secretary to John Lehmann in 1957, discovered in the files the teenage photo I had sent for *Penguin New Writing*'s 'Notes on Contributors' page. He told John, who had started a new venture, *The London Magazine*, that I was now living in London. John expressed an interest in meeting me, and invited me to one of his parties. We got on well, and after that I lunched with him occasionally, or spent weekends in the country at Three Bridges, where he shared a house with the dancer Alexis Rassine. Through John I met such interesting people as John Gielgud, Graham Greene, Harold Acton, William Plomer, Henry Yorke (the novelist Henry Green), Gore Vidal, W. H. Auden, and John's sisters Rosamond, Beatrix and Helen.

Early in 1958, only a few months after I had given up the theatre, John offered me a job as one of his two Editorial Assistants on *The London Magazine*. I accepted, and began work in March. I remained with the magazine for eight years, working with John for the first three years, and then staying on to become Assistant Editor when John sold the magazine to Alan Ross in 1961.

Shortly before receiving John's offer, I had applied for, and had been offered, a job with an international record company, to head their publicity department and be responsible for the provision of sleeve-notes for their records. I was on the verge of accepting when the company made the mistake of sending a private investigator to discover what my political affiliations might be. (I had, and have, none.) The investigator was stupid or desperate enough to ring my doorbell and ask me if I was a Communist. When I discovered on whose behalf he was asking, I wrote to the company telling them what they could do with their job.

My literary career began to gather momentum soon after I joined *The London Magazine*. Editors of other magazines commissioned me to write articles and reviews, and I was broadcasting now on as many book programmes as musical ones. One of the former was *The World of Books*, which, for a time, was produced by Russell Harty before he turned himself into a TV personality. At last I had both the freedom and the security to consider long-term writing projects, books rather than articles. I began to plan the book on the operas of Verdi which, in my view, was needed, and which I had always known I would one day write.

Publishers were always approaching me either with ideas for books they thought I might like to write, or with requests that I submit ideas for books to them. My first book to be published was a critical guide to Kafka, which I wrote for what was then a popular series, *Writers and Critics*, aimed mainly at students. *The Complete Operas of Verdi* was my first major work. (I mean it was major to me: I do not want to sound like those politicians who announce that they are about to make a 'major speech'. '*You* make the speech,' one wants to say to them, 'and *we'll* decide whether it was major.') It was critically well received, both here and in the United States, which I accepted as no more than my due. I was considerably more delighted when it was translated into Italian and when I had to travel to Parma to hear it being praised at a 'Tavola rotonda' of the Institute of Verdi Studies. '*La critica Verdiana Inglese: attualità del libro di Osborne*' (English Verdi criticism: topical interest of Osborne's book) was the headline of the newspaper report the following morning. It was the first time I had been called upon to speak publicly in Italian, and nervousness robbed me of vocabulary and grammar. *The Complete Operas of Verdi* has been frequently reprinted, and has kept in print ever since its initial publication. I have added to it volumes in a similar format on the operas of Mozart and Puccini, and am in the process of continuing the series with Strauss and Wagner.

Having now written more than twenty books, and had them published not only in the United Kingdom and in America but also in Italian, French, German, Spanish, Dutch and even Finnish translation, I am no longer especially pleased by favourable reviews or upset by unfavourable comment. I know when I have done well, and when I have done less than well. My own favourite children are my books on Verdi, on Auden, and on Agatha Christie, but there is none that I would disown, not even *Ned Kelly*, which I wrote in 1969 only because the engaging Anthony Blond tempted me against my better judgment.

Ned Kelly came into existence because Anthony, having learned that Mick Jagger was to star in a film based on the life of the Australian bushranger, asked me if I would be interested in writing a biography of Kelly which he would publish on the day of the movie's première, to cash in on the expected success of the movie.

My first impulse was to say, 'Sorry, Anthony, you've asked the wrong Australian. Russell Braddon is the kind of chap you want.' In fact, I seem to remember I did say this, but Anthony persisted and offered me a sufficiently large advance for my greed to vanquish my common sense. I ought to have realized that Mick Jagger would be absolutely awful as Ned Kelly, but I did not: that is, until the day dawned when my book (written during a summer holiday at a friend's house in the south of France) was published and the movie was released. I had to attend the première, and when I was interviewed on TV later that evening and asked whether I agreed that Mick Jagger had 'a certain spiritual quality', common sense was vanquished by frankness. 'Mick Jagger,' I informed BBC viewers, 'is about as spiritual as an Australian outdoor dunny.' (Antipodean slang for lavatory.)

The film was, of course, a ghastly flop. Its American release was cancelled, and the American publishers who had paid for the right to publish my book in the United States hurriedly paid me even more to be freed of the obligation to publish.

Ned Kelly, hastily cobbled together from nineteenth-century newspaper reports of the activities of Ned Kelly and his gang which a friend in Australia had sent to me, sold surprisingly well in Great Britain (and even better in Australia, where books about that country, however bad, always succeed). I think Sidney Nolan's jacket had a lot to do with it. It subsequently went into a paperback edition. When I was asked to revise and expand it for republication, I refused, for I was already feeling somewhat ashamed of having written it in the first place.

I had, however, taken the precaution of inserting secretly into the first edition of the book my real opinion of its hero; an opinion which I am now prepared to reveal to the world. At the end of the book I had included a section of ballads and songs known to have been sung in Victoria during the lifetime of the Kelly gang. One of these eight poems, a twelve-line fragment called *Stringybark*, is spurious. My opinion of Ned Kelly can be discovered by reading the initial letter of each line:

Four of them rode away, that day,
Under a summer sky,
Carrying rifles on their backs.
'Kelly,' they said, 'must die.'

Ned and his three mates kept alert,
Eager to join the fight.
Dan, Joey Byrne, and young Steve Hart
Knew all the police by sight.

Evening it was, at Stringybark,
Light faded from the sky.
Lonigan, drowsing by the fire,
Yawned, while the gang passed by.

I consolidated my position in literary and musical circles during my *London Magazine* years. John Lehmann once said of me that I never made a move that was not precisely calculated well in advance, but I cannot remember ever having planned anything very much, at any period in my life. During the sixties, as at other times, I tended to accept things as they came to me. Alan Pryce-Jones, when he was editing the *Times Literary Supplement*, took me on as a regular (and in those days anonymous) reviewer, and I continued to write for the *TLS* under Alan's successor, a smooth old journalist named Arthur Crook, though I dealt usually with the much more agreeable Ian Hamilton, who became a good friend. The *New York Times* invited me to be its London music critic. Because of the five-hour time difference, I could attend an opera performance at Covent Garden, come home and dictate my review over the phone to the London bureau, and have it appear in the following morning's newspaper in New York. I never ceased to regard that as miraculous, especially since, whenever I reviewed performances for the London *Guardian*, I would have to leave well before the end in order to make the deadline, and even then would occasionally find that the paper had gone to bed early and my piece appeared twenty-four hours late. I used in those days to be irritated by the sloppy proof-reading at the *Guardian*, and the numerous misprints in virtually every article. Now, of course, the unholy alliance of new technology with old union bloody-mindedness has enabled every other newspaper to catch up with the *Grauniad*. Also, we are a quarter of a century further along the road to mass illiteracy. (When, not very long ago, I gave an editor at Hutchinson's a list of several hundred misprints I had found in a volume, he was not particularly interested. The firm, he said, had been congratulated by a *Daily Telegraph* reviewer on having had fewer misprints than usual in that particular book!)

For a time, while Robert Conquest was its Literary Editor, I reviewed books regularly for *The Spectator*. The amiable, highly intelligent and extremely cynical Bob Conquest was a permissive editor, which was fine in a way, though I sometimes wondered how much he read of what his contributors wrote, either before or after he had printed them. But when he attempted to persuade me to review a book which he thought was just my cup of tea and about which he was keen to have my views, I gave up, for I had already reviewed it and my piece had appeared in his pages some weeks previously.

Reviewing books is a sordid and unrewarding activity, and I abandoned it as a regular occupation as soon as I began to earn enough from my own books to be able to do so. I thought I would be able to utilize the time I thus saved by writing more poetry, but that did not happen. To write poetry one needs time for reflection, and combining a full-time job with the career of a writer of books left me very little spare time. I am pleased with a few of the poems I have written over the years. A small selection of them was published in 1968, entitled *Swansong*. Sidney Nolan contributed a drawing to illustrate each of the poems, and the book is now a collectors' item mainly because of Sidney's beautiful drawings. I did not publish another volume of poetry until *Letter to W. H. Auden and other poems*, which appeared in 1984.

My journey to Moscow in 1957 had given me an urge to see more of the world, and so I began to travel regularly. I found I could manage two or three trips abroad each year, usually to cover a music festival for one or another newspaper. When I began to write books which necessitated research in foreign libraries, I would plan my visits accordingly, so that I could find what I wanted in the appropriate libraries in Berlin, Vienna, Paris, Rome, New York, Washington, Prague, Budapest, Tel Aviv, Cairo and so on.

After Moscow, my next trip abroad was to Berlin in 1958. The city was divided but the wall had not then been built and, although I stayed in West Berlin at the Hotel Steinplatz, I could visit the Staatsoper in the Eastern sector by walking under the Brandenburger Tor and down the Unter den Linden. Many of the old-timers were still singing at the Staatsoper. I heard Helge Roswaenge as Alvaro in *La forza del destino*, or rather *Die Macht des Schicksals*. 'He has to pull his voice up to the note sometimes,' I wrote, 'but the notes are still there.' In the western sector of the city I heard for the first time Mussorgsky's *Boris Godunov* in the composer's orchestration (untampered with by Rimsky-Korsakov). Mussorgsky's scoring has a freshness and edge that makes Rimsky's smoothness sound irrelevant.

Since those days I have travelled to every West European country, and to most of Eastern Europe. (Bulgaria is, so far, the exception.) I have been visiting the United States at least once a year for the last quarter of a century, to attend performances of opera, or to lecture, or to promote my books. I have seen more of America than most Americans, from New England to Key West, from Atlantic City to San Diego. I have driven from New York to Los Angeles, have tasted the delights of Chicago, Dallas, San Francisco, Memphis, Nashville, Chattanooga, have cruised down the Ohio and Mississippi rivers on the *Delta Queen*, an old paddle-wheel steamer, from Cincinnatti to New Orleans, have driven (oh, all right, for the most part *been* driven) over most of California, across Nevada and Utah, and over the Rockies to Denver. Only a few months ago, I was hearing opera in the semi-open-air opera house high up on a *mesa* three or four miles outside Santa Fe, and losing money at the races in Ruidoso Downs. I have stayed in luxurious resort hotels in Palm Springs and Palm Beach, and in the dingiest of motels in Little Rock, Arkansas, and Odessa, Texas. In Nevada I know Tonopah as well as I know Las Vegas, and, in Pennsylvania, Westchester and the Amish country as well as Philadelphia. And I have by no means exhausted my interest in America.

South America is still a closed book, and I cannot get as interested in Asia as I am told I should. (Stop-overs at Raffles in Singapore are all, so far.) I can do without the Japanese. What a shocking example of racial prejudice, you say? Not at all. I have not pre-judged them, I have judged them, and have decided that, as a race, I dislike them. I imagine that most Australians old enough to remember World War II or to have known people who did not survive capture by the Japanese feel the same way. It is different from Germany. There you could direct your loathing towards the Nazis. In Japan there were no Nazis, only Japanese.

While we are on the subject, what is wrong with racial prejudice (or rather racial dislike, for prejudice, or prejudging, of anything is clearly unfair)? Races differ from one another, and one cannot be expected to like everything and everyone in the world, can one? To say to yourself, 'I dislike Australians or Jews or Arabs or Boers or Japanese, and therefore I shall have as little to do with them as possible,' is, in my view, perfectly permissible. What is not permissible is to say, 'I dislike them and therefore I shall attempt to pass discriminatory laws against them and, if possible, kill them.' On the rare occasions when I have found myself meeting Japanese people socially, I believe I have always behaved politely, whether or not I have liked them. And it is, of course, possible to like individual members of a group one dislikes. But I regard the Japanese as a cruel and unusual race, and I have no desire to visit the land of the cherry blossom and the Toyota.

Sometime in 1959 I received a letter from an old friend, Max Oldaker, who had just returned to Australia after a period in London. Max was an operetta and musical comedy tenor who kept being 'discovered' in London at ten-yearly intervals. He wrote to me from Sydney, where he was starring in a revue, to bring to my attention a young comedian who was leaving the company to try his luck in London. 'He's very strange in many ways, and I'm not sure I understand half of his material,' Max wrote, 'but, you know, I think he's got genius. He's coming to London and I've told him to get in touch with you, as my dearest, kindest and wisest chum there. Do give him any help you can with introductions. His name is Barry Humphries.'

Some weeks later a letter arrived from Barry Humphries in Rome, announcing the imminent appearance in London of himself and wife, and proposing a meeting on the day following their arrival. This was the beginning of a friendship which has endured and grown stronger over the years. Barry's humour, as distinct from that of his most famous characters, Dame Edna and Sir Les, has a black edge to it. He is the one person who can always make me laugh: in his presence the malice and absurdity of others become harmless objects of hilarious derision.

I treasure the memory of those few occasions on which we have actually performed together, the first of which was at the ICA in 'An Evening of Innocent Austral Verse'. For the TV transmission of Dame Edna's 'Last Night of the Poms' at the Albert Hall I wrote the 'voice-over' introduction about the many great Australian musical dames who had performed in that historic hall: Dame Nellie Melba, Dame Joan Hammond, Dame Joan Sutherland, leading to the greatest of them all, Dame Edna Everage. When Edna played a season at Drury Lane in 1982, mine was the recorded voice which, as the house lights dimmed, made the Theatre Royal Drury Lane Public Service Announcement, instructing the audience in how to behave in the event of 'paranormal activities' in what is known to be a haunted theatre: 'Should a particularly *malign* manifestation occur near you, kindly desist from drawing attention to yourself. Fully qualified exorcists are stationed throughout this auditorium and will make themselves known to you if and when necessary.'

In *Dame Edna's Bedside Companion* (Weidenfeld & Nicolson, £6.50, she has asked me to add) I am proud to find myself credited as the Dame's 'Literary Advisor by Appointment'. Our mutual friend Max Oldaker died a few years ago, and my biography of him is about to be published in Australia. Appropriately, it contains an Introduction by Barry Humphries.

My *London Magazine* years were also the years of the conferences. I was frequently invited to attend this or that international literary or musical conference: in Italy, in East Germany, in the United States, in Australia. I soon grew tired of them, though at first I was intrigued to be able to meet and talk to the famous: the Sartres, the Moravias, the Mauriacs, the Felsensteins. Unfortunately one had to meet the infamous as well. At the Palazzo Vecchio in Florence, when I found myself shaking hands with Alexei Surkov, the leader of the pack of wolves that hounded and killed Boris Pasternak, I realized that protestations of international friendship and understanding at gatherings of this kind were not for me. There are writers who are natural *congressisti*. Let them get on with it.

At that Florence 'Congresso Internazionale', organized by something called the *Comunità Europea degli Scrittori* (or COMES), I found myself mingling with, among others, Marguerite Duras, Max Frisch, Tristan Tzara, Carlo Levi, Alberto Moravia, Anna Seghers, André Chamson (in my view one of the most boring men imaginable), Salvatore Quasimodo, Giuseppe Ungaretti and André Voznesensky. Why do writers of stature waste their time in these junketings? Here is a possible answer. I extract from my files one of the many invitations I have refused. It asks me to participate in an international conference on the theme of 'The Writer in the Twentieth Century'. It mentions that the other participants will include Chinua Achebe, Heinrich Böll, Mordecai Richler, Günter Grass, V. S. Naipaul, Wole Soyinka, Robert Penn Warren and Viktor Nekrassov. It offers a pleasant ten days in an agreeable part of the world (Honolulu), and its final paragraph reads:

> Round-trip transportation, apartment-style accommodation, plus a stipend of twenty-five dollars per day, evening receptions and an all-day beach picnic, as well as an honorarium of 350 dollars for a presentation, are included in the offer.

That one was so attractive an offer that I almost accepted it. But, really!

When Alan Ross took over *The London Magazine* in April 1961, and appointed me his Assistant Editor, I told him I would in turn need help, as my colleague Barbara Cooper had decided not to continue under the new régime. 'Your new assistant will start next week,' Alan said. 'He's very beautiful, apart from his other qualities!' 'What are his other qualities?' I asked ungratefully.

His name was Hugo Williams, he was a nineteen-year-old poet, and a son of the actor-playwrights Hugh and Margaret Williams. I do not know if he justified Alan's description, for we never entered him for any beauty competitions; but he proved a delightful colleague. He rode a motor cycle around London at high speed and could not understand why, after the first few times, I declined further invitations to ride pillion with him.

About a year after he took over the magazine, Alan became ill. For the greater part of 1962, with Hugo's help and later that of a young Australian playwright, Barry Pree, I continued to keep *The London Magazine* appearing monthly until Alan was well enough to take charge again. Then, towards the end of 1962, I took off for a long holiday in Australia. On the plane to relieve the tedium of the journey, I amused and excited myself by writing a pornographic novel, *Sadie Girl*.

It was my first visit to Australia since leaving in 1953, and I was surprised to find that so little had changed in the intervening years. I was expected not to have changed, too, and I think that some of my old friends were disconcerted to find that I had. I was not sure how to behave. I wrote in my diary: 'I seem to have behaved fairly destructively in Brisbane and Melbourne, and mechanically, as though I were a marionette that had merely to be set against its old familiar décor of ten years ago to begin behaving like its younger, dottier self.'

Part of the trouble was that I coped very badly with media attention on that first return visit to Australia. I suppose I was not used to it. It is not that I was incapable of switching on the charm, or of producing the soft answer that turneth away wrath. I was and I am. But I did not, and still do not, always care about my 'public image'. If, on occasions, I cut a *brutta figura*, then so be it. After the Aldermaston march in 1961, a photograph appeared in one of the London newspapers of thousands of us squatting in Trafalgar Square, daring police to remove us. An Australian TV interviewer either recognized me in the photo, or had me pointed out to him (the other Osborne was in the photo as well: those were the days, eh, John?), and when he was interviewing me on live TV in Melbourne, he asked me what I was doing, squatting with Communists in a London demonstration.

'What Communists?' I asked. (I disapprove of Communism, Fascism, and all other forms of coercive government. I believe firmly in the mob rule of democracy.)

'You're not going to deny there are Communists in that photo?'

There must have been more than a hundred recognizable faces in the photo. 'Yes, I suppose there are Communists,' I said. 'There are also actors, Methodists, lesbians –' I discovered later that, at that point, we lost sound for a few seconds until it became clear that I was not going to use any more dirty words. I became increasingly irritated with the interviewer, and when he asked me what part of Australia I had originally come from, I snapped, 'I was born in a concentration camp called Brisbane.' For a time the switchboards were jammed with calls from old friends and acquaintances and indeed strangers in Brisbane offering me piquant advice, some of it difficult to follow.

Almost everyone I met on that 1962 visit wanted advice, or an assurance from me that I could steer them to success in this or that field if they came to Europe. 'I feel like a great sponge that everyone from afar imagines to be a rock,' I confided to my diary. 'Lean on me and collapse.' I had occasionally tried to help fellow-Australians who had made themselves known to me in London; and, in an attempt to promote Australian writers and artists, I had edited a special number of *The London Magazine* which appeared in September 1962, containing new stories by Patrick White and Hal Porter, poems by Judith Wright and Randolph Stow, and pieces by younger writers such as Ray Mathew and Alan Seymour. For my pains I found myself referred to in the Sydney weekly magazine, *The Bulletin*, as having a fondness 'for truckling to the prevailing London cult of Australiana which has inflated the reputations of Nolan and Patrick White'. (I think both these artists were doing reasonably well without any help from a London cult.)

Now, in *The Courier-Mail*, the Brisbane morning newspaper, I found an article on my Australian issue of *The London Magazine*, under a huge headline, 'UN-AUSTRALIAN ACTIVITIES BY EXPATRIATES IN LONDON'. 'Osborne and his fellow "patriots" in London,' I read, 'are out to present a new image of Australia to the world.' I was castigated for not having returned to live in Australia, 'just as Patrick White did, because he became afraid of turning into "that most sterile of beings, a London intellectual".' (Years later, when a Sydney journalist asked Patrick why he lived in Australia, since he wrote so viciously of its society, he replied, 'If you want to study rats, you have to live in a sewer.')

In Sydney, I was interviewed for the *Sydney Morning Herald* by a young journalist to whom I remember having given some help and advice during his London years. He took me to a pub in King's Cross, plied me with whisky, and switched on his tape recorder. The piece that appeared in his newspaper was headed 'Portrait of a Pundit'. The accompanying photograph, taken just before closing time in the pub, was of a somewhat sloshed-looking pundit, and the article made me sound a real jerk:

> Mr Osborne ordered another whisky. He ran a hand over his thinning hair. 'I suppose you could call me a permanent expatriate,' he said . . . 'I have to keep a strict check on myself not to let the magazine become too weighted with Australians . . . No, I don't think there's an Australian cult overseas. Perhaps ten years ago, when we were sufficiently remote to be exotic. But not now.'
>
> I noticed two men were eavesdropping with mild interest at the other end of the counter. Osborne, an incredibly fluent talker, was creating an audience even in the bar. [Osborne by this time had about half a bottle of the *Sydney Morning Herald*'s whisky inside him.] It was

> not always so. Born in Brisbane, Osborne was one of a group of young Queensland University poets who set up their own magazine but failed to attract an audience large enough to keep it going.
>
> ... Ten years of close in-fighting in the London literary world have left their mark on Mr Osborne. Balanced, urbane, only slightly brittle, he has acquired a ten-year patina of imperturbability. Even so, returning to Australia has been a traumatic experience for him. 'I flew straight back to Brisbane to see my family, and at first it was wonderful,' he explained. '... But I had changed; after a while I couldn't bear the place. It's just like a sleazy frontier town; the Deep South of Australia. Most of the people are so conformist, so damned dull. Even those I knew talked about nothing but their cars. Some of my friends held a party for me, and unfortunately invited one of the most rabid expatriate-baiters along. It was rather nasty. After three days I fled to Melbourne ...'
>
> ... The two blokes at the end of the bar had stopped listening. We walked out into the crowded street, men in singlets drinking beer on the pavement, girls in high heels stepping gingerly over dusty piles of bluemetal, taxi windows reflecting the garish glint of late sunlight. 'I love Australia,' Mr Osborne said. 'In a foolish way, I'm quite sentimental about it. But I could never live here.'

The moral of that story is that one should never get drunk in the company of journalists (though it would take more than a bottle of Scotch to make me use phrases like 'rabid expatriate-baiters'). It took me many months to make peace with my Brisbane friends. I have been back to the country of my birth many times since that first visit, but now when I enter the arrivals lounge in Sydney, smelling of the insect spray which is squirted over all visitors before they are allowed to step off the plane, I mutter to myself as an incantation Peter Porter's clerihew:

> In Australia
> (Inter alia)
> mediocrities
> think they're Socrates.

I do not regret, however, that I spent those weeks in Australia in 1962, for it was there that I met Ken Thomson. He came to London three months later, and we have lived together ever since.

*

I had worked for *The London Magazine* for eight years, and had been its Assistant Editor for five, when Eric Walter White, a senior officer at the Arts Council of Great Britain, invited me to lunch in order to ask me if I would be interested in joining the Arts Council's Literature Department, which was about to be formed. I had met Eric on several occasions; he was an engaging, eccentric, and in manner extremely baroque individual, from whom benevolence positively oozed. I warmed to him, and to the idea or working with him at the Arts Council. I said yes.

The London Magazine gave a splendid farewell party for me at the Carlton Tower Hotel on 30 March, and on the following Monday, 4 April, 1966, I joined the Arts Council. I left the Council twenty years later.

I describe my Arts Council experience in the next chapter. My life in the last twenty years has revolved around Arts Council business and my own writing. What else has occupied my energies or my thoughts during those years that should be mentioned here? I jot down three headings: travel; music; thinking.

Let us start with travel. I have never felt an urge to write about travel, and I do not intend to begin doing so now. I do not enjoy travel, as such; I do not see how anyone can, nowadays. But I enjoy being in new places, so I have to subject myself to the rigours of present-day travel. Air travel is squalid, whether one travels Ambassador, Business or Economy class. (Note the modern adjectives that have replaced the more honest first, second and third.) The days are long since past when Noël Coward's quip was apt. ('Air travel,' he said, 'is like homosexuality: it's quicker, cleaner, and you meet a nicer class of person.') Trains are dirty. Sea travel by ocean liner I do actively enjoy, but when can one find time for it? I have travelled on the old *New York*, the *Vistafjord*, the *Sea Princess*, and once crossed the Atlantic on the *QE II* (a bit of a disappointment). I would rather take a stately five days to travel to New York than as many hours on a crowded jet, but I tell myself I cannot afford the time, and apparently I convince myself. I don't understand people who find sea travel boring. It is whatever you make of it. If you want to be gregarious, drink, gamble, play deck sports, chat to other passengers, you can. If, like me, you prefer to read, write or lie about on deck, gazing at the ocean and rejoicing in the circular horizon, uninterrupted by land, that, too, is allowable.

Much of my travel is in order to attend music festivals or performances of opera, usually in Europe or America. I used to make almost annual pilgrimages to Salzburg and Vienna, but I now tend to diversify. Two of my favourite restaurants were the Franziskaner (gone, alas) in Vienna, and the

Goldener Hirsch in Salzburg. At Festival time, one needs to have booked at the Goldener Hirsch months in advance (being resident in the inn itself does not help), so when Lord Goodman, whom I encountered one evening at the Grosses Festspielhaus, offered on impulse to give me lunch at the Goldener Hirsch next day, I said, 'You'll never get a table.' But of course he did, and we had a delightful lunch. At the next table, I remember, Karl Böhm, surrounded by friends, was celebrating his eightieth birthday. (My current favourite restaurants include, in New York, the River Café, which is located on a barge under the Brooklyn Bridge on the Brooklyn side, with a stunning view of Manhattan; in Hollywood, Chasen's; and, in London, the Caprice, where they serve a Champagne Asta, named after my highly intelligent, neurotic wire-haired terrier.)

I made the first of my (so far) three visits to Israel in 1971, to act as sheepdog to a team of British poets whom I had chosen to give readings there. Our party consisted of Ted Hughes and his wife Carol, Peter Porter, D. J. Enright, Jeremy Robson, Dannie Abse and myself. Our journey began, I remember, with a nervous flurry of jokes about hijacking as we were each carefully frisked before being allowed to board the El Al plane at Heathrow. A suspicious bulge was discovered in Ted's pocket. 'It's a tiger's tooth,' he explained, producing it. None of us being religious, we were distinctly unreassured to discover that the folder of pamphlets distributed to us as we strapped ourselves into our seats included a prayer for our safety, 'O deliver us from every enemy, ambush and hurt by the way . . .' But five hours later we had arrived in Israel, and were being driven from Lod Airport into Tel Aviv. 'Over there, to your right, is the tomb of St George.'

In eleven days we gave six performances. (I say 'we' because I was part of the act, reading English translations of the Israeli poets who joined us, and on one occasion at a *kibbutz* even uttering an introductory speech in Hebrew *pour étonner les poètes anglais*.) We were also shown much of their country by the immensely hospitable Israelis. Impressions showered upon us continually, far too many and confusing for the mind to assimilate, but I shall not easily forget my first glimpse of the walled city of Jerusalem from the top of the Mount of Olives, surely one of the world's most emotive sights. Those primitive notions of the Last Trump are given 'a local habitation and a name' by the green hillside liberally sprinkled with graves whose dead shall rise and enter the holy city, Paradise, through that particular gate. And there, just outside the walls to the south, is the valley of Gehenna, or Hell.

Other memories of Jerusalem crowd in: Dennis Enright and I rigid with fear in the back of Carmi's Volkswagen, as that nicest of men, most excellent of poets but most vicious of drivers whirled us round the hills at dead of night, reliably stalling at each precipitous corner and rolling backwards towards Gehenna; myself, puritanically shocked that Peter Porter had not visited the Holy Sepulchre, dragging him up the Via Dolorosa to see it; the party given for us by Jerusalem's Viennese mayor, Teddy Kollek (who got in on the Arab vote, they say), at which the food was so delicious that Ted and Carol Hughes and I descended upon it like a plague of locusts, devouring it within seconds; an afternoon spent at Yad Vashem, the moving, strangely unharrowing museum which records the Holocaust; the casual urban amity of Jew and Arab.

'Tel Aviv dances, Haifa works, Jerusalem studies,' we were told. And it is true that the differences between the three cities are sharp. Haifa seemed thoroughly bourgeois, and our audience in the Municipal Theatre would not have looked out of place in Vienna or Munich. Tel Aviv, slouching along the Mediterranean front from Herzlia, where the diplomats have their villas, to picturesque Jaffa, the only place in Israel where they do *not* grow oranges, is by no means a beautiful town. But it is alive, and is where the concerts and theatres flourish. Our amiable impresario, Yaacov Agmon, and his beautiful film-star wife, Gila Almagor, took us one evening on a whirlwind tour of the theatres. In and out of darkened stalls we passed, from Ionesco to Ibsen to Albee. It was in Tel Aviv that Jeremy Robson, Dannie Abse and I, on our way to visit a painter, passed Ben-Gurion's modest house. Jeremy, who had been rhapsodizing over an earlier meeting with the great man, was decidedly embarrassed when Dannie and I suddenly rounded on him and insisted on being taken in and introduced. He was brave enough to go through with it, but unfortunately Ben-Gurion had already left to attend a conference in Brussels.

All of us were staggered by the beauty and the variety of the landscape, as well as by the disconcerting tendency of our experiences to zig-zag between the sublime and the ridiculous. In so many of the mosques the muezzin no longer bothers to climb up to the minaret to summon the faithful: he uses instead a microphone at ground level, with a speaker up on the minaret. Sometimes he is not even there: he is a gramophone record. And, if the Arab town of Bethlehem manages to survive in one's memory, it is despite the birthplace of Christ on Manger Square. Yet the Sea of Galilee certainly has *mana*. I had that odd feeling of having been there before, but did not mention this to the others, who had already commented on my messianic complex.

Most memorable of all is the day we travelled down into the desert of the Negev, through harsh, arid, mountainous country like the moon, or

Nolan's Australia. Past so many biblical sites, Hebron, Sodom, Beer Sheva to the Dead Sea and, rising starkly from the surrounding hills, the palace-fortress of Masada, built by Herod: it was besieged by the Romans in AD 73 when, rather than surrender, nearly a thousand Jews killed themselves. In a land full of holy places, this was perhaps the holiest. It was also spectacular silent, vivid.

The poetry readings which were the purpose of our visit? As it happened, they were successful. Ted Hughes stunned audiences with *Crow*. Dennis Enright delighted them, Dannie's humanity and Peter's sensitive observation made their mark, and Jeremy was encored. The Israelis, as a nation, are tougher, more resilient than their relatives of the diaspora, but Jewish humour, thank God, remains Jewish: at our press conference, one of the poets gave a long and complicated reply to a question about the directions being taken by poetry, ending by admitting that the answer could not really be given for a number of years to come. 'That's all very well,' said the journalist who had asked the question, 'but what am I going to put in tomorrow's paper?'

I have been back to Israel twice since then, most recently in 1981 when Patricia Beer, Edwin Morgan, Michael Schmidt, Robert Wells and I read our poems, and I made the third of my totally unsuccessful attempts to float in the Dead Sea, which everyone else in the world is able to do. Is this some kind of miracle in reverse?

In 1970, at the end of a visit to the Vienna Festival, Ken Thomson and I drove all over Romania, from the Hungarian border to the Danube Delta. The most fascinating part of our journey was our exploration of Transylvania. (This was before Romania started advertising 'Dracula tours'.) Travelling in Transylvania was like stepping back in time a good fifty years. The old town of Oradea (Grosswardein, to me), Cluj (Klausenberg), Sibiu (Hermannstadt) and Brasov (Kronstadt) were so evocative, the country with its Carpathian mountains and pine forests quite beautiful, and the villages rather like Universal's old sets for *Frankenstein* and *Dracula*. The peasants performed all the peasant-like tasks as though they had been directed by James Whale: washing clothes in the brook, chasing geese, travelling in carts drawn by oxen, even crossing themselves at nightfall as they looked up at the sinister castle on the hill. Everywhere there were gypsies on the road, in beautifully painted wagons.

Tucked away behind the Carpathians, Transylvania had managed to retain much of its old identity. The rest of Romania was less fortunate, Communism's dead hand lay over the country, and Bucharest had become just another glum Socialist capital. The Black Sea resorts were ghastly, and though the Danube Delta was attractive it seemed odd that no local fish was to be found on any menu, only the ubiquitous pork chop.

An image which has remained with me is of a peasant squatting in the marshes by the Danube, his head sunk between his legs. As we drove by, the link between the Chinese poetry and the Danubian music of the *'Abschied'* from *Das Lied von der Erde* seemed to be symbolized by this passive figure in the landscape.

My visits to Australia in the seventies were less traumatic than my first return there in the sixties, though the local press continued to goad me for being an expatriate (God, you hear that word often in Australia). 'It's rather absurd,' I appear to have told *The Australian*, the major national newspaper, 'to keep on thinking that returning here involves some sort of perilous journey of the psyche.' That particular interview appeared under the heading, 'Expatriate Poet Drops In But Won't Stay':

> 'I could envisage myself living in Sydney if you could pick it up and take it over there, to all the opera, the theatre and concerts,' Mr Osborne decided, looking out over the trees of Centennial Park in Sydney, through the french doors in Patrick White's house.

That was in the days when Patrick and I were friends, and I was his house guest for a week in Sydney. Since then, he has published his memoirs, in which he has written so insensitively of Sidney Nolan that I feel it is unlikely that I shall see Patrick again.

In 1977 I was invited to take a group of British writers to the Soviet Union. One or two writers whom I approached made it clear that they disapproved of the visit. 'Dear Charles,' replied Harold Pinter to my invitation, 'Just back from a long haul in America to find your letter about a proposed trip to Russia. I must tell you that I wouldn't set foot in that bloody country, for obvious reasons. So you can count me well out. All the best.'

I respect Harold Pinter's attitude, though I do not share it. I disapprove of the government of the Soviet Union, and of all dictatorships whether they describe themselves as being politically left or right. But I have nothing against the Russian people. I have visited Greece under the Colonels, and Spain while Franco was still alive (in fact, one evening Franco and I stayed under the same roof, a *parador* in Santiago de Compostela), on the grounds that, if I were to confine my travel to those countries of whose politics I wholeheartedly approved, where on earth would I go? Copenhagen? But people are constantly throwing up their hands in horror at the thought of going to South Africa, while cheerfully dashing off to the Soviet Union, or vice versa. And we all, pinkos and crypto-fascists alike, continue to visit the good old U.S. of A., don't we? And Australia, where they practise a non-violent form of apartheid.

The team which visited the Soviet Union in 1977 consisted of Elaine Feinstein, novelist and poet; Brian Aldiss, novelist; Jon Stallworthy, poet; Ted Whitehead, playwright; and me. Elaine and I had been there before (I twice, first in 1957, and more recently as a tourist), but for the other three it was a first visit. Although our tour was organized at official level, the idea arose from a conversation between the Russian poet Yevgeni Yevtushenko and myself a couple of years earlier, and Yevgeni (Zhenia) himself was to prove personally a most generous host to us in the Soviet Union. We were asked to let the Soviet authorities know in advance of particular writers we wanted to meet, or parts of the country we wanted to visit. The names of writers presented little difficulty, as most of them lived in Moscow or Leningrad. But we five had widely differing desires as far as places were concerned. Everyone wanted to visit the two major cities, of course, but after that the geographical spread became rather alarming: Siberia, the Asiatic republics, the Ukraine, Georgia and, in my case, the Baltic states, the former countries of Estonia, Latvia and Lithuania. In the end, an itinerary was mapped out for our two weeks' stay which was based on Moscow and Leningrad but which also allowed us six days in the South, in Georgia.

We flew from Heathrow on a Japan Air Lines flight. When the hostess announced, 'Your pilot on this flight is Captain Kamikazi,' Brian Aldiss and I exchanged glances of dismay. But we got there. Among the friendly faces who greeted us at Moscow Airport, four were familiar to me: those of Zhenia Yevtushenko, his girl-friend Jan Butler, Anatoly Melnikov of the Writers' Union (whom I had last encountered in Australia), and William Marsden, cultural attaché at the British Embassy in Moscow. Soon, in the three large cars which were to be laid on for us and our retinue of guides and translators throughout the entire visit, we were on the way to our hotel. Would it be the plush, faded, still oddly glamorous Metropol, where I had last stayed? No, it was a more modern piece of marbled grandeur, the Sovietskaya. Zhenia came to the hotel with us, and waited while we sorted out rooms and freshened up. Then, on to the house of the Writers' Union, where he was giving a supper party for us. Some days later, we were formally to meet the bosses of the Moscow Writers' Union. But this first evening was Zhenia's, and he made it a memorable one for us. The club premises of the Writers' Union are in an attractive old house, and the dining room would seem familiar to anyone who had just finished reading *War and Peace*, for Tolstoy made use of it to describe the ballroom of the Rostov house. We sat at a large table in a corner, where we were joined by Zhenia's other guests. 'There are no bloody Communists at this table,' he shouted merrily, more for the benefit, one felt, of those sitting at other tables than for us.

The meal that evening set a pattern for those that followed: endless quantities of the most delicious food, and no shortage of vodka, wine or champagne. The meals were invariably punctuated by toasts. We reticent Britons, not given at home to such extrovert junketing, soon entered into the mood of it, leaping to our feet as the spirit (or, perhaps more correctly, spirits) moved us, to invite the assembled company to join us in yet another ingeniously phrased toast.

Throughout our tour, and especially in Moscow, Leningrad and Tbilisi, we were entertained informally, in their homes or in restaurants, by writers and artists, but at least once in each town there was a formal meeting at the local branch of the Writers' Union, which usually took the form of a meal preceded by an hour's discussion. The Soviet writers had questions they wanted to put to us about literary life in Great Britain, and we certainly had many questions for them. Some of the people we met obviously found it difficult to grasp that we, as a group of five writers, did not share a political, philosophical or moral viewpoint. They were, it seemed, surprised that we did not all have to trot out the same 'government line' on the subjects we discussed, and were perplexed when, as frequently occurred, we disagreed strongly with one another. They had not necessarily assumed that we would be five political Conservatives, but I think they did assume that we had been chosen to be sent to the Soviet Union because we were 'safe'. How wrong they were. No one chose me, I simply happened to be the chap in charge of literature at the Arts Council. I chose the others, on the basis that they were writers and that I expected they would make agreeable companions. I had no idea what their politics might be. It was in the presence of a group of Russian writers that we five from Great Britain made the discovery that as capitalists and Christians we made a pretty poor showing, for we appeared to have no political or religious commitments (with the possible exception of Ted Whitehead, further to the left than the rest of us).

Some of our questions must have caused embarrassment to our hosts, but they were answered cordially, if not always satisfactorily. There was, for instance, our meeting at the offices of the *Literaturnaya Gazeta*, a weekly newspaper which perhaps one could describe as a cross between the *Times Literary Supplement* and the *New Statesman*. We sat around a table with the Editor, Chakovsky, and his senior staff, and discussed various literary matters. Then Chakovsky announced that, if we had any other questions about Soviet life, not necessarily confined to literature, he would try to answer them. I had one question, for I felt we had been far too prissily polite with one another. 'Surely, by now,' I said, 'the Soviet Union ought to have sufficient confidence in itself to allow its citizens to travel abroad freely, even to emigrate if they wish to, as we do in the West. Even though, initially, you might lose a great many citizens, many of them would return once they realized that they could come and go freely. This seems to me to be the major difference between our ways of life, and to many people in the West it is a stumbling block in the way of their appreciation of your government's achievements.'

I got a lengthy reply, which took in traditional Russian distrust of foreigners; the intervention of the Western world in the Russian Revolution; the five-year-plan; Stalin; the war; Yalta; Churchill's cold war speech; and the difficulties of foreign exchange. 'All of these,' I said, 'are interesting reasons why Russian citizens might not be keen to travel abroad, but none of them are good reasons why they should be forbidden to do so.' The old fox of Socialism, as Chakovsky had described himself to us, smiled and left to go to a committee meeting at which his presence, he discovered, was urgently required.

One evening, Jon Stallworthy, Ted Whitehead and I went to the Bolshoi. I was delighted to be back again in the beautiful gold, cream and blue auditorium I had first visited in 1957 and then again in the early seventies, but as we took our seats in a box Ted glowered, 'This is the kind of place I'd like to burn down.' The Russians fortunately take a different view: they have never wanted to clear away all their pre-1917 babies with the Tsarist bath water. In fact, they are proud of the architecture of the past and have preserved a good many less delightful examples of it than the Bolshoi Theatre. The opera we saw was Rimsky-Korsakov's *The Tsar's Bride* in an attractive, traditional production, and well sung, especially by a mezzo who sounded like Christa Ludwig. ('The Soviet reverence for high bourgeois culture is a bit of a bore,' wrote Ted in *The Spectator* when we got back to London.)

Our flight from Moscow down to Georgia, over the snow-capped, mysterious Caucasus, was exciting. ('There are villages in those mountains,' said one of our minders, in wonderment, 'where they have not yet heard of the Revolution!') Our arrival in Tbilisi (or Tiflis, as some of us remembered it from our school-days) coincided with the arrival of spring, but a spring which was like high summer to us. The darker, slighter Georgians made a strong contrast with the Russians, and their charming capital city combined elements of Italy, the Balkan coast and the Middle East. The Russians had spoken in fear and trembling of Georgian hospitality, and indeed we found we needed all our stamina. The toasts, many of which, if the Tamada or chairman of the table so decreed, had to be drunk 'bottoms up', came thick and fast. After wine had loosened tongues, it became clear to us that Russians were not popular in Georgia, for they were seen as representatives of the Soviet Union, which had swallowed up the smaller country.

Paradoxically (or perhaps not: *vide* Hitler and Austria) Stalin was a Georgian, and it is in Georgia that one still finds him remembered. In Tbilisi one can (and did) buy Stalin postcards, and taxi-drivers often had his portrait fixed to the dashboard, just as a taxi-driver in Rome might display an image of the Virgin. One day we found ourselves driving through the small town of Gori, Stalin's birthplace. We stopped to visit the house in which he was born, a wooden hut now preserved under a concrete superstructure. We visited, too, the nearby Stalin Museum, which was an unusual experience. On the walls, huge social-realist paintings in which Stalin is featured at various climactic moments of his career; in cases along the walls, the usual memorabilia. But, when I went down to the basement in search of a lavatory, I found a huge store-room in which about a hundred discarded busts of the dictator lay sadly about, on benches, on tables, on the floor. They must have been returned from all over the Soviet Union after his death. There they all are, silently awaiting the inevitable day of the old monster's rehabilitation.

In Georgia, we were taken to a state farm. I do not know what we expected, but what we got was a charming old estate which might have provided a setting for *The Cherry Orchard*. We strolled in the gardens, imagining ourselves Gayev, Trofimov, Madame Ranevsky, and lunched in the cool dining room of the *dacha*. I rose, towards the end of the meal, to respond to a toast, and found myself saying how very Chekhovian all this was. As I spoke, there came from outside that unexplained sound, as at the end of *The Cherry Orchard*, like a string snapping, resonating and dying away. 'It must have been a plane,' someone said.

One of the highlights of our stay in Georgia was our overnight visit to the spa of Borjomi, high in the mountains in a beautiful pine forest. The sanatorium was an old hunting lodge which had belonged to a Crown Prince, brother of the Tsar. We stayed in *dachas* in the grounds, and were shown over the royal hunting lodge, which had been well preserved. We all tried a few shots, if that is the correct term, on the Crown Prince's billiard-table, and I was coaxed into testing his piano as well. Emboldened by vodka, I played the old Tsarist National hymn, and was greeted not only with laughter but with the voices of our Soviet friends joining in. The taste of the water at Borjomi itself is as foul as at any other spa, but the bottled Borjomi mineral water sold throughout Georgia is excellent.

The friendliness of the Georgians never ceased to enchant us. One morning at breakfast in our Tbilisi hotel, two young men at a nearby table who were beginning their day with champagne sent a bottle over to us when they heard us speaking English. When we thanked them, they sent over a second bottle, and a third. Finally they joined us, with more bottles, and Brian Aldiss went up to his room and came back with some souvenirs of the Queen's Silver Jubilee, which he and I then proceeded to distribute to our newly-found friends as though they were medals conferring some kind of distinction. The Georgians explained that, though they detested capitalism, they felt sympathy for us, its victims. There were more toasts, and one of them, proposed by the more ebullient of the two young Georgians, was 'To the three greatest Englishmen: Turner, Newton and Aldridge.' We dutifully drank, though we had our doubts about these three. Was Newton the right Newton, i.e. Isaac? He was, for our Georgian friend was a chemist, and Newton was one of his heroes. But was Turner the artist or merely a member of some earlier British delegation to visit Tbilisi? He was indeed the artist, for a Turner exhibition had recently toured the Soviet Union. We remained perplexed about Aldridge, even after we were told that he was a contemporary novelist called James Aldridge. Still, it would have been churlish not to drink to him.

After Georgia, we flew back to Russia, to Leningrad, one of the most beautiful cities anywhere. Our sight-seeing here had to be crammed. We drove quickly through those back streets Dostoevsky described in *Crime and Punishment*, went through the Hermitage at a *Schweinsgalop*, and took in a dull modern ballet, *Hamlet*, at the Kirov, which is the old Maryinsky Theatre and which rivals the Bolshoi in beauty. We found time to look over the cruiser, *Aurora*, which fired the shot to begin the 1917 revolution. I enjoyed sauntering alone down the Nevsky Prospect, browsing in the bookshop near our hotel (the Yevropaiskaya, with its echoes of the past), or just watching the river from the windows of the palace now occupied by the Leningrad Writers' Union. I recommend the cafeteria at the Yevropaiskaya. (Not the restaurant, whose Boeuf Stroganoff is excellent but for which you have to wait hours.) In the cafeteria, for one rouble you can eat your fill at breakfast: the blinis are delicious. And for one rouble, seventy-five copecks, as much lunch as you can manage.

At the Writers' Union, I was asked how I managed to control my group so well. 'They're not my group,' I explained. 'We're just five individuals.' 'But they all seem to do what you tell them to.' 'Ah, that's because I tell them to do only what they want to do.'

For at least three of us, Elaine Feinstein, Jon Stallworthy and myself, I think the most memorable of our experiences must have been on our last night in the Soviet Union. We left a Moscow party after midnight, to be taken by Zhenia Yevtushenko miles into the country, arriving, after several adventures, at the village of Peredelkino at about two in the morning. In the middle of a forest, with a nightingale singing nearby, we walked by moonlight to a cemetery and found the grave of Boris Pasternak. Here we sat and drank the wine which Zhenia had thoughtfully purloined from the apartment of the British cultural attaché the previous evening. Then we drove on to Zhenia's *dacha* for more food, drink and talk, finally arriving back in Moscow as dawn was breaking. A few hours' sleep, a farewell lunch in the apartment of the poet Margarita Aliger, and then on to an otherwise completely empty British Airways flight to London.

On my visits to the United States I usually try to combine relaxation with a little business, promoting my books through interviews and signing sessions in New York or Key West or Washington or Los Angeles; or participating in the Saturday afternoon Metropolitan Opera Quiz which is broadcast nationally under the sponsorship of Texaco, and which is great fun to do; or lecturing on opera in San Diego and elsewhere. Three or four years ago in New York, I got caught up in a delightful and doomed attempt on the part of hundreds of Broadway actors and directors to save two theatres. My involvement began in the bar of the Algonquin. I had checked into the hotel an hour or so previously, and was in the bar awaiting the arrival of my American publisher's publicity manager. The Algonquin bar, lobby and the Oak and Rose Rooms usually have familiar faces dotted about – on a good day, Bette Davis or Robert Redford, but on a bad day one can become dizzy through swerving to avoid British publishers. In the bar this evening were two Broadway producers, Joseph Papp and Harold Prince, and they seemed to be in a state of intense excitement. Eavesdropping, I pieced together from their talk the information that two Broadway theatres, the Morosco and the Helen Hayes, were under threat of immediate demolition, and that Papp and Prince were in the throes of organizing a last-ditch demonstration by all the actors they could round up at short notice. Papp thrust a brochure at me. 'Every star on Broadway will have a part in the read-in,' it said; 'every producer, director, stagehand and kid in the chorus.' 'Be there,' ordered Mr Papp.

Later that evening, on my way to the Alvin Theatre to see a revival of

George M. Cohan's *Little Johnny Jones* (which opened and closed that night), I went out of my way to pass the Morosco, just west of Broadway on 45th Street. The site next door, on which, when I was last in New York some months earlier, the elegant little Bijou Theatre had stood, now contained rubble and a huge earth-mover which looked like a dinosaur, its mouth gaping hungrily open at the east wall of the Morosco.

The Morosco itself already wore a vanquished look. In front of the theatre a platform had been erected. On it sat an impressive array of Broadway stars, before whom stood Joe Papp, now wearing a construction-worker's tin hat. (Americans like to wear funny hats.) He told an assembled crowd of more than a hundred onlookers that New York's actors were determined that the Morosco and the Helen Hayes, which backed onto it from 46th Street, would not be demolished to make way for a huge hotel. For the next two days, at the end of which a judge's decision was expected to be announced, the actors would give readings, right round the clock, of the many Pulitzer Prize-winning plays which had first been performed at these two theatres. To begin, however, the stars on the platform would each read a short speech from one of these plays.

Martha Scott, who had played in Thornton Wilder's *Our Town* in 1938, read the Stage Manager's opening speech from that play. Christopher Reeve contributed some lines from Eugene O'Neill's *Beyond the Horizon*. A fur-hatted figure – it had been a cold March day, and by now it was snowing – revealed himself to be Arthur Miller and read a speech from his *Death of a Salesman*. Lauren Bacall delved back to a 1926 Pulitzer Prize winner, *Craig's Wife* by George Kelly (which I remembered as a thirties movie with Rosalind Russell), and Madeleine someone, who had been in the original production of *Cat on a Hot Tin Roof*, spoke some lines from that play. By now the air was filled with emotion and snowflakes. Actors thrust petitions at us which we signed, urging Mayor Ed Koch to come to his senses. When Jason Robards moved to the front of the platform and, holding a copy of the play, to which he never once needed to refer, began James Tyrone's great confessional speech from *Long Day's Journey into Night*, even the traffic a block away on Broadway seemed to fall silent. It was a moving performance. Some of us greeted it with applause, some with silence. Joe Papp, however, leaped to the front of the platform, shouting 'O'Neill lives! O'Neill lives!' In his excitement he exclaimed that, if the bulldozers moved against the Morosco, they would first have to mow down himself and all the actors who would form a line in front of the theatre.

It was at that moment that I suddenly knew nothing was going to save the two theatres. Those marvellously sentimental extroverts were still declaiming as I walked off to see *Little Johnny Jones*. I was humming its best-known number, 'Give My Regards to Broadway', as I returned to the Morosco after the performance. The stars of *The Pirates of Penzance* were on the platform now, and they were followed by the lyricists Adolph Green and Betty Comden, who sang, to the tune of *Romola*, a lyric they had just written about the Morosco. (Did I really hear the line: 'Let's give some thoight/To keep New York unlike Detroit'?) Around midnight, the readings (by casts of lesser-knowns) of Morosco and Helen Hayes successes began. I listened to the beginning of *Strange Interlude* and made my way back to supper at the Algonquin. The readings continued through the night.

Next morning after breakfast I returned. They were well into *Cat on a Hot Tin Roof* now. At midday the play in progress was *The Shadow Box*, and I was allowed to read a few lines. I signed the petition again, using my sixth or seventh pseudonym (I think it was something Verdian, probably L. di Vargas, which I did not expect Mayor Koch to recognize), though I did not believe the actor who assured me it was now certain that the theatres would be saved. The Supreme Court in Washington had issued an order preventing demolition until after the weekend, and the demonstrators were jubilant. When I next passed by early in the evening, on my way to see Katharine Hepburn in *West Side Waltz* at the Ethel Barrymore, the read-in was over and the actors had departed. No one was about, in front of the Morosco, to hear me utter my final contribution, a line from Noël Coward's *Blithe Spirit*, which had played at that theatre in the forties.

Back in London a week or two later, I read in my newspaper that among more than a hundred demonstrators arrested when they moved into the path of the bulldozers in a vain attempt to protect the two theatres were Celeste Holm, Tammy Grimes and Richard Gere. The celebrities were hauled away, the demolition crews worked through the night as enthusiastically as had the actors, days earlier, and the Morosco and Helen Hayes Theatres are no more. They will live on, for a time, in people's memories, as Jason Robards's 'magnificent fuss' will in mine, and there is no sense in regretting that those buildings, that performance, have not survived. As the man in *Death of a Salesman* said, 'It comes with the territory.'

Enough of travel. What of music? Music is difficult if not impossible to write about, but I continue my attempts to do so. I think about music a great deal, about Mozart, Schubert, Verdi, Mahler and Britten, for instance. And I listen to it, which is, after all, the most sensible thing to do with music. I regret that, as far as creativity is concerned, we are at present in a downward curve, not only in music but in the arts generally, but I know that eventually we shall emerge from it. Meanwhile, there is more than enough music, art poetry and fiction already in existence to keep me occupied for the rest of my life.

What else do I think about and indeed write about? What 'gets my goat'? Many things, I fear. Several of the accepted attitudes of today. The nonsense, for example, that is talked about 'élitism' in the arts. Did I not think it monstrous, asked the drama lecturer at an educational institution in the north, that the Royal Shakespeare Company should be performing *Coriolanus* in Newcastle, rather than some new work which related to the local community? When I replied, 'On the contrary, I think the local community should make an attempt to relate to *Coriolanus*,' he smirked and said, 'Of course that's the élitist position.' (Meanwhile the citizens of Newcastle were sensibly packing out all performances of Shakespeare's élitist play.)

Only one example out of many. Indeed, I have encountered the non-word 'élitist' so frequently that I recently peered into my big OED to confirm that it had not crept in there while I was not looking. It had not. 'Élite', of course, is all right: it anglicized itself some time ago, and apparently still means 'the choice part'. It is perfectly respectable, therefore, to say that a list of the poetic élite would include Shakespeare, Dante, Goethe, Keats, Baudelaire, Yeats, Pushkin, Eliot, Auden and so on, but would exclude, well, me, for instance, and all but, at the most, two living poets. Frankness, however, compels me to add that I suspect there may be others, too, who are not part of the artistic 'élite', and that some of them are probably the very same people who shake that word 'élitist' in one's face like a fist. If, like my drama lecturer, what they are asserting is that one would prefer the arts to be the preserve of a choice few, then surely they are tilting at windmills, for who today holds so absurd a view? But if all they mean is that one is a person who recognizes some artists to be better than others, then it is hardly worth mentioning.

Apparently, however, these truths are not self-evident to all, for the world of the arts contains an increasing number of what one might call the gullers and the gulled. The gullers include those minimally talented, self-proclaimed artists who consider intention a reasonable substitute for achievement: poets, for instance, who are incapable of actually making a poem; prose writers who cannot even understand Swift's concept of 'proper words in proper places', let alone achieve such style, and who may even have convinced themselves that any old words truculently splattered onto the page will do; painters who – but why go on, for we all know they are the most successful confidence-men of all?

The fact remains that words are only the raw material of literature. Without the ability to use them skilfully and imaginatively, one is no writer. Nor does the possession of a stack of canvases and pots of paint in itself make one a painter, any more than a pile of bricks can call itself a house (or, for that matter, a piece of sculpture). As Cervantes puts it, *'Del dicho al hecho hay gran trecho.'* (It's a far cry from speech to deed.) Truisms a decade ago, these are now almost heretical statements.

What is one to say of the gulled, other than that without them there would be no gullers? They divide into those who are fearful of being thought ignorant or philistine, and those who are genuinely ignorant or philistine. The former should learn to trust their own temperamental preferences; the latter should head for the nearest Adult Education classes, though I cannot guarantee that even there they will not fall into the hands of one or the other category. Let us face it, some people are just incorrigibly gullible.

And why not? After all, one must leave room for divergences of taste. Those who prefer William MacGonagall or the Reverend Cornelius Whur to Shakespeare or Chekhov are likely also to prefer Wilson (Snoo/Robert: cross out whichever you think does not apply) to Pinter or Ayckbourn. God is no aesthete, so there will be no prizes awarded in heaven for having preferred the right names. Nor are they morally superior who find comfort in Brahms rather than in Barnabás von Géczy. Ask any survivor from Hitler's camps about the musical tastes of the commandants.

Perhaps worse than those two categories, certainly more boring, are the dunces who confuse the arts with politics: not only those actual politicians who would like to see the arts become more Conservative or more Socialist, whatever they may mean by that, but also the artists who choose to interpret criticism in political terms. The right-wing novelist who thinks you must be a Communist if you do not appreciate his novel; the left-wing poet who calls you a fascist pig when you tell him why his poem is awful. Use the terminology of literary criticism to these characters and you will be answered in the language of the political farmyard. This makes for a colourful exchange, but is hardly intellectually rewarding.

It is monstrously unfair that some people should be more talented than others. Those who fulminate against the notion of an artistic élite often invoke democracy to their aid, as though the least unfair and therefore most admirable system of government so far devised could possibly have the slightest relevance to excellence in the arts. Democracy can do many things, but it cannot, alas, vote a bad poet into being a good one. The jest once made by Toscanini, whose democratic credentials were impeccable, needs to be repeated every so often: 'In life, democracy. In art, dictatorship.' Skulls being as thick as they are, it needs also to be repeated that it *is* a jest.

The majority is not always wrong, and the most popular is not always the least good. Some novelists who sell in tens of thousands (Graham Greene, Patrick White, for example) are considerably better than some others who sell in hundreds (I am not fool enough to name them here, but you know whom I mean, the kind of writer to whom the Arts Council used to love giving bursaries). On the other hand, for my money Seamus Heaney as a poet is superior to Pam Ayres, though I dare say Mistress Ayres would win in a democratic show of hands. I also happen to be convinced that Schubert has the edge on Paul McCartney, though I respect Mr McCartney's achievement on its comparatively low level. After all, he is not as awful as Lloyd Webber. As Count Danilo said to Hanna Glawari when she complimented him on his dancing (*The Merry Widow*, Act I finale): *'Man tut was man kann!'* ('One does what one can.')

The illiberal attitude towards sex, which Australians call wowserism (the word 'wowser' comes from 'We Only Want Social Evils Remedied'), and which in Great Britain we have come to associate with Mrs Mary Whitehouse, is something even more reprehensible than phoniness in the arts. To the impure, like myself, all things are pure, and I have never fully understood how other people arrive at their definitions of obscenity. Words, like visual images, are at once powerful and harmless, but in what sense obscene? The act of murder is surely obscene, but no one flinches from pronouncing the word 'murder' in public, or from discussing the subject of murder.

It ought not to be part of anyone's job to interfere with the harmless pleasure of his fellow citizens. If a few people really do entertain the absurd belief that they can be harmed by speaking or reading certain words, they should have complete liberty to refrain from contact with the offending words. But that they should be able to insist on everyone else becoming lunatic with them is really unacceptable. '*I* do not like this, therefore *you* shall not read or see it' (see under Mary Whitehouse) is too similar to the cry of 'Better dead than red', which does not mean 'I would prefer to die rather than to live under Communism' (an acceptable, if unreasonable statement) but 'I would prefer that we all die rather than that I should live under Communism' (an unacceptable statement).

People who accept party political lines are among my *bêtes noires*. How can one accept a package of opinions from the Conservative or Liberal or Labour parties, or from anywhere else? While we have minds, do we have to delegate our thinking to others? In any case, a political system which depends on one half of the population thinking the other half fools or rogues, and voting accordingly, can hardly be taken seriously. Away with political parties.

It suddenly occurs to me that when I was younger I derived more pleasure from poetry than from prose. Now it is the other way around. I find the novel one of the most richly satisfying of art forms. I like to quote Jane Austen's sardonic defence of fiction in *Northanger Abbey*: '. . . only a novel . . . only some work in which the most thorough knowledge of human nature, the happiest delineation of its varieties, the liveliest effusions of wit and humour are conveyed to the world in the best chosen language'. It is for these qualities that I am a fiction omnivore. As a child I missed out on the fiction written specifically for children, and it's too late now, but from the masterpieces of Proust, Dostoevsky, Patrick White and Thomas Mann to the first-rate works of Svevo, Musil, Joseph Roth and dozens of living novelists, among them Philip Roth, Brigid Brophy, Melvyn Bragg and Joseph Hansen, I continue to read novels for delight, for information, and also for reasons of sloth, for when I am not reading a book in my spare time I would expect myself to be writing one.

However, I draw the line at the mediocre: at about nine-tenths of what is published and respectfully reviewed in the weeklies. With Henry James I share the belief that 'the only obligation to which in advance we may hold a novel, without incurring the accusation of being arbitrary, is that it be interesting'. Verdi expressed it differently. In operatic composition, the boring, he said, is the worst of all styles.

The novelist I admire does not have to be a person of the broadest liberal sympathies – look at Céline, or at Kingsley Amis – but it probably helps if he is. He does need imagination, wit, and to be able to write a decent, flavoursome prose. Too many novelists today – certainly more than in the past, it would appear – expect to be able to write without being able to write, if you see what I mean. Intention is nothing. Intention is those Irishmen sitting around in the Dublin cafés telling one another about the novels they are going to write (it happens in Melbourne, too, though not in large cities like London or New York, where writers do not huddle together for comfort and reassurance). Intention is also those *nouvelle vague* plodders and their English followers. Achievement is all.

Reviewers of novels now are not much cop, but perhaps they never were. They are superb, however, compared with drama reviewers (or critics, as they prefer to be called). I know it is no use longing for the golden days of Bernard Shaw, or even the silver days of James Agate. I do not suppose, either, that it is much use remembering the comparatively recent past when we used to be entertained on Sunday mornings by what someone called the sound of Harold Hobson barking up the wrong tree, or by Kenneth Tynan with his extraordinary ability to describe so vividly what it was like in the theatre when Olivier played Macbeth or Peggy Ashcroft Hedda Gabler. That, surely, is the most valuable function the reviewer can perform for his readers: to describe in lively fashion just what happened in the theatre, and what the play was like, whether it was entertaining, or boring, or offensive, or whatever. The reviewer also needs to be absolutely honest in his reactions. Since J. W. Lambert stopped reviewing in the *Sunday Times*, that honesty is something I miss.

Whom can you respect now? Milton Shulman appears to suffer from the belief that he is the kind of tough New York critic whose reviews can close a show. He is not, nor are any of the others. Plays which receive unanimously ghastly notices have been known to run for years in London, and the public has often stayed away in impressive droves from shows which all the reviewers have recommended.

Who has good taste in plays? Well, for a start, no one on the staff of *Time Out*. The more embarrassingly awful the play, the more inarticulate the dialogue, the more uninviting the characters, the more enthusiastic the review. The *Daily Telegraph*'s man is so bland and flavourless that one finds oneself almost looking forward to Shulman's sub-*Standard* wisecracks later in the day. Bernard Levin for a time added drama criticism to his already formidable list of accomplishments. He wrote more wittily and elegantly than any of his colleagues, and more memorably. I still recall with affection his scathing review of a Royal Shakespeare Company production of Ben Jonson's *The Alchemist*. Levin's view was that, between them, the director (Trevor Nunn) and an unnecessary 'adaptor' had botched Jonson's masterpiece, a view which he developed in detail and with great relish. He ended by admitting that he had lost his temper in describing the production. 'But,' he concluded, 'I plead intolerable provocation on the part of Barnes the Booby [he was the adaptor] and Nunn the Noodle, and it would serve them right if I refused to say another word about this bastard production, in which Jonson's work is butchered on the altar of Mr Barnes's vanity with the blunt knife of Mr Nunn's misunderstanding of his function.' That's the stuff. (And that is the way I feel when I encounter those Stoppardizations of perfectly charming Austrian or Hungarian plays.) I should add that I have enjoyed many of Trevor Nunn's productions, the most recent being *Les Misérables*.

The reason why most of the drama reviewers cannot be relied upon is that they regard themselves as part of the theatre industry. Time and time again, they have proved to be absolutely incapable of admitting that Edward Bond or David Mercer or John Arden or John Osborne or some other distinguished contemporary British playwright can possibly have written an absolute stinker. To say so, they feel, would be tantamount to admitting that our glorious crop of dramatists is not exactly all it is cracked up to be. It would be letting down a profession of which they feel themselves to be part. Occasionally, someone will say that perhaps that last play of Mercer's – the Lord in his infinite mercy has removed even the title from my mind – may not have represented the playwright at the very peak of his powers; or that it is possible that there may be one or two (no more, mind you) dull moments in Edward Bond's *The Woman*. But no one will tell you that an admired name has written a bloody awful play. The best drama reviews appear when a paper's regular drama critic is on holiday, and someone completely outside the world of the theatre is temporarily brought in. I instance the period when Ian Hamilton, poet, literary editor, biographer, and now TV 'front man', did a stint for the *New Statesman*. He was not interested in bolstering reputations, and it was refreshing to read him. (I except Francis King, novelist and *Sunday Telegraph* drama critic, from the above tirade.)

Of course, drama critics have other ways of being silly. They are absolute suckers for production gimmicks. I was once moved to comment, in the *Sunday Times*, on a particularly asinine review:

> Your drama critic praises a current production for being re-set in Ireland, thus removing from Chekhov his 'Russianness', which the critic seems to find annoyingly exotic. Could not repatriation of this kind be made mandatory in all productions of plays and operas, so that critics need no longer feel intimidated by the *italianità* of Verdi, the *Oesterreichischkeit* of Mozart, the Scandinavishness of Ibsen, or the Americanacity of Tennessee Williams? All that is necessary to achieve such critical peace of mind is a simple statute enacting that all productions of foreign works be set within the confines of the British Isles.

In 1981 Tom Stoppard, who had 'adapted' Nestroy's charming *Einen Jux will er sich machen* for the National Theatre, was quoted in the *Observer* as having 'confessed to never having heard of the said Nestroy until the project was suggested by his friend and frequent director, Peter Wood'. 'Stoppard,' the article continued, 'doesn't read German, and "adaptation" means that he takes the plot and the characters and writes his own dialogue.' ('Precisely what you had once done with Chekhov,' I imagine some churlish reader muttering.) Hence the transmogrification of a delightful little comedy-with-music into the ghastly Stoppardization of *On the Razzle* (which is now being translated into German for production in Vienna!). The Hungarian-born, non-German-speaking, Nestroy-ignorant British playwright has gone on to adapt plays by Schnitzler. Perhaps I should confess, before I am found out, that, although I have translated three Schnitzler plays, I had not only heard of the dramatist before doing so, but also, to compound the felony, I had a reasonable knowledge of the German language. The Royal Exchange company in Manchester produced my translation of *Der Reigen* (*The Round Dance*, better known as *La Ronde* because of the French film version), and I wish someone would stage *Anatol* (a very funny play) in my translation before Stoppard gets his hands on it.

I had thought of including in this book more about politics than I have done, and indeed I made copious notes for that purpose. But the subject really does bore me. What is so awful is that politics thinks it is so important. It seeks to dominate our lives, whereas ideally it should occupy no more than 0·5 per cent of our waking hours. It is the mechanics of life, not the whole of life. What is it about politics that bores me? It is people ignorantly flinging the term 'fascist' about at random; people who talk like socialists but live like capitalists; the Labour Party's Gadarene gallop over the cliffs; the Conservatives' utter ineffectiveness; the bullshit that all parties utter on the subject of the arts and ethnic minorities; the virtual disappearance of common sense from public utterance. I find myself frequently having occasion to mutter two quotes, from Goethe and Schiller. The Goethe, which follows on from my boredom with the continual two-party mutual abuse, is *'Lieber will ich schlechter werden/Als mich ennuyieren.'* ('I'd rather be ill than be bored'). The Schiller, which comes to my lips even on occasions when politics is not the subject under discussion, is the line uttered by Talbot in *Die Jungfrau von Orleans: 'Mit der Dummheit kämpfen Götter selbst vergebens'* ('Against stupidity even the Gods battle in vain').

The world is divided into countries which are clubs, and are thus difficult to get into, and countries which are prisons, and thus difficult to get out of. I know which I prefer. To fellow liberals contemplating the various moral dilemmas thrown up by the modern world, I address the words of Tolstoy: 'The antagonism between life and conscience may be removed in two ways: by a change of life or by a change of conscience.' The inadequacy of the terms 'left' and 'right' in politics is revealed if one stops thinking of them as being positions at opposite ends of a straight line. The line is not straight, it is shaped into a circle, and where the left and right ends meet, there you find Communism and Fascism meeting. Both are systems based on oppression. Who is oppressor and who oppressed is important only to those directly involved. In moral terms, one can hardly indicate a preference. If you are being held in prison without trial, you can hardly be expected to care whether your captors are men of the right or of the left. A bully is a bully, whatever his political colour. I am not going to indicate a preference between South Africans persecuting blacks and Russians persecuting Jews. My lack of admiration is equally divided between both governments. In my book, nobody should be persecuting anybody. As for the less important question of politicization of the arts, when people rabbit on to me about the need for the working classes to have their own community arts to replace the 'upper class' fraudulence of the 'high' arts (believe it or not, you hear a lot of this kind of thing at the Arts Council), I like to quote the American radical labour leader, 'Big Bill' Haywood, who said, 'Nothing is too good for the proletariat.' The gist of my message to the world is that pragmatists are infinitely preferable to dogmatists.

When the Soviet Union invaded Czechoslovakia in 1968, the European writers' organization, COMES, to which I then belonged, issued in Rome a manifesto expressing its indignation at 'this atrocious and absurd murder of liberty'. I see from *The Times* of 9 September that 'among the first writers to sign the manifesto were Philip Toynbee, Angus Wilson, Charles Osborne, Ignazio Silone, Eduardo di Filippo, Bernard Wall and Giuseppe Ungaretti'. The Secretary-General of COMES said that 'he, Signor Ungaretti and a group of leading writers were ready to leave for Prague to meet President Svoboda, Mr Dubcek and Mr Cernik to show our admiration for what they have done for their people'. What naive, meddling Poloniuses we were. I would sign no such manifesto today, for I have lost the taste for meaningless, grandiose gestures. In other words, I think I have lost the pomposity of youth. What I have gained is a decent embarrassment at seeing myself listed with the famous, such as Silone, Di Filippo, and Angus Wilson.

I have also lost the concern I used to have for my own moral purity, and am never likely again to say that the end cannot justify the means. The end must justify the means, or we shall never have change for the better. Some months ago, Bernard Levin and I agreed to take part in two separate evenings at the Royal Festival Hall, for the charity, Arts Liaison. Mr Levin was to interview Elisabeth Schwarzkopf, and I was to interview Kenneth Williams. (Both of us had done this kind of thing before, for Arts Liaison. My earlier performances had been with, among others, Joan Sutherland, Nicolai Gedda, Hermann Prey and Barry Humphries.) Informed that Ken Livingstone's GLC required us to sign an undertaking never to perform in South Africa, Mr Levin and I reacted in different ways, though I imagine we share an abhorrence of the present South African regime. Mr Levin, being a man of principle, refused to sign, and his evening with Madame Schwarzkopf had to be transferred to the Barbican. I, however, was not prepared to be unjustly denied the use of the South Bank concert halls. It is not illegal to travel to South Africa from this country, and if I choose ever to do so, it will be no concern of Mr Livingstone. Not being a man of principle, I agreed to sign the undertaking, but to my mind my agreement was no more binding upon me than if, in order to be allowed to sing at the Berlin Staatsoper, I had promised Hitler I would never perform to Jews.

I have no plans to visit South Africa, and I probably never shall see that country. I would have reacted in the same way to Livingstone if he had required me to swear I would never again visit Soviet Russia. My attitude coincides with the position stated most eloquently by Bryan Magee in a letter to *The Times* condemning similar totalitarian behaviour on the part of the Camden Council:

> The question is not whether one is for or against the regime in question but whether one is for or against fundamental freedoms in our own society. Most of us regard most of the Communist countries as repressive police states, but we would not dream of suggesting that our performing artists should not visit them. The more unfree and unjust a society, the more important it is that it should be penetrated by art and ideas from outside.

I enjoy doing those occasional evenings in the South Bank, talking to famous musicians and entertainers. I suppose that kind of thing helps to satisfy the residual performing instinct which is still with me, nearly thirty years after I ceased to be an actor. I also keep it fed with poetry readings, and like to test my skills by performing alongside artists of the calibre of John Gielgud, Vincent Price, Irene Worth, Constance Cummings, Michael York, Elaine Stritch and Alan Jay Lerner. I have also had some success with my lecture-recital, *The Vertical Man*, in which I talk about W. H. Auden and read some of his poetry. When I tried this out for the first time at the Little Missenden Festival some years ago, I was surprised and delighted to receive a rave review from Basil Ashmore. 'Osborne saves the day' was his heading, and I feared that he was being satirical. But no: 'Charles Osborne's contribution was worthy of the Edinburgh Festival. Though his lecture-recital was only being given for the first time, it had professional polish. Mr Osborne read his friend Auden's poems with poised elegance. He also made Auden the man spring to life. Though I had to sit in an agonizingly uneasy chair for ninety minutes, I was spellbound by Mr Osborne's virtuosity.'

Yes, I know it is vulgar to quote praise of oneself, but there it is, I *am* a trifle vulgar. And, anyway, doesn't the Talmud say something like 'If I am not for myself, who will be for me?'

In 1967, Brigid Brophy, Michael Levey and I wrote a *jeu d'esprit* called *Fifty Works of English Literature We Could Do Without*. Nothing that the three of us wrote separately has ever received anything like the amount of publicity accorded to this little volume, or the venom with which it was received in some quarters. (Venom was fine: it increased sales.) Bernard Levin called us 'incomparably the three biggest twits in Britain'. When Bryan Magee asked me on TV if we were offended by this, I was able to say that we felt it to be a compliment, coming as it did from someone who was, without doubt, the smallest twit in Britain. All good clean fun, as was the book. After all, we were not advocating the ritual burning of *Moby Dick*, Gray's *Elegy* and the works of Trollope, but merely putting forward a contrary view to generally received opinion.

'The play has no development, either of incident or of character,' we wrote of Jonson's *The Alchemist*. 'So charmlessly pronounced is its lack of personality that it might have been conceived by a computer.' And, as for Wordsworth's daffodils: 'It's harder to guess what (can it have been just the need of a rhyme to "crowd"?) made him consider "lonely as a cloud" a simile telling enough for an opening line. Lonely clouds are rare in all parts of the British Isles. In the Lake District they must be as rare as "golden" daffodils.' We were extremely rude to Thomas Hardy ('Perhaps it was Wessex clay that clogged Hardy's pen'), and among other old favourites whose works we dismissed were Defoe, Scott, Elizabeth Barrett Browning, Melville, D. H. Lawrence and Virginia Woolf: 'Those who praise Mrs Woolf's work,' we concluded, 'should be honest with themselves. They are a potential audience for today's equivalent, *Mrs Dale's Diary*.'

Fifty Works was fun to write, and it was launched joyously with a party on the motor vessel, *Connaught*, cruising up the Thames from Westminster. The late and greatly lamented Kenneth Allsop, in the *Evening News*, greeted our labours in the right spirit. 'It's a healthy bit of hooliganism,' he wrote. 'The noble heads of the innocent, the genuinely august (take your pick which they are) will survive the brickbats of Brophy-Levey-Osborne unbowed. The stature of the bogus (your choice again) may be beneficially shrunk.'

At the time we were writing *Fifty Works* (and for many years before and after) the two family units of Brophy-Levey and Osborne-Thomson were close friends. The book is dedicated to Ken Thomson: the four of us used to take holidays abroad together. But an odd, Antonionian undertow was at work in the complex of relationships, and Ken and I found ourselves drifting away from Brigid and Michael. We now rarely meet them, and I still miss their gaiety and wit.

It was in 1969 that Marina Warner revealed herself to be a woman of taste and discernment when she described me in *Vogue* as 'a suave twentieth-century version of the universal man'; that a manic-depressive film producer John Sutro, tried to revive *The Yellow Book* with me as its editor; and that my book on the operas of Verdi was published. Two years later, my translation of a volume of Verdi's letters appeared both here and in the United States, and my American publisher received this letter from a literary press-cutting service: 'Dear Mr Verdi, Congratulations on the publication of your new book, *Letters of Giuseppe Verdi*. We know from talking to our clients what a thrill it is for an author to see his latest work come off the presses and move into the stores . . . We hope your book is a great success and that you will let our clipping service keep you informed about the good news.' I was asked to undertake a second volume of Verdi letters, but I declined, for by this time I was at work on my book on the operas of Mozart. In due course, Puccini followed.

I found time in 1971 to marry a Czechoslovakian girl in order to procure her a British passport. It all ended in tears when, having got to California, she began to write me aggressive letters. Lord Goodman very suavely extricated me from the mess I had landed myself in. In the seventies I also broadcast regularly for the British Forces Broadcasting Service, which was a much more sensible thing to do, and which brought me appreciative rather than threatening letters, mainly from members of the British forces serving in Germany. My books, by this time, were also bringing me fan mail at the pitiful rate of a trickle of two or three letters a week. I should confess that I categorize as 'fan mail' all letters from readers or listeners or viewers with whom I am not personally acquainted, whether they write to praise, to castigate, or simply to communicate, to share a thought, a comment or a memory.

The book which has brought me the greatest volume of correspondence so far is *W. H. Auden: the Life of a Poet*, which my friend Michael O'Mara, at that time Managing Director of the Rainbird Publishing Group, commissioned from me. Actually, the first suggestion that I should write a biography of Auden was made to me very shortly after the poet's death, in the autumn of 1973, and I refused without giving the matter much thought. There seemed so many reasons to say no: Auden had died so recently that I had not adjusted to the fact of his absence, and surely in due course someone of his own generation, someone who had known him better and longer than I, would undertake the task of writing his life. Stephen Spender, I expected. There was the much-talked-of Auden dislike of prying biographies, and the request, made by Auden to his literary executor Edward Mendelson in a letter of 9 May 1972, that a notice appear after his death 'in the American and British Press requesting any friends who have letters from me to burn them when they've done with them, and on no account to show them to anybody else'.

Auden died on 28 September 1973, and some weeks later the notice that Auden had requested was published in various magazines and newspapers in Great Britain and the United States. Some of the poet's friends felt called upon to comment. Stephen, Wystan's oldest and most faithful friend, said he thought Auden's request superfluous for 'he was in no way a letter writer – the average letter was two lines'. Well, that may be. I certainly have a large number of two-paragraph letters of no great interest from Auden, of which this is a representative example:

> Dear Charles,
> I forgot to ask you when I saw you if, as in previous years, there will be a reception on the Monday at the Martini place in Canada House for the participants.
> I hope so, as both Chester and I want to have the opportunity of meeting Theodorakis.
>
> Yours ever,
> Wystan

'The Martini place' is the terrace room in which Messrs Martini and Rossi often give receptions, and Canada House is New Zealand House. (When you have seen one Commonwealth country, you have seen them all.) But Auden also wrote longer letters, of two or three pages. Those to Stephen Spender, especially several written during the war, from America, are of enormous interest and fascination, and it would have been as great a disservice to literature for Stephen to have burned them as it would have been for Max Brod to have destroyed all of Kafka's manuscripts as the author requested. Another friend of Auden's, Geoffrey Grigson, was quoted in the press as saying that he had a large collection of Auden letters, 'but if he says they should be burnt, I shall burn them'. He did not add that he had already sold a number of them!

Although I did not expect that I would ever write a life of Auden, I did not at any time take very seriously the poet's supposed dislike of biography.

In fact, I simply did not believe it. Auden loved gossiping to the press, and he enjoyed being written about. 'Look what they've said about me in the *Sunday Times*,' or wherever, he would exclaim as he thrust the article at one to read. Years after his death, when I began to read through almost everything he had published, I was surprised at the amount of autobiographical material Auden had embedded in articles and book reviews, as well as in his poetry and in his commonplace book, *A Certain World*. He liked to read biographies of artists and public figures, though he made it perfectly clear that psychological analysis of character was not what he wanted to find, but facts and gossip. Reviewing *The Diaries of Tchaikovsky* in the *New York Times* in 1954, he regretted that the composer had not entrusted to his diaries any details of his homosexual activities. But Auden ended his review by pointing out that the hero of the diaries

> works, travels, goes for walks, worries. He doses himself with castor oil, he gets drunk, he loses his temper at cards. One could write it all one's self. But it doesn't matter. After all, he wrote the most beautiful ballet music in the world and detested Brahms. He is our friend. And who does not enjoy reading a friend's diary?

Auden approved of, and reviewed favourably in the *New York Review of Books*, my translations of *Letters of Giuseppe Verdi*. Of the two-volume *Letters of Thomas Mann* (his father-in-law for a time), he wrote: 'Anyone who is interested not only in Thomas Mann himself but also in the problems which confront every writer will hunt through these letters eagerly.' Of course. And one day, no doubt, anyone who is interested not only in W. H. Auden himself but in the problems which confront every writer will hunt eagerly through a volume of Auden's letters. I think the poet's posthumous message to his friends was really that any embarrassing indiscretions in his letters should be suppressed, at any rate while other people referred to might still be alive. After that, he will take his chances with the rest of the great writers. And rightly so.

Some months after Auden's death, I was approached by the *Harvard Advocate* and asked to write something about the poet for a special memorial issue. I contributed a not entirely pious account of his funeral, which I hope would have made Wystan chuckle, and which brought me renewed requests from publishers for a book about him. I said yes to Mike O'Mara, after consulting Charles Monteith at Faber & Faber, and Edward Mendelson to satisfy myself that they did not feel their projects in any way threatened. Professor Mendelson did not, as Auden's literary executor, in any sense authorize the book which I then proceeded to write, but he was enormously helpful to me, read my finished typescript, to which he reacted with great enthusiasm, corrected a few errors he found, and made very useful editorial comments. (After the book was published, his behaviour left much to be desired, but that is another story, and those interested to pursue it should consult the correspondence columns of the *Times Literary Supplement* throughout 1980, where they will find Professor Mendelson and myself snidely slanging away at each other. Expect bitchy behaviour from envious academics, and you will not be disappointed.)

As soon as I had agreed to write a biography of Auden, I set myself certain hurdles to surmount. My main concern, without avoiding the less sunny aspects of his personality, was to write a book which Wystan would not have found objectionable. Also, I wanted my book to be informative, to reveal where Auden was, and when, and why, and I was determined that it should be readable. (A number of biographers, to judge by results, must set out with the opposite aim.) The review which pleased me most was *Time*'s comment that 'Auden would probably have grudgingly liked this book'.

The first of the hurdles I set myself was, as far as possible, to write with the aid only of my own notes and recollections, and of published sources, without attempting to interview the hundreds of people who had known Auden at various periods of his life, from his schooldays to his last years in New York and Vienna. To talk to all of them would have necessitated my taking several months' leave from my full-time job at the Arts Council, and this I was not prepared to do. I proceeded to collect material on Auden from libraries in England, America, Austria and elsewhere: material in the form of interviews, articles, reviews, essays and news items, in newspapers, books, leading literary journals and little-known student magazines. Clearly, there were two or three of Auden's old friends whom I needed to speak to, and of these by far the most important, from my point of view, was Stephen Spender. Not only had Stephen not destroyed his letters from Auden, he was also willing to let me see them and quote from them without restriction. Of course I needed the permission of the Auden Estate as well, and this was readily given.

A major problem was the assessment of material and information sent to me in response to my published request. A number of people who had gone to school with Auden or his elder brothers, or who knew him at Oxford in the twenties, or were colleagues of his in the thirties, or were taught by him in America in the forties, wrote to share their memories with me, and most of these were extremely helpful after one had made due allowance for lapses of memory, discrepancies between different accounts of the same incident, and so on. But some of the material I was offered was too scurrilous to be used, and some was presented (and in some cases, I am certain, concocted) out of sheer malice, usually towards Chester Kallman, Auden's close friend and lover, who outlived him by no more than sixteen months. Some curious jealousies came to light: I made use of none of these.

During the course of writing the book, I made a few serendipitous discoveries, and I also found that some people's published memoirs ought to be re-catalogued under fiction. Another hazard, which came to light after publication, is that sometimes people regret their indiscreet admissions when they eventually see them in print. Rather more serious are the things one can get wrong, or slightly out of focus, when one relies on what people who ought to know tell one, instead of checking for oneself. An example: the house in Middagh Street, Brooklyn Heights, where in 1940–41 Auden presided over a Bohemian household whose members included Carson McCullers, Benjamin Britten, Peter Pears and Gypsy Rose Lee. Relying on information provided by New York friends, I wrote that, in 1945, 'all the houses in Middagh Street were destroyed in the construction of a new automobile approach to Brooklyn Bridge. No trace of the street or the former atmosphere of the neighbourhood remains.' When I was in New York for the publication of my book, I took the opportunity to wander about in Brooklyn, something I had never done on any previous visit to the city. There, in Brooklyn Heights, was Middagh Street, looking much as it must have looked forty years ago. All that had been destroyed was the short block which had contained the Auden house, in order to facilitate the construction, not of the Brooklyn Bridge approach, which is a good half-mile away, but of a freeway. After publication, I received two good-humoured complaints from present inhabitants of Middagh Street, one of whom offered to show me some of 'that old-time Brooklyn Bohemian atmosphere' next time I was in New York.

Knowing personally the subject of one's biography has its advantages, of course, but it also has its pitfalls. Auden was a truthful creature, but his memory was highly selective, and it tended at times to select what Auden would have liked to be true instead of what was, in fact, true. One day, in the garden of his house at Kirchstetten, he gave me to understand that he had composed what he claimed to be the longest palindrome in English: 'T. Eliot, top bard, notes putrid tang emanating, is sad. I'd assign it a name: gnat dirt upset on drab pot toilet.' I duly mentioned this achievement of his in the penultimate chapter of my book. It appears, however, that Auden had simply, over the years, assimilated that palindrome unto himself, for in Brendon Gill's delightful volume of reminiscence, *Here at the New Yorker*, which I read some months after my Auden biography appeared, I was dismayed to find it attributed to the Scottish poet, Alistair Reid. Brendon Gill subsequently assured me that it was quite certainly by Alistair Reid. 'He is a close friend of mine,' he said, 'and I was practically beside him when he wrote it.'

A major difficulty, when you contemplate writing about a living or recently dead person, is how to deal with your subject's close personal and sexual relationships. If, by being truthful, you are going to distress your subject's family, it is surely better to wait for time to solve the problem, even if time solves it by assigning, years later, another biographer to the task. What is pointless, surely, is to distort the picture by omission of important detail. A generation ago it would not have been possible to speak frankly of Auden's homosexuality without giving offence to many people. That is no longer a problem, and I found I was able to present an important aspect of Auden without embarrassing anyone who had not already embarrassed himself in print. It would, for instance, have been absurd to write guardedly of Christopher Isherwood, two years after publication of *Christopher and His Kind*. But that does not mean that it is necessary to identify in print every one of Auden's sex partners. It is the job of the biographer to assess and select from the mass of material which is presented to him. The writer who throws at his reader every piece of information in his possession, down to the colour of the shirt which Mr X wore when he called on Miss Y, is simply incompetent. I know the man who, when he was a schoolboy, was the dedicatee of 'Lay your sleeping head, my love ...', but to have revealed his name (not one which the general public would recognize) would have embarrassed him, his wife and his family, without adding anything of significance to my biography.

The kind of biographer I do not enjoy reading is the humourless know-all who insults his readers' intelligence with what he calls 'interpretation'. When I saw a review of my book which began, 'For long one has felt that the life-history of Auden, if one could interpret it right, would tell one more than almost any other about mid-century British experience', I knew that the reviewer was someone whose tastes and temperament were diametrically opposed to my own. Though the review in question was a perfectly fair one, I found myself disagreeing with virtually every opinion expressed by the reviewer, who professed to know Auden's sub-conscious motives for almost every move he made, and who, with the confident arrogance of the amateur psychologist, suggested that Auden fell in love with Chester Kallman shortly after he, Auden, arrived in America because he had to at that moment, and because he had 'just exiled himself from England, in the knowledge that a war with Nazi Germany was certainly imminent, and he was aware that many people (including friends) would condemn him'. In fact, Auden exiled himself from England in the belief that war had been averted, and in any case these are not the reasons why, in the real world as distinct from the world of academic lit.crit., people fall in love.

There was much to-ing and fro-ing in the columns of the *Times Literary Supplement* and elsewhere over whether Auden had or had not gone to bed with this or that male contemporary at Oxford. The names of Betjeman and Spender, among others, were prominently featured. I tried to end it with a brief note – 'Dear Sir, Let sleeping poets lie' – but, if I remember correctly, that was thought too flippant for publication in so dignified a magazine.

A story came to me, indirectly from Robert Lowell, too late for inclusion in my book. At one time in New York Auden and Lowell were patients of the same doctor. Lowell encountered Auden leaving the doctor's surgery after a check-up, and Auden, who must then have been about sixty years of age, said to Lowell: 'Good news! I've just been given a clean bill of health. The doctor tells me that with my constitution I'll live till I'm eighty-five.' The doctor subsequently told Lowell that what he had said to Auden was that he already had the constitution of a man of eighty-five.

My Auden biography was even accorded the accolade of being satirized in *Private Eye*, whose response to the book's being serialized in the *Observer* was to publish an extract from '*Bysshe* by Charles Osbore'. This began:

> Keats and Shelley took an instant liking to each other, and agreed to become intimate the following spring. Sex was not important to them, but it was a logical extension of their shared interest in oriental cooking, nightingales, and messing about in boats.

It continued in the same vein. Could have been funnier, but the idea was not bad.

My American publishers, Messrs Harcourt Brace Jovanovich, invited me to lunch in a smart Manhattan restaurant in the week of the book's American publication. I arrived at the restaurant at the appointed time, but the Harcourt Brace people were more than half an hour late. It transpired that their office building, a skyscraper on Third Avenue, had been under siege in a rather unusual manner. An eccentric Australian author, dissatisfied at the way in which his book was being promoted by Harcourt Brace, had been buzzing the office building from a small plane, which he threatened to crash into the building if his demands were not met. The building had to be evacuated and, as it was in the vicinity of the United Nations Headquarters, the UN was also evacuated just as a session of the General Assembly was about to begin. Police helicopters finally managed to force this nutcase to land at La Guardia, where he was promptly arrested.

This bizarre incident made headlines in the New York press, of course, but it also got into the TV news in Great Britain, where viewers learned only that a crazy Australian author had flown a light aircraft around the Harcourt Brace building, threatening to crash into it. My London publishers and several of my London friends knew that I was supposed to be lunching with Harcourt Brace that day, and I was disconcerted on my return to London to discover that they had automatically assumed me to be the lunatic pilot.

There *are* some crazy authors about. There are even more crazy publishers. After my Auden volume appeared, several publishers attempted to commission books from me on the most unlikely subjects, and one actually offered me a large sum of money for my next book, 'whatever it is'. Mike O'Mara, more sensibly, asked me to follow up Auden with a life of T. S. Eliot. However, although I admired Eliot as a poet, I hardly warmed to him as a man, had met him only on two or three formal occasions, and for a variety of reasons did not want to become involved in the Eliot industry. Eventually Peter Ackroyd was chosen, and I went on to write *The Life and Crimes of Agatha Christie* for the Rainbird Group.

I was attracted by a suggestion, made to me by Peter Grose of Secker & Warburg, that I write a book about the proposed production of Wagner's *Ring* at Bayreuth by Peter Hall, which was to be conducted by Georg Solti. 'We had quite a success with John Higgins's book *The Making of an Opera*' (about Peter Hall's Glyndebourne *Don Giovanni*), Peter Grose wrote, 'and . . . we would be very interested in commissioning you to produce a similar book on the Hall production at Bayreuth.'

I indicated that I was willing to discuss the proposal, but when my name was mentioned to Lady Solti she issued a veto, presumably on the grounds that I had occasionally written critically of her husband's opera performances. (He is a superb Strauss and Wagner conductor, not so impressive in Mozart.) Someone else wrote the book, and when I heard of the reception accorded the Hall–Solti *Ring* at Bayreuth I could not help succumbing to a certain *Schadenfreude*, despite my affection and admiration for Peter Hall, and my occasionally modified admiration of Solti.

By this time, I had written a book on the operas of Puccini, which won the *Yorkshire Post* Music Award for 1981. (The runner-up was Donald Mitchell's *Britten and Auden in the Thirties*, a fascinating volume to which I would have given the prize; and I am not, as the reader will by now have noticed, a person to indulge in false or even genuine modesty.)

About a year ago, a volume of my poems was published, under the title *Letter to W. H. Auden and other poems*. Friends warned me to expect vicious reviews, for my Arts Council work had necessarily led to my being unpopular with a number of whingeing poets who were also reviewers. The knives, they said, would be out. In the event, the disaffected poets appear to have found it impossible to justify sufficiently nasty reviews, and chose instead a different tactic. The book received, to my knowledge, only two reviews in Great Britain. (I was not used to that, but on reflection I realize that a great many published books never receive even the smallest mention in the press.) One reviewer praised my 'beautifully moving lyrics', while the other thought I wrote 'self-regarding, incompetent drivel'. A number of friends, among them a handful of our finest poets, wrote appreciatively to me about the volume, and I treasure their letters, especially those from Ted Hughes and Philip Larkin. One does not, after all, write for reviewers. 'The whole book is very true to you', one of my correspondents summed up, 'seasoned, unflappable, complicated and amused.'

My books have all been written early in the mornings. By eight I am usually out of the bath and at my desk, and by ten thirty or so I have finished writing for the day. For twenty years, from 1966 until a few short months ago, I spent the remainder of each working day at the Arts Council of Great Britain. For the future, my pattern of work will be more varied, though I shall continue to write. My next four books have already been commissioned. I shall, however, now have time to take up again some of my free-lance activities in musical and literary journalism, for which I have not been able to find time in recent years, mainly because of the Arts Council. Let me now try to describe the years spent as an arts administrator employed by that organization.

3

THE ARTS COUNCIL

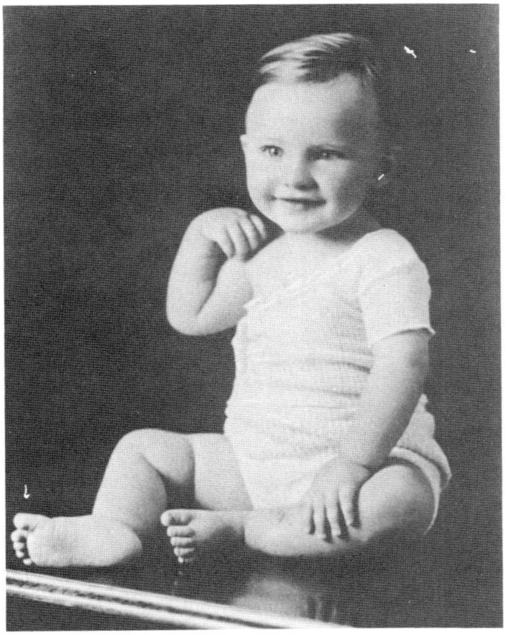

1. The infant Charles (1928)

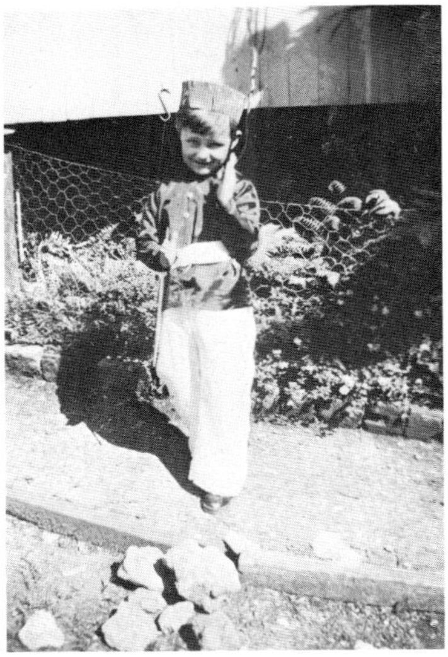

2. Rehearsing for an early stage appearance (c. 1933)

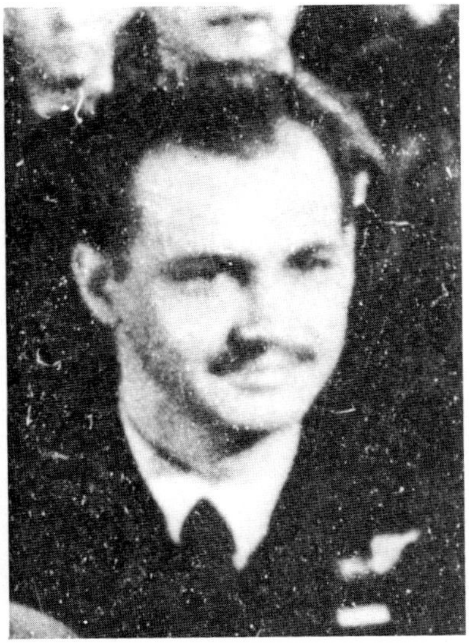

3. As Pilot-Officer Foxlee in *The Dam Busters* (1954) (photo: Associated British Picture Corporation Ltd)

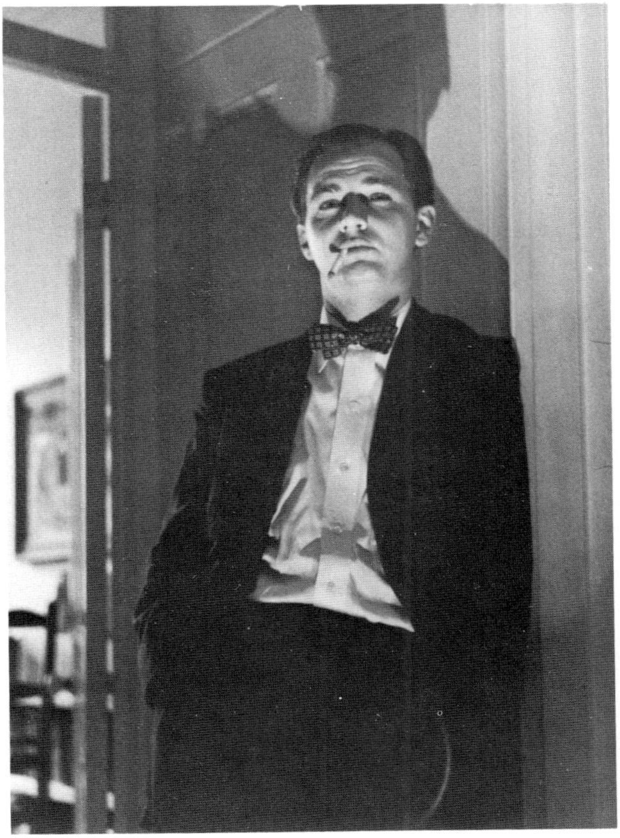

4. The moody actor, photographed by John Schlesinger (1954)

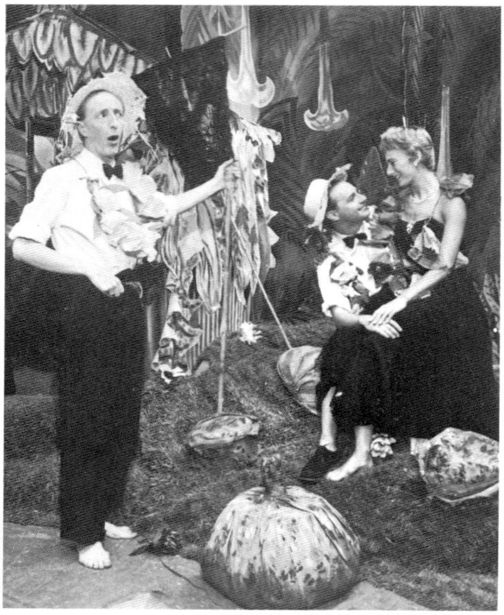

5. In André Roussin's *The Little Hut*, at Tunbridge Wells, with Peter Thorpe and Sheelagh Tiffany (1955)

6. The sensitive pianist, photographed by John Schlesinger (1954)

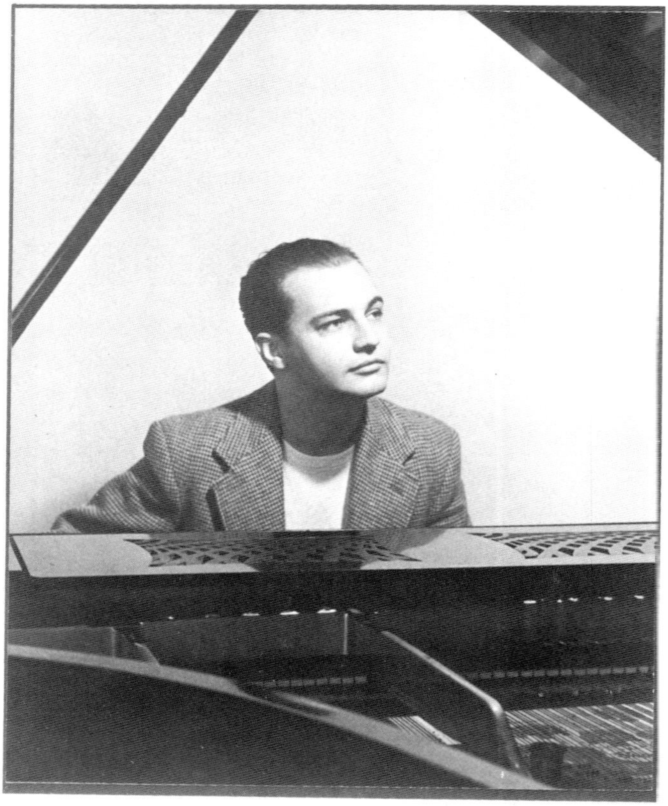

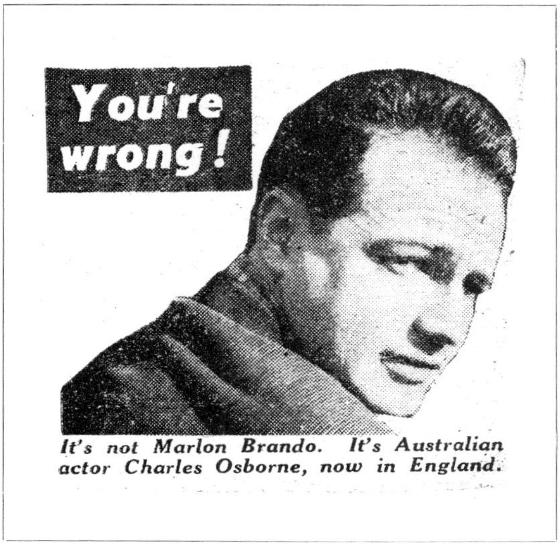

7. Unnecessary caption in a Melbourne newspaper (1956)

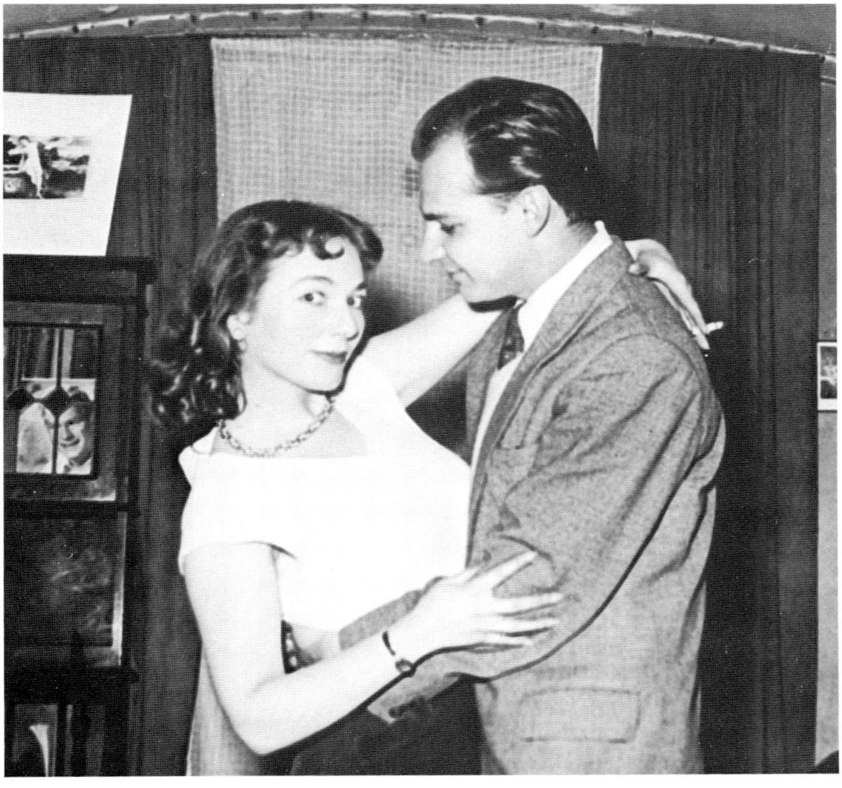

8. Sexy repertory juveniles: with Barbara Shaw in *Happier Still* by Mark Haywood (1955)

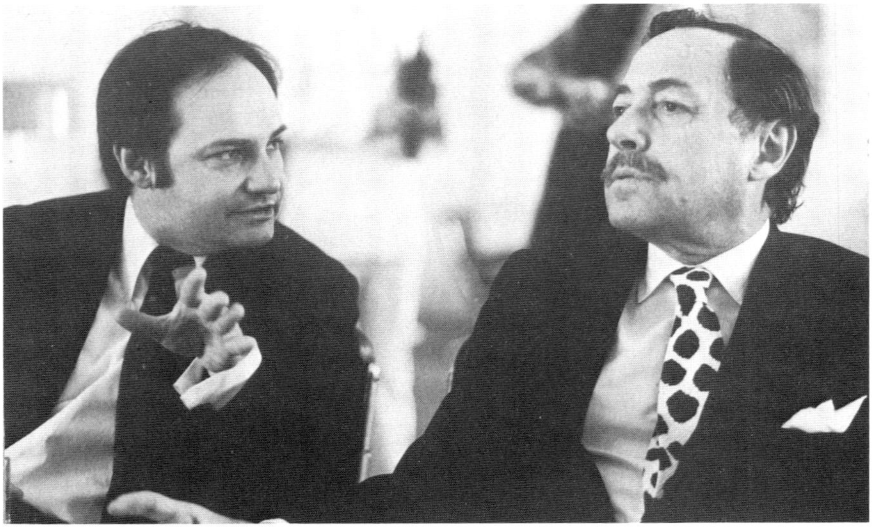

9. With Tennessee Williams (1970)

10. Poets in Jerusalem: Ted Hughes, Charles Osborne, Dannie Abse (1971)

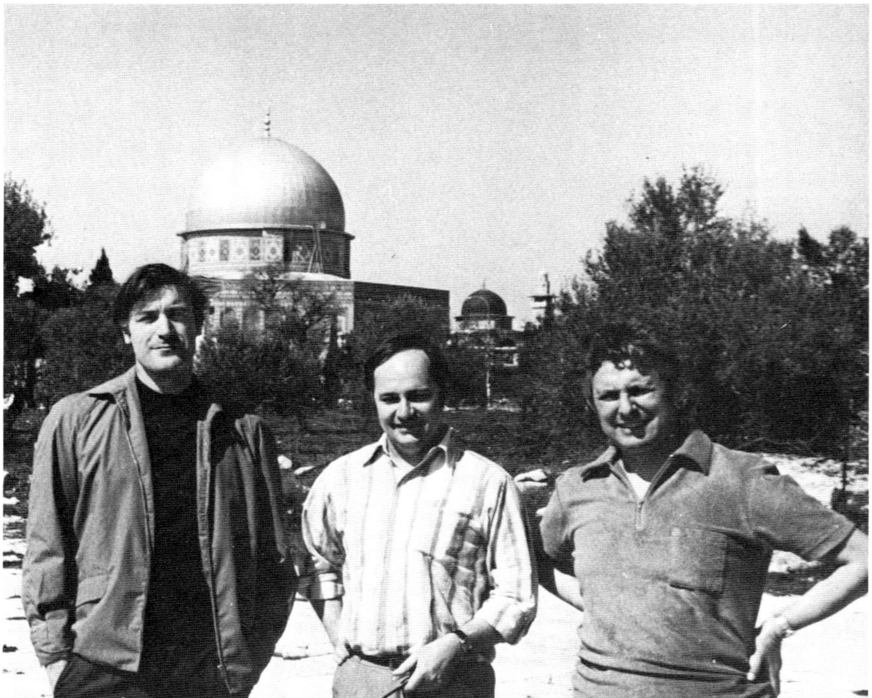

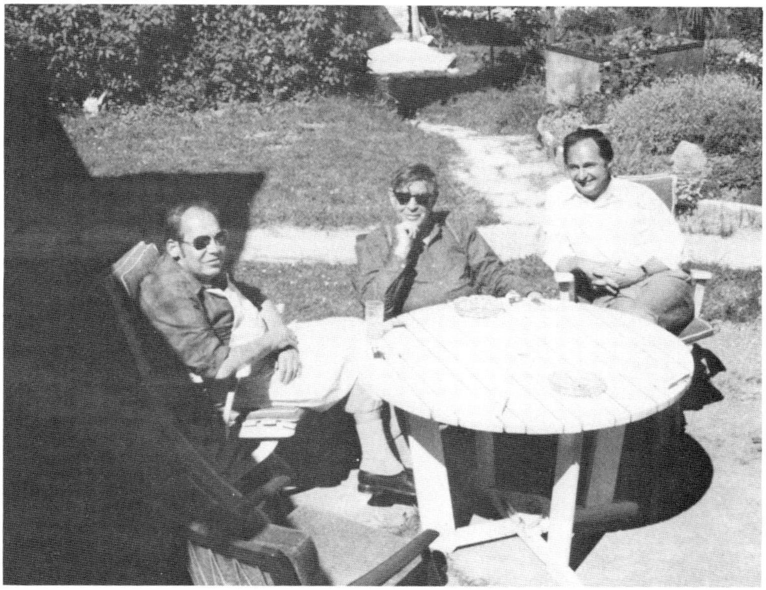

11. With Chester Kallman and W. H. Auden in their garden at Kirchstetten, Austria (1973)

12. *Poetry International* televised: Sir John Betjeman about to present gladdies to Dame Edna Everage. Others present include (l. to r.) Jill Balcon, Charles Osborne, Allen Ginsberg, Patrick Garland (1973) (photo: London Weekend TV)

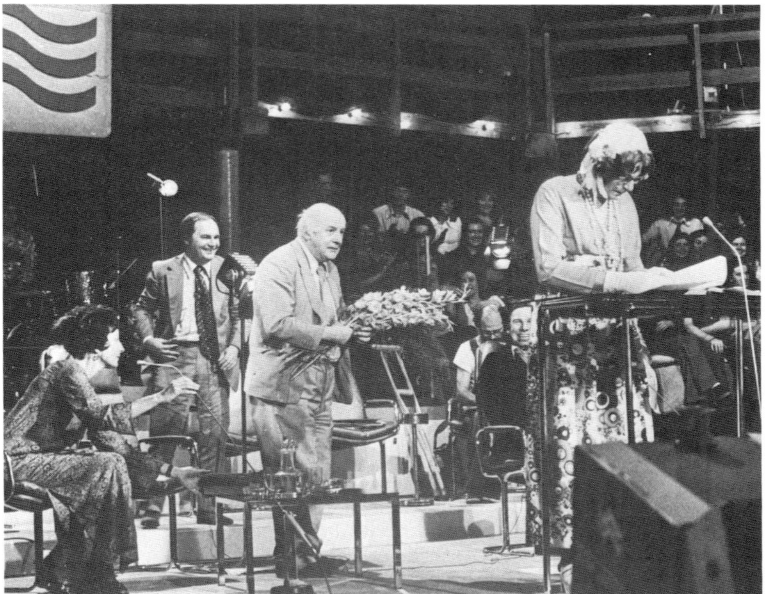

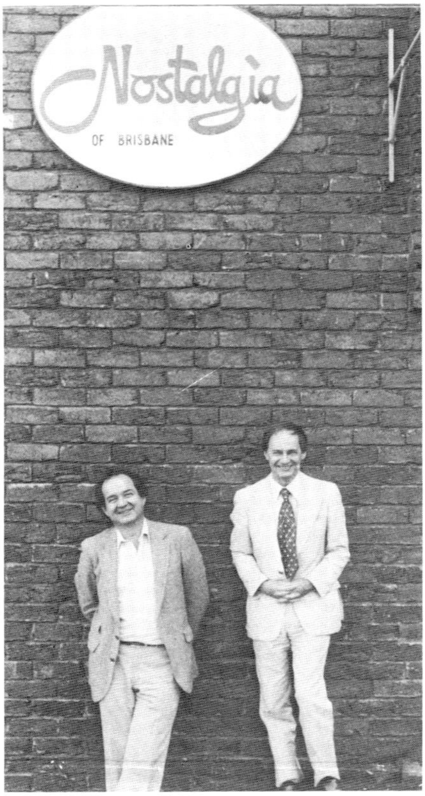

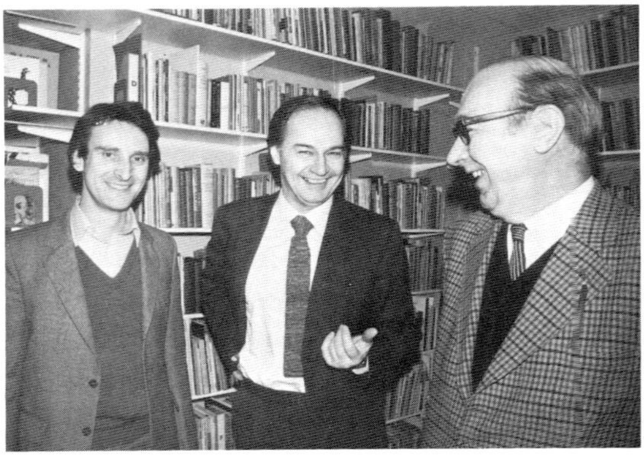

14. With Jonathan Barker and Philip Larkin, in the Arts Council Poetry Library (1981)

13. Ken Thomson and Charles Osborne, photographed in Brisbane by Barry Humphries (1979)

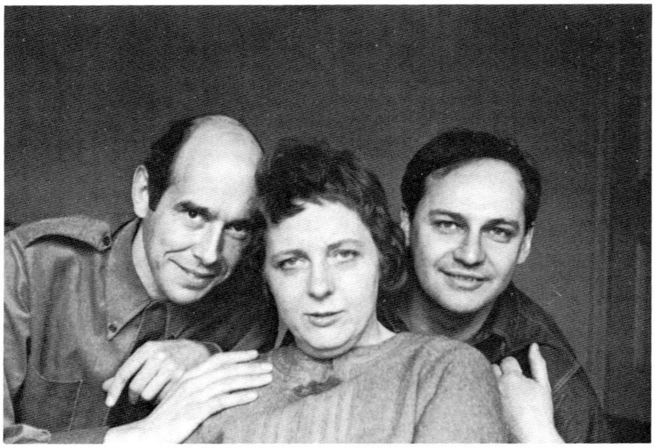

15. Michael Levey, Brigid Brophy and Charles Osborne (1967)

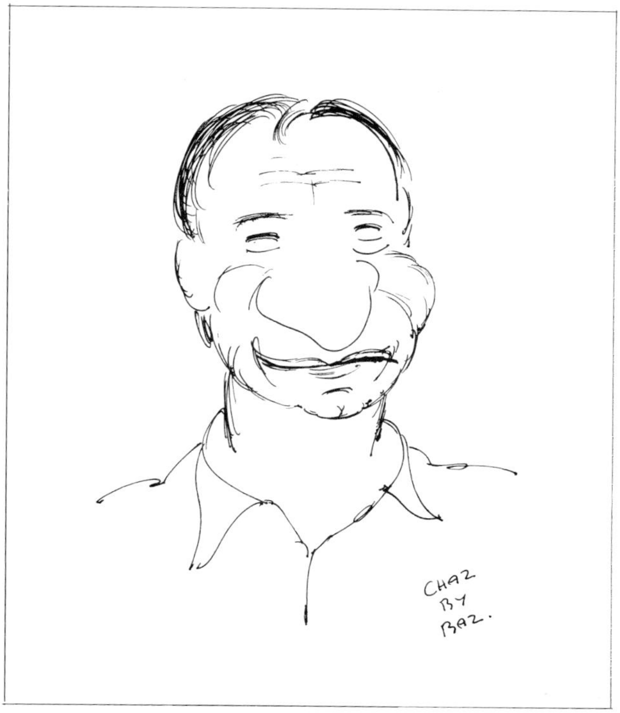

16. Charles Osborne by Barry Humphries
(1984)

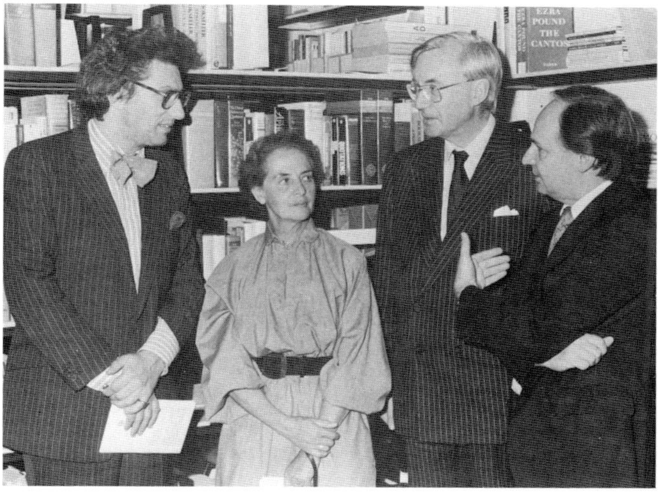

17. With Lord Gowrie, Marghanita Laski and
Sir William Rees-Mogg, at the Arts Council
(1984)

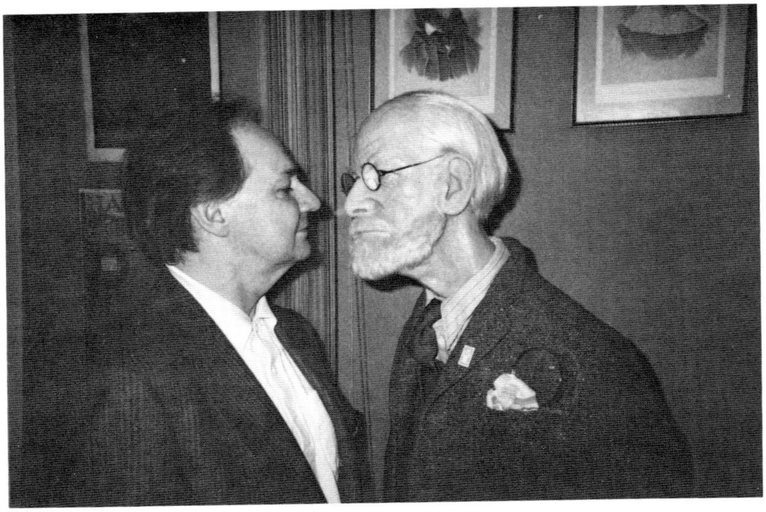

18. With Sigmund Freud at the Turret Bookshop, London, on the occasion of a poetry reading by Charles Osborne (1985)

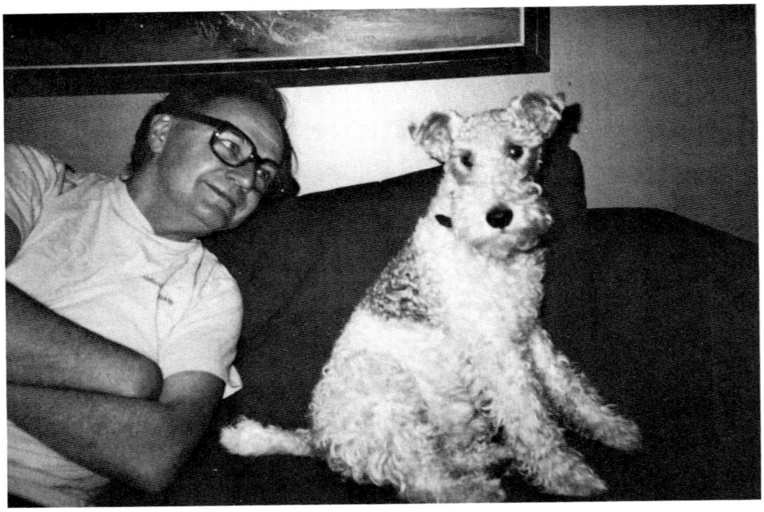

19. Charles and Asta at home (1986)

□ □ □

THE ARTS COUNCIL IS an organization whose function is to subsidize the arts in Great Britain. For the last fifteen years of my time with the Council I was a director of the organization, and must therefore accept a reasonable share of responsibility for its decisions, even though it has, over the years, made several of which I disapprove. When I joined it at the beginning of April 1966, the Arts Council had been in existence for twenty years, but it was still a relatively small, youthful body. Its grant from the government in 1965–66 was £3,910,000. In 1985–86 the grant was £101,900,000, and the Council is a much larger and more complex organization than in those comparatively early days.

In 1966 the Council was a body of which, in general, I approved. It seemed to me that it made, for the most part, sensible decisions. There came a time, however, some four or five years ago, when I began to realize that I was no longer certain of my feelings about the Council. It had squandered large sums of money on 'Community Arts', that perversion of the aesthetic urge invented by bored arts administrators yearning to become social workers; it had dished out funds annually to, God help us, the Notting Hill Carnival at a time when artistic institutions were finding their already inadequate grants being further eroded by inflation; and it had given thousands of grants to individuals for such purposes as the following (I choose my ludicrous examples from those awarded in one particular month: they could be multiplied almost indefinitely): £500 to Jill Bruce 'towards the cost of a study visit to Australia to look at the journeyings of Aboriginal women and visit sites of special significance'; £78 to Annabelle Lanyon 'to enable her to undertake thirteen voice lessons to develop and strengthen her voice'; £150 to Victoria Steer 'to enable her to undertake a series of bass guitar lessons with Steve Shone'; £100 to Iris Walton 'to enable her to undertake classes in acrobatic technique with Eugene Balla'; and £334 to Peter Yates 'to enable him to undertake a week's advanced tuition in hurdy-gurdy playing with Valentin Clastrier, in Ennordes, France'.

This same Arts Council refused a grant to the D'Oyly Carte Opera Company on the grounds that the company's standards were too low and its repertoire not sufficiently varied. The company, unable to cope with the present costs of touring, went out of existence, though it continued to the end to attract capacity audiences of those tax-payers so much of whose money was being spent on enterprises of, at best, dubious artistic worth. As it happens, I used to derive little pleasure from D'Oyly Carte performances of Gilbert and Sullivan (though even less from street and community theatre). Chamber music played by groups of the standard of the Amadeus Quartet are more in my line, but they are not in need of public subsidy.

Did I, I wondered, want to continue working for this Arts Council, which appeared to have lost its way? At that point the Council, somewhat surprisingly, began to take steps to attempt to put its house in order, and I decided to stay on and see what would happen. Now, having finally left, I can look back on my years with the Arts Council and attempt to give some account of the Council's progress during those years: a progress from, as I see it, small funds fairly sensibly disbursed, through a period during which the funds increased while, disconcertingly, the sense decreased, to the present time, where funding has levelled out and is, in real terms, decreasing, thus forcing the Council to take, albeit reluctantly, some common-sense decisions. If it had not done so, there was a real danger that it would, like the dinosaur, have ceased to exist. (The present Labour Party spokesman for the arts has already announced that the next Labour Government will abolish the Arts Council, though this will no doubt prove as reliable as any other promise made by a politician.)

I take it for granted that there should be, in any civilized country, some form and degree of public funding for the arts. Without it we would be no better than, to use the colourful phrase from David Mamet's *American Buffalo*, 'savage shitheads in the wilderness'. Many of the Arts Council's problems in the 1970s derived from the fact that, although it was a public body with certain specific aims and objects, more often than not there were precious few members of the Council at all well placed to forward those aims and objects. In other words, there were times when the Council could not count among its members very many who knew anything about the arts. This, however, was not the case a decade earlier, in the sixties.

When I started working for the Arts Council of Great Britain, I had very little knowledge of the organization I was joining. I knew, of course, what its main purpose was, but I had no idea of how, on a day-to-day basis, it went about achieving its objects. More than once, before agreeing to become his assistant, I asked Eric Walter White exactly what my job would entail. In reply, Eric was characteristically flowery, and less characteristically vague. 'We subsidize the arts,' he would say to me. 'Your job will be to help me advise the Council on a feasible literature policy, and then help to implement that policy.'

What I wanted to know, however, was something much more basic. 'Look,' I said to Eric. 'It's nine am. I arrive in the office. I sit at my desk. Then – what do I do?' But he was not accustomed to being questioned on so mundane a level. 'You help to advise on literature policy,' he repeated.

I began to wonder exactly what I could be letting myself in for. With foresight, would I have said yes? If I had known that, within months, every talentless lout who fancied himself a poet and who considered he had a God-given right to public subsidy would be howling for my blood, would I have accepted the Council's offer of employment? I suppose it would not have made much difference to me. I have never been one to seek out trouble, but if it comes my way in the natural course of events I deal with it as best I can.

A few years later, the Arts Council became somewhat more highly organized, and as it began to attract, from year to year, a larger share of government funds it eventually found itself having to behave more like a Civil Service Department. At this later stage, it would have felt it necessary to advertise the job of Assistant Literature Director. In 1965, however, the Council rarely advertised to recruit staff. It was all managed on what is nowadays sneeringly referred to as the Old Boy network.

I was not much of an 'old boy'. I was an arts journalist who had worked in Great Britain for twelve years but who had somehow managed, without being strident about it, to retain his identity as an Australian. (Australians do not *have* to sound like Sir Les Patterson, Germaine Greer or Clive James.) I had worked for the previous eight years for a literary magazine, and had revealed a reasonable flair as editor and critic. I had not shown any special gift for administration: indeed, at the time I hardly knew what that was.

Eric Walter White, Assistant Secretary of the Arts Council and number three in the hierarchy, had been handed an additional responsibility, that of Literature Director, to which he thought he would be able to devote not much more than two-fifths of his time, or two days a week. He would need a full-time assistant, and it must have seemed to him a good idea to choose someone in his thirties who, though still young, might five years later be thought mature enough to take over as Literature Director from Eric when he retired at the age of sixty-five.

I don't know why Eric chose me. We did not know each other very well. I had read his excellent volumes on Stravinsky, on Britten, and on English opera, and we had first met a year or two earlier when he had invited me to join the committee which was organizing a Commonwealth Poetry Festival. I considered carefully his offer to me to join the staff of the Arts Council. Financially, it was not especially attractive: a full-time job with a salary of £1500 per annum, as compared to the £1000 I was earning at *The London Magazine* for what was effectively a half-time job which gave me my afternoons off for my own writing.

I realized, however, that I could not go on working for the magazine for much longer. I was aware that our losses were borne personally by Alan and Jennifer Ross, so I felt inhibited from asking for salary increases to keep up with the cost of living. Soon, I knew, I would have to go out into the real world. Was the Arts Council the real world? I had my doubts. But at least it was a move. I could describe it to Alan and Jennifer as an attractive offer, and they would not want to stand in the way of my improving my situation. If it did not work out, then I could always move on from the Arts Council in a year or two.

In the sixties the Arts Council occupied an elegant eighteenth-century town house at 4 St James's Square, a former residence of the Astor family. The house was not really a suitable home for the Council: its senior officers occupied rooms which were luxuriously appointed and far too large, while the junior staff were squeezed into a number of cubicles in what had once been Lady Astor's squash court. There was a splendid reception room on the first floor which was used occasionally, not only for receptions but also for recitals, and there was sufficient space on the ground floor for the Council to mount small-scale art exhibitions to complement the larger and more prestigious shows which were put on at the Tate or the Royal Academy or, in due course, the Hayward Gallery.

Mr Arnold Goodman had become Chairman of the Arts Council in May 1965, and by the following April, when I joined the Council, he had been ennobled. I took to Lord Goodman instantly and, although I was a comparatively junior member of staff, he seemed to have a lot of time for me. I think I amused him, in those days. I probably still do, for when we had a most enjoyable lunch together a few months ago at the Oxford and Cambridge Club, we found ourselves laughing a great deal as we contemplated our early years at the Arts Council when it was still fun to work there. Arnold Goodman was, and is, very good company. One of the most life-enhancing of men, he has a well-stocked mind and he has always been generous in sharing its contents with his fellow-workers, be they artistic directors or temporary typists. He acknowledges barriers of intelligence, but not of class.

In 1966–67, the government grant to the Council was increased from £3,910,000 to £5,700,000. This was a generous increase, and it was widely believed at the time to have been achieved not only by virtue of the influence wielded by the then Labour Minister for the Arts, Jennie Lee, but also because of her close and friendly relationship with Lord Goodman.

Of that £5,700,000 it allocated £63,000 to its Literature Department, which spent only £50,000 of the allocation.

As the disingenuous and the unscrupulous have in recent years made great play with the fact that I have occasionally underspent my literature budget, perhaps I should explain how it comes about that *all* Arts Council departments can find themselves, at the end of the year, with part of their allocation unspent. Each allocation is broken down into a number of different areas of spending: in Drama Department, for example, so much for grants to annual clients like the National Theatre, the Royal Exchange Theatre in Manchester, the Bristol Old Vic, and so on; so much for New Writing in the Theatre; so much for bursaries to playwrights, actors and technicians. In Literature Department, if the Council allocates, say, £100,000 of my total grant to writers' bursaries, then I can spend that £100,000 only on bursaries. If, as a result of the applications received, our literature advisers want to give bursaries totalling only £85,000, then that part of the allocation will be underspent by £15,000. Similarly, if £200,000 is allocated to literary magazines, and at the end of the year it is seen that the magazines cost us only £190,000 to subsidize, that leaves another £10,000 unspent. The grants to organizations, whether the Royal Opera House or the Poetry Society, are made by way of grant and guarantee. This means that if, say, I have £100,000 allocated to the Poetry Society, it may be offered as a grant of £90,000 and a guarantee of £10,000. If the Poetry Society's accounts at the year show a loss of £101,000, they will get the entire £100,000 allocated to them. If they show a loss of, say, £97,000, they will get the grant of £90,000 but only £7000 of the £10,000 guarantee. If they show a loss of only £83,000, they will still get the grant of £90,000 (in fact, by the end of the year they will already have had it), but of course they will not get any of the £10,000 guarantee.

At the end of each financial year, therefore, there are always sums of money which fall back into the Council's general reserves. This money is used by the Council to help finance the arts in the following year. It is not given back to the government to buy nuclear missiles with. However, though I have now, for the umpteenth time, made this clear, I expect I shall continue to find the usual two or three disaffected ex-panellists or beneficiaries of the Arts Council failing to grasp the point. (I never expected to be praised for having occasionally overspent, nor was I ever disappointed in my non-expectation.)

The Literature Department in 1966 consisted of Eric White and myself. We shared an office and a secretary, and in those early days of literature funding much of our time was taken up in trying to find ways of spending the money. Part of his time was spent by Eric in angrily chasing away the pigeons which innocuously gathered on our window-sill. Eric was the most amiable person, impeccably polite and most equable of temperament, but he used to undergo an immediate Jekyll-Hyde change of temperament whenever the pigeons appeared. One morning, after I had been working for the Council for no more than a few days, he suddenly rose from his desk and lunged across the room towards me, brandishing a telephone directory and shouting, 'Get away, you filthy creature.' 'What on earth have I done?' I wondered nervously, and was relieved when he dashed past me to the window, still shouting at a pigeon, which flew indolently and haughtily away.

Many of the problems and much of the controversy surrounding the Arts Council and its Literature Department in recent years have arisen from the manner in which the Council began to fund literature in the mid-sixties. For the first twenty years of its existence, the Arts Council did not subsidize literature at all. (Yet literature was as available in those dark ages of the forties and fifties as it is today.) This was not because anyone took the view that literature was not a legitimate art: English literature is, after all, one of the glories of the world. It was not subsidized, prior to 1966, because it appeared not to be in need of subsidy. All the good novelists and poets, as well as far too many of the bad ones, were published commercially, and there simply was no group of people exerting any pressure on the Council to intervene in the commercial processes.

With hindsight, the Council probably wishes it had never decided, in 1965, to venture into the domain of literature. Nevertheless, venture it did; and that was why, the following spring, Eric White and I sat looking at each other across our office in St James's Square.

Before 1966 small sums of money had been disbursed, but only to poets, or organizations connected with poetry. When the Arts Council initially arose, Phoenix-like, in 1945 from the ashes of the war-time agency, CEMA (Council for the Encouragement of Music and the Arts), whose Chairman was John Maynard Keynes, it inherited CEMA's three advisory panels for music, art and drama. In 1949–50, a Poetry Panel was created, largely at the instigation of Eric White, whose responsibility it became. The members of that first Poetry Panel were Joseph Compton (Chairman), Richard Church, G. Rostrevor Hamilton, Christopher Hassall, John Lehmann, C. Day Lewis and L. A. G. Strong. A very impressive line-up: whoever one thinks their equivalents are today, they are not to be found on the present Literature Panel. (Members of the Drama Panel in 1949–50 included Sir Bronson Albery, Peggy Ashcroft, John Burrell, Dame Edith Evans, Leslie Banks, Sir Lewis Casson, John Gielgud, Hugh Hunt, Sir Laurence Olivier, Hugh Beaumont, Noël Coward, Tyrone Guthrie and Benn Levy. For a list of some of the nonentities advising the Council on drama in 1986, see the current Annual Report and despair.)

In those early days, the Poetry Panel disbursed grants to the Apollo Society, which gave polite readings of verse interspersed with music (£200 in 1951–52), and to the English Festival of Spoken Poetry (£136.50, or £136.10.0 as it was expressed in the pounds, shillings and pence of the time). The year 1953 was a good one for poetry. In May, the Arts Council opened its Poetry Library, which it housed at the National Book League in Albemarle Street. The speakers at the opening were Lord Justice Birkett, Joseph Compton, T. S. Eliot and Sir Herbert Read, and (I quote from the Annual Report of the Arts Council) 'they all welcomed the fact that here was the nucleus of what it is hoped will in course of time become a specialized reference library of considerable importance'. Both Eric White and, later, I did our best to ensure the realization of that hope. I think it will be generally agreed that we succeeded. After 1973, I was greatly helped by the present Librarian, Jonathan Barker, who pursued an amiably aggressive policy of bullying me into making more than adequate provision for book-buying. When I appointed Jonathan, there were six thousand books in the Library. At the most recent count there were more than 30,000, and the Poetry Library, thanks to Jonathan, has now an enviable international reputation.

In December 1953, the Council accepted the Poetry Panel's recommendation to bring into existence a Poetry Book Society. The Society was accordingly incorporated as an independent company limited by guarantee, with Joseph Compton as its Chairman and a board of management which included Basil Blackwell and T. S. Eliot. Like the Poetry Library, the Poetry Book Society initially operated from the premises of the National Book League.

By 1964–65, the Arts Council was spending just under £5000 a year on poetry. In that year, the grants went to the Apollo Society, the Poetry Book Society, a few Poetry Festivals (among them the engaging Little Festival of Poetry at Cley-next-the-Sea, which cost us £11), a handful of poetry magazines, and one poetry bursary (£750 to Martin Bell).

In the autumn of 1964, representatives of the Publishers' Association persuaded the Poetry Panel to recommend to the Arts Council that it should broaden its policy to cover literature in general, as well as poetry. The Council agreed, and turned the Poetry Panel into a Literature Panel by increasing its membership. The new Panel, which was brought into existence during the 1965–66 financial year, was charged with the responsibility 'of advising the Council on ways of helping literature – particularly imaginative literature, including poetry'. It was at this point that I appeared upon the scene.

Unfortunately, or at least it appears to me to have been unfortunate, by the time I joined the Arts Council in 1966 the new Literature Panel had already met once, and had laid down the lines along which it wished to develop the Council's policy for literature. The Panel in 1966–67 consisted of Cecil Day Lewis (Chairman), Patricia Beer, Charles Causley, Leonard Clark, Reg Davis-Poynter, Patrick Garland, Giles Gordon, John Hall, Ted Hughes, Frank Kermode, Edward Lucie-Smith, Julian Mitchell, Iris Murdoch, Ian Parsons, Peter Porter, V. S. Pritchett, Alan Ross, Stevie Smith, Charles Tomlinson, C. V. Wedgwood and Angus Wilson. Twenty-one people: far too many, of course, for sensible discussion, but it took me years slowly to reduce the number to twelve. And some of those names are more impressive than others. Iris Murdoch joined at my urging, but did not stay long. Leonard Clark was a funny little chap, a poet and Inspector of Schools whose main concern was to promote the poetry of Leonard Clark. John Hall was also a poet, and sold advertising space for *Encounter*. The remainder were well-known literary names, with the exception of Reg Davis-Poynter, who was a publisher with the engaging air of a wide-boy. Not all were assiduous in their attendance at meetings, and of those who did come regularly one or two hardly ever opened their mouths except to sip the dreadful Arts Council tea. The most useful members of the Panel in those days were Patrick Garland, Ted Hughes, Frank Kermode, Peter Porter and Angus Wilson. Cecil Day Lewis was a sweet man and an amiable Chairman, but his invariable response to any suggestion which he feared might involve him in action of any kind was a tired 'Oh, Lor'!'

The Literature Panel began its work in January, 1966. Instead of attempting to decide how best to subsidize literature, and to discover precisely how, when, where and why subsidy was necessary, the Panel lazily agreed merely to extend the help formerly given to poets. Grants and bursaries would now be available for novelists, biographers, autobiographers and translators as well. 'One major difficulty facing the Panel,' the Arts Council's Annual Report for 1965–66 stated,

> is that writing, in prose or verse, is a one-man job. The other advisory Panels of the Council receive many applications for grants through organizations and groups – repertory theatres, drama and ballet schools, orchestras and musical societies, art galleries and so on. The Literature Panel, concerned very much with the individual writer, must think out how best the Council may use its money for the benefit of Literature, and then *go out and find* the writers most deserving of financial help.

This was sheer nonsense. To begin with, if writing is a one-man job, so are composing and painting. Of course the composer requires musicians to perform his music. Similarly the painter needs galleries to exhibit his paintings. But the writer, too, depends upon the collaboration of others: in his case, publishers to publish what he has written. If the Literature Panel had, from the beginning, set itself the task of identifying, not the individual writers, but the organizations which required subsidy, it could have persuaded the Council to embark upon a more sensible literature policy, and one which today might well have been in a state of expansion rather than acute contraction.

To say, as the writers of that statement of policy did, that the Panel had to think how best to advise the Council to use its money, and then go out and find the writers most deserving of financial help, was to produce the most ridiculous *non sequitur*. The best use of the Council's money would have been to identify the areas of literary publishing in need of subsidy, and then to subsidize them. Spending hundreds of thousands of pounds on encouraging mediocrities to think of themselves as 'full-time' writers was both pointless and cruel. Also, it did absolutely nothing for the condition of literature in Great Britain.

I should, at this stage, draw attention to one of the several anomalies connected with the Arts Council. The name of the organization is the Arts Council of Great Britain, and it is responsible for public funding of the arts in England, Scotland and Wales. (There is a separate Arts Council of Northern Ireland, in Belfast.) When I joined the Council in 1966 it had, as it has now, several panels and committees. Two of those, in 1966, were the Scottish Committee and the Welsh Committee. For some reason which I was never able to discover, there was no English Committee. In 1986, the situation has not altered except that, several years ago, for reasons of national pride, the Scottish and Welsh Committees were re-named Scottish Arts Council and Welsh Arts Council. They are, in reality, still committees of the Arts Council of Great Britain; there are not three Arts Councils, but one.

Theoretically, therefore, a Director of an Arts Council Department (Music, Drama, Art, Literature) is responsible for his or her art-form throughout Great Britain. In practice, virtually complete autonomy is given to Scotland and Wales, and the influence of a Director of the Arts Council of Great Britain beyond the borders of England is negligible. So, in effect, in the continuing absence of an English Committee, the full Council of the Arts Council of Great Britain acts as a purely English Committee, and confines its business effectively to English concerns, even though it includes among its members at least two from Scotland and two from Wales, who are the Chairmen and Vice-Chairmen of the Scottish and Welsh Arts Councils. Thus, discussion of and decisions concerning English matters have a Scottish and Welsh input, and not always a welcome one, whereas it would be more than any non-Celtic member's life was worth for him to infiltrate himself into, and attempt to influence, decision-making north or west of the English borders. This seems to have bothered successive Chairmen of the Arts Council of Great Britain not at all.

At the time of writing, the Council is coming to the end of an organizational review into every aspect of its activities, so there is the possibility that, from the new structure being proposed, more sensible decisions may flow. But I would not hold my breath: the radicals on the Council's staff are of that conservative variety that is in theory insistent on the need for change and in practice strongly resistant to any change. The Council itself is no better. It has cheerfully agreed to all the changes proposed which concern its staff, but rejected the proposed change to its own structure and frequency of meetings. It prefers the *status quo.*

That digression will, I hope, have explained why my comments on the literature policy of the Arts Council must be understood to apply only to England. The Scots have pursued a path even more lavishly strewn with grants to individuals than ours has been, while the Welsh, aided by the fierce nationalism of their literary officer, have, on occasions, gone wild and spent their money on sermons, comics, and almost anything in print, provided it is in Welsh.

Cecil Day Lewis, as Chairman of the Council's Literature Panel in 1966, wrote:

> The layman, while he may realize that poets cannot begin to make a living out of the art, often does not know that many serious prose-

writers are in almost equal difficulties today; he is apt to judge a writer's income in terms of the best-seller. In fact, a fiction writer is unlikely to make more than £150–£300 on each of his first few books (each book taking a year or more to write); and there are good writers who, after ten or twenty years' work, do not earn above £1000 a year. If we are prepared to pay more than lip service to the art in which our nation has always excelled, we have to do something about the writer's situation today.

This strikes me as being faulty reasoning. Did Cecil seriously think that, by distributing (as it did in 1966–67) the sum of £17,950 in bursaries to a few out of the hundreds of eligible applicants, the Arts Council was doing anything at all useful for literature? When I was appointed Assistant Literature Director I tried to say, as frequently as possible and to anyone who would listen to me, both inside and outside the Council, that the basis on which the literature policy had been conceived was entirely inappropriate. Literature, I argued, should have been handled in precisely the same manner as the other art-forms. In music, drama and the visual arts, we at the Arts Council did not direct our efforts primarily to providing handouts to individuals. Instead, we subsidized the artistic organizations which, in turn, commissioned and employed the creative artists. In music, we subsidized the opera companies and the orchestras; in drama, the theatres; in the visual arts, we provided (and subsidized others to provide) exhibitions of art. Nor did we, in those departments, confine our patronage to the contemporary arts. We allowed the Royal Opera to perform the work of dead foreigners with names like Mozart, Verdi and Bizet. We offered no objection when our theatre companies put on plays by Irishmen such as Shaw, Sheridan and O'Casey, or translations of Ibsen, Chekhov and Pirandello. Nor did we ourselves hesitate before mounting exhibitions by Picasso or Renoir, exhibitions which, in fact, made profits for us which we were able to plough back into the arts.

The newly formed Literature Panel, however, took the parochial view that 'literature' meant only 'contemporary English literature', and further chose to interpret 'contemporary English literature' to mean 'living English writers'. Thus the Panel missed a unique opportunity to initiate the Council's new Literature Policy on a much larger scale. Instead of recommending that, to complement the Royal Opera House and the National Theatre (and, later, the Hayward Gallery), there should be brought into existence a Royal or National or State Publishing House, at an initial cost of, say, £500,000 and an annual subsidy of (at 1966 figures) £100,000, the Panel spent in the financial year 1966–67 the sum of £50,123, which it frittered away on bursaries, awards and prizes to writers (about £30,000), and small grants to such organizations as the Lewes Poetry Group (£25), the Apollo Society (£500), the Barrow Poets (£600) and many others. Twelve literary magazines were offered annual grants, which was a more useful way to spend the money, but they received only £5000 in total.

These decisions had been made before I arrived. One of the magazines in receipt of grant-aid was *The London Magazine*. When, some weeks after I joined the staff of the Council, I found the *Times Literary Supplement* implying that there was some discreditable connection between my working for the Arts Council and the Council's offer of a grant of £2000 to my previous employer, *The London Magazine*, I realized that in my new career I was, no doubt, frequently going to be dealing with the disingenuous and the malicious.

The fact that the Arts Council was now spending money on literature greatly excited, not the Publishers' Association, whom one might have expected to display some interest since the expansion had occurred largely at their instigation, but the writers' organizations, the Society of Authors and, later, the Writers' Guild. The Society of Authors was the first to come sniffing around. They took the view then, and I believe they still do, that the Arts Council should allocate a sum of several million pounds to literature, and spend it by dividing the sum among all of the Society's members. The Poetry Society wanted money for themselves as well as for their members. Addressing an audience mainly of poets one evening, I said, 'Poetry is both a way of life and a part-time occupation. What a poet needs in order to write, therefore, is either to be cushioned from care for the whole of his life, or to be provided once a month with a notebook and a new biro.' The howl of rage which immediately arose is still echoing somewhere in Earl's Court Square.

In July 1966, a mere three months after I joined the Council, I appeared on a BBC TV programme together with the Minister for the Arts, Jennie Lee, and two others, the writer B.S. Johnson and the publisher Anthony Blond. We discussed novelists' earnings. Brian Johnson, having earned only a few hundred pounds from his two novels, considered he had been exploited by his publisher. Anthony Blond was able to explain to him that, on the contrary, his publisher had in fact subsidized him from profits made on non-fiction books. It is good, of course, that some publishers are willing to set profits from *The Cats' Calendar*, or whatever, against losses incurred in publishing some young avant-garde novelist. But, finally, the only real solution to the problem is to sell more copies of the novels. Perhaps one could never sell a 'difficult' novelist in sufficient quantities to enable the author to live on the proceeds. But it may be to the novelist's advantage to earn his living from some extra-literary activity. What is important is that his work, if it is of high quality, should continue to be published. If it can be published only at a loss, then there is a strong case for subsidy. This, it seemed to me, was where the Arts Council should come in, instead of dribbling out hundreds of small grants here and there to enable a number of good, bad and indifferent writers to lead marginally more comfortable lives for a few months while working on their current projects.

The Arts Council in 1966 was a considerably less solemn body than it was later to become. When Lord Goodman gave it as his opinion that 'one of the most precious freedoms of the British people is freedom from culture', he shocked many of his more doctrinaire friends, but made me realize that he was a man after my own heart. Arnold Goodman even managed to spread his gospel to Jennie Lee, who was quoted in the *Sunday Times* on 20 February 1966 as having said: 'My function is merely a permissive one. I keep repeating that like a gramophone record . . . permissive, permissive, permissive. I want simply to make living room for artists to work in. It isn't my job to tell them what to do in it.' But even Jennie seemed unclear about her priorities. Was arts subsidy intended primarily for the benefit of artists or of audiences? She never made up her mind, nor did the Arts Council. Most of the argument about subsidy was concerned with such suspect topics as artistic freedom, which most people took to mean whether or not you could write 'fuck'. Meanwhile, our Panel Chairman, Cecil Day Lewis, while obliged to support the Council's policy of giving hand-outs to writers, was able to say publicly: 'I do not myself believe that the young writer, however talented, should have things made too easy for him. A period of struggle, adversity and discouragement is a good test of his vocation, integrity and stamina (too early success is a stern test of integrity too).'

I found, very early on, that the possession of a sense of humour was highly dangerous for an Arts Council employee. Nevertheless, I decided to retain mine in case I should need it again in some post-Arts Council career. George Wightman, who ran an organization, 'Poets in Public', used to write me very long and, I thought, excruciatingly tedious letters. To one of them I replied that its tone was 'noticeably boorish'. By the next post I received from Wightman a huge list of errata and addenda to his letter ('for "so-and-so" read "such-and-such"'). I sent a postcard acknowledging receipt of this, and added, apropos of my earlier letter, and in imitation of his style, 'for "noticeably boorish" read "suicidally impertinent"'. Mr Wightman complained to *The Times* that my statement was 'disturbingly sinister' (the construction of adverbs modifying adjectives was obviously catching), and so my evil Arts Council persona made the first of its countless appearances in the public prints. The Council's Secretary-General of the day, a civilized ex-Civil Servant named Nigel Abercrombie, was amused, but Wightman continued for some time to pursue him, and even Jennie Lee, with letters complaining about me. To one such letter, which Wightman wrote while I was in hospital recovering from a car accident, Jennie Lee rather foolishly replied that he must understand I had written 'under conditions of severe shock'. I had not, and quite rightly Wightman would have none of this. He wrote again, stating that he had it on good authority that my mental condition while I was in hospital had been perfect.

The novelist Anthony Burgess argued strongly in public against bursaries for writers, which he thought a waste of public funds, but then sponsored a West Indian novelist for an Arts Council bursary. In rejecting his candidate, on the advice of the Panel, I wrote to Burgess: 'Since you are so solidly against the whole business of state subsidy for writers, you will be relieved to hear that you are now free from, for you, an embarrassing situation. In other words, your sponsorship of Wilson Harris for one of the bursaries has been unsuccessful. I am so glad to be able to give you this heartening news.' Within days, I was able to read my letter in the *Guardian* and the *Daily Mail*. How quickly writers rush to newspapers to complain when they think they are being addressed disrespectfully.

Under Arthur Crook, the *Times Literary Supplement* decided to mount a campaign against the Council's new literature policy. It was difficult enough at the time to discern precisely what the complaint was, and I have now completely forgotten. Looking at the press cuttings is no help. The row spilled over into other newspapers, and the *Daily Mail* devoted a half-page to a story headed 'There's fighting talk at the Arts Council':

> A splendid row is blazing up over the way the Arts Council hands out money to writers. On one side is the Council itself and its Literature Panel, headed by Mr Cecil Day Lewis, the Chairman. On the other is the *Times Literary Supplement*, which has attacked both Lewis and the Council, to mingled cries of approbation and horror from onlookers.
>
> For connoisseurs of both consistency and prose style it is a memorably instructive dispute. Consider the interchange between the Council and Mr Anthony Burgess, one of Britain's leading novelists.

The *Mail* then printed in full the text of my letter to Burgess, referring to me as 'a balding, Australian-born poet and music critic'. I found from the beginning of my time at the Council that the press liked to personalize matters. I was told that under no circumstances must I ever publicly reply to criticism. We at the Arts Council were expected to behave like civil servants and maintain a dignified and discreet silence. This, however, was never my style, and I made it perfectly clear to the Secretary-General of the time, and his successors, that I intended to behave like the creature in the adage: *'Cet animal est très méchant; quand on l'attaque il se défend.'*

I think that what the *TLS* probably wanted was less money to be given to writers, or at any rate to that 'pack of dunces, charlatans and scroungers that swarms upon all literary horizons'. It was piquant to observe Mr Crook referring to others in these terms, yet I rather sympathized with him, though I could hardly say so at the time. I was, after all, the new boy at the Arts Council, and although I seemed to attract more publicity than my boss, the Literature Director, or the Directors of those more stable art-forms, Music, Painting and Drama, I felt that the only proper course for me to pursue would be to attempt to warn the Council away from its sentimental regard for 'starving' authors, by discussion within the Council itself.

Meanwhile, the correspondence columns of the *TLS* were, for a few weeks, uncharacteristically lively, and the noise of axes being ground was quite deafening. The ludicrous Wightman of 'Poets in Public' published his edited version of my correspondence with him in the 'hippy' (remember them?) newspaper, *International Times*. Alas, he edited it so badly that he became the laughing stock of literary London for some weeks. Our correspondence came to an end with his threatening to have a question asked 'in the House'. What might the question be, I wondered. I am still wondering.

In that first year of spending money on literature, our main problem was the one which has continued to beset the Council: 'What on earth shall we spend it on?' When I consider the absurd rows I have had over the years with the Poetry Society (a kind of poetic equivalent of Bottom, Snug, Starveling, Peter Quince and those other luminaries of the Athens Amateur Dramatic Society), I derive a certain ironic amusement from remembering how the Arts Council first became involved with the Society. It was a rainy summer day in 1966. Eric White and I were staring gloomily out of our window in St James's Square, and Eric was taking what satisfaction he could from the fact that at least the rain had kept the pigeons at bay. We had been discussing possible recipients of Arts Council aid, but were having difficulty in choosing any. 'What about the Poetry Society?' said Eric.

'What about them?'

'Perhaps they'd like to be subsidized.'

'They've existed since 1912, or whenever, without subsidy. And, in any case, surely they'd approach us if they needed anything now.'

'The poor dears may not realize they need help. Let's have them to lunch.'

We invited the Secretary of the Poetry Society to visit us. He was an elderly, retired something-or-other named Robert Armstrong, whose job at the Poetry Society was an unpaid one. Eric persuaded him that the Society was in need of an annual subsidy of £1500 so that it could pay him a salary. It is from such acorns that the most monstrous oaks grow: in 1986–87 the Arts Council's subsidy to the Poetry Society exceeds £100,000.

Another of our bright ideas in 1966 was that there should be Arts Council Prizes for Literature. We awarded four such prizes, the winners being chosen not by committee but by individual members of the Literature Panel. The prizes of £1000 each were awarded to John Bowle for a book entitled *Western Political Thought* (on the recommendation of Veronica Wedgwood); Rayner Heppenstall (recommended by Angus Wilson), whose excellent novel *Blaze of Noon* had just been reissued; Edgell Rickword for his *Collected Poems* (recommended by Cecil Day Lewis), and James Stern for a volume of stories, *Something Wrong* (recommended by V. S. Pritchett).

We announced the prizes at a ceremony at 4 St James's Square, presided over by Jennie Lee. Jennie handed over the cheques, and made a speech in which she said that Great Britain was feeling its way towards the best means of making more room for the arts and the artist, and was doing so without 'the shadow of political direction of any kind'. This was the spirit in which the present awards had been made, and this was how she hoped it always would be in this country. A society which was essentially liberal and permissive had its faults, but it was infinitely more desirable than one in which artists were expected to reflect the views of the government.

It was a well-intentioned but illogical speech, and no one can have been surprised at the response it brought forth from the *Daily Telegraph*'s satirist, Peter Simple:

> The Arts Council will gladly subsidize plays of extreme left-wing, even pro-Communist tendencies, and if anyone objects, Miss Lee will remind him piously of the evils of State control over the arts . . . Could anyone who tried to put on in London a political play with an extreme right-wing or 'Fascist' message expect a subsidy from the Arts Council and a liberal, permissive pat on the back from Miss Lee? He would be lucky if his theatre were not burned down and he himself got away with his life.

When my views were sought, I made it clear that I thought the political question irrelevant, and that the introduction of such silly labels as 'left-wing' or 'right-wing' into discussion of the arts was totally unacceptable. I supposed that Shakespeare and Terence Rattigan could be described as right-wing playwrights, and Shaw and Arnold Wesker as left-wing, but that the important thing was to understand why Shakespeare and Shaw were great dramatists, while Rattigan's and Wesker's talents were something less than protean.

In the autumn of 1966, Jennie Lee went up to the Lake District to address a meeting at which the creation of a Northern Arts Association was to be decided upon. The Arts Council sent me to address the same meeting. I drafted my speech in advance and, as a courtesy, sent a copy of it to Miss Lee's office. On the day of the meeting, Miss Lee and I and one or two others, among them the Chairman of Cumberland County Council, walked onto the platform of a hall in Penrith. The County Council Chairman introduced Jennie and myself to the audience, and invited Jennie to speak first. Sitting behind her on the platform, I listened in increasing panic as I heard her deliver my speech with great conviction. I followed it from my own typescript: there it was, word for word.

When she sat, to great applause, I murmured to her, 'That was my speech.'

'Yes, dear, very nice.'

'No, no, you don't understand. I wrote it.'

'Yes. You drafted it for me.'

'No, I drafted it for me. What am I going to do?'

In front of us the Chairman had concluded his thanks to Jennie, and was saying, 'And now I shall ask Mr Charles Osborne of the Arts Council to –'

Jennie leaped up again. 'Forgive me for interrupting, Mr Chairman,' she exclaimed, 'but I'm sure Mr Osborne won't mind if I say that it's all very well for people like us to come up from London, and tell you what you should be doing for the arts. But what is more important is that you yourselves should decide, from your knowledge of local conditions . . .'

She improvised for another minute or two, then sat down to applause which was even more voluminous than before, applause in which appreciation of her words was strengthened by relief at not having to endure another long speech. 'There you are, dear,' said the Minister for the Arts, patting me on the knee.

Jennie Lee, as everyone who knew her during her time as Arts Minister will agree, was a darling. She was not very knowledgeable about the arts, but she had an auto-didact's enthusiasm, and she was an astute politician. Her popularity knew no political barriers, and when we gave a party for her at the Arts Council in the autumn of 1966, the assembled gathering of more than two hundred included the Countess of Albemarle, Lord Annan, Sir Edward Boyle, Viscount Chandos, Richard Crossman, Bernard Delfont, Lord Drogheda, Lady Fermoy, Michael Foot, Reginald Maudling, Henry Moore, Laurence Olivier, Victor Pasmore, Paul Scofield, Lord Thomson of Fleet and Dame Ninette de Valois.

An obvious consequence of a literature policy based on *ad hoc* hand-outs to a few writers and magazines was that one was subjected to a continual barrage of sniping from those who were not fortunate enough to be among the recipients. A certain 'dog in the manger' attitude soon revealed itself among our younger poets. When we announced the names of the poets to receive grants in 1967, those who had been given grants in 1965 assembled outside our windows in St James's Square to burn the books of the 1967 winners.

A typical 'sixties' fracas was the following (I reproduce the *Sunday Telegraph* account: there were others):

> ROW OVER STORY ON MRS KENNEDY
>
> The American Embassy is considering asking the Arts Council why it pays £100-a-year subsidy to a magazine named *Ambit* whose current issue carries an article entitled 'Plan for the assassination of Jacqueline Kennedy'.
>
> A spokesman said yesterday that someone had written to the Ambassador, Mr David Bruce, saying he was 'disgusted and revolted' by the article, and thought the subsidy a 'disgrace'.
>
> *Ambit* (circulation 2000) is edited by Martin Bax, a North London children's doctor, and backed mainly by his own money. The writer of the article is Mr J. G. Ballard, author of a number of books which critics have reviewed with awe, reserve and perplexity.
>
> He said he could not agree that there was any lapse of taste in personal comments on Princess Margaret, Mrs Kennedy, Brigitte Bardot or Madame Chiang Kai Shek.
>
> Or anything strange about preparing a montage photograph of the four women to show an 'optimum victim', and subsequently showing the photograph to disturbed children.
>
> 'You mustn't take the plan literally,' Mr Ballard said. 'The story is about the popular image of Jacqueline Kennedy as translated through all the television, newspaper and magazine media. These

images of public figures become mixed up and reverberate with each other.'

He saw no harm in writing about the 'increasing incidence of sexual climaxes among persons cleaning automobiles'.

Mr Charles Osborne, Assistant Literature Director of the Arts Council, said: 'I've read the article and take no exception to it myself. Is there anything wrong with sexual climaxes or cleaning automobiles?'

He said *Ambit* had received £100 for payments to contributors in several years, but each year was considered afresh. No request had yet been received for a 1967–68 subsidy.

Unfortunately, one was continually having to defend rubbish on grounds of principle. This is the kind of thing that gives principle a bad name.

As early as 1967, members of the Council's Literature Advisory Panel were beginning publicly to question the role of the Panel. Giles Gordon, now a literary agent but then a publisher, wrote an article in the monthly *Socialist Commentary* in which he complained of the system:

> I joined the Panel (and have been trying for two years to discover why I was invited) as a convinced believer in State subsidy for literature. I leave it holding the view that the idea is untenable, at least without there being *a policy for literature*. I confess with despondency my own inadequacy in contributing towards one. The Literature Panel, in keeping I think with all Arts Council Panels, is advisory merely. In practice this means that the two full-time Council employees seconded to the Literature Panel make the decisions. They decide what should be discussed, what should be 'tabled', and thus – more significantly – what should not; consequently an ordinary Panel member has little if any knowledge of what has transpired in the period since the last meeting, and meetings take place only every few months; the officials draw up the agenda and, perhaps most important, compile the minutes. Whether this is appropriate, inevitable, intelligent or otherwise, I am not prepared in print to express an opinion. The two gentlemen in question I consider as friends or at least as acquaintances, and infinitely more knowledgeable about the arts than myself. (Apart from the fact that the London literary scene in 1967 is so small, in every sense, that everyone is either your Friend or Enemy: no half-way houses.)

Giles Gordon is still a friend, and if he cares to ask me why Eric White and I invited him to join the Panel, I am as willing to tell him now as I would have been then. I understood the frustration felt by some Panel members at not being allowed to make the day-to-day decisions, but that was not their function. The Arts Council is a professional organization with a staff of more than three hundred, giving several thousand grants each year. The grant applications have to be professionally assessed, and that is not a task one can entrust to someone who is not devoting his full time to it. We always made it clear to new members of the Panel that they were being asked to serve on a purely advisory committee, and they invariably accepted this – at first. As the months went by, however, many of them began to hanker after a little executive decision-making.

The trouble was that, usually, they were so bad at it. For a few years we did, in fact, allow two or three members of the Panels to join the professional staff in making decisions (technically, these were not 'decisions' but 'recommendations to the Council', which was and remains the executive body), more often than not with results which I had predicted at the start of the experiment. What almost invariably happened at meetings of the Literature Finance Committee, as it was called, was that, if we were discussing an applicant organization, let us say a little magazine, the Panel members might well be unanimous in agreeing that the magazine was completely worthless and utterly unreadable, and its Editor virtually illiterate.

'Very well,' I would say. 'Thank you for your advice. So we don't offer any subsidy.' At that point, the Panel members' sentimental hearts would take over from their comparatively rational heads. The people who, minutes earlier, had been denouncing the magazine, now rushed to its defence. The Editor was such a nice man, and his wife had behaved so badly to him in the recent divorce. Could we not offer subsidy in the hope that, during the year, the magazine's standards would improve? Conversely, Panel members had a great aversion to quality. The better the magazine, the less keen they were that the Council should support it. Protecting our leading literary magazines against pompous hacks may well have been the most useful task I performed at the Arts Council.

If we were considering an individual writer who had applied for a bursary, the Panel members would behave in an even scattier fashion. They could never agree simply to offer bursaries to the writers they thought first-rate and to reject the second-rate. They used instead to devote hours to attempting to persuade me that, if the good writer needed and was offered £1000, then perhaps the bad writer, who also claimed he needed £1000, should be offered £500 rather than nothing, on the grounds that he was half as good as the first writer. On countless occasions I found myself pointing out that it cost bad writers as much to live as good ones; that we should either fund a writer's current project or not fund it; and that throwing away hundreds of pounds on writers whom we all agreed were of no interest to us was an irresponsible use of public money. However, I was but one voice on a committee of four or five, and though I was persuasive enough to win some of those arguments, I must carry my share of responsibility for the squandering of quite large sums of money on bursaries to the untalented. As I am accurately quoted in the *Standard* as saying, 'If a third of all the novelists and maybe two-thirds of all the poets now writing dropped dead suddenly the loss to literature would not be great.' (Incidentally, I have just read in Stephen Spender's *Journals* that, at a Writers' Conference at the 1962 Edinburgh Festival, 'Rebecca West said it would have been no loss to the world if most of the writers now writing had been strangled at birth.' I am delighted to find that Dame Rebecca had made my point even more strongly than I.) The good Lord, being no democrat, does not dole out talent in equal portions among the citizenry; those who approach the Arts Council for help are all too frequently the less favoured.

'Untalented' was not a word to be lightly uttered at the Arts Council. Nor was it safe to make value judgments. I remember being rebuked by a novelist, Maureen Duffy, for having said that, of two writers we had been discussing, one was considerably better than the other. 'Better,' Maureen growled, 'is an élitist word.'

Giles Gordon, to do him justice, never indulged in that kind of nonsense. Nearly twenty years before the Arts Council itself came to something like the same conclusion, he had arrived at a position where State subsidy for individual writers seemed to him, at best, an irrelevance. 'The Arts Council,' he wrote,

> is the Arts Council of our Labour Government. Its Chairman [Lord Goodman] was handpicked by our Prime Minister [Harold Wilson]. But the socialism that therefore should permeate and dominate the Arts Council's policy for literature seems as much stop-go-stop as the socialism that is being applied to Britain in most other respects. Once again, the ideas have run out. Perhaps they weren't there at the beginning, two years ago. The overall, all-embracing vision is lacking. I would suggest, for a start, that the Literature Panel should advise the Arts Council to stop paying money to individuals.

Giles went on to argue that the Literature Panel should be dissolved and its allocation spent on indoctrinating teachers with the thought that reading books was a worthy pursuit. Putting aside his misconception of the Council as the creature of one political party and thus committed to a socialist policy, whatever that might be, his complaint that, as far as literature funding was concerned, ideas were lacking, was completely justified. The Panel's principal idea was that money should be handed out to writers and to would-be writers in order to encourage them to write.

I was opposed to this. In vain did I argue that we had no need to encourage people to write more: our task was surely to encourage people to read more. We already had far too many writers chasing far too few readers. We needed, in my view, a two-pronged policy: (a) a means of improving the distribution of literature, and (b) a non-profit-distributing publishing house to publish those first-rate works of literature.

My concept of a State Publishing House, however, seemed to frighten members of the Council and its Literature Panel. They feared that what I had in mind was something on the Soviet model, and that, were I to get my way, my next move would be to put our commercial publishers such as Hamish Hamilton, George Weidenfeld, André Deutsch and John Calder against a wall and shoot them.

Not necessarily. For years the commercial theatre in Great Britain had quite happily co-existed with the subsidized theatre. Why could this not happen in literary publishing? But, though I carried this King Charles's head about with me for some years, I found very few allies. And eventually, when I undertook detailed research on the subject, I began to be less certain that my National Publishing House was needed. The literature of the past was increasingly available in cheap reprints, and when I looked for evidence to support the contention, put forward by the writers' unions, that there existed in manuscript form a large number of novels of publishable quality by new young writers, which were being rejected by publishers because they were unlikely to sell in sufficient numbers to be profitable, I could find no such evidence.

I contacted all the literary publishers and agents that I and our advisers could identify, asking the publishers to let me have details of any novels they had rejected within the previous two years which they would have published had literary quality or even promise been the only consideration. I asked the agents to tell me of any such novels they had been unsuccessfully submitting to publishers. If, as a result of this trawl, I had been able to compile a list of a hundred titles, it would surely have been worthwhile setting up a subsidized publishing house to get these books into print. Even if there had been only twelve or twenty such books each year, we could have initiated a scheme, perhaps with an existing publisher, to make them available. Unfortunately, however, there were not a hundred such books, nor were there twenty, nor even twelve. There were none.

To forestall the howls of frustration and rage that will no doubt greet the preceding paragraph, let me make it clear that I am talking about books which someone – some one agent or publisher – other than the authors themselves considered worth publishing, but which for economical reasons were not accepted. I repeat, there were none.

Giles Gordon's views received a wider circulation than they were given in *Socialist Commentary*, where they were initially aired. His article was quoted extensively in the national press. 'Arts Council panel attacked' was *The Times*'s headline, while the *Guardian*'s was 'Stop State aid for writers, says publisher'. Cecil Day Lewis, as Chairman of the Literature Panel, was asked to respond, but unfortunately he merely trotted out our party line: 'Of course the Panel could not always be right in its choice, but its purpose was to help writers of whatever age by giving them time to write. Nothing was arbitrary: the choice was by vote. To stop giving personal awards would be a negation of the Council's whole policy.'

My reply to that would be, and was, 'So much for the Council's policy.' But, of course, the Council rarely, if ever, discussed arts policy; nor did the Council's management body, its Directorate. I attended the weekly Directorate meetings right from the beginning of my employment with the Council. I was not entitled to do so, not being a Director, but Eric White had become bored with his chore of writing the minutes every week, and introduced me into Directorate to relieve him of that task. I frequently deputized for him at Council meetings as well, in those early days, long before I began attending Council meetings in my own right. When I did, I often sat next to Lord Snowdon, who opened his mouth once or twice at each meeting only to ask me to lend him two shillings for the parking meter outside in St James's Square. I never got any of those two-bob pieces back.

In those days, Council members tended not to question what they were told by their officers. Nowadays, they like to believe they are thinking for themselves, but they do not easily reach agreement even on what subjects they should be thinking about. The livelier debates in the sixties took place outside the Arts Council, either in the pages of magazines, or at meetings which were occasionally organized to protest against some aspect of Council policy, or sometimes in the unsavoury gossip columns of the newspapers. A typical example of the columnist's art is this, by John Gordon, in the *Sunday Express* on 17 March 1968:

> The Arts Council is an outfit worth watching. Currently it gives the Institute of Contemporary Arts a hefty subsidy of £23,000 a year, part of which, as I have disclosed, is spent on a bulletin stuffed with immature-minded pornography.
>
> Now W. H. Smith, the booksellers, have raised the matter of another publication, *New Worlds*, which recently had a £1800 grant from the Arts Council. Smiths say that some of its contents are so deplorable that they hesitate to sell it. Having read the magazine, I agree. It is well down in the filth class.
>
> But what does the Arts Council say in defence of spending public money on this sort of degradation? I quote its Assistant Literature Director, Mr Charles Osborne: 'We are interested only in the literary standard of the magazine, and we have a high regard for it.'
>
> If the magazine represents Mr Osborne's literary standard, I suggest that it's time he had his bumps read. The Arts Council, and its guardian angel Miss Jennie Lee, should take a hard look at what it is doing with our money.

New Worlds was a perfectly innocuous science fiction magazine whose literary standards were not especially impressive. However, enough members of our Literature Panel liked it, and so we subsidized it. Though I was prepared to argue, within the Arts Council, against supporting the magazine, I had, of course, to come to its defence when it was attacked by a philistine journalist.

Defending the bad against the worse can become lowering to the spirits if indulged in over a long period of time. What I found particularly tiresome, however, was having to go on saying the same thing to the same people, who seemed incapable of understanding what they were told.

For example, someone had worked out that the Arts Council spent only 1% of its total budget on literature, and at meetings organized by various interested parties I was thereafter continually asked if I did not think this monstrous.

I tried to explain that the percentage figure was totally irrelevant. The issue was whether the actual amount of money spent on literature was adequate. If it was, then it hardly mattered whether it was 1% or 90% of our total spending on the arts. In 1969–70, our literature allocation was £75,000. That was either the right amount to devote to literature, or it was not. If we had been spending £75,000 out of a total of £750,000, we could have boasted that we were devoting 10% to literature, but the £75,000 would not have stretched any further as a result. What I explained, I hope patiently, on innumerable occasions in public halls, in print, on television and on radio, was that the Arts Council did not receive a sum of money from the government and then decide how much of it to spend on music, how much on drama, or how much on literature. The process was the reverse of this. We decided how much we needed for each art-form (and these decisions were reached separately by each department of the Council) and for administration (rent, salaries etc). These amounts were added up, and the sum total was the figure we requested from the government. If we received the full amount that we had asked for, that was fine. If we got, however, only 90% of that figure, then each department in turn received 90% of its bid.

In other words, the Directors of Music, Drama, Art and Literature were never at any time forced into the position of having to fight one another for a larger slice of the cake. We each ordered, in advance, as much cake as we thought we could consume. Those vociferous and greedy writers who kept complaining of the huge sums being given to, for example, opera were misguided. If the Council had spent less on opera, it would not automatically have spent more on literature. It would, instead, have received a correspondingly lesser sum from the government.

Why then, I used frequently to be asked, did I not demand a larger sum for literature? Time and time again I explained that it was necessary for me to tell the Council why I wanted the money, and for the Council to agree. And there was never any chance of the Council agreeing (or of my asking it) to request the government to produce a few million pounds extra in order to share it out between unsuccessful authors. (A recent diary column in the *Standard* about my shortcomings quotes Michael Holroyd, 'one of Osborne's foes', who appears to have said of me, 'He wasn't the writer's best possible representative at the Arts Council . . . the man in the job should be generous.' Oh, really? The Literature Director of the Arts Council is not appointed as 'the writer's representative' nor does his job description require him to be 'generous' with the public purse. He is appointed to advise on and to implement Arts Council policy. The Music Director of the Council, similarly, is not there to represent composers, nor is the Drama Director there to represent playwrights. It is only writers who imagine that the Arts Council's job is to hand over their fellow-citizens' money generously.)

Being given grants seemed to bring out the worst in many of the writers who received them. I remember the unpleasantness which surrounded our awarding a grant to the novelist, Olivia Manning. A woman friend of Olivia's, a novelist whom Olivia herself had, the previous year, recommended to us for a grant, contacted a *Times* journalist and told him that the Arts Council's grant to Olivia Manning was scandalous because Miss Manning had no need of money, having just disposed of some lucrative film rights.

The Times man rang me to confirm this story. I checked, and said it was incorrect. I then wrote a sternly worded letter to the lady, telling her I was appalled to discover that she had appeared to be stirring up trouble about the Arts Council grant to Olivia Manning, and suggesting that, as a writer who had herself benefited from Arts Council grants, she might have taken some pleasure in knowing that other writers were benefiting from the same source.

Olivia Manning was upset at her friend's behaviour. But when I was next invited to lunch at her house I discovered that the magnanimous Olivia had also invited the friend. I declined the invitation. The friend had replied to my letter, incidentally, by returning it to me with the following lines typed at the bottom of the page:

This is totally offensive
This is totally inaccurate
This is totally libellous
Consequently totally uninteresting
And is therefore returned
to the totally silly sender.

The bursary committee gave her another grant quite recently, to help her with whatever she's supposed to be writing now. I shall be pleasantly surprised if any book sees the light of day as a result of the grant.

In 1970, the Council set up an Experimental Projects Committee to deal with applications relating to multi-media activities, principally the kind of thing which soon came to be called 'performance art': harmless lunatics wandering across East Anglia with poles on their heads, and the like. I was asked to be the senior member of staff responsible for this area of work. My committee was chaired by Michael Astor, and its members included the amiable Richard Attenborough. Richard, even in those pre-*Gandhi* days, was an extremely busy film director and actor, and it was not easy to catch him for meetings. But I valued his good sense and good humour very highly. I was reported in the *Daily Mail* as saying, 'Our job will be to sort out the sense from the senseless,' but not very much sense was to come our way.

and I divested myself of my responsibility for these 'experimental projects' as soon as I decently could.

A delegation representing these so-called experimenters attended an Arts Council meeting in order to put their case for more funds. Lord Goodman was in the chair, and welcomed the delegation, which was headed by a young woman in her twenties named Jenny Harris. Invited by Goodman to speak, Jenny looked around at the assembled Council, and then said, 'I don't know what to say to you, or how to communicate. When I look around this room, you all seem so old.'

Michael Astor bridled angrily (it was always easy to upset him), and one or two other Council members looked distinctly displeased, but Arnold Goodman was, as usual, equal to the occasion. 'It's the light, my dear,' he assured her. 'Don't let it worry you.' Even Jenny Harris laughed, and the angry confrontation she had initially wanted to manoeuvre everyone into was avoided.

By 1971, the year in which the part-time Literature Director, Eric White, reached retirement age, the Arts Council had moved in the direction of greater formality, and had also, having grown larger, moved physically from St James's Square to a house in Piccadilly which the 1967–68 Annual Report described thus:

> Aesthetically, the building lacks most of the qualities that grace our former headquarters, but it is extremely impressive, and is in process of becoming agreeable inside. Its history began in 1780, and is not without interest. As the Pulteney Hotel, in 1814, it housed the Tsar (in preference to St James's Palace) for his state visit to London. The 4th Marquess of Hertford is supposed to have housed in it the nucleus of what is now the Wallace Collection. In the nineteenth century it became a part of the Hotel Splendide. At least one member of the Council's staff enjoyed in it the amenities of the King George V Club for Officers during the Second World War.

Eric White's retirement raised the question of the future of the Council's Literature Department. As the date of his departure approached, I was asked if I would be interested in applying for Eric's part-time job of Literature Director, and, if so, whether I would consider combining it with some other senior post, perhaps assuming responsibility for Arts Festivals.

My answer was that I would not. I was no more interested in becoming the Council's part-time Literature Director in 1971 than when the opportunity presented itself again, more recently, in 1985. It seemed to me that, if the Council was to take its Literature Policy seriously, and develop it into something more than an *ad hoc* scattering of grants, its first move ought to be to appoint a full-time Director. This was agreed by the Secretary-General and by the Council, but our paymasters in the Civil Service had to be consulted. At that time, our grant came from the Department of Education and Science (a separate Office of Arts and Libraries was set up much later), and I understand that the Council did not find it easy to convince the Department that a full-time Literature Director was a *sine qua non*.

However, they did eventually succeed. That did not mean that the job was automatically mine. Senior posts at the Arts Council now had to be nationally advertised. An advertisement appeared in the leading newspapers and magazines, and more than a hundred applications were received. A large number were from the lunatic fringe, but many quite respectable characters also applied. I remember that George MacBeth, poet and BBC producer, was among them. And so was I.

I had by now become quite friendly with our Chairman, Arnold Goodman. I liked him enormously, and we seemed to share the same sense of humour, though he had, and has, by far the greater patience and gentleness of spirit. Arnold took me aside one day and warned me that I should by no means take it for granted that I would be appointed Literature Director. 'The view of the Department of Education and Science is that you are something of a wild man,' he said. The DES, having reluctantly agreed to the establishment of this new, full-time post, would expect to approve the successful candidate, who therefore was unlikely to be me.

There seemed no point in staying on as Assistant Director, so I began to make contingency plans. The Gulbenkian Foundation was advertising for a new Director, and I promptly applied for the job. I was short-listed, and interviewed by a committee, one of whose members was Patrick Gibson (later Lord Gibson), who, it was already known, was shortly to succeed Arnold Goodman as Chairman of the Arts Council. Tricky. As I arrived back in my office from the Gulbenkian interview, I was told that I had been short-listed for the Arts Council job. 'I should bloody well think so,' I replied ungraciously.

Some days later, I was interviewed by a small committee of Council members which included Lord Goodman, Lady Antonia Fraser and Lawrence Gowing. As Chairman of the Literature Panel, Frank Kermode should have been present but was abroad. He told me much later that, when asked by telegram to adjudicate between the merits of the two leading candidates, George MacBeth and myself, he had wired back, 'The devil you know'. At the interview, Arnold Goodman disconcerted me at the outset by saying, 'You're the last of the short list, and we shan't need to spend very much time with you, as we all know you.'

That made me determined to ensure that they would spend as much time with me as I felt I merited. I began to outline my ideas on literature funding. The advertisement to which I had responded required applicants to be over thirty-five years of age (I was forty-three), to have a thorough knowledge of the problems of authorship (as the author of several books I knew something of these problems), and to 'be alive to current developments in the field of contemporary literature' (I was not sure what this meant, but I did read living writers). I pointed out to the Selection Committee that I possessed a further qualification which I thought should be taken into consideration, although it had not specifically been asked for: a firm belief in the necessity of state aid for literature, though not in the necessity of grants to individual authors. I drew their attention to the penultimate paragraph of the three-page letter I had written to support my application:

> Intervention is required at three points: those at which our literature is written, is published, and is bought. The writer, the publisher and the bookseller should, therefore, all be brought into consultation on these matters. My own suggestions would include attempting to find wider outlets for the writer (through the creation, perhaps, of a first-class, purely literary magazine – none exists at the moment; also through use of and collaboration with the communications media, particularly TV and radio); changes in techniques of publishing, especially in the areas of creative literature, i.e. fiction and poetry; discussions with booksellers in an attempt to set up some kind of agreed training scheme for young people going into book-selling (the trade's staff recruitment methods are at present hopelessly haphazard, and so bookshop staffs are as often as not completely lacking in even the most superficial knowledge of contemporary writing); serious consideration of the possibility of selling books in public libraries (we have a splendid public library system with branches in very many localities where no bookshop exists).

I expanded on these subjects, talking at the committee for a good half-hour before giving them a chance to ask any questions. When it was all over, I was thanked and told that I would be hearing from them in due course.

As it happens, they must have come to a decision soon after I left the room. Arnold Goodman phoned me after lunch, and said, 'You're not supposed to hear this until it's confirmed by the Council, but you'll be pleased to know we decided unanimously to offer you the post of Literature Director. Never was a choice made so easily on the merit of the applicants.' Before I could think of a suitable response to this, he continued, 'I shan't deflate you by saying anything further.'

I rang the Gulbenkian people, who had not yet made up their minds, and withdrew my application. A few days later, Lord Goodman told the Arts Council that the Selection Committee had 'fallen over backwards' in an attempt not to appoint me, for they wanted to avoid the criticism that the Council was a self-perpetuating body by bringing in someone from the outside. 'However,' he assured them, 'we were unable to find a better candidate.'

The Arts Council had by now acquired a new Secretary-General in Hugh Willatt, an amiable Nottingham solicitor who had been the Chairman of the Council's Drama Panel. Nigel Abercrombie's initial term of appointment as Secretary-General had expired and, although Lord Goodman felt that he must go, the post of Chief Regional Adviser was created for him; he filled it adequately by travelling the provinces, attending meetings, until he reached retirement age.

Apparently the applications received when the post of Secretary-General was advertised were an even more depressing collection than the Literature Director batch. 'Why didn't you apply?' Arnold Goodman asked me on a railway platform in Leeds, where we had gone to represent the Council at some dreary luncheon or other. 'Have you no ambition?'

'Not in that direction,' I said. 'But are you suggesting that, had I applied, I would have had a reasonable chance of being appointed?'

He was saved by the approach of the train, and by a voice which announced over the public address system, 'Due to industrial action, there is no restaurant car on the London train. There is, instead, a miniature buffet.'

Arnold, a large man, cast a sad glance upon me and said, 'I'm afraid nothing miniature will be of the slightest use to *me*.'

The manner in which Hugh Willatt underwent a transformation from unpaid adviser to chief executive officer at a reasonably high salary was hilarious. At the Council meeting at which it was announced that the response to our advertisements had been disappointing, Hugh removed his pipe from his mouth long enough to murmur, 'I would be willing, if Council wishes, to assume the duties of Secretary-General, if no other suitable candidate can be found.'

The Council immediately rolled over on to its collective back, waved its collective feet in the air, and accepted his offer. Earlier, they had been persuaded by Arnold that it was imperative to find a younger man than the sixty-year-old Nigel Abercrombie. They had succeeded: Hugh was fifty-nine and a half.

Hugh Willatt proved to be a perfectly competent Secretary-General. He did not do much, other than disappear behind the huge piles of paper on his desk (one knew he was there if smoke could be seen rising from the other side of the papers), but with Arnold Goodman as Chairman it was almost inevitable that we should have had a virtually invisible Secretary-General.

My appointment as Literature Director was greeted with joy in some quarters and dismay in others. The Society of Authors (of which I was a member) immediately began to offer me advice in the pages of their quarterly magazine, *The Author*. First, there was an 'Open Letter to Charles Osborne'. This was followed by an article. 'Do we need a Literature Panel?' by – you have guessed it – Giles Gordon. 'How can the thing be expected to work?' Giles asked:

> On paper, the Literature Director is the servant of the Panel. In practice, he is wheeling and dealing day in, day out, to push through what he thinks should be pushed through. But if he is the right person for the job (and Mr Osborne is an honorable man, as well as a Gollancz author [Giles worked for Gollancz at the time]) the farce of the Panel meeting for tea and rhubarb six times a year should be dispensed with, even if it can't be seen to be dispensed with. If the Arts Council's charter has to be altered, have it altered. If the Literature Director cannot be allowed that much freedom, then the Panel should meet much more frequently, and its members should be paid for their services.

Giles had correctly identified the weakness inherent in the Arts Council's Panel system. I did not, of course, at any time envisage myself as 'the servant of the Panel'. I knew that some of my colleagues among the Council's Directorate liked to hide behind their panels, but this was never my style. If the Arts Council, I argued, had wanted their Directors to be mere secretaries to Panels, they could have described them as such and appointed competent people at less than half the salaries they were paying us Directors. I intended to earn my salary, and if the Council did not like that, it would presumably say so. As I read it, the function of advisory panels was to advise. The function of the Literature Advisory Panel was to advise me and, through its

Chairman and myself, the Council. I set about reducing the 'tea and rhubarb' occasions from six times a year to four.

It was not unnoticed in the world outside the Arts Council that its only two Literature Directors, Eric White and myself, were both trained musicians and musicologists who had written books on music, with an emphasis on opera. That unofficial Poet Laureate of our times, Gavin Ewart, published a poem, 'The Phantom of the Opera':

In a world full of Thomas Hardy-type ironies
what could be properer
than that a Literature Director should be
a man who only cares about music –
Charles Osborne,
the phantom of the opera.

There had been several Panel Chairmen since Cecil Day Lewis, who had retired at the end of 1967. Cecil was succeeded by Angus Wilson, lovable and effervescent, who in turn was followed by the thoughtful and courteous Professor Frank Kermode. At that time, when Arts Council Directors had considerably more authority and prestige than they have now as a result of the recent changes in the Council's structure, it would have been unthinkable for a new Panel Chairman to have been foisted upon a Director without prior consultation. Until the appointment of the present Chairman of the Literature Panel, I was always consulted when a change was being proposed. I remember, for instance, that when the question of a successor to Frank Kermode came up, and the name of Stuart Hampshire, distinguished philosopher and Warden of Wadham College, was mentioned, Arnold Goodman gave lunch at the Garrick Club to Frank, Stuart Hampshire (whom I had not met) and myself, principally to give Stuart and me a chance to discover whether we could bear the sight of each other. It was a very civilized way of doing things.

As it happens, Stuart and I got on extremely well from the beginning. I appreciated his ironic detachment, and I look back with pleasure on the period in which he chaired our Panel meetings. We also sat next to each other at Council meetings, able to make the occasional snide remark, *sotto voce*, to each other. It was Stuart who said to me, shortly after he had attended his first Council meeting and listened to discussions concerning the large annual subsidies to the Royal Shakespeare Company and the Royal Opera House, 'I begin to realize, Charles, that what we lack in Literature Department is a large, loss-making institution. We must acquire one.' He became a firm, if flippant, advocate of my National Publishing House. Together, however, we were still unable to persuade anyone else that it was a good idea.

One of the questions to which we had given high priority from the earliest days of the Literature Department was that of a Public Lending Right. A Working Party, chaired by Cecil Day Lewis, on which Eric White and I sat, was set up, and in due course made its recommendations to the Council. What we proposed was that the Secretary of State for Education and Science should establish a Library Compensation Fund Committee, to administer a Fund provided by the DES. In order to compile figures relating to library usage, on the basis of which the Committee could effect the distribution of benefits, we thought that a sampling system, based not on issues of books to borrowers but on stocks of books held, should be used.

These proposals were approved by the Council and forwarded to Jennie Lee in the spring of 1967 for her consideration. A delay of two years then ensued, at the end of which, discouraged by the lack of response from Miss Lee, the Council's Working Party reassembled, now under the chairmanship of Angus Wilson, to consider what further action should be taken.

At this point the DES awoke from its slumbers and set up its own Working Party, eventually producing a Public Lending Right scheme which was a variant of the Arts Council plan. This was discussed with the interested parties, including, this time, the Library Association, which had been, and indeed remained until it realized the battle was lost, staunchly opposed to a Public Lending Right.

In June 1969, Lord Goodman headed a deputation to the Chancellor of the Exchequer, who assured us that he accepted the principle of Public Lending Right as a matter of equity. A series of meetings was held at the DES, but as late as February, 1970, the librarians and, indeed, the local authorities were still in total opposition. The Arts Council then proposed an alternative scheme which would not have required the co-operation of librarians, and submitted it to the new Minister, Lord Eccles, who set up yet another committee, on which I represented the Arts Council.

Public Lending Right eventually arrived, and most of us writers are now a few hundred pounds a year better off as a result. But there were some amusing hiccups along the way. One of these arose as a result of a question I asked in a letter to *The Times* (in March, 1977), the body of which was on a quite different subject, the question of whether the Arts Council should subsidize the public libraries' purchase of modern serious fiction. The penultimate paragraph of my letter read thus:

> In the view of many, the dark person in this interesting literary woodpile is the public library system, which leads me to the question of Public Lending Right. Representatives of the major political parties, the Society of Authors and the Writers' Action Group have all assured me that the possibility of borrowers paying for their books is simply not on. They may, of course, be right. I observe, however, that no one has bothered to ask the borrowers. I should like, therefore, to put to the readers of *The Times* this question: Would you be prepared to pay, say, £2 per annum, or less than 4p a week, for your reader's ticket? A word on a postcard to me at the Arts Council, whether yes or no, would be very gratefully received. An argument would not.

I received 756 postcards saying 'yes', and two saying 'no'. I thought this interesting, but the then Minister for the Arts, Hugh (now Lord) Jenkins, was so incensed at my daring to raise publicly the question of payment that he rang the Arts Council in an attempt to have me sacked. He succeeded only in incurring my enmity, and in persuading our Deputy Secretary-General, Angus Stirling, to write the following letter, which *The Times* published:

> Charles Osborne, Literature Director of the Arts Council, in a letter which you published on March 11th, invited your readers to let him know if they would be prepared to pay a subscription for the right to borrow books from public libraries.
>
> In the absence of the Secretary-General, I should like to make it clear that this personal initiative of Mr Osborne's in no way represents a change of policy by the Arts Council on the question of the Public Lending Right. The Council has always supported the cause for legislation in Parliament to bring about an effective Public Lending Right for authors, and continues to do so.

It began to be believed that I had, somehow, spoken against Public Lending Right. What I was attempting to do, of course, was to discover whether there might be a more effective way of financing it than from public funds. A modest charge, with the usual exceptions for the old, the young, the indigent and the bludgers (see the *Macquarie Dictionary*), would have produced a much larger annual sum than that which the government has so far seen fit to allocate to Public Lending Right, and we authors might now be one or two thousand pounds a year better off, rather than a few hundred.

*

In April, 1972, we said goodbye to Lord Goodman as Chairman of the Arts Council at a dinner at the Café Royal. It was not a sad occasion, for the wit at that distinguished gathering flowed as readily as the Piesporter Goldtropfchen 1970. Among those present were Angus Wilson, Stuart Hampshire, Myfanwy Piper, George Harewood, Richard Attenborough, William Coldstream, Peter Hall, Michael Astor, Antonia Fraser, Frank Kermode, Henry Moore and William Glock. I knew I would not be losing contact with Arnold Goodman (apart from anything else, his firm were my solicitors), but I also knew that I would miss our frequent exchanges of scrawled office memos, his in a GP's illegible scrawl (and sometimes in a GP's Latin), mine less sparkling but easier to decipher. (*'Bis dat qui cito dat'* ['He who gives quickly gives twice'] was the message he sent to me when he considered I had been dilatory in arranging for the payment of a grant. 'I require no admonitions from Publilius Syrus,' I replied.)

Our new Chairman, Patrick Gibson, was very different from Arnold Goodman. His was not an expansive personality, but he gave an impression of quiet competence. He was cold, polite, and occasionally lost his temper. He once lost it with me, over something absurdly unimportant: his photograph in the Annual Report, of which I was the Editor. We were shouting at each other over this until finally, in exasperation, he exclaimed, 'You're so stubborn! Why don't you just admit you're in the wrong, and I shan't mention the subject again.' Although I was convinced I was right, I agreed that I had been in the wrong, in order to end the fruitless argument. Lord Gibson immediately forgot his promise not to mention the matter again, and continued to harangue me. I liked him, though no one could say he was a charmer.

It was during Pat Gibson's period of office as Chairman that I found myself beginning to be at loggerheads with my employers, the Council. Through the Secretary-General, Hugh Willatt, I was informed that two complaints were being made about me. One was that I earned money outside the Arts Council with my books, articles and broadcasts; the other was that my epistolatory style, in communications with the press and the public, was not that of a po-faced civil servant. (This latter complaint was not communicated to me in precisely those words.)

I rejected both, and continued to have to do so, intermittently, throughout my entire time at the Arts Council. In my view, the Council should have been grateful to have the services, as Director of one of its art-form departments, of someone active in the relevant art-form. If my books, I told the Council, brought my employers into disrepute, they would have valid cause to require me to refrain from publishing them. But, on the contrary, my books were favourably received, they were not pornographic novels but critical works on musical and literary subjects, they reflected credit on my employers, and they were written in my spare time. If I chose to *earn* money in my free hours instead of *spending* money on a leisure-time activity (the very concept of a 'hobby' appals me), it was none of the Council's business.

Similarly, the efforts made by successive Secretaries-General to encourage me to drain my public utterances of personality have met with the failure they deserved. I have always tried to match style not only to subject but also to surroundings. For example, I would never employ in *The Times* the style I used in *Time Out* when, in August, 1973, I replied to a comment from a gentleman named Asa Benveniste, who ran a small publishing venture, Trigram Press:

> Trigram's founder, Mr Asa Benveniste, who has had several Arts Council grants, is quoted as saying 'It's kind of a humiliating business. You have to give them [the Arts Council] a list of past work, plans for the future, finances . . . and it's a thing I find boring to do.' I have thought long and deeply about Mr Benveniste's dilemma, and find I can most appropriately comment by quotation from *Gypsy*: 'Tough titty', Asa!

To me, one of the Literature Department's finest achievements in the 1970s was our support, for five years from 1973 to 1978, of the literary magazine, *The New Review*, edited by Ian Hamilton. For some years prior to this we had subsidized Ian's poetry magazine, *The Review*, and when the Literature Panel was persuaded to encourage into existence a new literary magazine of national stature, we eventually found ourselves asking Ian to build upon the success of his smaller venture and edit *The New Review*.

At first, we cast about elsewhere in an attempt to land a distinguished editor. I remember trying to tempt Karl Miller into taking on the editorship of a new literary magazine. Karl was reluctant, but recommended Ian very highly. And so we helped *The Review* to die and *The New Review* to live. Ian, who has since those days shown himself to be also a superb biographer and a surprisingly good presenter of TV literary programmes, was a brilliant editor. Those fifty issues of *The New Review* stand as a remarkable achievement, and one of which the Arts Council's Literature Department can be proud. The magazine folded after four-and-a-half years, not only because its business management was poor, but also, and mainly, because of the envy of a number of people in the literary world (some of them members of our Literature Panel) who had not been invited to contribute to its pages.

I seemed to have to fight for *The New Review* both inside and outside the Arts Council. Finally and inevitably I lost the battle. But at least I helped to keep the magazine afloat for fifty issues, and I am much prouder of that, and of having, over the years, protected our other first-rate literary magazines, *The London Magazine* and *The London Review of Books*, than of having presided over the awarding of grants to writers.

I had become used to finding scathing references to myself in the satirical magazine, *Private Eye*, and had no objection to their continuing to give me publicity, as long as they spelled my name correctly. But I was annoyed when, in 1975, they began attempting to club *The New Review* to death, and I still fail to understand why a funny magazine should have felt the need to behave so viciously to a serious magazine which was in no way its rival. *Private Eye* had, at least until recently, a source of information within the Arts Council's Literature Panel: there are always plenty of people in the literary world eager to offer information to journalists, and our Panel was usually notoriously leaky, as was the Council generally.

The following appeared in *Private Eye* in July, 1975, under the heading, 'Literary Supplement':

> Towards the end of his editorship of *The London Magazine*, John Lehmann met a young Australian, Charles Osborne, and took him on as his assistant. Thus began a remarkable career in the tangled world of English literature which has continued now for more than fifteen years. Osborne is himself a writer of sorts – he has published privately several volumes of verse, and has also written a book on Verdi – but his main roles have been editorial and administrative. He remained at *The London Magazine* until he was appointed assistant to Eric Walter White, Literature Director of the Arts Council, whom he succeeded in 1970 [actually 1971]. Recently he came close to higher power yet: when Sir Hugh Willatt retired as Secretary-General of the Arts Council, Osborne applied for the job with the powerful backing of Lord Goodman. *Eye* readers will recall that Hugh Jenkins appointed instead the obscure Roy Shaw.
>
> As Literature Director, Osborne has very considerable powers of patronage. He is answerable to a Literature Panel [wrong], but the Panel only meets [I am not responsible for *Private Eye*'s incorrect placing of the adverb 'only'] four or five times a year (the last meeting scheduled was cancelled at the last moment) and its composition is not designed to produce critical restraint of Osborne. Some members, such as Francis King, have been personal friends of Osborne's. Others

have been recipients of the Panel's *largesse* in the form of grants and 'bursaries': Maureen Duffy, Colin Falck, Paddy Kitchen, Alexis Lykiard, Derwent May, Piers Paul Read. (None of these, of course, received money while they were actually on the Panel, although a publisher's grant was made to Jonathan Cape while Tom Maschler was a Panel member.)

Previously the grants to writers were detailed: thus for example the public could learn that £2000 of its money had gone to Rayner Heppenstall in 1968–69, £1000 each to A. Alvarez and Ian Hamilton in 1969–70. Coincidentally with Osborne's succession as Director, the Arts Council's Annual Report ceased to print the figures, so that we know that Brigid Brophy received a grant in 1972–73, but not how much. (Hamilton is a friend of Osborne's; Miss Brophy used to be a close friend – they collaborated, with Miss Brophy's husband Michael Levey, on a particularly frightful squib called *Fifty Great Works of Literature We Could Do Without* [*sic*] – but they seem subsequently to have fallen out violently.

Figures are, however, available for grants to 'little' magazines. Osborne has been consistent in his support for two of them, his own old *London Magazine* and Hamilton's *The Review* (now *The New Review*).

For several years the *London Magazine* has received £2000 or slightly more per annum; in 1973–74 this rose to £3000, and it has now gone up to £6000. [I don't want to give the Editor of *Private Eye* apoplexy, but the grant in 1984–85 was £37,300.] *The Review*'s subsidy rose steadily from £400 to £2200 per annum, until last year, glossily revamped as *The New Review*, it hit the jackpot with £12000, more than half the total allocation for literary magazines (the *Eye* has commented on this previously, as on the fact that Osborne is a regular, pseudonymous contributor to *The New Review*).

The normally quiescent members of the Arts Council Literature Panel have come as close as they are capable to open criticism of Osborne over this issue. At the last Panel meeting, in March, Hamilton attended to 'exchange views' with members. Elizabeth Thomas expressed the views of many members that *The New Review* editorial base was 'small and restricted, with the same flavour as the former *Review*'. Alexis Lykiard hoped for a diversification with the 'feeling commonly expressed that "the same old people" were contributing to *The New Review*'. Tom Maschler observed that 'sales were a little disappointing, and that since many people did make a charge of cliquishness against *The New Review*, there might be some truth in this criticism'. Hamilton dismissed these criticisms with, of course, Osborne's support.

> Hamilton has probably nothing to worry about, as Osborne habitually gets his way. There are a number of recent instances of his making arbitrary decisions, naturally without reference to the Panel, dictated by his personal preferences. He vetoed a reading by Bob Cobbing at the Arts Council Bookshop; he withdrew a subsidy to the Coelfrith Arts Centre in Sunderland, apparently because of his disapproval of the poet Basil Bunting, who was giving readings there; he has reduced the grant to the Arvon Foundation because of his dislike of some of the writers chosen by Arvon (eg Auberon Waugh, who has quoted Osborne's letter to the Foundation's organizer in the *New Statesman*, 20 June); he has conducted a running feud with the Poetry Society and its head, Michael McKenzie; privately, he promised an Arts Council colleague that he would 'snuff out the Poetry Society within a year'; at the last Panel meeting he spelt it out, saying that the 'Council could be recommended to offer subsidy only for those aspects of the Society's work which appeared worthwhile'.
>
> He did not say worthwhile to whom, and that is the nub. Writing to the *Eye*, Clive James, another friend of Osborne, accused us of furthering the aims of a cabal (of 'talentless regional poets who run in and out of Peak District pubs with carrots stuck up their noses', presumably a roundabout attack on Elizabeth Thomas, who is responsible for literature in the regions). This is a remarkable example of projection, for the Hamilton-James-Osborne connection is nothing if not a cabal. Osborne ('a man of wit, accomplishment and courage', Clive James *op cit*) has told the *Sunday Times* that 'I'm not going to hand out money just to keep poets alive.' He has certainly kept his word as far as many poets are concerned, but others who 'appear worthwhile' are very much alive and will continue to thrive while Osborne is responsible for seeing that public money goes to the right cabals.

That is a typical *Private Eye* mishmash of distortions, inaccuracies, half-truths and occasional whole truths. It's all too remote to be raked over now, except perhaps for the references to *The London Magazine* and *The New Review*. It never ceased to amaze and sadden me that, when I visited universities or literary communities in the United States, Australia, Israel or various European countries, I would invariably be told of the high regard in which these two leading English literary magazines were held, whereas on my return to London all I heard about them from my Panel and elsewhere was the usual bitchery.

Private Eye was right about one thing. Remembering that Arnold

Goodman had gently castigated me for not having applied for the post of Secretary-General in 1967, I decided, when it fell vacant again in 1974 upon Hugh Willatt's reaching retirement age, that this time I would apply, not because I thought there was any real danger of my being appointed, but in order to flex my muscles, annoy a few people, and remind the successful applicant that there was at least one member of his staff who would be keeping a critical eye on him.

I was short-listed, but the person appointed (not by the Minister, as *Private Eye* had claimed, but by the Council itself) was Roy Shaw, in my view by far the least satisfactory Secretary-General the Council has had, so far. Roy the Obscure, as he was known, was a professor of adult education at the University of Keele. Faced with the complexities of the Arts Council job, he chose to concentrate on his own subject, adult education, bringing into being an Education Section, and bringing on to the staff an Education Officer, a woman with a manner which reminded me of Anna Neagle as Queen Victoria. The women on the Arts Council's staff never really felt at ease with Roy, taking offence at some of his banter. Many of the men felt he was trying to bully them. He never got on with our gentle-mannered Musical Director, Basil Deane.

Roy confined his criticisms of me to our private meetings. He had two major arguments and, as I pointed out to him, they could hardly both be valid. One was that I behaved dictatorially with my Panel; the other was that my heart was not in the job and that I was too busy pursuing a career outside the Arts Council. The truth was that I led the Panel as much as I could, precisely because of my interest in and enthusiasm for the job of trying to steer the Council towards intelligent decisions.

Occasionally I had difficulty in discerning whether Roy was bestowing praise or blame upon me. When I described an eminent Council member as 'a closet idiot in imminent danger of "coming out" ', our Secretary-General looked at me searchingly. 'I don't suffer fools gladly,' he said, 'but, Good Lord, you don't suffer them at all!'

Actually, it was kind of *Private Eye*'s anonymous columnist to quote Clive James's over-generous assessment of me from a letter Clive had written to the Editor. The full version reads: 'If you are sincere about asking for additional information on Charles Osborne, let me provide some. He is a man of wit, accomplishment and courage – an ideal appointee for the difficult job of backing a small number of worthwhile projects while being harried by a large number of mediocrities on behalf of an infinite number of fools.'

Throughout 1975, and for several years thereafter, though they have still not entirely given up, *Private Eye* regularly published scurrilous and even legally actionable stories about me. I am not by nature litigious, and on the one occasion when I consulted Arnold Goodman, as my solicitor, about an article in *Private Eye*, he advised me not to pursue the matter.

'But they say I've been giving grants to my friends. Surely they must retract that.'

'In court, their defence would be that you are a well-known person with a number of friends among writers. It would be strange if you did not have friends in the literary world, and surprising if some of your friends were not among the recipients of Arts Council grants.'

'But that isn't what they mean. They clearly imply –'

'Yes, of course they do. But, alas, the law allows it. It isn't worth pursuing. No one believes anything they read in *Private Eye*, and by taking them to court you would merely be giving more publicity to the article you object to.'

I'm sure that Arnold's advice was sound, but I'm equally sure that a number of ingenuous people do believe everything they see in print.

One gets no sympathy from one's friends when one is hounded by *Private Eye*. They seem to think one should look on such a campaign of mendacious abuse as an accolade. Oddly, the only time that people did commiserate with me over a reference to myself in that magazine was on an occasion when I thought that the wild flight of fantasy published in the 'Grovel' column was genuinely funny:

> Bookworm's amusingly Philistine campaign against Charles Osborne, the Arts Council squanderer, has so far ignored the story of how Osborne happens to be here in the first place. Mr Osborne 'raffled' his body in Australia, promising those who bought tickets that, in the event of winning, the lucky person – male or female – could do whatever they liked with it for 24 hours.
>
> To his chagrin, a housewife was the winner, and she made the unattractive pseud wash dishes round the clock.
>
> With the proceeds of this distasteful competition, Osborne bought a one-way Qantas ticket to London.

References to me as 'the dreaded Queenslander', 'the gritty Australian' and so on continued to grace the pages of *Private Eye*, sometimes in columns written anonymously, sometimes in a diary contributed by Auberon Waugh. (Philip Larkin once suggested to me that I should write a book about talentless sons of famous fathers, and give pride of place to the Waughs.) Waugh's anti-Osborne outpourings still continue, and have now spread far beyond the pages of *Private Eye* to the *Spectator*, the *New Statesman*, *Books and Bookmen* and several other journals, among them, most recently, the Australian *Bulletin*.

What, the reader may wonder, is the reason for this? To the best of my knowledge I've never met him, but in 1974 he took umbrage at references to himself in a letter not intended for his eyes, but which he read among the papers on someone else's desk. What I had written (to the Director of the Arvon Foundation at Lumb Bank in Yorkshire) was:

> I have considered the list of writers that you invite us to engage for the months of May and June. Presumably you have already engaged the May writers, so I do not see that I can meaningfully deal with these. My only comment on the entire list, in any case, is that I do not think the Arts Council will wish to engage A. Waugh if he is the gentleman who writes the silly piece in *Private Eye*. So I suggest you dig your hands in your own pockets for him.

The Arts Council, at that time, made an annual contribution towards the costs incurred by the Arvon Foundation in engaging writers as tutors for their courses. Our contribution was never intended to cover the entire costs. As a matter of form Arvon regularly sent to me a list of writers they intended to engage; our subsidy covered some, but not all of them, the shortfall being made up by Arvon's revenue from students. I used to indicate which of the writers could be assumed to be those paid for by the Arts Council. It was a paper exercise, and in no way affected the amount of subsidy Arvon received from us. What Waugh pathetically claimed, in article after article in various magazines, was that I had attempted to stop the Arvon Foundation from employing him, by reducing their grant by the amount of his fee. This was completely untrue. Arvon's Director corrected Waugh's facts in a letter which *Private Eye* was forced to publish, but Waugh chose to ignore this, and eleven years later was still screaming.

If one were really to worry about everything one reads about oneself in the press, one would have a miserable passage through life. I prefer, against all the odds, to enjoy life, so I do not worry. I am not very good at worrying, nor do I see the point of it. If you can change an unsatisfactory situation, then do so, or at least make the attempt. If you can't, then you must live with it. It is important not to turn into the kind of whinger who is forever blaming others, friends, employers, the government, the Russians, for this or that state of affairs. Turn thine eyes into thy very soul, as Hamlet might have said to Gertrude.

It was more than ten years ago that I first read in the press of my imminent departure from the Arts Council. 'Ian Hamilton, boring editor of the *New Review*, is likely to succeed the diminutive Aussie, Charles Osborne, as the head literary man at the Arts Council,' wrote 'Will Waspe' in the *Spectator*. Variants of that have been appearing with monotonous regularity ever since, the most recent being a flurry of new items at the beginning of 1985. I returned to the Arts Council in March of that year after a holiday in Australia and America, to find my desk littered with press cuttings announcing that I had quit. (By the time this book is published, however, I shall have left, at the beginning of 1986.)

One of the most fragrant versions of this long-running news story appeared in a weekly magazine, *What's On In London*, a few years ago. The (anonymous) columnist on that occasion (I was later told his name was Kenneth Hurron) wrote that, when I left the Council, Britain's poets and writers would dance in the streets for sheer delight. A TV interviewer in Los Angeles recently quoted this to me, and asked me if I agreed that on my departure from the Arts Council there was likely to be dancing in the streets. 'In the streets?' I replied, 'Oh, no, I hardly think so. In the sewers, perhaps.'

An agreeable piece of light relief from the rigours of Arts Council life was provided in 1974 when the Maltese Ministry of Education and Culture contacted me. They were setting up a European prize, the Malta Cultural Award, to be competed for by most European countries. The prize would be given for a book of essays published within the previous twelve months. Would I nominate the British entry?

I thought for a few moments. Who wrote essays any longer? Ah yes, Ian Hamilton had published a book of literary essays. I nominated Ian. Some weeks later I was informed that Ian had won the Malta Cultural Award. He and I were invited to Valletta, air fares and all expenses paid, for a weekend in May as the guests of the Maltese Government. We flew out on a Friday, were met at the airport and driven to our hotel. On Friday evening there was to be an official dinner given by the Minister of Industry, Trade, Agriculture and Tourism. Ian and I decided to skip this, and 'do' Valletta instead. We felt that honour would be sufficiently upheld by our presence the following morning at the prize-giving ceremony in the Palace of the Grand Masters.

Valletta is a dump. We ate a mediocre meal at an Italian restaurant in a sleazy street (is it called 'The Cut'?), and then, since there was nothing else to do in Valletta, we began a tour of the bars. At some point in the evening I seem to remember we separated. But we later ran into each other again in an otherwise deserted bar whither Ian's taxi driver had taken him as being the most likely scene of action.

Ian was later to recall that we left that bar together, having called for a taxi to take us back to our hotel. He apparently stopped for a moment at the cloakroom, and emerged just in time to see the taxi disappearing, with me in it. I remembered nothing of this.

The next thing I did remember was being shaken awake by Ian. I looked around me. I was in our hotel, but in a strange room, neither mine nor his. My clothes were strewn about on the floor. 'Thank Christ you've awakened me,' I said to Ian, 'or I'd have slept through, and missed the prize-giving. Hold on. I'll have a quick shower.'

'Have a slow shower,' Ian replied. 'It's afternoon. I had to go to the ceremony without you. I told them you were ill. Here's what they gave me.' And he waved in my face a cheque (for several hundred pounds, I subsequently discovered) and a hideous, phallic-shaped statuette, the Malta Cultural Award.

'Why didn't you wake me before you left the hotel this morning?'

'I came to your room, but you weren't there, so I assumed you'd gone on without me. But you weren't at the ceremony, so I improvised an excuse for you, but then I began to be worried. I thought you might have been kidnapped by that taxi driver last night.'

'Perhaps I was. I don't remember a thing. Where am I now? Whose room is this?'

'It's an otherwise unoccupied room. When I came back after the ceremony, I insisted that the hotel people search for you. Then the night porter remembered you coming in late. You must have given him the wrong room number, and he gave you the key you asked for. You staggered in here and passed out, I suppose.'

And that is how I failed to attend the Malta Cultural Award ceremony in the Palace of the Grand Masters, 'in the presence of the highest authorities of the State, Diplomatic Corps, economic leaders and the international press corps'. Ian and I made it to the Gala Dinner on the Saturday evening, but opted out of lunch with the Ministry of Education and Culture on Sunday, as well as a party given by the Governor-General. Instead, we decided to spend the day on the beach. But we had to take a taxi to the other end of the island to find a sandy beach, on which we fell asleep, only to be awakened by having sand kicked in our faces by Royal Navy ratings playing football. 'Christ,' muttered Ian, 'we might as well have gone to Blackpool for the weekend.'

Surprisingly, the Maltese asked me the following year to nominate another writer. This time I chose Clive James, whose recently published volume was the best (if not the only) book of essays to appear that year. As a nominator of prize-winners, I obviously possessed the Midas touch, for Clive was given the Malta Cultural Award for 1975. I made it perfectly clear, however, that nothing would induce me to spend another weekend in Malta, and Clive refused to go alone. The British Council representative in Valletta collected the statuette on Clive's behalf, and in due course handed it over. I think the Malta Cultural Award did not survive for a third year. It was just as well, for I was running out of essayists.

In many ways, 1975 was Poetry Year at the Arts Council. To begin with, a poet became Chairman of the Literature Panel. 'Since you don't appear to mind working with an aged sceptic,' Roy Fuller wrote to me, 'I accept the invitation right away, with thanks for being so honoured.' Other poets, however, wrote less agreeably to or about the Arts Council. When a group which called itself 'Poets' Conference', under the leadership of Bob Cobbing, an amiable but, in my view, talentless 'sound poet' (if 'talentless sound poet' is not a tautology), put out a belligerent press statement, it received much light-hearted comment in the press. The statement, a rambling affair, complained that I had been rude to the Poetry Society: '*The Times* reported Charles Osborne as describing the Poetry Society's National Poetry Centre as "that rag-bag down in Earl's Court". Osborne later took the trouble to phone up the Society to say, "I have been wrongly reported. I did not say 'that rag-bag'. I said 'Those ratbags down in Earl's Court'." '

The following is from the *Guardian*'s account of the *affaire*:

> The Poets' Conference, a trade union of poets, last week threatened militant action if the Arts Council does not 'see sense' and cough up more money for the rhythmic word. In the verbal firing-line is the secretary [*sic*] of the Arts Council's Literature Panel, Charles Osborne, the arbiter of who gets what in the poetry world.
>
> The poets are threatening to confront Mr Osborne in his office at 105 Piccadilly and force him to listen to the words which he will not sponsor – such as a tape recording of 'Kurrirrurrirri', a sound poem by Bob Cobbing. Although in fairness it should be heard, not written, the sounds of 'Kurrirrurrirri' are something like 'Twonk, rol rol rol, twonk twonk rol rol rol twonk rol rol rol rol rol twonk twonk rol rol rol rol rol rol'.
>
> This might be followed by the more measured cadences of the other spokesman for the Poets' Conference, Lawrence Upton (from his

collection, *How to Make Money*): 'Where were you this morning?/I was out in the sun./Where were you this morning?/I was out having fun/In leagues of deepening air.'

Mr Osborne, unimpressed by this show of militancy, could then read from his own slim volume, *Swansong*: 'So I sit here and watch them watching me./They think I'm sullen. I suppose I am,/only because I don't get angry any more./When I screamed at them, they laughed/and were frightened.' [This is from a poem about Guy, the London Zoo's gorilla.]

The Poets' Conference met in London this month and issued a document called 'The State of Poetry'. The aim of Charles Osborne, it said, 'is to control poetry from one point of view which is not shared by the great number of poets and readers in this country'.

The confrontation did not take place, and I can't recall that anyone ever heard again from Poets' Conference. My reaction to 'The State of Poetry' was reported in the *Guardian*: 'I can't really say that I've taken the report all that seriously. If you're in the business of subsidizing what you think to be good, then you're going to come in for criticism from those whom you think to be not so good.'

During the year, I demonstrated that I did not want to do anything so impossible and so ludicrous as 'to control poetry from one point of view' (whatever that may have meant) by publishing the first of the Arts Council's series of annual poetry anthologies, which continued to appear for the next ten years. *New Poetry I* was edited by Peter Porter and myself. When we advertised nationally for poems, we expected to have to plough through about 5,000 entries. In fact, we received 42,000 poems from 10,000 poets, a handful of established names but most of them, of course, unknown.

Is not that a frightening thought? Ten thousand poets? Most of the stuff was junk, but my co-editor insisted that we should both read all of the poems, and then confer. We did. The extent to which we found ourselves in agreement was both remarkable and fortunate. We chose, finally, 224 poems by 170 poets, and paid generous fees. This came as a surprise to some of the poets, who, victimized by vanity publishers, had expected to pay us for the privilege of appearing in an Arts Council anthology.

When *New Poetry I* was published, it was widely and favourably reviewed. 'It is *the* book of modern British verse,' wrote Martin Booth in *Tribune*, 'and should in the future establish itself as the standard text on the art above all others.' In the *Guardian*, Peter Redgrove said: 'The Arts Council anthology ought to have the word "life" somewhere in its title. We've been cheated too often by things called "new" and things called "poetry". This is certainly poetry – there's hardly a bad poem in the book – and it's certainly contemporary, since it speaks with the accents, and springing, and rhythm of our time – but its roots are both natural and ancient . . . the verse is full of things to see, touch, bite, taste, bark your shins up against. Nobody must be put off by "Arts Council". This is highly unofficial poetry.' 'It sets out to do,' said Gavin Ewart in the *New Statesman*, 'what *Poetry Review*, organ of the Poetry Society, should be doing and isn't, because of its excessive devotion to tenth-rate American material . . . Apart from typewriter poetry and concrete poetry most kinds of verse are represented. The editors were "careful to judge whether it was good of its kind – not whether they liked that kind".'

Emboldened by the success of *New Poetry I*, I also began an annual short story anthology, and edited the first issue with Margaret Drabble. For the next four years, I chose two different editors annually for each anthology, but thereafter changed to a single editor for each. I made this change after disagreements with two editors. When I appointed Fleur Adcock, she decided she wanted a friend as co-editor and offered the job to a poet and magazine editor, Jon Silkin. I pointed out to Fleur that I had already chosen her co-editor, Anthony Thwaite, at which point Silkin complained to the Secretary-General, Roy Shaw, who thought I should let him have his way. I thought it important not to, and refused. Having won my battle, I then magnanimously (or weakly) engaged Silkin the following year to edit *New Poetry V* with Peter Redgrove, after which I mentally crossed Silkin off my list.

At the Cheltenham Literature Festival in the autumn of 1975, I made two appearances. One was at Cheltenham Ladies' College as a reader of poetry in a programme I had devised, 'Hail, Horrors, Hail', an evening of macabre verse by Poe, Webster, Thomas Hood and others. (It was to have starred Christopher Lee, but he was ill and his place was taken at short notice by Kenneth Haigh.) My other appearance was as one of a panel of writers discussing 'Literature, the Poor Relation'. 'Six well-fed writers,' said the *Gloucestershire Echo*,

> sat for an hour and a half in Cheltenham Town Hall last night, discussing the plight of their starving brethren.
>
> The distinguished cast of the Cheltenham symposium consisted of the novelist, Ronald Harwood (the Festival's artistic director) as Chairman; Norman St. John Stevas, former Minister for the Arts; Maureen Duffy, novelist; J. W. Lambert, literary editor of the *Sunday Times*; Lord Willis, writer; and Charles Osborne, writer and Literature Director of the Arts Council.

> The theme was that writers are the lowest paid members of society. Unfortunately, the audience was small, as this is not a topic so dear to the public as it is to the poverty-stricken writers themselves.

Everyone said what one would have expected them to say, some more succinctly and articulately than others. What this occasion, and so many similar ones, revealed to me, however, was that no pressure was ever going to be applied to the Arts Council to increase its literature budget by any group representing the consumers of literature, the readers. At every so-called public meeting at which I spoke on the subject, the public was conspicuously absent. The same old faces were present, and they were those of the interested parties, members of the writers' associations, plus an occasional sympathetic publisher. I recall one occasion when Joan Bakewell on BBC-TV simultaneously interviewed myself and one Derek Parker, who represented the Society of Authors, on the subject of grants for writers. Parker, whose disapproving expression underlined his resemblance to the Duchess in *Alice in Wonderland*, began to talk about writers 'starving in garrets'. This was too much for me. 'Oh, come off it,' I exclaimed. 'When did you last see a garret, let alone a writer starving in one?'

In 1976, the Arts Council acquired a sympathetic new Chairman in Kenneth Robinson, who had been a Labour Minister of Health and, later, Minister of Housing, and who was the author of an excellent book on Wilkie Collins. Kenneth is now a Social Democrat. At the Arts Council he was the most open-minded and undogmatic of individuals, and an agreeable and stimulating colleague.

In October 1977, Roy Fuller decided he could bear no more of the Council's sillier decisions, and resigned. He was quoted in the *Evening Standard* as saying, 'It's just that there comes a moment when I felt I couldn't go on answering the question people kept asking me: "What the hell did you spend money on that for?" One can only put up with a certain amount of this.'

It had been a year in which some Arts Council clients had excelled themselves in offensive lunacy (Miss Cosey Fanny Tutti's dirty underwear exhibited at the Institute of Contemporary Arts, for example). 'I can't pretend I wasn't upset by that sort of thing,' Roy announced. He made it clear that he had no quarrel with the Council's Literature Department, but only with 'performance art'. In fact he had written me the following letter on the day that he resigned:

Dear Charles,

I have written to the Chairman and Roy Shaw telling them I am resigning from the Council. I disagree with many of the Council's decisions and I see no prospect of getting them amended or reversed – so what point is there in being unhappy and frustrated at meeting after meeting? I am sorry to let down you and your assistants, and the Literature Panel – that part of the work I have enjoyed and felt was making progress.

Yours ever,
Roy.

Roy received support in the *Sunday Times* from J. W. Lambert, who had been a member of the Council, and Chairman of its Drama Panel from 1968 to 1976. Jack Lambert charged Council and Panel members with displaying 'timid silence, worse than indifference and amounting to moral cowardice'. Too few members had been willing to 'ask the necessary questions or to speak their minds', and he did not absolve himself from blame.

One of my more enjoyable tasks in the late sixties and early seventies was my involvement with the annual Poetry International summer festivals of spoken poetry which the Council, through the Poetry Book Society, presented in London. These festivals had grown out of earlier occasions at the Mermaid Theatre or the Royal Court: the first Poetry International proper was directed by Ted Hughes and Patrick Garland in 1967. A designer called Edward Tuersley produced posters and programmes which were completely illegible, but we had a splendid line-up of poets: Auden, of course, and Spender, Neruda, Empson, Hans Magnus Enzensberger, John Berryman, Charles Olsen, Allen Ginsberg, Robert Graves, Anthony Hecht, Yehuda Amichai, Hugh MacDiarmid and several others. They were not all first-rate poets but they were all worth hearing. Some of them were better value off-stage than on. The continually drunken Berryman kept wetting and soiling his bed at the Sixty-Nine Hotel ('Sounds promising' said Anthony Hecht), where we had accommodated some of the poets, and was thrown out. On one evening, William Empson delivered a very long introduction to the poem he intended to read, and then sat down having forgotten to read it. While she was reading one of her dreadful confessional pieces, Anne Sexton was audibly heckled from the stage by Auden, and Bella Akmadulina simply didn't turn up, having failed at the last moment to get out of Russia. There were, not surprisingly, clashes between the engaging though minimally talented Allen Ginsberg and the charming Malcolm Muggeridge, whom, inappropriately, we had asked to introduce the poets on the first and last of the five evenings.

Those first Poetry Internationals were biennial events. We invited John Betjeman to appear in 1969, and his acceptance letter was written in the highly specialized franglais he habitually used in his correspondence with Patrick Garland: 'Oui, si vous voulez, the festival, but the whole idea of it depress moi somewhat, and I will be afraid of rotten apples or no one at all. Pour moi je prefer poésie morbide et seul.'

It was in 1969 that, at the urgent insistence of a member of the Poetry Book Society's board of management, we agreed to invite a Swedish poet named Gunnar Ekelöf. I dutifully attempted to contact him, but found myself later having to write to Patrick: 'This is just to let you know that Mr Gunnar Ekelöf will not be able to attend Poetry International this year, as he has been dead since March, 1968. P.S. Perhaps he will be with us in spirit.' Looking through the files, I find also a letter from Christopher Logue which begins: 'Dear Garland, Why do you fuck me about?'

1969 nevertheless contrived to be a vintage year: Auden again (he was our mascot, and came every year, even the year when I wrote specifically to explain why we were not inviting him!), Miroslav Holub, Ogden Nash (at the inspired suggestion of Ken Thomson, though Wystan characteristically claimed it was his idea), Janos Pilinszky, Pier Paolo Pasolini, Derek Walcott, Robert Bly and others. As in 1967, the young Peter Jay acted as our dogsbody, ferrying poets across London, running errands, and remaining sunnily pleasant while temperament raged around him.

In 1970 we decided to turn ourselves into an annual event. Ted Hughes did not want to continue, so I became Patrick's co-director. Sidney Nolan produced a stunning poster for us, which was so sought after that most of those to whom we gave it to display simply took it home and framed it. So I turned it into a programme, printing the details of performance on the back, and selling it for a mere two shillings. That was the year I persuaded my old acquaintance Tennessee Williams to fly from Key West, Florida, to join us and read his poems. Our other poets included Wole Soyinka, Thom Gunn, Octavio Paz, Allen Tate and Sandor Weöres. At the end of the week, I flew up to Edinburgh with five of the poets, including Auden, and we did a final performance in the Assembly Rooms. (This venture had its amusing moments, which I later described in my biography of Auden.) The following year we tried to do something similar in Cardiff. It was not a great success: the Welsh were interested only in hearing the one local poet they had foisted upon us, a dim old preacher whose name I've forgotten.

In 1971, at a press reception to launch the festival, I introduced Wystan Auden to Mary Wilson, wife of the then Prime Minister, and herself a published poet. They did not find a great amount to say to each other. As for the performances, 'the breathy platitudes of Denise Levertov induced a bit of unseemly shifting in the stalls', frowned the *Times Literary Supplement*, though Auden was appreciated as greatly as ever, and Patrick and I were complimented by the *Guardian* on our readings of the English translations of the foreign-language poets.

During the festival week, I chaired a discussion at the ICA between Wystan and Stephen Spender. It was a bizarre occasion. 'Poetry can change the world,' said Stephen.

'Nonsense,' replied Wystan.

'You can't just say "nonsense", Wystan. What about Blake?'

'What did he change?'

'I can't be expected to itemize,' retorted Stephen, 'but there's Shelley as well.'

'A detestable poet.'

'But many of the Labour Party's ideas derive from Shelley –'

'That,' interrupted Wystan, 'is what's wrong with the Labour Party. It isn't the poets who are the unacknowledged legislators of the world, it's the secret police.'

Of his own work, he said, 'Nothing I wrote in the thirties saved one Jew from Auschwitz. Let the poet be political if he wants to be, but the only person who's going to profit from it is himself.' When Stephen suggested that poetry existed to oppose the evil society, Wystan replied, 'It opposes all societies.'

He soon tired of the discussion, looked at his watch, declared that it was nine-thirty and 'way past my bedtime', and shuffled off the platform. Stephen and I sheepishly followed him.

In 1972 we expanded our programme. The visiting poets (this time from the United States, Hungary, Austria and Yugoslavia) read at the Queen Elizabeth Hall, but we also put on a number of 'sideshows' at the Institute of Contemporary Arts, involving Edna O'Brien, Harold Pinter. Judi Dench, Diana Rigg, Annie Ross and Dudley Moore. I surrounded a reading (by Vivian Merchant, standing in for Marianne Faithfull, and Edward Woodward) of poems by Sidney Nolan with an exhibition of portraits by Nolan. Patrick and I introduced a programme of highlights from our week in Humphrey Burton's TV show, *Aquarius.*

1972 was also the year in which the Russian poet Joseph Brodsky was expelled from the Soviet Union. Though he had never expressed any great interest in Jewish culture or religion, Brodsky was threatened with imprisonment in the Soviet Union if he did not agree to emigrate to Israel. He had already suffered years of Arctic exile from his native Leningrad, having been tried as a 'parasite', so he wisely chose Israel, but hopped off the train in Vienna and made his way to W. H. Auden's house at Kirchstetten. 'Dear Charles,' Wystan wrote to me on 6 June,

> A few days ago Joseph Brodsky was expelled from the Soviet Union. At the moment he is here in Vienna waiting for a U.S. visa
>
> If it comes through in time, he would be able to come to the Poetry Festival, and if so we *must* invite him, as he is the best living Russian poet, and his first appearance outside would be a great coup for us.

I was touched by Wystan's identification with Poetry International, but even more so by Brodsky's plight. Patrick Garland and I had more than once attempted to invite him, but the Soviet cultural attaché in London had refused to admit his existence. 'We have no poet named Brodsky,' he had said. 'There was at one time a parasite of that name.'

Somehow I managed to pull the right strings and procure a British visa for Brodsky very quickly. He arrived from Vienna with Wystan at Heathrow, to be met by a barrage of press photographers. How difficult it must have been for him to understand. For years he had been persecuted, for no better reason than that he was a poet. Now he was being lauded, for the same reason. He had first fallen into disfavour in the Soviet Union in 1964 when he was accused by a Leningrad newspaper of corrupting the youth of the country with nihilistic, pessimistic and pornographic verse. (Brodsky is the least likely poet I know to write pornographic verse.) A district court, apparently composed of neighbours and private citizens in Leningrad, tried him under a law which provides for the banishment from cities of persons who have no visible means of support. The presiding judge sentenced him to five years' labour as a manure-spreader on a state farm in Archangelsk.

'I spent three months in a mental home before the trial,' Brodsky told a *Guardian* journalist. 'They put me in a hospital for psycho-criminal tests. They simply kept me there, giving me injections and so on. I can't say it was pleasant. It was quite difficult to endure, but I told myself I had to endure it. Afterwards they said I had some traces of schizophrenia, but nevertheless that I was OK for work in the conditions of the Arctic regions.'

Brodsky read his poetry at the 1972 festival to great acclaim. Some months later, he wrote to me from New York (I had sent him a photograph of himself on TV, declaiming a poem):

> Dear Charles,
>
> Thank you so much for sending that photograph: it recalled those nights in London – the happiest nights in my life, I guess. Although I couldn't respond properly, partly because of my English (which isn't any better, as you see), mostly because of a certain shock (not cultural one) in which I was after Russia.
>
> Because life is such a mixture, a hodge-podge, I never will have another chance, probably, to tell how grateful I was and am to you for that invitation and everything you did for me . . .

After the 1972 festival, Patrick Garland decided not to continue as a director, so I became the sole director from 1973. As usual, Wystan Auden was the star attraction, and at Wystan's request I also invited his friend Chester Kallman to read. For my sideshows I engaged John Betjeman (who was then the Poet Laureate) and Roy Fuller to present 'Homage to C. Day Lewis: poetry and prose by the late Poet Laureate', a programme in which Cecil Day Lewis's widow, Jill Balcon, also participated. I encouraged Ian Hamilton and Clive James to devise and present 'The Poetry International Revue' (out of which grew those long narrative poems of Clive's).

I also presented a programme, 'The Poet as Lyricist', in which the lyrics of Noël Coward, Cole Porter, Lorenz Hart, Ogden Nash and others were introduced by Benny Green and read by Constance Cummings, John Gielgud, Vincent Price and me. I asked Jack Lambert to chair a discussion on 'The Poet as a Librettist', but on the night he was indisposed and I had to step in and do it myself. The other participants included Auden, Kallman, Ronald Duncan, Elizabeth Lutyens, Nicholas Maw, Myfanwy Piper and Malcolm Williamson. The most enjoyable of the sideshows, however, so people told me, was 'An Evening of Innocent Austral Verse', in which Mrs (as she then was) Edna Everage was assisted by Mr Barry Humphries and myself.

It was a highly successful week. *The Times* wrote: 'This has been the most various and ambitious season of Poetry International, which can now be regarded as a miniature poetic equivalent of the Proms. Nursed through infancy by Patrick Garland, helped by Ted Hughes, and now in the capable and imaginative hands of Charles Osborne, it was a triumphant week, Ginsberg or no Ginsberg.' Auden declared that Poetry International was 'the most important event of its kind in the world'. Alas, he died a few weeks later, robbing the event, thereafter, of much of that importance.

In 1974 I presented a programme, 'The Politician as Poet', in which I induced four politicians to appear together at the ICA and read their poems. They were Lord Hailsham, Lord Gowrie, Tom Driberg and Enoch Powell. I was sorry not to have achieved a fairer political balance, but it had proved difficult enough to find four politicians of any stature who wrote poetry (of any stature!), and Tom was the only Labour man to present himself. A group of hecklers in the audience tried to stop Enoch Powell's innocuous academic verse from being heard. From the stage I identified my friend Adrian Mitchell, who appeared to be responsible for the most vociferous booing and shouting, so I castigated him ironically and, I hope, elegantly, and eventually Mr Powell was given a hearing. Adrian wrote to me a few days later, unabashed, and even complaining that 'seven demonstrators are no match for Powell with a microphone, and the audience solidly on his side'. I know that political extremists are not fond of the concept of free speech, but that one poet should try to stop another from reading his poems (which were not even political) saddened me. I would have expected Adrian to agree with me that Mr Powell was better employed writing and reading classical poetry than stirring up racial prejudice.

Poetry International 74 was the first without our beloved mascot, Wystan Auden. I presented 'The Vertical Man', a programme of Wystan's poetry chosen and introduced by me, with John Betjeman, Irene Worth and Michael York. People seemed to find it an interesting and enjoyable occasion, but I was disappointed with the performances of the three readers I had engaged. John, who had refused to rehearse, stumbled his way through the poems, fluffing and mispronouncing all over the place; Irene over-acted outrageously (perhaps in a well-intentioned attempt to compensate for John), performing one of the poems in a strange imitation of Humphrey Bogart; and Michael, though he gave the most sensitive readings, was simply very nervous, and showed it. ('This is the first live audience I've played to since my Old Vic days', he muttered apprehensively to me as we walked on stage.)

In 1975 I initiated an additional poetry festival in London, with 'Poetry Week at the Wigmore', which occupied the final week of July. On each of seven evenings, I allowed a different organization to present its own event. On Monday, the Poetry Society; Tuesday, the Poetry Book Society; Wednesday, *The New Review*; Thursday, the Arts Council (we featured poets from *New Poetry I*); Friday, the Apollo Society; Saturday, the Barrow Poets. On Sunday, to end the week, we presented my choice of 'Poetry of the Macabre', a rehash of the programme I had already presented at Cheltenham and was shortly to do also for the BBC. My readers at the Wigmore Hall were Vincent Price, star of countless horror films, and Fenella Fielding.

Our six visiting poets at Poetry International 75, later in the summer, included the elderly Nicolas Guillen from Cuba, Stefan Aug Doinas, from Romania, and Atukwei Okai (whom I had known years earlier in London as John Okai) from Ghana. One of the most popular events of the week was 'An Evening Without Philip Larkin', in which Harold Pinter, Ian Hamilton and I read verse and prose by Philip. Other attractions included 'The Fate of Felicity Fark in the Land of the Media', a scurrilous verse epic with a message for our times, by Clive James, read by the author and Russell Davies; 'The Poetry of Lust', perverse and licentious verse introduced by that master of the genre, George MacBeth, and read by Susan Musgrave and myself; and 'Grouping-Groping', a programme devised and presented by Cicely Berry with actors from the Royal Shakespeare Company, and less sexually arousing than might be inferred from its title.

Poetry International came to an end with the 1976 festival. We had six not very good American poets (who had been touring Great Britain under the auspices of the Arts Council to celebrate the American Bicentennial Year), as well as poets from Italy, Jamaica and the United Kingdom, among them Robert Graves, who was by then virtually in his dotage but who still exuded 'star quality'. The ICA sideshows involved, among others, Clive James, Kingsley Amis, Maxine Audley and Richard Pascoe. We were losing impetus, we were finding it difficult to procure foreign poets of sufficient stature whom we had not already engaged in previous years, and the younger, lesser-known poets were not attracting audiences. I felt it was time to 'reculer pour mieux sauter'. Unfortunately, the times have not, since then, been propitious, and we never managed to *sauter* again. I was glad, however, that, in addition to the poets we had advertised in advance, we were able to present Natalya Gorbanevskaya from the USSR. She had survived two periods of arrest in Moscow for her ardent support of Siniavsky and Daniel, and her participation in the brave Red Square demonstration against the Russian invasion of Czechoslovakia. After enduring detention in the notorious Kaschenko mental hospital, she had escaped to Paris. Reliable critics regarded her as one of the best contemporary Russian poets, and it was perhaps fitting that she should have been the very last poet to appear on the Poetry International stage.

In 1976 I visited Australia at the invitation of the Adelaide Festival of the Arts, to give the opening address in their Writers' Week, but also to advise the Australia Council in Sydney on various matters of organization and policy. I made myself unpopular in some quarters by expressing my doubts as to the wisdom of their spending large sums on grants to writers. Nothing could stop writers from writing, I assured the Literature Board of the Council. The writers needed help with publication and distribution of their books, not handouts to encourage them to write. I could have saved my breath, for the Australia Council continues to fling money indiscriminately at the talented and the untalented. They then frequently have to thrust grants at publishers to coerce them into publishing the books that have been written, which the bookshops fail to sell and which no one even wants to borrow from libraries.

It was during 1976 that a form of civil war broke out in the ranks of the Poetry Society. At my instigation, the Arts Council had investigated the Society and its affairs, and had produced a highly critical report, in which I had no hand, but which, of course, the Poetry Society rejected. The Society's Executive Council was, in those days, a strange assemblage. There was a handful of talented poets in the Society, but they rarely got a chance to make their voices heard.

If the Society was to survive (and I always wanted it to survive, not to be 'snuffed out'), the non-talents and eccentrics had to be weeded out of the governing body. As the Arts Council's assessor, it was my duty to attend meetings of the Executive Council, which were not only absolute torture but were also usually held on Saturday afternoons. The level of debate was subterranean, and it was only rarely about poetry. Usually they were arguing and shouting at one another about the most inconsequential matters imaginable.

Attempts by the Arts Council to bring a respectable Poetry Society Executive Committee into being were stoutly resisted. One Saturday afternoon, I found myself yet again at a meeting, waiting for it to begin. I was accompanied by Tony Field, our Finance Director, whom I had cajoled into sharing my wasted afternoon. They were nearly half an hour late in starting, because they were too busy shouting accusations at one another about the Chairman's desk being moved without permission, or something equally ridiculous. Finally, having had enough of this, I took a deep breath, projected my voice as though I were declaiming at the Theatre Royal, Drury Lane, and managed to make myself heard above the clamour. 'For Christ's sake pull yourselves together and start the bloody meeting,' I yelled. 'I have better things to do than waste my weekends here.'

What the Arts Council's investigating team had failed to achieve in months I accomplished in seconds. One of the poets, Jeff Nuttall, stood up. 'I am not going to bow down to this kind of official censorship,' he exclaimed. 'I resign in protest.' 'So do I,' said another, Bob Cobbing. And, one by one, their followers said the same. They marched out of the room, and I asked the Secretary to be certain to record their resignations in the minutes, for fear they should come to what senses they possessed and march back in again. But they didn't return. Was ever a victory so easily, so inadvertently achieved?

The *Guardian* reported the affair in jocular vein:

> Shelley would get a nasty shock if he could see the Poetry Society now. The latest schism [occurred] at the weekend when 12 of the members resigned from the 30-strong Council of the Society, and asked all fellow-rhymers to boycott their proceedings . . . The affair seems to have been brought to a head by an impatient interjection at Saturday's Council meeting from Mr Charles Osborne, Literature Director of the Arts Council and charged with overseeing how the Society spends £54,000 of the Council's and taxpayers' money.
>
> The initial sticking-point was apparently whether a desk and chair should be provided for the secretary of the Association of Little Presses at Earl's Court Square. 'It was really a matter of great principle,' said Mr McSweeney [Chairman of the Poetry Society]. 'I discovered after instructing the General Secretary to do this four or five weeks ago that it still hadn't been done. There was an argument . . .' Mr Nuttall and Mr Cobbing said that they feared Mr Osborne taking control of the Society.

What silly billies, as Mr Healey might or might not have said. But, for some weeks after this delightful walkout, I received frequent phone calls at home in the middle of the night. When I answered, no one was there, not even a heavy breather, except once, when a voice said, 'Charles Osborne? A bomb has been planted in your flat, and it is timed to explode ten minutes from now.' I thought that unlikely, but it seemed prudent to call the police, who arrived within five minutes and made a cursory search of every room, by which time the ten minutes were up, and there had been no explosion. 'Who might have made such a threat to you?' the officer-in-charge asked me. Was I involved in Irish politics? Arab–Israeli conflicts? No, I told him, but there were these poets in Earl's Court . . . He looked sceptical. 'Poets are not usually violent people, are they, sir?' he asked. 'I can think of no more violent group of individuals,' I replied.

Later in the year, Auberon Waugh began to raise his shiny head again.

In the *Spectator* he referred to me as an 'odious literary buccaneer' because he disliked some of the magazines subsidized by the Arts Council. And, in *Private Eye*, I was an 'opinionated, second-rate and ineffably conceited power maniac' who was forcing the Arts Council to pour thousands of pounds 'into something called the Commonwealth Community Writers' Workshop'.

'Not true: not even a penny. Please ask him to apologize,' I wrote in the next issue of *Private Eye*. 'On the other hand,' I continued,

> please do not ask him to apologize for referring to me in the same piece as ignorant, illiterate and loutish, for in addition to possessing all these qualities, I am also so ridiculously vain that I would much rather he continued his schoolboyish abuse than that he should ignore me. I am delighted to be his obsession, though I fear that he can never be mine.

That silenced the funny little fellow for a time.

In the summer of 1977, we mounted another 'Poetry Week at the Wigmore', since our previous year's events had been so enthusiastically received. We opened the week with 'What, All This for a Song?', a programme of verse by Poets Laureate through the ages, read by Anna Calder-Marshall and William Squire. This was to have been compiled and presented by the contemporary Poet Laureate and myself. However, at short notice Betj went off to make a TV film instead ('I hate to let an Aussie down, old cock, but . . .') and I found myself having to compile, write and introduce the programme. Our week ended with a dramatized reading of the Auden–Isherwood play, *The Dog Beneath the Skin*, which I directed. Tony Beckley was excellent as the Dog, William Squire and Jonathan Cecil played the other leading roles, and Rohan McCullogh and I handled all the smaller parts.

When Roy Fuller resigned from the Arts Council in 1977, a woman called Elizabeth Thomas (not the Elizabeth Thomas who is currently a Council member) showed interest in being appointed Chairman of the Literature Panel. After I had suggested to the Chairman of the Council, Kenneth Robinson, that the Minister be asked to appoint Melvyn Bragg to the Council, so that he could subsequently be made Chairman of the Panel, Mrs Thomas informed Melvyn that the Panel wanted her to be its Chairman, and suggested that he should not accept. The subsequent debate led to her leaving the Council and Melvyn Bragg being appointed.

The press attempted, sourly, to brand Melvyn purely as a 'TV personality', the *Guardian* claiming that his appointment marked a breach in tradition. 'Recent holders of the Literature Panel's chairmanship,' it said, 'have been critics or academics like Professor Frank Kermode and Stuart Hampshire.' When this point was put to me by a *Guardian* reporter, I agreed with him. 'I would say,' I replied, 'that the appointment is a conscious attempt to bring a creative writer to the post.'

Melvyn and I had been friends for many years when he became Panel Chairman in 1977 (we had first met when I appeared in a TV panel game he produced for the BBC in the sixties), and we were both pleased at the prospect of working together to hammer out a realistic and practicable literature policy for the Arts Council. We were jointly interviewed in *The Times* by Ion Trewin, at that time its Literary Editor and a member of the Council's Literature Panel:

> Charles Osborne, Literature Director, thinks the Panel set its sights too low in the past. What attracted Bragg to the job? He could well have turned it down on the grounds that his new job – editing and presenting London Weekend's *The South Bank Show* after a long spell with the BBC – was taking up all his time. But Bragg is also a writer.
>
> Says Bragg: 'Publishing is in a funny state – partly booming, partly in difficulties, and it's literature that is in none too healthy a condition. You can see it in fiction, first novels in particular. Perhaps we need a national publishing house? Or perhaps we should simply increase the chance of new writing rewarding a publisher with a bigger public.'
>
> Therefore he believes that the first aim of the Literature Panel should be to identify what is best in contemporary writing and then ensure it reaches more people.
>
> Charles Osborne agrees: 'We don't just mean "little press material", but mainstream fiction and poetry.' Bragg would like to see help going to small bookshops who want to sell literature – not just best-sellers – but find it economically difficult or impossible. 'Why can't the Arts Council subsidize a special section or room in a shop for fiction and poetry?' he asks. 'It could say that this space wouldn't be there, but for the Arts Council's help.'

The relationship between Director and Panel Chairman at the Arts Council could sometimes be a difficult one; for, in theory at any rate, both were the same kind of person (by which I mean that both were assumed to be experts or practitioners in their appropriate art-form), and so there was a danger of their treading on each other's toes. This was perhaps less of a problem in some of the other departments, especially if the Director saw himself or herself simply as the 'servant' of the Panel.

There were never any problems thrown up by the professional relationship of Melvyn and myself, and I think this was not only because we knew each other well, but also because we liked and respected each other. We could, when necessary, differ, without either of us taking offence. In fact we differed very seldom, for we shared many of the same ideas about the sponsorship of literature. When Melvyn was appointed, we thought of ourselves as likely, in tandem, to achieve a number of objectives. If we did not, in the long run, achieve many of them, this was in large part due to intransigence on the part of some of the Panel and the bureaucratic pusillanimity of some Council members.

During Melvyn's time at the Council we did make determined efforts to lead first the Panel and then the Council to the adoption of a properly considered literature policy. (Actually, although one has to use this kind of language at the Arts Council, I'm really not keen on the word 'policy', or on the concept.) Melvyn and I did improve the procedures, due mainly to him, for as Chairman he proved much more adept at persuading the Panel through patience and courtesy than I through amused exasperation.

In 1978 the Council, in an attempt to put its house in order, set up a Working Party to examine its organization and procedures. The Working Party was headed by Lord Hutchinson, Vice-Chairman of the Council and one of its most popular members. Jeremy Hutchinson, QC is a man who combines sharpness of intellect with good humour. It is impossible not to like and admire him, and I was not at all surprised when, in due course, he produced a superb report, with a number of proposals for improving our practices. The Council acted upon far too few of them, which is why in 1984 it found itself compelled to undertake a much wider-ranging review of its structure and procedures. In 1985, at the end of this exercise, when it came to consider the changes proposed, the Council still found it difficult to approach the proposals with an open mind, for it prefers complacent reminiscence and prejudice to concentrated, unfettered thought. It finally contrived to pull itself together, perhaps having realized that, if it had failed to do so, an exasperated government – either the present Conservative administration, or the next one, which will, one imagines, not be Conservative – would pull the plug on it.

In giving evidence to Jeremy Hutchinson's Working Party in 1978, I concentrated on two procedures which I thought most urgently required attention: that by which recommendations to offer or to refuse grant-aid were made to the Council; and that by which such recommendations were considered by the Council.

The system in operation at the time, whereby a large panel of 'advisers' considered general policy, while a smaller group with quasi-executive status made direct recommendations to the Council regarding specific grants (bypassing the Panels) was not only cumbersome but also apparently confusing to some of the members of both groups. Members of the large group, the Panel, sometimes felt they were missing the real action if they were not also members of the smaller group, the Finance Committee, while members of the Finance Committee were not always clear about their relationship to the Panel.

A further problem was the familiar difficulty of extracting firm decisions or even firm views from a body too large to be anything but a forum for discussion. Melvyn and I moved towards a solution of that particular problem by continuing to reduce the size of the Literature Panel (and when Marghanita Laski succeeded Melvyn, we continued this process). But, in my view, a more sensible procedure would have been to combine the functions of Panel and Finance Committee in one small Executive Committee of about six members, at least three of whom would need to be numerate as well as literate. (Our Finance Director, Tony Field, was heard to declare more than once that he despaired of ever finding on our Literature Finance Committee anyone capable of understanding a balance sheet.)

I also told Jeremy Hutchinson's working party that I thought the Council's Finance and Policy Committee would function more efficiently if those of its members who were Panel Chairmen were replaced by the departmental Directors. The highly specialized task of this committee is, I still feel, too important to be left entirely to part-time Council members. However, this suggestion did not commend itself to anyone. Both my proposals were for a mix of professional paid staff and unpaid Council members or advisers on committees which could be given executive status. If one has to have advisers, I still consider this would be the best way to use them.

Meanwhile, the arts debate continued, widening to include the question of grants to individual artists in general. When the Australian composer Malcolm Williamson, Master of the Queen's Musick, failed to obtain one of our commission awards (of £5000), his disappointment was expressed with a certain Antipodean vigour. The Arts Council, he said, had heaped a long list of humiliations on him over the years. What annoyed him particularly was 'this vexed Anglo-Saxon habit of glossing over matters concerning money'.

The *Guardian* was moved to run a series of articles on state patronage.

John Cunningham, the author of the articles, quoted the Council's Deputy Secretary-General, Angus Stirling, and myself. Angus explained the reasons why the Council concentrated its resources primarily on supporting the performance (or publishing) of the art-form rather than on grants to individual artists. I was quoted, directly and indirectly, on the subject of grants to writers:

> The most sanguine view comes from Charles Osborne, Literature Director of the Arts Council. He knows of no writers who would have given up simply because they were unable to get a public grant while producing a novel.
>
> The Literature Panel is interested, he says, in being sure that any creative work has 'a more than reasonable' chance of being published before an award is made. And some evidence of success helps an application. 'We don't like to think we're taking on an Arts Council pensioner when we take on a new writer.'
>
> Even so, Mr Osborne isn't as hard as nails, because he realizes that writers can go on having good novels published yet not make any money from them. With poets he seems a little harder, because too much bounty is going in that direction for his liking: 'We're in danger of breeding a race of lyric poets who are incapable of putting pen to paper unless the Arts Council waves a large amount of money in front of them.'
>
> Part of the answer to making the system more effective is to realize that we need mixed patronage for a mixed economy. The state won't bear all the burden. Writers could be better helped, according to Mr Osborne, if there was official help in the distribution of their books. The book trade, he reckons, is pretty inefficient – many more copies could be sold if they were available in places presently without good bookshops.

Now, some years later, a couple of distribution schemes have finally been brought into being with the help of the Council's Literature Department (one of them with the involvement of Regional Arts Associations). Ironically, they have been born at a time when the Arts Council has decided to diminish its role in the funding of literature. They will have to be nourished, somehow.

Roy Shaw's five-year term of appointment as Secretary-General came to an end in 1979. It was open to the Council either to advertise for his successor or to extend Roy's term for a further four years, which would take him up to retirement age. In the opinion of the senior staff, he had proved to be an unsuitable Secretary-General, a view which was shared by a large number of our members of staff just below senior level (Deputy and Assistant Directors, and what the Council calls officers). A member of the Music Department Staff (who is now Music Director) reported to the Chairman, Kenneth Robinson, that if Roy Shaw were to be re-appointed there would be several resignations.

The senior members of staff (that is, those of us who comprised the Arts Council's Directorate) chose not to threaten the Council with resignations, but we were united in our desire to see the Council take this opportunity to make a more suitable appointment, and we met to discuss how this could be brought about. I suggested that we seek the advice of a former Chairman of the Council, Lord Goodman, whom I knew shared our doubts about Roy Shaw.

It was important, thought Arnold, in order to convince the Arts Council, that we gain the support of the Council's most prestigious clients, the Chairmen and Artistic Directors of the national companies: the Royal Opera House, the National Theatre and the Royal Shakespeare Company.

Unfortunately we had come together rather too late to be effective. We had the sympathy and support of a few Council members, one of whom, Lawrence Gowing, agreed to make the anti-Shaw case at the Council meeting at which a decision was to be made. The Secretary-General and Directors were asked to leave the meeting while the question was under discussion, but of course we heard about it immediately afterwards from several Council members. (The Deputy Secretary-General, Angus Stirling, was with us *en principe*, for he was especially disturbed by the low level of staff morale, but since he hoped to be appointed to replace Roy Shaw he did not think it proper that he play an active role in our campaign.)

At the Council meeting, apparently, Lawrence Gowing lost the argument by over-stating his case against Roy Shaw to such an extent that Roy gained some sympathy from one or two members who had entered the meeting intending not to support him. The question was put to a vote, and by a majority of one it was agreed to extend Roy's term of appointment.

The following Monday, the Chairman called my fellow-Directors and myself to his office. 'This is it,' I thought. 'He will say, "Gentlemen, your plot is discovered, and has failed. May I have your resignations by the end of the day?" ' But he did not say anything of the kind. Instead he announced the Council's decision, adding that he knew this would be a disappointment to us but that he hoped we would rally round and support the Secretary-General.

Roy, at our next weekly Directorate meeting, confessed to some of his shortcomings, and said he hoped, with our help, that future relations between us would be happier. They were not. He continued to be more interested in adult education than in the arts, and his plain, blunt Yorkshireman style remained as off-putting to everyone else as it had always been. The Music Director for instance, had left to run an Arts Centre in Hong Kong.

I continued my style of passive resistance. I once had occasion to prevent a chum of Roy's, whom most of us considered an inappropriate candidate, from being appointed Deputy Secretary-General to replace Angus Stirling, who had decided to leave us and join the National Trust. The post had been advertised, and a short list of candidates had yet to be interviewed. Roy's friend had been unwise enough to inform several people at dinner parties that he was to be the next Deputy Secretary-General of the Arts Council, and this gossip made its way back to two of my fellow-Directors, who passed it on to me. At the next Directorate meeting, therefore, I simply announced to Roy and my colleagues that I had heard a very amusing story: poor old so-and-so was telling the world that he was to be Angus Stirling's successor at the Arts Council. Everyone but Roy hooted with laughter at this, and we heard no more of the matter.

In 1979 I finally had to yield to pressure from that gathering of *tricoteuses* known as the Literature Panel, and announce that the Council was to withdraw subsidy from *The New Review*. The press, which had done nothing but publish criticism of the Council, and of me personally, for supporting the magazine, now wept crocodile tears and said how monstrous it was of the Arts Council to let this magazine of international reputation die. There did not seem at the time much to be gained from castigating either the press or the Panel. The damage had been done, and it was true that the magazine had not been managed as efficiently as it had been edited.

'Why is it,' Roy Shaw asked me one day, 'that I'm always reading about you in the press, or seeing you quoted? The other Directors don't stick their noses over the parapet to the same extent.' I could only reply that perhaps writers leaped into print to complain about the Arts Council more readily than composers, painters or dancers, and thus I found myself having to comment in public on Arts Council affairs much more frequently than my colleagues.

I certainly have never courted publicity in my capacity as an Arts Council Director. (As a writer, yes: when my American publisher asks me to make myself available for publicity purposes, naturally I agree.) Much of my Arts Council publicity was unwelcome, and some of it was quite ludicrous. For instance, one day in 1980, I read over someone's shoulder in a bus the headline of the Londoner's Diary in the *Evening Standard*: 'CHARLES OSBORNE ACCUSED OF CENSORSHIP'. How amusing, I thought. There's someone with the same name as myself, and he's been censoring something. But when I bought a copy of the newspaper, to show to a friend as a joke, I discovered that the story was about me:

> No sooner had Charles Osborne extricated himself from the row over his biography of W. H. Auden than he walked slap into another one – this time in his infinitely more powerful capacity as Literary [*sic*] Director of the Arts Council.
>
> He has been accused of using Arts Council grants as a method of censorship by Anthony Rudolf, who has just had a £3000 grant application for the Menard Poetry Press turned down by Osborne.
>
> According to Rudolf, this is the second time Osborne has rejected one of his applications. 'Last time I got up a petition of well-known people and I managed to save the Press,' Rudolf told me.
>
> Mr Osborne's letter to Mr Rudolf did in fact suggest another list of publishing projects would get serious consideration though the most Mr Rudolf could hope for was £1500 . . .

In fact, as I had occasion to inform the newspaper's readers a few days later, we had offered Mr Rudolf £1500, a generous increase on the £1120 he had received the previous year. How many *Standard* readers, other than Mr Rudolf and myself, could have been in the slightest degree interested in whether Charles Osborne had been accused of censorship, or even aware of who Charles Osborne was?

At Roy Shaw's instigation, in March 1980 we held at 105 Piccadilly an Open Forum on the subject, 'The Arts Council and Literature'. Roy chaired the event, and Melvyn Bragg and I were there to lead the discussion and to answer questions. We advertised the Forum widely, and well in advance, hoping that a few members of the general public, actual readers with an interest in the subject, might turn up to augment the usual contingent of writers, journalists, and small-press publishers. But, of course, they didn't, and Melvyn and I found ourselves facing the familiar and hostile few. It continued to be a disappointment to me that, whereas one could interest the general educated public, the consumers of the arts, in questions concerning the subsidizing of theatre, music or the visual arts, the only people interested in the subject of literature subsidy were those queuing up to apply for it.

There were also, in 1980, a few more fights within the Arts Council. I had occasion to admonish the Panel collectively. 'Once again,' I wrote to them all,

> certain members of the Panel have chosen to disregard the requirement that Arts Council business be considered confidential. As a result, statements have appeared in the press to the effect that the Panel has 'decided' to discontinue offering grants to writers. (It is, of course, not within the Panel's power to make decisions on behalf of the Council, which will be considering the Panel's advice in due course.)
>
> All members of the Arts Council Advisory Panels undertake upon joining to respect the confidentiality, where appropriate, of business discussed at meetings. If it is not possible to keep Literature Panel business confidential, then the range of subjects placed on Literature Panel agendas may have to be restricted to non-confidential matters.
>
> It is unfortunate that the work of the Literature Panel should be shown in such a negative light before the Arts Council's overall policy for literature has been agreed, and the recommendation to terminate grants to writers can be seen in relation to the whole picture and to any new schemes to be implemented.

One member in particular, the novelist Margaret Forster, admitted to being one of the sources of the leaks, and in due course I found myself having to contradict her in the columns of the *Standard*. Margaret honourably resigned from the Panel but subsequently withdrew her resignation. To me, she wrote:

> Wow – poor old *innocent* other panel members getting that shot across the bows. I feel even more guilty. The thing is, I couldn't stick to resigning without seeming ungracious, and the Queen Mum and I, tho' dreadful blatherers, find that so hard. I wasn't at all offended by yr reprimand (fully justified) – I'm just amazed I've got through 3 years without incurring yr wrath before. Anyway, I will now reform for my final year.

Margaret Forster stayed on for her final year, and then published an article in *The Times*, entitled 'Why I Quit the Arts Council's Literature Panel'. 'Charles Osborne has told *The Times*,' she complained, 'that he doubts whether I ever understood what the Literature Panel was about in the first place. In a flash of divine anger he said at our last meeting that I had never grasped that the Panel's function was *advisory*. There I was, he said irritably, forever making trouble over utterly trivial matters like individual grants when the Council needed me, in these troubled times, to help it decide on much weightier matters.' The rest of her article made it clear that, after four years, she still seemed incapable of directing her attention to such questions as whether the Council should give individual grants, should support literary magazines, should subsidize publishers. All she wanted was to be allowed to decide whether Michael or Fay or Edna or Paul got the bursaries for which they had applied.

I felt it important that she should be replied to publicly and at length. Although the Council would have preferred a dignified silence, I published my article in *The Times*. I had given it the title, 'Why I do not quit the Arts Council's Literature Department', in consonance with Margaret's title, but *The Times* printed it under the terser headline, 'No Time to Quit the Arts Council':

> Margaret Forster's resignation from the Arts Council's Literature Advisory Panel, of which she wrote in *The Times* on September 21, under the headline, 'Why I quit the Arts Council's Literature Panel', comes at a time when certain policy shifts are being implemented, to the dismay of a small but vociferous faction in the literary world.
>
> More interesting than the policy itself is the fact that Miss Forster was one of its major instigators. I remember with affection her passionate outburst against the wastefulness of the former scheme of grants to writers and her articulate defence of standards, and am sorry that she should have left us as soon as her case had been accepted by the Council. Surely she did not think we were a sinking ship?
>
> As for the polite request by the Society of Authors that I resign, I expect my fellow Directors of the Arts Council would agree with me that working for it is distinctly less agreeable than it used to be, if only because the state of the visual arts, music, drama and literature is much less buoyant than it was 25 years ago.
>
> However, if that makes the job of an Arts Council Director more difficult, at the same time it makes it more interesting. This is no time to quit.

In addition to its specialist arts staff in each department, the Council has, for each art-form that it subsidizes, an advisory Panel of 12 or more members who meet approximately every three months. The members of these Panels are usually people with expertise in some area or another of the relevant art or its propagation. The Literature Panel, for instance, includes writers, publishers, a librarian, and even one or two readers.

I do not mention readers flippantly. It is not often understood that the Arts Council exists not to serve various sectional interests (musicians, composers, playwrights, theatre directors, writers, arts administrators) but the public.

The Panels advise the Council and the specialist departments. Margaret Forster implied in her article that the Council rarely took its Literature Panel's advice. The opposite is true: since I joined the staff in 1966 the occasions on which the Council has acted against the Panel's advice have been disquietingly few. The same could be said of the Council's relationship with its other Panels.

There is no Arts Council Literature Policy – rather a number of I hope, sensible decisions all taken at regular intervals, with shifts of emphasis to meet changing situations.

The Council's current thinking about the ways it subsidizes literature is set out in a paper appearing in its *Bulletin* to be published next week.

The paper makes the point that the success of an Arts Council 'policy' is not to be measured solely or even principally in terms of the money expended on it. That section of the public which cares – and I mean the public, not the 50 familiar, and by no means disinterested, faces who pop up to say the same things whenever the work of the Arts Council is discussed in public – will surely be relieved to learn that the staff of the Arts Council's literature department is doing its best not to squander public money.

The Council believes it can help the creators of literature, and those who read them, most effectively by increasing the opportunities for writers of merit to be published and, when published, bought. A sizeable portion of the sum allocated to literature is now being used to subsidize publishers in several ways, in order to help the production of certain books, and also their distribution.

It is ironic that, in a recent article in *The Times* (September 25), Mr Vincent Brome should have written of the Arts Council that 'At the point of greatest hardship they have seen fit to revolutionize their grant system and are now backing already successful writers in preference to those who still struggle to realize their potential', especially since, earlier in the same article, he bewailed the plight of several distinguished novelists whose works, he claims, 'are sitting unrealized in English publishing houses'. In fact, Arts Council grants are available to publishers *for precisely the kind of novel Mr Brome has described.*

I return to the matter of my position. I have worked with a series of distinguished Chairmen of the Literature Panel and maintained the most cordial relations with them all.

Our present Literature Panel under Marghanita Laski's chairmanship is at last a compact group of people from several literary fields. They give their time generously, and they argue constructively, for which I am grateful.

It is true that the writers' unions had called for my resignation. In reply I wrote to the Chairman of the Society of Authors, of which I had been a member for several years: 'In view of the tone of your recent letter to the Secretary-General of the Arts Council, I feel I have no option but to resign – not, however, from the Arts Council but from the Society of Authors.'

The call for my resignation had come as a direct consequence of a report we had asked a young sociologist to write on our scheme of grants to writers, which had been in operation for some years. (That was a mistake: steer clear of sociologists and economists, the witch-doctors of modern society.) The evidence which the sociologist had gathered from his interviews with grant recipients suggested that no books had been written with an Arts Council grant which would not also have been written without the grant. The sociologist didn't like the evidence he had unearthed, and ended his report with recommendations which owed more to his blinkered political sense than to his ability to draw conclusions from facts.

In discussing the report with a *Times* journalist, I appear to have said, 'A number of mediocrities have received grants from us in the past few years, and we ought not to have been handing out money to these writers,' It was no more than a statement of the truth, but it unleashed a great fury in the writers' organizations, and it ended up in the *Observer*'s 'Sayings of the Week', along with more contentious statements by Tony Benn ('Elections are so healing'), Sir Keith Joseph ('The way to full employment is to allow jobs to occur'), John Osborne ('Writers don't need love: all they require is money'), and President Reagan's remark to his wife, after he had been shot and wounded by a maniac ('Honey, I forgot to duck').

I was not, to put it mildly, the most popular creature in the British literary world. A few people, however, came to my defence. Peter Jones, Managing Director of Carcanet Press, wrote in *The Times*: 'No-one has approached us, long-standing clients of the Arts Council, for testimonials for the controversial Literature Director. If they had approached us, we would have told them that he has advised and assisted our developments always in a responsive and forthright manner, this last quality, forthrightness, being, it would appear, his chief offence.'

And Melvyn Bragg, in 'Arts Counsel', his regular column in *Punch*, wrote:

> Charles Osborne has become an increasingly controversial figure as Director of the Literature Panel. When I worked with him I found him helpful, blunt, knowledgeable and, understandably, a man of firm opinions. Once again, in the dogged continuation of the decision to declare any interest, I must say that I regard him as a friend.
>
> Why does he get so much stick from that literary world his job supposedly exists to serve?
>
> He is not the invisible civil servant. When attacked he responds often brusquely, sometimes fiercely. The general frustration many writers feel about literature policy focuses on him because he is there: chairmen and Panel members come and go; Charles Osborne, with his increased powers now given to all the Council's Directors, sits apparently forever. He is strict in his interpretation and expedition of Council policy and, when that is not concerned, will not bend and so far will not break either. The powerful pressure group claiming money for community writing workshops, for example, meets with little sympathy because the Council, he would say, exists to aid professional writers. He would also be likely to add that considerations of quality would wipe out such workshops from any serious concern. He is a poet and an élitist; an authority on Verdi; a broadcaster, a translator and able to write books on his friend W. H. Auden and on Agatha Christie. He is not only visible, he can appear protean – thus sinning against the English preference for single commitment. He rubs some people up the wrong way: who doesn't?
>
> The core reason for the criticism, I suspect, is that people still believe him to be the instigator of all literature policy. The fact is that he carries out a policy decided on by the Council. Consequently Osborne is too often regarded as the bad news and not as the messenger. After all this, it is only fair to say that he has a substantial number of supporters and admirers whose views, as is usual in this sort of thing, tend to be unvoiced and uncanvassed. He is certainly devoted to the job and will be there for a long time yet.

When he wrote those words, Melvyn had ceased to be Chairman of the Literature Panel, and had been succeeded by Marghanita Laski. The Chairman of the Council was now Sir William Rees-Mogg. In the autumn of 1982, as Roy Shaw's extension of his appointment as Secretary-General was coming to an end, the Council advertised for a new Secretary-General. Though it would have been unrealistic for me to imagine I was likely to be chosen, I decided to apply again, on the same principle as before. Arming myself with the sponsorship of Lord Goodman, Lord Hutchinson, Melvyn Bragg and Professor Karl Miller, I put in my application.

In due course, William Rees-Mogg courteously informed me that he proposed not to short-list me, for there were two or three preferred candidates, and he assumed, correctly, that I would not wish to be interviewed as a mere formality. It transpired that Arnold Goodman had agreed to act as sponsor for three of the candidates. In the chronological order in which he had given his agreement they were Luke Rittner, myself, and Anthony Field. I understand that this was not necessarily his order of preference.

After a hiccup or two, when Luke Rittner's appointment was prematurely announced and subsequently resisted by the Council, Luke was eventually appointed. Knowing that most of the Directors had made known their objection to the appointment on the grounds of Luke's inexperience and comparative youth, Marghanita Laski, as Vice-Chairman of the Council, asked me if I thought I could work with him. 'Why not?' I replied. 'After all, I've managed to work with Roy for nine years!'

Frankness compels me to admit that, although I had neither met nor had any form of contact with Luke Rittner, I associated myself with my colleagues' protest, and sent a strongly worded message by Western Union from New York, whither Ken Thomson and I had fled for Christmas (and where I was making one of my annual appearances on the Met-Texaco Opera Quiz). But when Luke settled into the job I soon came to appreciate his qualities. He manages the staff firmly but fairly, has proved perfectly capable of dealing with the Arts Council's clients, and so far hasn't even made any false moves in negotiating with local authorities, whose representatives can be, I am told by colleagues, tiresome creatures.

Shortly before he left the Council in the middle of 1983, Roy Shaw tried to persuade me to leave at the same time. 'I'm telling you this for your own good,' he said. 'I happen to know that Rees-Mogg and Rittner intend to sack you. I want to spare you that embarrassment. Why not resign now? You don't need to go on working for the Arts Council. You have your own career as a writer.' I thanked Roy for his kindly advice, but added that, as no one had any reason to sack me, I would stay on and take my chances. I later discovered that attempts had been made to persuade at least one other Director to resign.

Shortly before Roy's retirement, his friend Richard Hoggart came to the end of his period as a member of the Council. When he was not invited by the Minister to continue for a further term, he made a public fuss, claiming that his non-reappointment was 'a political act'. I doubt that it was, but even if he was right, had he taken into account the possibility that his original appointment to the Council may also have been a political act?

Marghanita Laski may not have proved to be one of nature's Chairmen during her time at the head of the Literature Panel (nor, I feel sure, would she wish to have been), but she was an endearing and stimulating colleague. We enjoyed working together and, though we occasionally differed, we more frequently found ourselves in agreement and at odds with the Panel. Eventually, Marghanita tired of the unfair attacks on herself in the press, and resigned from the Panel, though fortunately not from the Council, whose Vice-Chairman she remained until March 1986.

I attempted to dissuade her from resigning as Chairman of the Panel, not only because I did not want to lose her but also because the Council member most likely to be asked to succeed her was Robert Woof, a Reader in English at Newcastle University who had been appointed to the Council as a *bona fide* regional member. I thought it important that the Chairman of the Literature Panel be a person of some standing in the literary world. We had so far been fortunate in our Chairmen: C. Day Lewis, Angus Wilson, Frank Kermode, Stuart Hampshire, Roy Fuller, Melvyn Bragg, Marghanita Laski – people of disparate qualities, but all well-known literary names. And now, Robert Woof?

Robert Woof it was to be. A pleasant fellow, but not the best organized Chairman I have ever worked with. He often latched onto insignificant detail, to the exasperation of myself, my staff, and most of the Panel. Meetings now became an interminable and disjointed monologue by Robert. Three years after his appointment, people in the literary world continue to ask me who he is and what are his qualifications.

Another of those silly Literature Panel quarrels erupted in 1983 when a member of the Panel, a journalist named Michael Church, wrote a paper criticizing my Department and myself on grounds which he ought to have known perfectly well to be invalid, and then published articles about it, all over the place. I was forced to waste a great deal of time shooting him down whenever he popped up in various journals. (The details are too tediously parochial to be rehearsed in these pages.) My various replies to Mr Church brought me a number of congratulatory letters. 'Your response to the Church onslaught, both in *Publishing News* and in *The Bookseller*, put the record so very straight that I doubt that anyone would dare to bend it again . . . You do clearly justify the expression, "He who laughs last",' wrote one of the Arts Council's major clients.

William Rees-Mogg occasionally gives luncheon parties at 105 Piccadilly to which people prominent in the arts are invited, and at which subjects of current concern are discussed. At lunch one day in March, 1985, there were eight of us around the table in the Boardroom: Sir William Rees-Mogg, Luke Rittner, Sir Stuart Young (Chairman of the BBC), David Puttnam, Sheila Hancock, Lord Birkett (then working for the GLC), Sir Kenneth Robinson (William's predecessor at the Arts Council) and myself. We talked of, among other things, the Council's funding difficulties and how best to deploy our limited resources. A fairly wide range of political attitudes was represented, and it was a relief to find that there was no argument among us as to the desirability of adequate state funding for the arts or the need, in our mixed economy, to seek support from commerce as well. ('When Kenneth Robinson, in addressing William Rees-Mogg, referred jocularly to the Conservatives as 'your party', William was able to protest, plaintively, 'I haven't had a party in twenty years!') Where we differed was in the emphasis we placed upon the various art-forms and, within each discipline, the methods and aims of subsidy we would wish to adopt. What exercised us most was the urgent need to convince the present government that an increase in arts funding could be justified in business terms. Some months later, the Council launched its 'Prospectus for the Arts', initially conceived at that lunch, and written in a style which it was expected the Prime Minister would appreciate. As I write, we have yet to learn what sum will be made available to the Arts Council. If it falls short of £160 million, as I have no doubt it will, the Council will be in a more difficult situation than at any time since its inception. It would then have to take yet another look at its priorities. If it decided not to give any further grants to individuals, it could save approximately £1,400,000 (at 1985–86 levels of expenditure) in England alone, a sum which it could usefully devote to literature.

Even if it receives what it considers to be a satisfactory sum, the Council should give urgent consideration to the ways in which it spends its money. At a time when virtually all of Britain's major artistic institutions are under threat, it is shameful that the Council should still allow large amounts to be thrown away by its staff and its advisory panels on grants which range from the unnecessary to the ludicrous. Each month, the Council receives a list of the grants which have been offered in the preceding month. It can comment on these, though it rarely does, but it cannot reverse any decisions, for it has delegated authority to the Secretary-General and Directors to make grant offers, and by the time it sees the list most of the offers of grant will have been made and accepted.

The present Secretary-General is aware that, under the system which is currently operated, many unwise offers of grants are made, even before he sees the list. He is exploring ways of ensuring that grants which could bring the Council into disrepute are brought to his attention before the grants are actually offered. But he is finding it difficult, especially since he does not have the full support of certain members of his senior staff, who condone and support even the most obviously inappropriate recommendations.

At a recent meeting of the Council's Directorate, Luke Rittner queried one particular grant, which, in his view, was 'an absolute nonsense'. Two of my colleagues immediately said that they regarded that application as one of the best that had been considered in that month. I pointed out that, given the kind of applications we received, it was perfectly possible that both views were correct.

I have before me as I write (in October, 1985), the September Applications List, from which I quote, not because it necessarily contains a larger number of lunatic grants than usual, but because it is the most recent to be available. It gives details of the 129 grants awarded during the month of September, and I list below merely a few of those which, in my opinion, need not, and, in some cases, should not have been given:

Bruce Birchall: Grant £1000
to enable him to undertake a programme of training in typesetting to improve his standard of presentation in play-publishing projects.

Ben Haggarty: Grant £500
to enable him to visit the United States to research the traditions of storytelling there and develop his administrative and research skills.

Susan Haywood: Grant £500
to enable her to spend four weeks in Nicaragua observing various forms of visual communication there.

Stephen Homes: Grant £700
to enable him to visit flamenco dance schools and guitar teachers in Madrid to improve his knowledge and playing of flamenco guitar.

Paul Jackson: Grant £500
to enable him to visit New York to study the role of the contemporary dance accompanist there.

Shobana Jeyasingh: Grant £600
to enable her to visit Madras to undertake training in various types of folk dance.

Graham Marsden: Grant £700
to enable him to undertake training in Chilean and West Indian kite-making and -flying techniques.

Valerie Coffin Price: Grant £1000
to enable her to develop carving skills in relation to the use of coloured stones, and to learn the art of gilding and polychroming stone.

David Pugh: Grant £500
to enable him to undertake a series of piano/music lessons.

Jatinder Verma: Grant £900
to enable him to visit India to spend time at two major centres of theatre there, participate in workshops and undertake field research.

Each of these grants of a few hundred pounds costs the Arts Council a further £1500 to process. For instance, to give a grant of £500 costs £2000, because of the time spent by various people in considering the application, agreeing the grant and handling the paper-work.

The Working Party on Library and Booktrade Relations (known vulgarly as Libtrad) held a one-day conference in January, 1985, at the National Book League, under the title, 'The State v. Literature'. Martyn Goff was Chairman, and the first speaker was Richard Hoggart. 'Don't blame the Arts Council,' Richard urged:

> It is all too easy to lay all the blame on Charles Osborne, who has become the Norman Tebbit of the literary world, the man we love to hate. He likes a fight, it is true, and he likes making what he knows will be taken as outrageous statements. Some of his critics lead with their chins. And any Chairman of the Panel knows that, next to Charles Osborne, they will be the regular target for abuse. Marghanita Laski was right to talk of 'the literary pressure group's total lack of philanthropy'.

Later in his speech, Richard said:

> None of us, writers or others, are owed a living. We have no preemptive right to state support. We do not *have* to write and should be glad of that. As Auden reminded us constantly, writing is one of the few purely 'gratuitous' acts we can perform, thank God. And if enough money does not come in from writing, we can, most of us,

> look for ancillary work . . . I think that, in a society such as ours, most of us should be content to be less than full-time writers; or, if we choose to go full-time, we should be prepared to stake the best balance we can between our 'real' writing and that occasional work which pays the rent and grocers' bills . . . After all, so many good writers today do write in the margins of their time: Philip Larkin, this century's equivalent of the lens-grinder; Charles Causley, who was a teacher for decades; David Lodge; P. H. Newby, who had a very distinguished and taxing career right up to near the top of the hierarchy of the BBC; Raymond Williams. [Richard could well have added himself to this list.] There are many reasons why some people choose that way: some do not like the insecurity of living by the pen; some like the order and formalities of institutional life against which to brace themselves . . . And of course anyone is entirely at liberty to set out on the open sea and take their chances. That can be admirable. What I am doubtful about is their right to grumble as though it is someone else's fault if things do not work out well.

For saying this, Richard incurred the wrath of another speaker, literature's answer to the stage Irishman, Frank Delaney. 'I never thought,' lamented Frank, 'I would see the day when the man who wrote that fine book, *The Uses of Literacy*, would begin to sound like a high Tory.'

The other speakers included Tom Rosenthal, who referred to me as 'my old mate' (I *suppose* that's preferable to being the Arts Council's Norman Tebbit); Sir Frederick Dainton; Lord Donaldson; and Norman Buchan, the Labour party's spokesman on the arts. If Richard Hoggart made the most thought-provoking contributions to the day, Delaney and Buchan tied for the least sensible. Delaney began by saying, 'I am addressing what is largely an Anglo-Saxon audience, noted for its restraint, and I work under the burden of Celtic excess. If I again, as Charles Osborne has accused me in the past, generate more heat than light, it will be because of that Celtic excess.' He then proceeded to generate more heat than light.

I had occasion to shout an interruption from the floor to Norman Buchan's speech. He was advising me, from the platform, to ask the government for four times as much money as I really needed for the support of literature. 'You have always got to say your budget is never big enough,' he exclaimed.

'Not being a politician, I am not a liar,' I retorted.

In the discussion period which followed the formal speeches, I contented myself with correcting inaccuracies. This led to a second clash with

Buchan. All good clean fun, but utterly pointless. Approximately one hundred people, representing various organizations, paid £25 each for the privilege of wasting a day listening to all of this. *Cui bono?*

Some weeks after he succeeded Grey Gowrie as Minister for the Arts, my fellow-Directors and I lunched with Richard Luce at the Arts Council. That Mr Luce proved to be no brighter than the average politician was, I suppose, to be expected; but, if I had hoped that he might display some knowledge of at least one of the arts comparable to Lord Gowrie's informed enthusiasm for poetry and painting, then I was certainly disillusioned. During the meal, there was a certain amount of talk of Arts Council matters, and we all trotted out our usual lines. When the Minister said that he was constantly being asked why the Arts Council did not do more for literature, and asked for my comments, I gave him (politely I hope) the lecturette which I have delivered so frequently that I can now churn it out while thinking of more agreeable subjects. I was sure, I said to the Minister, that when people told him they wanted more money to be given to literature, he always asked them what they meant. No one would dream of demanding more for music, or more for drama, without being more specific. They might want more to be given to the Bristol Old Vic, or the Hallé Orchestra, or the Contemporary Music Network. They might feel deprived of orchestral provision in East Anglia, or neglected by drama and opera touring companies in the west country, but presumably no one could possibly say to the Minister, 'Sir, we in Budleigh Salterton are seriously deprived of literature. It must be given more money by the state.'

'Er, precisely,' said Mr Luce. I then asked him if these cries for more money for literature ever came from the audiences for literature. I suspected that, though he frequently heard from people who attended theatre performances and concerts, the only people who approached him on the subject of literature funding were not readers but the writers themselves. 'Er, precisely,' Mr Luce said again.

Occasionally at the Arts Council I had to do battle by letter. The artist Ian Hamilton Finlay, taking exception to the Arts Council's stationery, wrote to me, 'Your triangle looks silly, and as for you, you are an absolute cunt. If you come here again I will be pleased to fight you. P.S. Do not darken my Second Gate.' When I failed to reply to this, he accused me of arrogance. I don't think it was arrogance that caused me not to reply. I tend to adopt, in correspondence, the tone that has been used by my correspondent, and I feared I would not be able to match the level of Mr Finlay's abuse.

When I received an application for a grant, which was written in excruciatingly limp verse, I replied in kind:

Dear Mr Cuninghame, please go away.
Your poem is dreadful, what more can I say?
You've clearly no talent or feeling for verse
(Though some people say we give grants to far worse.)

I suppose that what has made me most unpopular with the writers' unions is not my epistolatory style but my scepticism as to the usefulness, or indeed the propriety, of many of the grants we have given to writers. For a time we were in danger of turning the Arts Council into a literary soup kitchen. Since 1985, we have restricted the number of writers' bursaries awarded annually to three, but the following are four examples, from 1984, of what I regard as a waste of public money.

Paul Hyland, a thirty-seven-year-old poet living in Devon, was given a bursary 'to help finance a journey up the river Zaire to retrace the steps of Joseph Conrad, Roger Casement, and his own ancestor, Dan Crawford, and work on an account of that adventure, which will be a travel book interspersed with poems'.

Pete Morgan, a poet who has earned his living as a free-lance writer for the last fifteen years, was given a bursary simply in order to encourage him to write more poems. A bursary for a similar purpose went to Penelope Shuttle. Both Pete Morgan and Penelope Shuttle are established poets, but why should they receive bursaries? They will go on writing poetry with or without handouts from the public purse.

James Berry, a fifty-nine-year-old poet living in Brighton, was given a bursary to enable him to visit his native Jamaica, 'to make fresh contact with its language, landscape and history, in order to enrich his work'.

Our advisers on the Literature Panel, however, easy touches though they may be, are nowhere near as gullible as some of those who advise other departments of the Arts Council. I have earlier drawn attention to a few representative examples of the so-called 'training' bursaries: I could have as easily chosen to take my examples from music, drama, dance, art or photography.

The axe fell on my Department when, in the spring of 1984, the Council announced its plans for the next decade in a 44-page booklet, *The Glory of the Garden*, its title taken, unironically, from the poem by Kipling. Development funds were to be found for Art, Dance, Drama and Music in the regions, at the expense of some London-based organizations, and also at the expense of the Council's involvement with Literature. To be precise, my budget for the Literature Department's spending on grants was cut from just under £1,000,000 (in 1984–85) to approximately £500,000 (in 1985–86).

The Council's reasons for taking this step are set forth in paragraph 100 of *The Glory of the Garden*:

> There can be no doubt that, without public subsidy, drama provision in this country would be radically different from what it is today: the network of repertory companies would simply cease to exist on anything like its present scale. If there were no public subsidy for opera, it is very unlikely that large-scale opera performance would take place at all outside a limited annual season at the Royal Opera House. English literature, on the other hand, is sustained by a large and profitable commercial publishing industry. It is a basic ingredient in the school curriculum. It is available to the public through the public library system. In these circumstances, the impact of the Arts Council's subsidy for literature other than poetry is highly marginal.

The announcement that the Arts Council was to reduce its spending on literature came as no surprise, for literature had always sat uncomfortably alongside the Council's other interests. I happen to think that the grants to non-profit-distributing publishers, to literary magazines, and to organizations such as the National Book League and the Poetry Book Society, are the right kinds of grant for the Council to continue to give; but the level of support needed for those areas is closer to the one million pounds I had in 1984 than the half-million I had in 1985.

A consequence of the Council's decision was that three jobs in my department, including those of myself and my deputy, were declared redundant.

(Appropriately, I have been interrupted at this point by a phone call from a *Standard* journalist planning a story on my departure from the Arts Council. A rumour was abroad, he said, to the effect that I was to receive 'a golden handshake of £100,000' from the Council. Could I confirm this? 'The Arts Council has rules regarding redundancy payments,' I told him, 'and they are being followed. I don't think I should mention an amount, for fear of upsetting those kindly souls who will think it too small, or those envious creatures who will claim it's too large.')

My deputy chose to leave precipitately when she was made redundant. I felt I should behave in a statesman-like manner and stay on until the appointment of my successor, a part-time Director who will work a two-day week. Theoretically I could have remained as the part-time Director, but after twenty years at the Arts Council I felt it was time for a change. Also, I did not relish the prospect of staying on to preside over an ever-decreasing budget. (When Tony Field, the Finance Director, left the Arts Council after about twenty-six years, to go to another job, his mother said, 'You can't go on chopping and changing like this, you know.')

I suppose I should not have been surprised to read, in so many of the news stories and articles following the publication of *The Glory of the Garden*, that I was to blame for the Council reducing the level of its commitment to literature:

> Had the Literature Director, Charles Osborne, fought to retain his Department, things would surely have turned out differently. But Mr Osborne, who has been sceptical about literature subsidy, seems to have colluded in his own departure. (The *Observer*)
>
> The Literature Department, which put its own head on the block, as promised, had it cut off! (The *Sunday Times*)
>
> Charles Osborne, little-loved Arts Council Literature Director, left for an Australian holiday yesterday – to recover, it is suggested, 'from his exertions in undermining his Department'. (*The Times* Diary)
>
> The immediate response, both of the staff union at 105 Piccadilly and of the Society of Authors and the Writers' Guild, has been to try to get the decision debated by the Council. My impression is that Mr Osborne, who is not a member of the staff branch of ASTMS, would not be particularly grateful for their efforts on his behalf. (*Times Literary Supplement*)

The *Guardian* managed to publish something completely untrue and defamatory, as a result of which they found themselves paying my legal fees and publishing a retraction and an apology. I corrected the *Sunday Times* statement, just to set the record straight, but I saw no point in defending myself everywhere against the charge that I was sceptical about subsidies for literature. Instead, I published in the *London Review of Books* an informal *apologia* or statement of my position, of which the following is an abridgement:

> A few weeks ago, in New York, I accompanied a friend on a shopping expedition. While we were in a novelty gift shop on Columbus

Avenue, she bought me a rubber stamp which she said I'd find useful when I got back to my Arts Council office in London. I know what she means, though, in fact, I've found myself using it, not on office memos (strong at times though the temptation has been), but on press clippings relating to the Arts Council. The stamp reads 'BULLSHIT' and it has recently been slapped on articles in the *Sunday Times*, *Publishing News*, and the *Times Educational Supplement*. As the 1940 Deanna Durbin song says, 'It's foolish but it's fun.'

It is nearly twenty years since I was invited to join the Arts Council (it would never have occurred to me to *apply* for a job there), and I still remember W. H. Auden warning me against accepting the invitation: 'You'll go mad, having to deal with boring cultural bureaucrats.' 'Worse than that, my dear Wystan, I shall become one.' And if I did not become one, at least I can now give a reasonably good imitation of a faceless bureaucrat when required to do so. I think that what kept me going was my determination to continue to practise the art-form I was required by the Arts Council to preach: literature. Arts Council definitions of literature have varied and veered this way and that over the years. I like to think that good, non-technical writing on any subject can aspire to the condition of literature: the current official view narrows the definition to include little beyond poetry and fiction. Since I first slipped into print as a poet in 1941, my career has embraced biography, musical and literary criticism, journalism and writing for the theatre.

I was surprised, a few days ago, to read somewhere a description of myself as 'a heavily subsidized author'. Don't almost all authors subsidize their writings by doing other jobs? Actually (and I don't care if it sounds like boasting), I no longer have to subsidize my writing, which does very well, thank you. I've continued to work for the Arts Council, not only because I have had there a strong feeling of *Après moi, le déluge*, but also because the subject of state subsidy for literature still fascinates me. And there's another reason: like most writers, I can't write for more than a couple of hours a day, and I don't like being idle.

In one sense, of course, the less the state has to do with the arts the better. (The less the state has to do with anything the better: surely we all want minimal interference in our lives. Those of us who like being dictated to have presumably already buggered off to some Fascist or Communist country.) We are not prepared to be told by our rulers what music to listen to, what paintings to admire, what plays, novels or poems to enjoy. If we could be provided with all the music, theatre, art and literature we require without paying for it twice, once as consumers and once as tax-payers, clearly we would all prefer the Government to keep its hands off the arts. However, the need for subsidy has been demonstrated fairly conclusively. Without it there would be virtually no music (other than the pop rubbish the teenagers buy), much less theatre, less visual art, and perhaps a little less literature.

What would be at risk in the case of literature? Those who claim that the answer is 'nothing' point to this country's vast commercial publishing industry, but I think they overstate their case. I would concede that perhaps 95% of our literature is provided by commercial publishers (whereas in the theatre probably not more than 25% of our drama is provided by commercial managements). But the remaining 5% of literature is important. Much contemporary poetry and some (not much) new fiction will remain unpublished if there are no subsidized publishing houses to introduce it: publishers such as Carcanet, Anvil and Calder. And even such publishers, to say nothing of the commercial houses, will find new writers of quality more difficult to identify without such literary magazines as *PN Review*, *The London Magazine*, *Granta* or *Stand*, the majority of which could not exist without subsidy.

So there remains a public need for the Arts Council and Regional Arts Associations to continue to subsidize a few publishers and literary magazines. I imagine that, for the foreseeable future, they will continue to do so. What there does not appear to be any public need for is a greater state involvement in the subsidizing of writers. If there is, I for one haven't heard the public crying out for it. The voices I hear are those of writers, not those of readers.

The voices, especially, of poets. It is they who, with even less justification than novelists, clamour for more public money to be spent on grants and bursaries to enable them to buy time to write. A novelist, admittedly, does need to carve large and regular segments of time out of his life to devote to his craft. What a poet needs is not time but dedication, and that's something that can't be bought – not even with public money (as Lane did not say to his employer Algernon Moncrieff). Once upon a time, a poet needed a talent for poetry as well, but I shan't pursue that line for fear of being accused of 'talentism'.

It is wrong for the state or one of its agencies to decide which poets should be encouraged, and which should not. I do not want ever to be in the position of deciding which of my fellow-poets should be supported, nor would I be willing to allow a civil servant to make that kind of decision. Editors of magazines and of publishing firms should choose whom they wish to publish, just as theatre and music artistic directors choose their playwrights and composers. Subsidies are much more appropriately directed to institutions – the orchestras, opera and theatre companies, galleries, publishers and magazines – than to individuals.

There are those, prose writers as well as poets, who for reasons of *amour propre* insist on 'being a writer' and nothing else. And, as long as they're prepared to accept a wide definition of the writer's craft, they are able to do so. They accept all kinds of hack-work provided that it involves writing. Any writer of talent can live like this, if he has the temperament for it. I have not. I refuse more commissions to write books than I accept, I am not available to ghost the memoirs of this or that actor or singer, and I would never agree to work in advertising. On the other hand, I am perfectly prepared to do a full-time job which does not utilize my skills as a writer, and to get on with my writing in my spare time. I have a gift for organizing my time intelligently. But then (a bi-lingual pun for German-speakers), one man's gift is another man's *Gift*, and I would not dream of imposing my methods of work upon others.

In general, the better the poet, the more private he will wish to keep his art. Poetry is, after all, essentially reclusive in a way that fiction is not. Indeed, one of the finest living poets, Philip Larkin, has remarked that novels are about other people while poems are about oneself. But then Larkin has talked sense on so many aspects of literature. He is a real poet in that he writes poems only when he has to. It is those who fear (often, only too rightly) that they may not be real poets who keep up a large and uneven output. '*Of course* I'm a poet. Haven't I written a poem a day for the last ten years?'

Larkin has on more than one occasion voiced his fears about poetry becoming 'official and subsidized'. In *Required Writing* he says: 'I think we got much better poetry when it was all regarded as sinful or subversive, and you had to hide it under the cushion when somebody came in. What I don't like about subsidies and official support is that they destroy the essential nexus between the writer and the reader. If the writer is being paid to write and the reader is being paid to read, the element of compulsive contact vanishes.' I'm sure that Philip Larkin would agree there is no harm in subsidizing the magazines in which poets are published, as long as the subsidizing bodies do not interfere with the functions of the editors. I am equally sure that he is right to decry some poets' obsessive insistence on unnecessary and, in the long run, damaging handouts.

If those who, over the years, have been crying out simply for more public money for literature had been able to produce sound reasons for spending more, then literature would no doubt have featured in the Arts Council's development plans, and we could now be contemplating perhaps a doubling rather than a halving of its spending on literature. None of the Council's critics, however, has been able to make out a case for increased spending, nor have successive Literature Panels. The yelling of the poets and writers for more money, without substantiating a need for it, has brought much of the structure of the Arts Council's Literature Department down. I imagine that, in due course, the rest will come tumbling after. Then we can all go home and get on with our writing.

I knew it was time for me to go when I read in the *Guardian* an article, 'A Socialist Policy for the Arts', by a pair of Labour Party spokesmen. 'Since the arts are at present defined and mediated by a small handful of people, serving vested interests and a particular class,' Ms Steyn and Mr Sedgemore wrote, 'it is Labour's duty to take over and re-establish art so that it carries socialist meanings and becomes part of a collective socialist cultural drive.' There are those who will shudder with fear at such cultural bullying, which reads like a footnote from *Mein Kampf* or *Das Kapital.* But when I encounter the words 'take over and re-establish art so that it carries socialist meanings', I reach for my Bullshit stamp.

These final paragraphs on the Arts Council are being written during my last months as Literature Director. Despite occasional appearances to the contrary, I have enjoyed my twenty years with the Council and have thought (until it was halved) that my annual budget was at about the right level. If I had been allowed to spend it as I wished, without the encumbrance of 'advisers', I would have given more of it to publishing houses such as Carcanet and Anvil, literary magazines like *The New Review, The London Magazine* and *The London Review of Books*, and organizations which help to spread the reading habit, namely the National Book League, the Poetry Book Society and the short-lived New Fiction Society. I would, consequently, have spent much less, if I spent anything at all, on grants to individual writers.

What I have not particularly enjoyed are the formal meetings I have been obliged to attend: the monthly Council meetings, the weekly Directorate meetings, the quarterly Panel meetings, and the occasional meetings with the Literature Officers of the Regional Arts Associations.

At yesterday's (October, 1985) Council meeting, in the middle of a plodding discussion there was a sudden eruption from Sir Roy Strong. 'What this Council needs,' Roy exclaimed with some passion, 'are a few polymaths to heighten the intellectual level of debate.' He was right, of course. When I joined the Council in 1966 it was a perfectly respectable gathering of the great and the good. Actually it looks a little better now than it did a year or two ago. No body which includes among its members Marghanita Laski, Ronald Grierson, Jeremy Hardie, Mathew Prichard (Agatha Christie's grandson), Sir Roy Strong and Sir Brian Young can be all bad. And Donald Sinden not only contributes mightily to the gaiety of nations but can also be relied upon to produce some common sense when it is most needed. Sir Kenneth Cork is a valuable recent addition. But I have named half of the Council's members. I would guess that Roy's outburst was directed at the other half.

The Council's Directorate has, over the years, lost some first-rate members, and some of their replacements give us cause to lament their departure. I recall Tony Field, our Finance Director for many years, exclaiming as he rushed away from one Directorate meeting, 'No one in the outside world would believe we have such a nincompoop directing an Arts Council department.' The Director to whom he referred was one who resisted strongly a change in working practice some years ago because it gave Directors too much responsibility, and who later resisted changes because they removed the responsibility which was added on that earlier occasion.

One or two Directors seemed incapable of thinking as Directors of the Arts Council: they were concerned only to defend or expand their own little empires. However, that is as much a consequence of the Arts Council's hitherto highly departmentalized structure as of their own attitudes to the arts, and in the new management structure they will no longer be required to take the larger view. Those who failed to behave responsibly will no doubt complain the loudest when divested of responsibility.

What Roy Strong said of the Council is equally true of its advisory Panels. It is becoming increasingly difficult to find people of sufficiently high calibre willing to serve on the Panels. The regions, we are told, have to be represented, though I always resisted taking someone onto the Literature Panel merely because he or she had the right address, which nowadays is not S.W.7 but anywhere 'regional', and the more unsalubrious the area the better. I attempted to find first-rate advisers, and whether they lived in Belgravia or Bolton was, to me, completely irrelevant.

As for the meetings with representatives of the Regional Arts Associations, it is well-known within the Arts Council that I consider the blackest day in the Council's history to be the day in the late 1950s when it closed its own regional offices, and allowed to be brought into existence twelve separate autonomous organizations called Regional Arts Associations. Ever since that day, the Council has had no control over arts subsidies in the provinces, sorry, regions (it's inevitable that 'regions' will, too, become a dirty word), and has had to devote a considerable part of its energies to squabbles with those Associations.

In my department, we held as few meetings with the Regional Literature Officers as we decently could. To her draft minutes of one such meeting, my deputy, Josephine Falk, appended a note to me, which read: 'Do you want to edit these minutes before they are circulated? You will appreciate how difficult it is to produce a coherent record of what was largely incoherent waffle.' I would not, of course, want to leave the reader with the impression that it is only from employees of Regional Arts Associations that one hears incoherent waffle, which has also had its exponents among Arts Council Panel Chairmen.

At a recent meeting, we found ourselves considering how to provide concerts of orchestral music in rural areas. But should not rural areas be rural, and metropolitan areas metropolitan? No one in his right mind expects to find the amenities of cities in the country any more than he expects to find hosts of golden daffodils sprouting in Shaftesbury Avenue. I imagine a herd of cows huddled together at the furthest end of the field from the Arts Council's musicians. 'Not bloody Stockhausen again,' complains a Conservative cow, 'Brahms is much better' – only to be admonished by a left-wing cow for truckling to the cult of excellence.

The leading story in the Londoner's Diary column of the *Standard* on 30 October 1985 is another gratuitous attack on me, written, I suppose, by the journalist who rang me a couple of days ago and asked a number of silly questions. It says that 'Charles Osborne is at last leaving the job in which he has been surrounded by controversy and hatred', and it quotes anonymous opinions of me:

> 'Quite the most viperous person I've ever met,' says one who has served on the advisory Literature Panel; 'contemptuous and obfuscatory,' says another; 'appallingly rude,' I hear from a third.

I wonder if they heard any compliments as well! The story refers to 'the long-running scandal of the subsidy to *The New Review*', and goes on to say that I 'turned off the Poetry Society's grant after seventy years'. Why do they bother to write such rubbish? The Arts Council, which didn't exist seventy years ago, began to subsidize the Poetry Society, at the instigation of Eric White and myself, about nineteen years ago, and the Council is still subsidizing it. In other words, I helped to turn the tap on, and it has never been turned off since then. The grant has grown from £1500 in the early days to, in the current year, £95,000, and at no time has it ever been reduced. Why do these viperous, contemptuous, obfuscatory and appallingly rude creatures persist with their lies?

It is ironic that a newspaper should refer to 'the long-running scandal of the subsidy to *The New Review*' in a week which has seen the publication by Heinemann of *The New Review Anthology*, a handsome volume which reprints some of the best of the stories, poems and articles that appeared in the magazine. The only scandal is that, after five years, the Council abandoned *The New Review*. In his preface to the *Anthology*, Ian Hamilton writes: 'I would like to offer public thanks to Charles Osborne, Literature Director of the Arts Council throughout the magazine's brief life – without his unflinching personal support that life would have been far briefer, and quite a few of the items in this book might not have seen the light of day.' The pleasure I feel in reading Ian's words more than cancels out the mild disgust induced in me by the *Standard*.

That item in the *Standard* has brought me a number of letters from writers and publishers whom I have attempted to help during my time at the Arts Council. This, from a highly regarded novelist, is typical:

> This is just to let you know how deeply grateful I am for everything you did for me as Director of the Literature Department. It is no exaggeration to say that you helped to give me a sense of myself as a writer at very uncertain times, and helped me go on. I'm sure that many, many writers in England feel the same.

I hope that is so. Unfortunately my penchant for blurting out home truths will keep me unpopular with a good many writers.

Having now left the Arts Council, I am able to combine the writing of my books with a greater freedom of movement than I have been used to in the last twenty years. Meanwhile, at the Council a number of changes have been made as a consequence of the 1984 Organizational Review. The amateurs on the Panel will have, to use the distasteful jargon, 'more input into the decision-making processes'; the senior management team which meets weekly now does not include art-form Directors, who are relegated to an 'Arts Directorate' which meets at monthly intervals; the Directors no longer report directly to the Secretary-General but to a Director of Arts Co-ordination ('We have ways of making you co-ordinate'); as present Directors leave (most recently, myself and the Drama Director (Dickon Reed), their replacements are being recruited at lower salary scales. The Directors of Music, Drama, Art and Literature have much less authority, status and financial inducement.

I do not think that all these changes are necessarily for the worse, but they postulate an Arts Council into whose highly regimented structure I would have fitted only with the greatest discomfort to all concerned. The Autumn 1985 issue of a staff publication, *Image*, outlined the brave new world Arts Council Directors would inhabit in 1986:

> The great art-form departments are at the heart of the Arts Council's work, and their achievements during the post-war era have been remarkable. They have, however, come to resemble the semi-autonomous satrapies of the Persian Empire; the Great King lived in Persepolis and his messengers took months to cross his territories. The provincial governors were able to act more or less as they wished more or less all the time.
>
> Each art-form has its own needs and a diversity of approach is to be expected, and welcomed. But if it is wrong to impose conformity on the Arts Council's artistic policies, the arts communities and the public at large are right to expect a consistency in the ways in which they are implemented and presented; a demonstrable fairness in the allocation of funds among the art-forms; a universal application of assessment procedures; the identification and harmonization of common policies and programmes. The establishment of a Department of Arts Coordination to which the other arts departments will report will help to resolve these long-standing difficulties.

The Arts Council gave a farewell party to this provincial governor, in Persepolis itself, at which the Great King, William Rees-Mogg, made what one of my friends called 'a surprisingly affectionate speech'. I thought its tone more ironic than affectionate, but I enjoyed it and appreciated it, and reciprocated at some length.

Three months later, at the instigation of Michael Schmidt, one of the few Arts Council clients who has remained untainted with disaffection, my old friend Nicolai Gedda, one of the great singers of this century, gave a recital in my honour at the Wigmore Hall, with another old chum, Geoffrey Parsons, as his accompanist. It was a marvellous occasion. Nicolai was in superb form, and was accorded a terrific reception from a crowded audience. He sang a programme of songs and arias which we had chosen together, and he was generous with his encores, which included an expansively phrased '*Amor ti vieta*' from Giordano's *Fedora*. 'I'm Giving It Away to you, Charles,' he said as he introduced the item. Nicolai sang, that evening, like the great artist and superb stylist that he has been for the last thirty-five years, and Geoffrey accompanied him impeccably. About sixty people came to a reception backstage after the performance, and the evening ended with a supper party at the Caprice for the artists and four or five close friends.

This volume of memoirs has been occasioned by my leaving the Arts Council and twenty years of public life. It contains little about my private life, which has been a happy one, enriched by personal relationships, travel, enjoyment of music, books, good food and good health. I shall miss the friends I have made at the Arts Council and among its clients; and even several sparring partners, whom I do not regard as enemies, whatever their feelings may be towards me. (I am a man of few virtues, but I am aware of one, which is that I do not harbour grudges or resentments. Those with whom I am angry today I am, with one or two exceptions, perfectly prepared to greet amicably tomorrow.)

What I shall not miss is the talk of 'catchment areas', 'targeting', 'dance activity', 'arts product', 'forward-looking, multi-dimensional assessments' or 'arts coordination', and those who think in such terms. To them I utter a cheerful farewell, with the concluding lines of W. H. Auden's 'Song of the Devil', a poem its author wickedly enjoyed declaiming to audiences:

> Believe while you can that I'm proud of you,
>   Enjoy your dream:
> I'm so bored with the whole fucking crowd of you
>   I could scream!

4

NAME-DROPPING

□ □ □

Authors of memoirs are often accused of name-dropping, merely because they have scattered throughout their volumes comments or anecdotes concerning people they have known, of greater fame than their own. Unless one is a prime minister or a pop star, it is difficult to avoid doing this: one's readers, surely, deserve a few stories about people who are better-known and more interesting than oneself. Be that as it may, in order to facilitate the substantiation of any such charge against myself I have gathered together in this section a number of names which I shall now proceed to drop, alphabetically. (I had, in fact, thought of calling the entire book *Name-Dropping*, until I read in Cole Lesley's life of Noël Coward that 'the greater number of Noël's friends were and are famous – many of them world-famous – and name-dropping is therefore unavoidable. *Name-Dropping* was, in fact, going to be the title of one of the last books he ever planned.')

The following, however, is not an annotated list of everyone I know who is famous. A number of people about whom I have nothing to say, from Claudio Abbado and Richard Attenborough to Hilde Zadek and Franco Zeffirelli, are absent from these pages, while some of the names included are of people whom I may have met only once or twice, but about whom I have an anecdote to relate.

ACTON, Sir Harold. On my first visit to La Pietra, Harold's magnificent villa outside Florence, I met and was greatly charmed by his mother, the most elegant of elderly American upper-class ladies. I remember also the grubbiness of the butler's white gloves. Harold's house and his garden were, of course, overwhelming. Some of his local guests were, on the other hand, distinctly underwhelming. I think it was on a subsequent visit to La Pietra that Alberto Arbasino, a fellow guest at lunch, drove me to Rome afterwards at suicidal speed: a terrifying experience, and it went on for hours. What a crummy way to die that would have been, careering over the side of a mountain in a sports car whose driver was still singing bits of *Tosca* at the top of his unmellifluous voice.

It was Harold Acton who recited, at a luncheon party he gave at the Hyde Park Hotel, the following verse, inspired both by Mount Snowdon and by the husband of Princess Margaret (I cannot recall whether Harold also claimed authorship of the verse):

The hikers claim – they never stop –
That they have been 'up Snowdon's top';
But what of those who claim, God rot 'em,
That they have been up Snowdon's bottom?

In 1966, when an announcement that I was leaving *The London Magazine* to join the Arts Council appeared in the British press, Harold wrote to me from La Pietra. 'I am truly sorry,' he said, 'to hear that you are leaving the London Mag., after devoting so many years to its rejuvenation. You will surely be missed. But I hope the Arts Council will provide you with more power and prosperity and leisure for loving.'

Power, no. Prosperity, not much. Leisure, whether for loving or hating, insufficient.

ASHTON, Sir Frederick. The doyen of British ballet has very decided views about modern dance. When I encountered him at a gallery opening recently, he said of the Arts Council's Dance Director, 'What a dreadful woman that is, so prejudiced, and liking all that Riverside rubbish.' I could neither agree nor defend my colleague, for I am not party to her views on Riverside Studios or the dance groups which perform there. It's true, however, that the Council has squandered considerable sums of money on some very dodgy dance companies or, to use the jargon, 'dance activity'. There are also people called 'dance animateurs' all over the country, funded by the Arts Council to bully the natives into dancing. And there are plans now to provide a theatre as a National Dance House. Apparently it is considered scandalous by the ballet world that there is no theatre in this country exclusively set aside for dance companies. That there is no such theatre in any other country in the world is apparently neither here nor there.

AUDEN, W. H. The year after Auden's death, I invited his friend Chester Kallman to take part in London in a memorial programme at the

Institute of Contemporary Arts, in which Auden's poems would be read by John Betjeman, Irene Worth, Michael York and myself. Chester replied:

> Much as I would adore coaching Mr York in an intonation or two, the early date makes it out of the question. If only it could all be a few weeks later, and the ICA would provide me with widow's weeds covered with the *blackest* sequins, and a bottle of vintage champagne to sip indiscreetly under my veil in a corner of the stage, I *might* manage. But I'm afraid . . .
>
> P.S. Professor Mendelson, whom you met and whom *I* find rather yummy, arrives on Monday to 'evaluate' Wystan's papers and so get Austrian 'inheritance' settled. I'm afraid it will all be confined to paper work, though, as I am, at present, Hellenistically accompanied. That's life.

One of the two or three short lyric poems I am pleased that I have written was coaxed out of me by Wystan Auden. I had shown him, one day in 1962, some poems I had written several years earlier. He liked three of them, and was particularly struck by the opening lines of one, 'The poet's vacant/and engaging smile', but did not care for the rest of the poem. The opening, he said, promised one a poem about a poet's vacant and engaging smile, 'and then you go traipsing off into a pallid imitation of some minor Georgian'. He crossed out the remaining eleven lines, and handed it back to me. 'Describe the smile,' he said. 'Interpret it, if you like. But just do that, and nothing else. And it hasn't got a title. I like poems to have titles. Call it "The Smile". And keep it metrically regular. All those weak endings must go.' He jabbed a finger at 'betrayal', 'shadow' and 'reflection'. 'You can get rid of those, too.'

I went away and did as I was told. Next time I saw him, I showed him 'The Smile'. 'There you are,' he said. 'It's perfect now. It's small, but it's perfect. Well, almost. If you change the punctuation in the last stanza, and turn some of those commas into full stops, to get a more *staccato* effect, that would do it.' I changed the punctuation:

The Smile

The poet's vacant
and engaging smile

is even falser now
than once it was.

Ingredients: love,
mirror, hate and cold.
(Amused self-pity
is an added spice.)

He's bored and fretful,
lazy, gentle, proud.
And anxious. Frightened.
Scared to death of life.

BARBIROLLI, Sir John. A *Guardian* reporter told me that, when the Australian pianist Noel Newton-Wood died, he (the reporter) had rung Barbirolli to get a comment from him on Noel, who had frequently played under Barbirolli's baton. 'What kind of comment do you require?' asked the great conductor. 'Well – I thought you might want to utter some kind of tribute to him –' 'I'm sorry,' said Sir John, 'but I am not in the habit of issuing testimonials to homosexuals.' A distinguished Mahlerian, but also a very silly Antiqueerian.

BARRYMORE, Diana. It was in the mid-1940s. I was a teenage Assistant Stage Manager in Melbourne, and a famous American star had arrived to play the lead in our next production. She was Diana Barrymore, daughter of John, and although only in her twenties she was already a hopeless alcoholic. (She died of it in 1960, at the age of 39.) We sat in a circle for the first reading. I was opposite Miss Barrymore, who fascinated me because she wore only a dress and shoes (no stockings) with absolutely no underwear whatsoever. She sprawled in her chair with her skirt hitched up, and I could see – well, more of the lady than I had expected to see. I was acutely embarrassed but I couldn't take my eyes off her, until she noticed my gaze and snapped at me: 'Don't worry, it's only a cunt. It won't bite you.'

BATES, Alan. I had devised a programme of poems by Philip Larkin to be read by Alan Bates, Patrick Garland and myself. The BBC sent a producer and camera crew to the performance, at the Odette Gilbert Gallery in Mayfair, to film some of Alan Bates's readings for a subsequent TV show. During the interval, a slightly nervous female producer made her way to our dressing room and said to Alan, in an impeccable old-style BBC accent, 'I hope there won't be any difficulty over some of the lines. We'll be using only two of the poems. What do you think is less likely to cause offence: "They fuck you up, your mum and dad", or "Books are a load of crap"?' Neither Alan nor I felt able to advise her.

BETJEMAN, Sir John. Everyone knows John Betjeman was a fine poet and a lovable teddy-bear on TV. Not so many will realize how irritating a correspondent he could be, especially if one was trying to coax him into doing something he was reluctant to do. His response to my invitation to something or other in the summer of 1973 was:

> Dear Charles,
>
> Oh, Alas, I have to go to some event in Sloane Square at that time and won't have the time to cross the river. I love your writing-paper. It must be the only thing of its kind in S.W.11. I like the yellow ink, too.
>
> Yours,
> John.

The following year, I asked him to sign copies of a newly published volume of his poems at the Arts Council Shop, which was then in Sackville Street:

> Dear Charles,
>
> It's very kind of you to suggest this arrangement with the Arts Council Shop. It's no good my saying I want to do it, I don't want to do it at all. In fact I so dread publication day I am arranging to be at sea on my way to St Helena from Southampton if I can coincide publication date with the voyage. Across the road in Albemarle Street is my publisher Jock Murray and I have sent him a copy of your letter and of this my reply. I don't want to seem ungracious and ungrateful and if Jock Murray and you think I ought to do it, then I will. All the best,
>
> Yours ever,
> John,
> Baron Betjeman of Moonee Ponds.

(John was a great fan of Dame Edna Everage, who comes from Moonee Ponds, Melbourne.) Jock Murray and I agreed that he ought to do it. And, of course, he didn't.

Two years later he replied thus to an invitation to take part in Poetry International, 1976 (I had been in Australia, graciously opening a literary festival):

Dear Charles,

I'm so glad you enjoyed Adelaide. Colonel Light was a genius to make those broad streets and the green belt round the city. I became very fond of Gawlor as an untouched Australian town. I have just returned from Romania and up country there is Chaucer with ox-carts and wooden huts and richly beautiful Orthodox churches much more like High C of E than anything you will find between this island and the Black Sea. I've had rather firm medical instructions not to hold forth in public. I am under a course of pills for high blood pressure and I'd better not risk it. I really am more of a nuisance than an asset to the cause of poetry I know it is my duty to espouse.

Yours in the sure and certain hope of a speedy resurrection,

John

artiste (ex)

On another occasion, ducking a similar assignment, he ended: 'I can't suggest anyone else, but you know all our good poets, and one of the least good, and far the luckiest, is your old Pommy friend, John.' As often as not, however, he said 'yes' without being coaxed. He was a marvellous performer of his own poems. 'Here's another by yours truly, and not much cop,' he would announce by way of preface.

We spent occasional hilarious mornings in his study at 29 Radnor Walk, off the King's Road, exchanging stories and sipping champagne. Once, in his publisher John Murray's office, whither we had, for some reason, ventured after a lunch together, Betj introduced me to a man we found there, a tall, ravaged-looking individual wearing a cloth cap. 'Charles,' said John B., 'I want you to meet John Huston.' We shook hands, and Huston began to talk in his strange American-Irish accent of the most recent film he had directed. Had I seen it? I had, and began to discuss it enthusiastically.

After a minute or two, John Betjeman got a fit of the giggles, which also infected Jock Murray. Only Huston kept a grave face, as he and I continued to talk about Hollywood. But when John B. collapsed into an armchair, helpless with laughter, John Huston's face began to crease as well, and he confessed to me that his name was not John Huston, whom he somewhat resembled, but Tom Driberg.

One evening, at a party at the Festival Hall after a Poetry International performance, John, who was no linguist, found himself talking to the East German poet, Peter Huchel, who spoke no English. John came across the room to me, and asked, 'Charles, how do you say "popular" in German?' Involved in conversation with some other foreign poet, I did not stop to consider what kind of 'popular' he meant, ie the opposite of 'unpopular' or the opposite of 'classical'. I assumed the latter, and answered *'Volkstümlich'.*

'Volkstümlich,' John muttered to himself as he made his way back to Huchel. It suddenly occurred to me that perhaps he needed more help, so I followed him, and arrived in time to hear him say to Peter Huchel, slowly and laboriously, with much use of gesture, *'Ich – bin – nicht* – gut, – *aber – ich – bin* – volkstümlich.'

We had a little contretemps in 1980 when my biography of W. H. Auden was published. I had heard from both Auden (more than once) and John the story of how, as undergraduates at Oxford in 1925, they had been discovered by a servant in bed together. John gave me his permission to mention this in my book, and indeed the incident is briefly described in a couple of lines in the American edition, which was published in the autumn of 1979.

No one was at all shocked by this not very startling account of the sexual experimentation of a couple of eighteen-year-olds. However, a few weeks before publication of the English edition in the following spring, John informed me that he wanted the offending passage removed. His old friend Lady so-and-so had decided that it was undignified to have this kind of youthful indiscretion mentioned. So there is an interesting minor difference between the American and British editions of *W. H. Auden: the Life of a Poet.* In the American edition, one reads: 'And they experimented sexually. One morning, they were found in bed together by Wystan's "scout" and he had to part with a five-pound note to buy the man's silence.' In the British edition, faced with the task of filling the two-and-a-half lines with different words, I altered this to: 'They discovered and read together the works of the Rev. Dr E. E. Bradford, who wrote bad verse which Betjeman has described as "innocent and touching about the love of 'lads'."'

On one of the occasions when Wystan Auden told me the story (in his sixties, he tended to repeat a small repertoire of well-tested anecdotes), I asked him if he thought the five pounds had been well spent. 'No, it was not,' he snapped.

In 1979 I asked John Betjeman to judge the entries in the children's book category for the Arts Council's short-lived National Book Awards. He agreed to do so on payment of a large fee and provided he did not have to read very many of the books submitted. I agreed to have the entries slimmed down for him, and in due course delivered a carton of books (perhaps twenty out of nearly two hundred submitted) to him in Radnor Walk. It was after eleven in the morning, so the champagne flowed, and John chose the winner by a curious process of osmosis, holding the books, one by one, in his hand, as though weighing them. Occasionally, he sniffed a volume. 'The smell is important,' he giggled. Always fascinated by the sexual proclivities of the famous, he would interrupt his own casual reading aloud of a paragraph from one of the children's books to say, for instance, 'Did you know that Sargent was as queer as a coot?'

'Sir Malcolm? I think you're mistaken, John –'

'No, no, the painter. Queer as a coot.'

He was delighted when I told him Melvyn Bragg had informed me that Captain Bligh and Fletcher Christian were lovers.

'I say!'

Tiring of the children's books, he tossed one at me, saying, 'I should think this is probably the best of the bunch. Now you can help me decide something different. The Queen's Medal for Poetry. I've narrowed it down to Eric Walter White, Edgell Rickword and Seamus Heaney. You and Philip Larkin are both very wise about poetry, so advise me. I'm seeing Philip this evening, so you have first go.'

I advised him, and he then began immediately to talk about 'forgotten best-sellers', about Warwick Deeping and Charles Morgan. He was delighted when I praised Morgan's *The Gunroom.* 'This blonde goddess,' he said, waving at his secretary, who was at that moment re-filling our glasses, 'is Morgan's granddaughter.'

His death robbed the literary scene of much good-humoured gaiety (of the old-fashioned kind). A final letter is signed, 'Your old Pommy cobber, John, *artiste et flâneur*'. It is an accurate piece of self-description.

BIRNEY, Earle. I sat next to Laurence Cotterell at a poetry reading at Canada House, held to launch a tour of Great Britain by three Canadian poets, none of whom could be described as a major talent. The first poet to read was the elderly Earle Birney, who, in the middle of a not very good and far too long poem, suddenly succumbed to what turned out to be a fortunately minor heart attack, and collapsed. As people in the front row rushed to his aid, I turned to Laurence and murmured, 'One down, two to go.'

BRITTEN, Benjamin. I had not spoken to Britten more than four or five times, and then only briefly, when, early in 1963, he agreed to my interviewing him for a Fiftieth Birthday Symposium I was planning for the *London Magazine*'s October 1963 issue, my other contributors to which were Michael

Tippett, Norman del Mar, William Plomer and Basil Coleman. Britten had so seldom ventured into print on the subject of his own music that I feared that to talk to him about it might prove to be a difficult and hesitant affair.

I was wrong, and our conversation ranged widely, though much of what he said was too personal to be used in my published account of the interview. It was clear, despite my trying to categorize him as continuing a tradition that, as I put it, 'comes through Mozart, by-passing Beethoven but including Schubert, re-emerging in Mahler', that Britten considered himself to be a local composer with strong roots in the English language and folksong. The contemporary composers whom he said he most admired were Stravinsky, Shostakovich, Copland and Tippett.

When I said that I thought of him as primarily an opera composer, he replied very promptly, 'Well, I don't know that I do. Certainly I respond very deeply to words but not necessarily only opera.' We agreed that *Gloriana* was an unjustly neglected piece, and Britten was obviously looking forward to a concert performance of it, planned for his fiftieth birthday on 23 November. On that day I was in the audience at the Royal Festival Hall. It was during the interval that we heard President Kennedy had been assassinated.

Britten's *War Requiem* was then quite new, having been first performed the previous year. He had strong feelings about the work. 'Some of my right-wing friends loathed it,' he told me. ' "Though the music is superb, of course," they'd say. But that's neither here nor there to me. The message is what counts.'

There, surely, he was wrong. The music *is* the message, and those who begin by loving the sound are in dire peril of having to admit the sense.

Sidney Nolan once told me that Britten had recounted to him a dream in which he, Britten, had met Schubert and had been blessed by him.

BROPHY, Brigid. There arrived at *The London Magazine* for review, one day in 1962, a huge book called *Black Ship to Hell* by Brigid Brophy. I had never heard of the author, though she had previously published two novels, but I was fascinated and appalled by the task she had set herself in this work of non-fiction, an examination of the self-destructive impulse in mankind, which she traces to its origins in our biological nature. I began to read it, and when I emerged from my reading of its 500-odd pages a week or two later I was as exhilarated as when, twenty years earlier, I had made my first contact with the mind of George Bernard Shaw.

The dust jacket informed me that Brigid Brophy lived with her husband, Michael Levey, in a flat in Old Brompton Road. I looked her up in the telephone book to discover her exact address, and I wrote to her. It was during the period that, in Alan Ross's absence, I was Acting Editor of the magazine, and I invited Miss Brophy to call on me at our office, which was then in Charing Cross Road, and discuss the possibility of her reviewing books for *The London Magazine.*

Brigid became a regular contributor to the magazine: I think I was responsible for her literary career as a critic, at least for initiating it. I hope that is so, for it is something of which I would feel proud. She and Michael Levey became my close friends. Both of them dedicated books to me – Brigid her novel *The Snow Ball*, and Michael his *History of Western Art*. After all three of us had collaborated on *Fifty Works of English Literature We Could Do Without*, we resisted a tempting offer from Sol Stein, our American publisher, to do *Fifty People We Could Do Without*.

BROWNE, E. Martin. Friend of T. S. Eliot and producer of most of his plays, including the first and most famous, *Murder in the Cathedral*, Martin Browne was a competent director of the old school. In other words, he could move actors around on a stage so that they did not bump into one another, and he could instruct them in the art of speaking their lines as though they understood the words. This kind of director is now sadly missed.

He was a gentle soul and, when he directed the York Mystery Plays in 1957, he found it impossible to come up with images of violence when he needed them. Rehearsing a scene in which three devils are dragging Lucifer back into hell, he took the four of us aside and said: 'It needs to be much more horrifying. Lucifer must be savagely manhandled in such a way as to shock the audience. He is, after all, being dragged down into hell. It has to be awe-inspiring, tremendously frightening. I want you to convey a sense of – of –.' He searched for the vilest thing he could imagine, and eventually produced it: 'A sense of – "Come on, chaps, let's scrag him." '

He had cast me in the Mystery Plays without an audition, although he had never seen me act, purely because he had enjoyed my conversation about the plays of T. S. Eliot at a dinner-party. 'I thought you were intelligent and sensitive and had a nice voice,' he explained to me. 'What more would one require?' Quite a lot more, I should have thought. But I was glad of the job.

BURTON, Richard. At the first night of Lena Horne's 1984 London season at the Adelphi Theatre, I found myself during the interval talking to a woman who was a friend of a *Guardian* arts journalist whom I used to refer to at the Arts Council as Nicholas de Wrongh. 'It's such a shame,' said the lady. 'Poor Nicholas was so looking forward to seeing Lena Horne, but at the last minute he's been forced to stay at home to write Richard

Burton's obituary for tomorrow's paper. Isn't that infuriating?'

'It certainly is,' I replied. 'In fact I think it's monstrously unfair. I would much rather Richard Burton were at home writing Nicholas's obituary.'

Incidentally, I'm delighted to learn from one of his colleagues of the Critics' Circle that, when tired and over-emotional, young Nicholas is given to stabbing at the table-cloth with his knife, muttering, 'I wish this were Charles Osborne.'

CALLAS, Maria. Though I heard her sing on a number of occasions, I met the lady only once, some years after she had ceased to sing in opera. Our encounter took place in Chicago in 1974 at a conference on Verdi, organized by the Italian *Istituto di studi verdiani* and the Chicago Lyric Opera. A number of musicologists and Verdi specialists had been assembled from all over the world to read papers on various aspects of the composer. Hearing of this, Miss Callas, who had been in New York giving master classes at the Juilliard School of Music, let it be known that she would not be averse to addressing the conference. The organizers considered this to be an offer they could not refuse.

When she arrived in Chicago, it became clear that Callas had nothing in particular that she wanted to say about Verdi. She had not prepared a paper, but she graciously condescended to be interviewed in public by one of the *congressisti*. We did not draw lots for this honour: in fact several of us, myself included, refused to conduct the interview, feeling that the nature and purpose of a scholarly conference were ill-served by pandering to the whims of a superannuated prima donna. One or two sycophants, however, offered themselves for the task. In the event, the luckless William Weaver was chosen to act as interviewer.

We assembled, twenty or thirty critics and musicologists and a few hundred members of the general public, in the Civic Theatre one morning at eleven. A few minutes later, Maria Callas strolled onto the stage followed by Bill Weaver, and it was not long before, to quote the colourful prose of the next morning's *Chicago Tribune*, 'world scholars were quizzically tapping their translation headphones, and critics rolled their internationally incredulous eyes'. For the lady, to the surprise of some but by no means all of us, revealed herself to be as silly, coarse and egotistical as – well, as the next prima donna.

Opera, said Callas, had entered into a period of decline since she had ceased to sing. People were too concerned nowadays with authenticity, with performing the notes the composer wrote. She, Callas, had improved the scores of Bellini, Donizetti and Verdi with her interpolated high notes. 'The public loves the high notes, and when I had some very good high notes I gave them. Why not? If you're a wealthy man, why not be generous?'

She insisted we must return to the real traditions of Italian opera. 'Modern productions are boring the audiences by restoring the cuts that the great conductors used to make in the scores.' She made it clear that the guardians, no, the makers of this 'tradition' were herself and her mentor, the conductor Tullio Serafin. 'I want singers and conductors to respect these old traditions, instead of trying new gimmicks – like thinking Donizetti and Verdi are so perfect. I put my foot down. Cuts must be respected. I insist on that.' One of the cuts she would like to insist on in *La traviata* was of the baritone aria. Not the cabaletta (that too, of course) but the aria, '*Di Provenza*', on the grounds that it held up the action.

At this point, to quote the *Tribune* again, 'Charles Osborne, who wrote a marvellous Verdi book, rose to protect the sanctity of the composer.' 'You seem to forget, Miss Callas,' I said, 'that the composers are not there to serve you or your high notes. You are there to serve the composer. You are an interpreter, not a creator. Singers like yourself will come and go, but the genius of Verdi will outlive us all.'

The myopic, affronted gaze of the prima donna focused upon me. 'If Verdi were alive today he would agree with me,' she snarled. 'That we shall never know,' I replied, 'and I'm certainly not taking your word for it.' I was angry, not so much with Callas, an ignorant fishwife of a woman with an intuitive dramatic instinct which enabled her to give some extraordinary performances before her imperfect vocal technique got the better of her, but with those of my colleagues who, I knew, agreed with me, but were afraid to contradict so popular a singer. 'You have the right to disagree with me,' she graciously informed Bill Weaver, who had started her off with a question or two. 'I know I have the right,' Bill answered, 'but I just don't have the nerve.'

Someone had to have the nerve. Anyway, I had nothing to lose except, as it happens, my supper that evening. Callas let it be known that she would not attend a certain supper party if I were going to be there. I tactfully (or cravenly?) refrained from attending, for I did not want to embarrass our host and hostess.

Some years earlier, after Callas appeared in opera in London for the last time, I wrote an article about her for one of the monthly music magazines. The month after my piece appeared, the magazine printed a selection of letters from readers, prefaced by an editorial comment: 'Readers have written hundreds of letters about Charles Osborne's April article, "Is Callas really a great actress?" All were too long to print in full, and many were too rude – either to Callas or to Charles Osborne – to print at all.'

I asked the Editor, Evan Senior, if he could tell me what percentage of the total number of letters received were pro-Callas. His answer was that, while nearly 80% of the letters supported what I had written, the anti-Osborne letters from Callas fans were extraordinarily violent in their abuse. Among the letters sent on to me by the magazine were two containing death threats.

To the best of my knowledge, Callas was the only prima donna to attract fans who behaved like football hooligans. Gore Vidal claimed that, in addition to being stupid, the lady was also anti-semitic. I have no evidence of that. From my observation of her, on and off the stage, I would say she was, as a woman, neither better nor worse than many another temperamental soprano. When she sang, she could be very forceful, though (to me) never moving, for she allowed the bones of technique to stick through the flesh of her artistry. After she reached the age of thirty, her voice began rapidly to deteriorate. In her final concerts she sounded excrutiating.

CARDUS, Neville. The *Guardian's* great music critic spent most of the war years in Australia, which is where I first met him. It was after I had won some competition or other which involved my writing a short critical piece on, if I remember correctly, the Overture to *Tannhäuser*, that Cardus suggested I might consider becoming a music critic. He was a friend and great admirer of my friend Max Oldaker, a most stylish tenor, whose Danilo in *The Merry Widow* and Eisenstein in *Die Fledermaus* Cardus thought the equal of any he had seen. Cardus loved the singing voice, especially in opera, and when we met later in London, we would often talk of singers and singing. He had a particular interest in Australian singers, and a deep admiration for Florence Austral, Marjorie Lawrence, Peter Dawson and several others. When I reviewed his autobiography favourably on the BBC's *Music Magazine* programme, he wrote to thank me, not so much for having spoken well of his book but for having, during the course of my review, endorsed his appreciative comments on Joan Hammond, a soprano whom he thought had been underrated, not by the public but by 'the snootier critics'.

CHAGALL, Marc. Along with a number of other people, I was a guest at a luncheon given by *Ebony*, the black American magazine, in Chicago in 1974. Seated next to a charming old lady who spoke English with a foreign accent, I listened to her talk about her husband, who was, it appeared, an artist. Only towards the end of the meal did I realize that the husband, an even older man sitting at the other side of the table and frowning a great deal, was Marc Chagall.

After lunch, I said to our host, the Editor of *Ebony*, that I had noticed his organization employed only black people. 'But that isn't so,' he replied. 'We do have some whites, but you won't have seen them today in the editorial offices. They are the cleaning staff.' When this was explained to Chagall, he laughed for the first time.

CHAPLIN, Charles. If you were a child in the thirties, you couldn't escape Charlie Chaplin. Some kids loved him. I loved Laurel and Hardy, whose humanity seemed somehow less willed, but by the time I reached my teens I had learned to admire Chaplin. I took his films of the forties seriously, found the argument of *Monsieur Verdoux* unconvincing, and revelled in the satire of *The Great Dictator*. I saw it in Australia when it was first released in 1940. In 1948, walking along the Kurfürstendamm in Berlin, I noticed that it was playing in a cinema there for the first time. Curious to watch it with a German audience, I bought a ticket and went in. The Berliners stared at the screen in absolute silence. Were they outraged? Ashamed? I couldn't help laughing at Hitler-Hynkel's dance with the globe, and at him and Mussolini-Napaloni (Jack Oakie) upstaging each other, but I laughed alone and, after more than one head had turned to look at me (in reproach?), uneasily, I left the cinema before the end of the film. As I came out, the commissionaire on the door, an old man who looked like Emil Jannings in *The Last Laugh*, insisted on giving me a pass in case I was coming back. As he did so, he held my hand and squeezed it. I smiled, walked on, out, and into the nearest bar.

In 1957 I visited a friend who was filming in *A King in New York* with Chaplin, who was also, of course, directing. My sole purpose in visiting the set was to meet the great man. I took with me a photograph, a still from an earlier Chaplin film, *Limelight*, which I used to prop up against the mirror in my dressing room in the days when I was touring around Great Britain as an actor. It showed Chaplin as the old clown, the Great Calvero, staring in quiet desperation into *his* mirror in a theatre dressing room. I did manage to meet Chaplin, and asked him to autograph the photo. As he did so, he said 'Yes, that's the one, all right,' and smiled as he handed it back to me. He put my quite expensive biro in his pocket as he walked away, and I felt pleased that we had something of each other's. A sentimental, oddly Chaplinesque incident.

CHRISTIE, Agatha. I met Dame Agatha only once, on the occasion of a party in 1970 to celebrate her eightieth birthday and the publication of her latest novel, *Passenger to Frankfurt*. Finding myself alone with her for a minute or two, I became uncharacteristically tongue-tied. Though accustomed to meeting and talking to the great and the good, the rich and the famous (no one, incidentally, can be all four), I held Agatha Christie in a special kind of awe. Meeting T. S. Eliot, Jean Cocteau, Bruno Walter or Robert Frost had not reduced me to a panic-stricken silence, but Agatha Christie, whom I had begun to read when I was ten, long before I had heard of those Eliots and Cocteaus, for some reason had this power over me.

I realized I had to say something to her, but what? I began to speak. I heard myself telling her who I was and what I did, and before I could stop myself I was inviting her to join an Arts Council Writers-on-Tour group and tour the provinces for a week, talking to school-kids during the day and adult audiences in the evenings.

She let me down very lightly and kindly. 'I'm afraid I couldn't do that,' she said. 'I wouldn't be any good at it, and besides, one of the reasons I began to write, over sixty years ago, was to avoid having to talk to people.' Someone came up and rescued Agatha Christie and me from each other.

COCTEAU, Jean. I met him on two or three occasions in Paris in the fifties, and once in London. One evening in Paris I was one of a party of about a dozen people, among whom were Cocteau and his friend Jean Marais. We had supper at a restaurant on the Left Bank, in an alley somewhere between the river and the Boulevard St Germain-des-Prés. We sat at a long table, whose covering was of butchers' wrapping-paper.

After the meal, we sat on, drinking, and Cocteau, who was on my left, began to doodle on the 'table-cloth' with a biro. Then, glancing at me occasionally, he quickly sketched my face. I told him I intended to keep the drawing, and asked him to sign it. He signed it 'Henri Matisse'. I carefully tore it away from the table and, trying to roll rather than fold it, put it in my pocket.

For some months I displayed this curiosity on my mantelpiece, and then I put it away 'in a safe place', intending eventually to have it framed. I don't remember where the safe place was, and I now can't find the drawing. I have a feeling that I must have placed it between the pages of a large book, an art book of some kind, to keep it flat. However, it isn't in any of the books I've searched. Since, every few years, I thin out the books on my shelves and sell what I no longer have space to keep, I fear I must have inadvertently sold my Cocteau drawing as well.

COMPTON-BURNETT, Dame Ivy. I first met her when I accompanied Julian Mitchell to tea with her and her companion, Margaret Jourdain.

When she died, it was discovered that she had left small bequests of objects or sums of money to a number of people. I, apparently, was to receive an eighteenth-century mirror. One day, some months after Dame Ivy's death, Olivia Manning phoned me to say she had collected the mirror at the same time as she had collected her own bequest from Ivy, whatever it was. Would I come to tea or drinks one day and take my mirror away?

For months I failed to collect it, and Olivia regularly reminded me. Eventually, she tired of having the mirror sitting in her entrance hall. She rang again, and invited herself to lunch with me: 'I'll call at the Arts Council at one o'clock, and bring the mirror with me. I can't understand why you haven't bothered to take it, Charles. The glass is tarnished but it can be replaced, and the frame is absolutely gorgeous.'

Olivia and I had a pleasant lunch together. Then I accompanied her to her car, to be given my mirror with its elaborate and absolutely gorgeous eighteenth-century wooden frame. Olivia lifted it from the boot of her car by the wire screwed into its back, held it out to me, and dropped it. The absolutely gorgeous frame broke into several pieces, but the tarnished glass was unharmed.

'I'm sure you can have it repaired,' said Olivia as she drove off. But I doubted it. I placed the pieces of frame into a rubbish bin, and carried the mirror, which Ivy would have called a looking-glass, back to my office. I still have it. After all, the frame never reflected the eighteenth century, did it? And, although absolutely gorgeous, the frame was also positively ugly. I like the mirror, like seeing in a glass darkly, like looking into my eighteenth-century eyes.

CURZON, Clifford. One should never expect either a creative or an interpretative artist to be able to explain his art. There is a story that when Mozart, having played his new piano sonata, was asked what it meant, he sat down and played it again. However, Clifford Curzon provided me with a certain illumination when I complimented him, after a recital, on his performance of a Schubert sonata. I said that I sensed he had somehow arrived mysteriously at the heart or the meaning of the work. He thought for a moment, before replying: 'It's all in the sonority, isn't it?' He paused, then continued: 'But sometimes one gets *beyond* the sonority, and then –' He could not find the words to convey his meaning, but we both understood. Or in that moment we thought we did.

DAVIS, Allan. The distinguished director of a number of plays, Allan Davis will probably not be pleased to be best remembered for *No Sex Please, We're British*, which is now in its fifteenth year in the West End. When I misspelled his name in my book, *The Life and Crimes of Agatha Christie*, he sent me the following note in verse:

The Life and Crimes of Charles Osborne
Alun, Alain or Allan D
Or Allen with an E maybe,
Or if sometimes you use one L
I'll say, of course, well what the hell,
Variety's the spice of life,
And nothing causes me much strife
When I am mentioned in your tome
Which I'm enjoying here at home.
Forsooth your book you'll sign, methinks,
So let us fix a date for drinks.

I replied:

Oh what a dreadful thing, God save us,
To make a mess of 'Allan Davus',
Or is it Davies with an E,
Or even Dayviss? Can it be
That I've forgotten how to spell?
Have I upset him? What the hell!
It's true I mispell all my Allans,
Whether in English, Welsh or Lallans.
He really shouldn't be so petty,
It's not as though I'd called him Bette.

DOONE, Rupert. In my biography of W. H. Auden, I had occasion to mention Rupert Doone, the dancer and choreographer who was one of the founders, in the 1930s, of the Group Theatre, which staged the Auden-Isherwood plays. Doone died many years ago, but a friend of his, a self-promoting lady of fierce and formidable temperament named Vera Russell, saw an American copy of my book, and took exception to the following sentence, a fair summary of what many people had said to me about Doone: 'Doone is said by most people who knew him to have been a vain, arrogant man with a number of silly or pretentious ideas about theatre and an extraordinary ability to bully or charm others into accepting them.' (What Auden said about Doone was simply not printable.)

Mrs Russell, some weeks before the British publication of my book, sent this telegram to my publishers:

HAVING WORKED WITH AUDEN AND AS PARTICIPATOR AND LATER CO-ARTISTIC DIRECTOR OF GROUP THEATRE TAKE ABSOLUTE EXCEPTION TO CHARLES OSBORNE'S MALIGNING FALSELY MY COLLEAGUE THE LATE RUPERT DOONE STOP IT IS INEXCUSABLE AND SHALL BE VIGOROUSLY PURSUED

My Editor at Eyre Methuen, a nervous man at the best of times, went into a panic when I told him I would reply personally to Mrs Russell. However, after I sent her the following telegram, we heard no more from the lady:

THANK YOU FOR TELEGRAM TO MY PUBLISHER OFFERING VIGOROUSLY TO PUBLICIZE MY AUDEN BOOK STOP GRATEFULLY ACCEPT YOUR OFFER.

EDDY, Nelson. The American baritone, who began his career in opera (he made his début in Philadelphia in 1924 as Amonasro in *Aida*) and became a film star in the 1930s, was one of my childhood heroes. He first visited Australia in the mid-forties, when he toured the South Pacific entertaining American troops. I still have the programme of a production of *Candida* in which I played Marchbanks, on which he gave me his autograph, adding the words: 'Keep up the good work.' In 1962 he was in Australia again, appearing in cabaret in Sydney while I was briefly visiting my homeland. With a mutual friend I spent an evening with him, talking about opera, German *Lieder*, Lotte Lehmann and American folk song. He said he sometimes wished he had accepted Fritz Busch's offer and joined the Dresden Opera as leading baritone in 1927, if for no other reason than that he would at least have avoided Hollywood and Jeanette McDonald. He had never really enjoyed making films, and felt most at home on the concert stage or the radio.

In my teens I used to collect his 78 rpm records, eagerly awaiting the new ones and scanning the monthly lists of new releases for them. His duets with Jeanette McDonald, and his ballads and songs from films, are re-issued on LP, but does anyone other than me remember his Richard Strauss and Tchaikovsky songs, his Wagner (Hans Sachs and Wolfram), Mozart (Figaro's two Act I arias), *'Vision fugitive'* from Massenet's *Hérodiade*, or his Stephen Foster songs? My collection of 78s was destroyed by a fire in Australia, and I have never found another copy of a 10-inch record of two American folksongs, one of which was called 'Red Rosy Bush'. It began, 'Wish I was a red rosy bush/On the banks of the sea./Everytime my true love walked past/She'd pluck a rose off of me . . .', and it ended, '. . . Wish I had a golden box/To put my true love in./I'd take her out and kiss her, twice,/Then I'd put her back again.'

EMPSON, William. At a party in someone's house in Regent's Park, after a Poetry International performance, a rather inebriated young man tried to begin a punch-up with my co-director Patrick Garland. As people dragged him off, the poet William Empson came up to me and said, 'I must apologize to you for the behaviour of a member of my party, for which I accept the responsibility.' 'There's no reason for you to apologize,' I began. Empson interrupted me. 'But there is. He is my wife's lover.'

EVANS, Dame Edith. I used to encounter her, and a number of other theatrical Dames and quasi-Dames, at board meetings of the Apollo Society at the Arts Council in the sixties. Marie Ney, Margaret Rawlings, Irene Worth, Dadie Rylands were all value for money. I sometimes contrived to sit next to Dame Edith, so that when she fell asleep, which was often, I could unobtrusively awaken her with a murmur. She reacted in the grand manner to everything, even the most trivial incident or remark. 'Sit here, Dame Edith, I've reserved the arm-chair for you,' I said. 'The *Arm*-chair?' It might have been Prism's offending handbag. 'I don't know whether to be Pleased or Of*fend*ed!'

FELSENSTEIN, Walter. The great director of East Berlin's Komische Oper invited me, during a conference in Leipzig, to visit him at his house in Berlin. When I asked him for his address in East Berlin, he looked astonished. 'You don't think I live in that dreadful place, do you?' he said. 'I only work there. I live in the West.'

GARDNER, Ava. Always in search of starry names to increase the box office takings of Poetry International, I took advantage, in 1972, of the fact that I had once been introduced to Ava Gardner and that she lived in London. I wrote to her, asking if she would be interested in taking part in our international festival of poetry at the Royal Festival Hall. I wanted her to give a reading of poems by modern American female poets: the confessional school of Anne Sexton and the like.

I received a most gracious refusal from Miss Gardner. 'I am honoured, indeed flattered, that you should ask me to read poetry, especially at your annual Festival. And you shouldn't apologize for the fee being small. People should be proud to read the works of great poets – if they are able.'

'But,' she continued, 'I regret to have to tell you I am not. It is just not my thing. I do enjoy reading poetry, especially that of my dear friend Robert Graves, but I am not accomplished at reading aloud, and it would be quite wrong not to do it properly.'

She went on to thank me for asking her, said she was sure I would find someone better equipped, and wished me every success with that year's Festival.

Encouraged by the fact that she had replied at some length, rather than with a dismissive abruptness, I made the mistake of persevering, attempted to persuade Miss Gardner that it would not be too daunting a task, and offered to coach her in the art of reading verse. Her reply this time began, 'Full marks for persistence.' Reading verse might not be daunting to me, she said, but it certainly was to her.

I gave up.

GARLAND, Judy. It isn't fashionable to admit one's admiration for Judy Garland. If one does, one is in danger of being categorized as either a hopeless old square or a screaming faggot. There was a time when it seemed that the entire membership of the Garland Fan Club (I don't imagine there really is one) consisted of Paul Bailey and myself.

I fell in love with the young Judy (she was five years older than I) when, at the age of twelve, I saw *The Wizard of Oz* on its first release. As a teenager, I followed her through those films with Micky Rooney, and in my mid-twenties I finally realized she was not only a superb vaudeville entertainer but also a great screen actress, when I attended a preview of *A Star is Born.* I went to her stage show at the Dominion in Tottenham Court Road several times during the course of its season of a few weeks, and Paul Bailey and I were still with her at the end, at that sad cabaret appearance at *Talk of the Town* in 1968. The final, successful suicide bid a year later came as no surprise.

I met her during that Dominion Theatre season in 1957. She promised, when she was next in Hollywood, to dig out the poems she had written as a teenager, and let me see them. She never did, of course. I remember her spontaneous laughter when I told her I'd like to hear her sing Mahler – the *'Kindertotenlieder'* perhaps. 'Oh come *on*,' she said, through her laughter, and I began to laugh at myself, too. But I'd still like to have heard her sing Mahler. (Pseud's Corner please copy.) Oscar Levant, pianist, composer, actor and acerbic wit, said of Judy, 'When I like her, I think she's the greatest singing artist in the world. When I don't like her, I think the same thing, but grudgingly.'

GEDDA, Nicolai. Since at most periods of my life I've written about music and musicians, opera and opera singers, I have tended to avoid socializing with musicians and singers in order to be free to express my opinions in print. But a friendship which grows spontaneously is another matter, and since Nicolai Gedda is one of the great tenors of the century I have not felt any embarrassment at writing favourably of his performances even though we have been friends for more than twenty years. His wife Stacey, too, is a dear friend.

I first heard Nicolai on gramophone records, and was struck not only by the beauty of his voice but especially by his musicianship and technique. In due course I came to marvel at his versatility as well. Who else can encompass everything from Bach to Robert Stolz, taking in French, Russian and Italian opera and Russian liturgical music as well? (And American opera. When Nicolai sang in the première of Barber's *Vanessa* with a cast of American singers, the clarity of his diction showed up that of his American colleagues.)

He is a superb mimic, and it was his hilarious imitations of Otto Klemperer (a conductor he greatly revered and who admired Nicolai enormously, using him in several of his recordings) that led Ken Thomson and me to compile our book, *Klemperer Stories*, to which Nicolai provided a preface.

I first heard Nicolai live on stage when he made his Covent Garden début in 1954 as the Duke in *Rigoletto*, and have enjoyed countless performances of his since, in London, New York, Paris, Berlin, Vienna, Stockholm and Edinburgh. In December 1982, Ken and I were the guests of Nicolai and Stacey at his gala recital at the Metropolitan Opera House, celebrating his twenty-fifth anniversary with the Met. And, as I have said, I was enormously honoured by the recital which Nicolai generously gave, in April 1986, to celebrate my twenty years with the Arts Council.

GIELGUD, Sir John. When John Gielgud, Constance Cummings and Vincent Price agreed to perform in one of my Poetry International programmes, I rehearsed them at Sir John's house in Cowley Street, Westminster. I was, at first, nervous at the thought of directing one of our oldest and most distinguished actors, but was soon put at my ease by Gielgud's attitude, which was that we were there to perform as successfully as possible, and that all help would be gratefully received. 'When I don't understand the lines, I tend to sing,' he informed me. 'Do stop me if I begin singing.'

There was nothing he did not understand in our programme, for his contributions were all from the pen of his old friend and colleague, Noël Coward. Even so, he listened politely as I explained the shape of a particular Coward lyric to him. When I criticized him for imitating Coward in his rendition of one item, and suggested ways in which his performance could be liberated from Coward's own inflections, he immediately accepted my suggestions.

I gave him lunch one day, at *Chez Victor*, in Wardour Street. All through the meal, the waiters kept fussing over Gielgud, coming up to ask him if everything was all right, and hovering unnecessarily. This began to irritate me, and I said to him, 'I'm sorry, I can't imagine why they're all carrying on like this.' 'I think,' he replied, 'it's because I usually sit over there.' And he gestured to a table on the other side of the room.

When my book on Auden appeared, Gielgud wrote to congratulate me but also to point out that one of the photographs in the book, purporting to be of the George, a favourite Oxford restaurant of the twenties, was in fact not the George Restaurant but a completely different building, the George Hotel, in another part of Oxford. When my book went into its next edition I had the false George removed. No one could find a photograph of the real George at short notice, so I substituted Blackwell's Bookshop as it was in Auden's student days.

John Gielgud was once overheard to say to Harold Pinter, 'I must thank you for having written such a marvellous vehicle for me.' Harold Pinter's reaction to the description of *No Man's Land* as a vehicle is not known.

GIESEKING, Walter. When I first began, as a child, to listen to classical pianists, I admired Gieseking enormously, especially for his Mozart and Beethoven performances. I found the cool, crisp articulation of his recording of Beethoven's G major Piano Concerto infinitely preferable to the more traditional approach of Artur Schnabel. By the time I heard Gieseking play in person, however, although he could only have been in his fifties he seemed to have lost his unique quality. It was in Melbourne, around 1950, and he plodded his way through the E flat Concerto (the 'Emperor') like any one of a dozen other pianists in Australia.

I was taken by a Viennese friend to meet him a day or two after the concert. There had been talk of Gieseking's having been pro-Nazi, or at least of having remained in Germany to promote his career during the Nazi period. This did not unduly concern me, for I have never been very good at adopting a high moral tone from a distance. He appeared to be a very gentle soul, but I understand that appearances can be deceptive. What was most disconcerting was that he seemed to be somewhere else, listening to music we could not hear. I don't think it was simply that we were boring him, though we probably were. He was quietly distrait, I thought. Certainly something had happened to him, something catastrophic. God or someone had swooped down and punished him (for what?) by taking his great gift away from him.

GOBBI, Tito. I first met Tito and his charming wife Tilde many years ago, in the days when I frequently presented BBC programmes on musicians, especially singers. The most intelligent as well as the most dramatically exciting of Italian baritones, Tito was a joy to interview, or to discuss opera with. He always remained absolutely unflappable, whatever might be going on around him, on stage or off.

He gave a startling demonstration of this unflappability on one occasion when Ken Thomson and I gave him and Tilde supper at *L'Opéra*, after Tito's final performance in Verdi's *Falstaff* at Covent Garden. Rather than wait backstage for him, we had arranged to go to the restaurant, where Tito would join us as soon as he could. We had to wait a good half-hour for, as he explained later, he was besieged by autograph-hunters at the stage door. From our table I had been keeping my eye on the front door of the restaurant for some minutes when Tito eventually appeared through it and paused, looking around for us. As he caught sight of me, he waved, and then lowered his arm, dropping his hand into a frying pan of sizzling butter in which a waiter was about to *flambé* a minute steak.

Tito removed his hand smartly, but did not utter a sound. Wending his way through the restaurant, he arrived at our table, beamed genially at me, and asked, 'What do you do for a frying hand?' More butter, this time unsizzling, was applied to it by a nervous waiter, and then Tito promptly forgot about it for the rest of the evening.

GOLLANCZ, Victor. I loved chatting to Victor about opera. He had firmly-held views: the story of his rushing out of the Royal Opera House during Joan Sutherland's first *Lucia di Lammermoor* in 1959, exclaiming, 'My God, she's even duller than Melba,' is well-known. He once enlisted my aid in an attempt to persuade the Covent Garden management to mount Wagner's *Die Meistersinger von Nürnberg* with Nicolai Gedda as Walther, instead of the usual Wagnerian shrieker. 'Then,' Victor shouted at me, 'we'd hear the role *sung* for the first time.' I'm sure he was right, but now we shall never know.

When I worked for *The London Magazine*, I used to phone Victor every month to ask him to advertise Gollancz books in the magazine. He always said no. Then, one year, I ran into him at the Staatsoper in Vienna, during the Festival. We chatted about the performances we were attending. Every evening, for about a fortnight, we would encounter each other at the opera and argue about the merits of this singer, the defects of that conductor. On my last evening in Vienna before returning to London, Victor (who was staying on longer) said to me: 'To commemorate our pleasant talks here in

Vienna, the next time you ask me to take advertising space in *The London Magazine* I shall do so.'

The following month, back in London, I rang Victor as usual. No, he would not advertise. Next month I tried again. Still the answer was no. 'But Victor,' I complained, 'you did say, in Vienna, that you would take a page.'

'Ah,' said Victor, 'you have learned something about me.'

'What is that?' I asked.

'I am not a man of my word.'

Some time in the mid-sixties, I approached Victor with my plan to write a book on the operas of Verdi. He was immediately enthusiastic, and commissioned the book, which Victor Gollancz Ltd. published in 1969. But by then Victor had died, and the firm was being run by his daughter, Livia.

On the day on which my book was published, Livia gave me lunch at Rules'. 'You know, Charles,' she said, 'my father was very fond of you, and he had great hopes for this book. When we showed him the new season's catalogue, shortly before he died, he looked through it and singled out *The Complete Operas of Verdi*. He said he was so glad you had written the book, and he knew it was going to be a major contribution to Verdi studies.'

I was touched, and murmured something appropriate.

'But, of course,' Livia continued, 'his mind had already gone by then He died a few days later.'

GOODMAN, Lord. He is too nice a man for me to embarrass him by quoting his comments to me on others, except in the most general terms. As a senior civil servant hove into view one day, Arnold murmured, 'There's one of those nitwits from whose disastrous advice I'm forever extricating Jennie.' Is it indiscreet to reveal that he once confided to me his only theatrical ambition: to play Mr Knightley in a stage adaptation of *Emma?*

One morning when he had invited me to his flat for breakfast, he offered me several statements explicitly for my memoirs, which he said he hoped I would soon begin to write, and not wait until I had left the Arts Council. Looking at these now, I find the only one I can use is: 'You at the Arts Council are a helpless lot. If you were wrecked on a desert island, apart from a little nervous cannibalism you wouldn't know how to survive.'

At the Royal Opera House, during *Aida*, when Ramfis the High Priest stepped forward to demand the death of the Ethiopian prisoners, Arnold Goodman murmured, 'Rossetti.' Harold Rossetti was the Department of Education and Science's assessor to the Arts Council.

Shortly after Arnold had returned from Rhodesia, whither he had been sent by the government to try to talk the Rhodesians out of their unilateral declaration of independence, he and I lunched with Leonard Wolfson of Great Universal Stores, who was thinking of endowing a literary prize. It transpired that when he spoke of literature he really meant history, and was appalled when Goodman and I began to talk of poetry and novels. The lunch conversation became more general, and Arnold shared some of his Rhodesian experiences with us. He had been warmly welcomed by the Jewish community in Salisbury, but not so warmly welcomed by Mr Smith. 'I never got a meal out of him, or even spoke to him outside of committee.' In committee, however, Smith had said to him, 'Give me one valid reason why we should give these bloody niggers a vote.' 'Arithmetic,' said Goodman. He did not, he told me, meet one African (and he met a great many) who was not perfectly capable of exercising his franchise.

As we came away from lunch, he said of Wolfson: 'A most reactionary character. Could be the Jewish Colonel of a smart regiment. But we may as well take his two million pounds.' (A sample of Wolfson's conversation: 'My father was asked, at the age of seventy-four, "Why do you need Burberry's?" "I don't need it," he said, "I want it."')

When we lunched together a few months before publication of this volume, Arnold gave me *carte blanche* to say whatever I wanted to about him. 'My belief,' he had written to me some weeks earlier, 'is that, if everyone to whom you have sent an offensive postcard buys a copy, you will be a richer author than Mr Jeffery Archer or Miss Barbara Cartland.'

GRAHAME, Gloria. In her heyday in the cinema, she was never one of my favourites, though I could see that she had a certain sulky appeal. I think I liked her best in a film called *In a Lonely Place*, in which she played opposite Humphrey Bogart.

I was dragged out to Watford by Ken Thomson, who admired her inordinately, to see her play Sadie Thompson in *Rain* with the local rep, which she did reasonably well. Some weeks later I bought her a drink at a West End club, and months afterwards caught another performance of hers at a Hampstead theatre club. I encountered Gloria Grahame only once after that. As I was passing a betting shop in Jermyn Street, I glanced in the doorway and saw her with a man. She was crying, and the man appeared to be threatening her. I recognized her only after I had walked on a few yards, but then turned back to see if she needed any help. It was clear, however, that the quarrel, if that's what it was, was a domestic one, and I don't think she would have appreciated any interference. I turned away, and walked on.

GRAVES, Robert. He was over eighty, and his concentration came and went when he took part in Poetry International. He read his poems at the Festival Hall, standing erect at the microphone, and holding six typed pages each containing a short lyric poem. As he finished reading each poem, he placed the sheet at the bottom of the batch of papers, and began the next one without a break. Having got to the end of poem number six, he was about to begin on number one again, when I murmured to him that I thought he'd probably finished. He allowed me to lead him off the platform.

Backstage, someone gave me a message that the Italian Ambassador was in the audience, and would like to meet Robert Graves, whose poetry he greatly admired. I asked Graves if he was willing. He nodded, and began to tell me a confused story about World War I. The Ambassador entered, I shook hands with him and took him across to Graves, who was tired and remained seated. 'Your Excellency,' I said to the Italian Ambassador, 'this is Mr Robert Graves.'

Graves looked up at the Ambassador's outstretched hand. 'You're an eye-tie, are you?' he asked, but not at all belligerently, as he accepted the hand.

'Ah – yes,' said the Ambassador.

GUINNESS, Sir Alec. One cannot help being allergic to certain performers. This is not the same thing as considering them poor artists. For instance, I think of Alan Howard as a coffee-bar Olivier, but that's simply because I consider him an absurdly over-praised actor. I can't say I'm actually allergic to him.

Alec Guinness is an actor of great technical accomplishment, and he has written a splendid volume of autobiography. However, I'm convinced that, if I were to be exposed to him for more than a few minutes, I would come out in a rash. I once had to stay away from a play by Alan Bennett until Guinness had left the cast. I went to the play on the first non-Guinness night, and took Alan Bennett to supper after the performance, explaining why I hadn't come to his first night six months earlier.

Once, I rounded a corner in Mayfair and almost bumped into Sir Alec. He must have thought my involuntary exclamation of dismay somewhat over the top, but I didn't wait to find out. Another time, I spent a *mauvais quart d'heure* in Cecconi's Restaurant in Burlington Gardens, waiting for Melvyn Bragg. I sat at our table, horrified to discover Alec Guinness lunching alone at the nearest table, in my direct line of vision. When Melvyn arrived, I asked him to sit where he would completely obscure my view of the distinguished actor. (I hadn't intended to criticize his craft, but there *is* a residue of something smarmily Guinnessian in all of his performances, isn't there? I ran screaming from his Macbeth at the Royal Court, and it wasn't because of Simone Signoret and her 'Infirm of pur*pose*, give me ze dag*gairs*!')

HALL, Sir Peter. His *Diaries* are superb, and he is surely our most imaginative and most sensitive director of plays and operas. His *Don Giovanni* and *Le Nozze di Figaro* are so unobtrusively right, and his productions of Shakespeare, which I've been enjoying since Stratford in the fifties, are always illuminating. Verdi's *Macbeth* at the Met seemed to me to be a comparative failure, but even there I approved of what he was attempting to achieve.

Peter did not deserve to be saddled with the administration of the National Theatre, although I suppose he must have wanted it. When he came to talk about the National to the Arts Council's absurd Drama Panel, he was bitterly attacked by many of the panel members, especially the envious no-hopers. Peter wrote to me after the meeting, at which I had been present:

> I can't say I much enjoyed the Drama Panel Cricket Match. It is a melancholy fact that the radicals of the theatre no longer want a National Theatre. If they have to have one, they are obviously going to treat it with great suspicion. A hundred and fifty years of effort by their predecessors end in this. What would G.B.S. have said?!

HAMILTON, Gerald. When I knew him, the original of Christopher Isherwood's Mr Norris was nearly eighty, and was living in a bed-sitting-room above a Chinese restaurant in the King's Road. (For the story of his funeral, see under Stephen Spender.) He earned a little money in 1955 by posing for the sculptor Oscar Nemon, as the body of Winston Churchill. When I drive around Parliament Square, I derive a certain pleasure from glancing at the Churchill statue and recalling that, while the features may be the great war leader's, the body and stance are that of Gerald, the dreadful old crypto-fascist.

HAMMOND, Dame Joan. Like every other opera-lover of my generation, I derived great enjoyment from Joan Hammond's war-time recordings of Verdi and Puccini arias sung (because it *was* war-time) in English. 'O my beloved father', 'Love and music, these have I lived for', and 'One fine day, you'll notice', she sang in her impeccable diction and with that highly individual timbre. She once sang 'One fine day' at a fund-raising gala for the Sydney Opera House, not realizing at the time, she told me later, how apt the title of the aria would prove to have been: the opera house eventually opened years behind schedule.

Though she was an Australian (and we forgive her for actually having been born in New Zealand), she had studied in Vienna, had begun her career there before the war, and had then become a successful opera singer in England, so none of us in Australia had heard her sing in person. When she returned to tour the country in 1946, she was critically and popularly acclaimed everywhere. One Sunday afternoon in Melbourne, she gave a recital in the Town Hall to which admission was free. As we were not paying, Joan presumably felt she could sing what she wanted to, and not what her public most wanted (Verdi and Puccini arias). Her programme that afternoon consisted entirely of Schubert and Wolf songs, and I realized with astonishment that she was as fine a singer of *Lieder* as of opera.

We became friends much later, in London. After she retired, due to ill health, and returned to Australia to live, I continued to see her on my visits there. I remember on one occasion, when I was lecturing at Melbourne University, casting my eye around my audience and discovering Joan in the front row. She and Lolita Marriott lived in a splendid house overlooking the sea. Sadly, it was destroyed in a bush fire, and they now live in Melbourne, where Joan still teaches. She is the friendliest and most spontaneous of women, and I still consider her one of the best Aidas or Leonoras (*Il trovatore*) I've ever heard.

In her youth Joan was a champion golfer. When she left to study singing in Vienna, a newspaper wrote that her departure was 'the worst thing that could happen to Australian golf'.

HAMPSHIRE, Stuart. Some time after Stuart had ceased to be Chairman of the Arts Council's Literature Panel, we lunched together and chatted about the past. Stuart said that a certain female member of the Council was 'not very intelligent', to which I replied that she was an intellectual giant by comparison with Marina Vaizey (whom we had earlier been discussing). I recalled once scribbling a note to Stuart at a Council meeting while Marina was speaking. 'Inside that plump brunette,' I had written, 'there's a dumb blonde struggling to express herself.'

HAREWOOD, Lord. John Calder invited Lord Harewood and me to lunch at Wheeler's in Frith Street to discuss the possibility of our jointly editing for him a resuscitated *Opera Annual*. (Under Harold Rosenthal's editorship it had reached nine issues, after which publication had been suspended for some years.) We found ourselves gossiping about opera performances we had attended in various countries. George asked, 'Have either of you ever failed to get into a performance you wanted to see?' John and I confessed that we had occasionally failed to gain admission to a sold-out première. 'I've always got in,' said George. 'When all else fails, I point out that I'm the cousin of the Queen of England.'

At an Arts Council meeting during the time when Lord Eccles was Minister of the Arts, we were discussing what Lord Goodman might like as a farewell present. I said to George Harewood, who was sitting next to me, 'He'll probably opt for the head of Eccles on a silver platter. What then?' 'Then,' replied George, who was then head of English National Opera, 'we gladly put on a private performance of *Salome* – with the head.'

HATFIELD, Hurd. I had noted the fact of his existence as early as 1945, when he played Dorian Gray in a Hollywood film of Wilde's *The Picture of Dorian Gray*, with George Sanders as Lord Henry Wotton (a good piece of casting), Angela Lansbury as Sybil Vane (ditto), and Donna Reed (Donna Reed?) as Gladys Hallward. Hurd Hatfield possessed the decadent good looks for Dorian which was about all he needed, for it is hardly a difficult role to portray.

I was only eighteen when I saw the film. It stayed in my mind as a surprisingly good adaptation of Wilde. Hatfield went on to make a few disappointing appearances in movies for the next five years or so, and then faded into insignificance.

One evening in the summer of 1983, Ken Thomson and I set out to attend the performance of a play by Marghanita Laski, in a North London pub. We arrived, and were directed up a flight of stairs leading from the bar to a first-floor room where the play was to be performed. As we were about to enter, I experienced a sudden revulsion from the whole grotty business of plays in pubs. We fled. (I felt I was being disloyal to Marghanita, whose play I wanted to see, but I couldn't help it. One is allowed to be neurotic, occasionally, is one not?)

Since we were in his vicinity, we decided to pay an impromptu call on Angus McGill, the *Evening Standard* columnist. We found Angus in his garden, drinking with a small group of friends, one of whom was – Hurd Hatfield. Forty years on from Dorian Gray, Mr Hatfield had retained his elegance and charm, and sufficient of his looks for one at least to speculate on the condition of any portraits he might have in his attic.

HAYDN, Richard. A delightful actor and, to use Richard's own description, 'fish mimic', whom Noël Coward took to America in 1939, Richard Haydn played Charley in a film of *Charley's Aunt* with Jack Benny, and then remained in Hollywood for more than forty years, although he virtually retired from the screen after delivering a characteristically acerbic performance as Max in *The Sound of Music.* He was said to have become somewhat reclusive and to stir but rarely beyond his attractive house in Pacific Palisades, but when Ken Thomson and I visited him there in the summer of 1984 we found him to be friendly, welcoming and amusing. Though nearly eighty and virtually blind, he allowed us to take him out to lunch at a seafood restaurant in Santa Monica at the point where Sunset Boulevard hits the ocean. We drove in our rented car down the tortuously twisting streets to the sea, and Richard was able to direct us accurately, despite not being able to see where he was. We talked about his neighbours, who were various Hollywood stars; about his old friends Gladys Cooper, her son-in-law Robert Morley, and his son Sheridan (Richard's godson). We spoke, too, of our mutual friend Max Oldaker, whom Richard had known in London in the thirties when they were both in Coward's *Operette*, and whom I had first met in Australia in the forties.

Like all those Beverly Hills, Bel Air and Pacific Palisades characters, Richard had a splendid swimming pool. As I led him by the arm past it, I asked if the pool nowadays got much used. 'I was last in it at five-thirty this morning,' he replied indignantly.

It was less than a year later that I read his obituary in *The Times*, written by Sheridan Morley: 'He was one of the last of the Hollywood Raj, that remarkable breed of English actors and writers who went out to colonize American films of the 1930s as successfully as their parents and grandparents had colonized Africa and Australia.'

HUMPHRIES, Barry. I've written about Barry Humphries in the main narrative of this book. But you know what he's like: he will think that, if I don't mention him in *Name-Dropping*, I don't regard his as a sufficiently famous name to drop. Actually, it isn't Barry who would react so childishly, but his *alter ego*, the ebullient but highly sensitive Dame Edna.

Barry has extremely arcane tastes in music and literature; well, in most things, actually. He is envious of my collection of gramophone records, and I have more than once caught him attempting to sneak out of my flat (one of those rambling old Victorian mansion flats, near Westminster Cathedral) with my Malcolm McEachern album, or my *Dokumente* disc of Eduard Künneke's Biedermeier Suite, conducted by the composer. I have not yet allowed him to hear my records of flute quartets by the obscure nineteenth-century Danish composer, Dag Henrik Esrum-Hellerup, of whom

I first became aware after reading of him in the New Grove Dictionary. Esrum-Hellerup is the kind of composer Barry most admires, one who achieves *multum in parvo.*

KARAJAN, Herbert von. For many of Karajan's opera recordings, especially of Verdi, I was engaged to write the articles for the booklets accompanying the albums. When Karajan made a film version of his Salzburg production of *Otello*, I was invited to the film's première at the Royal Festival Hall, and to a reception for Karajan.

At the party, I had an opportunity to talk to the Maestro for quite some time. After we had spoken of other things, I congratulated him on the *Otello* film, and added, 'But tell me, was that you I saw amongst the crowd in Act I?' (When the camera had panned along the Egyptian citizens waiting to great Othello, it seemed to linger somewhat on one of them, who, although he was an swarthily made-up as the others, had very light blue eyes.) Karajan put his arm around my shoulders. 'Ah, my friend,' he murmured, 'you are the only one to have noticed.'

Some days later I asked Peter Andry of EMI, the distributors of the film, if he had spotted Karajan 'doing a Hitchcock' in the crowd scene. 'Oh, yes,' said Peter. 'I noticed that when I was looking at a rough cut in Munich some months ago. In fact I mentioned it to Karajan, and he said, "Ah, my friend, you are the only one to have noticed." '

KERR, Sir John. At a party in the Crush Bar of the Royal Opera House, Joan Sutherland introduced me to Sir John, the ex-Governor-General of Australia, who had caused a political storm in the Australian teacup by sacking the Prime Minister of the country, the well-meaning and highly engaging Gough Whitlam (who had been responsible for Kerr's appointment).

Kerr had been savaged in the recently published memoirs of Patrick White, and was still smarting from this when I met him. He began to fulminate against the great novelist, whom I felt called on to defend, although I think his memoirs, *Flaws in the Glass*, to be Patrick's least impressive work. 'You have to make allowances for Patrick White,' I said. 'I know he can be something of an old curmudgeon –' A florid-faced Sir John interrupted me impatiently. 'Curmudgeon?' he shouted, his nasal Aussie accent becoming stronger and his vinous complexion even ruddier. 'I'll tell you what he is. He's a proper bastard! That's what he is!'

KIPNIS, Alexander. Kipnis, the finest Russian bass of his time, and the possessor of a voice of rich velvet, was a greatly admired Boris Godunov in

Mussorgsky's opera. He sang in Germany until the rise of the Nazis, when, as a Jew, he found it expedient to leave. His later career was based at the Metropolitan Opera, from which he retired in the late 1940s.

Some time in the seventies I attended the first night of Karajan's production of *Boris Godunov* at the Salzburg Festival. The role of Boris was sung beautifully, though not very dramatically, by Nicolai Ghiaurov. Unfortunately, the elderly gentleman sitting next to me insisted on singing along softly, in Russian, during Ghiaurov's solos. Eventually I silenced him by digging him in the ribs.

In the interval I talked to an American singer whom I knew. 'My teacher is here this evening,' he told me. 'Who is your teacher?' 'Alexander Kipnis. Ah, here he comes. Let me introduce you.' And I found myself shaking hands with the greatest living Boris, whose singing I had so impolitely suppressed during Act I.

KISSINGER, Henry. At a reception given by the U.S. State Department in Washington, I was one of several people singled out to meet our host, Dr Kissinger, and had to stand in line to do so. The man ahead of me in the queue was an Indian or Pakistani academic who, as he shook hands with Kissinger, said effusively, 'Dr Kissinger, on behalf of my country I must thank you for having saved the world from the threat of destruction. We of the free world salute you, and thank you.'

'You're velcome,' replied Dr Kissinger.

KLEMPERER, Otto. All of my Klemperer stories, as well as those told to me by Nicolai Gedda, Alfred Brendel, Christa Ludwig and others, are to be found in the volume, *Klemperer Stories*, which Ken Thomson and I compiled and which was published in 1980. Klemperer's was a rough humour, and he was capable of using it cruelly. He did not always, however, have the last word. When Walter Legge, the producer of many of Klemperer's records took Maria Callas to a Klemperer concert, and brought her backstage afterwards to meet him, Klemperer said to Callas in his most forthright manner, 'I have heard you twice. *Norma*, very good. *Iphigénie*, horrible!' 'Thank you, Maestro,' said Callas with a charming smile. 'But I am sure,' Klemperer continued, 'that Mr Legge will agree to engage you to sing at a concert here with me. What would you like to sing?' Callas smiled again with great sweetness as she replied, 'The arias from *Iphigénie*, Maestro.'

A story which did not get into our book was told me by the tenor John Mitchinson. At a Festival Hall rehearsal, Klemperer said to Hugh Bean, then the leader of the Philharmonia Orchestra, 'I feel awful this morning. I think

I am going to die.' 'We are all going to die, Dr Klemperer,' said Bean. Klemperer's face brightened. 'Ja?' he queried. 'Even Walter Legge?'

The first time I encountered Klemperer was in Brisbane in 1950. He had come to Australia to conduct concerts with the symphony orchestras in the various states. (At his first sight of the Sydney Symphony, his jaw dropped in dismay. 'Womans!' he exclaimed, as he looked at the string section. 'Never haf I seen so many womans!') The Queensland Symphony Orchestra at that time was not a first-rate band, but Klemperer made them play like angels in Beethoven's Eighth Symphony and, with Alfredo Campoli, in the Mendelssohn Violin Concerto. At the end of the concert, although the applause was overwhelming, it appeared that the conductor did not intend to return to the platform to acknowledge it. We applauded all the more vociferously, until eventually the tall, gaunt figure of Klemperer made its way back to the platform, wearing an overcoat and a felt hat. He glared at us, nodded curtly, and disappeared again.

I had met Klemperer a day or two before that concert. The Australian Broadcasting Commission's publicity officer had rung me at the Ballad Bookshop (then Brisbane's only decent bookshop, owned and run by Barrie Reid and myself) to say that Dr Klemperer was 'short of reading matter', and to ask if I would come along to his rehearsal, bringing with me a selection of books in German. What, I wondered, would a distinguished German conductor read? He would already know the whole of Thomas Mann and Kafka, and most of the other German-language books on our shelves. But I selected two or three recent German novels of a distinctly literary kind, and a few other volumes which I thought might be sufficiently intellectual for him.

At a break in the rehearsal I was taken to the artists' room and introduced to the great man, who was seated in an armchair, smoking a pipe. We shook hands solemnly, and I began, feeling like a rather shabby pedlar, to produce books from the Gladstone bag I had brought with me, thrusting them at him, and nervously attempting, in German, to describe them. Klemperer glanced cursorily and scornfully at the first few books, and then looked up at me. Without removing his pipe from his mouth, '*Kein* Agatha Christie?' he asked, incredulously.

LAING, R. D. The maverick who, for some years, convinced a number of people that he had revolutionized psychiatry, was once invited to read his own poems at a Poetry International event. His reading was interrupted by a fierce commotion outside the doors of the auditorium, and Patrick Garland, Jamie Muir (the attractive and amiable son of Frank: then our general dogsbody, now a TV producer) and I had to use strong-arm tactics to prevent the interrupters from pushing their way through into the audience. Patrick, Jamie and I wondered whether the demonstrators were ex-patients of Laing, furious with him for not having cured them, and delighted at this rare opportunity to attack him in a public place.

LARKIN, Philip. He was not only one of the finest poets of the century; he was also, behind that misleadingly dour façade of his, the most amusing and life-enhancing of men. His manner could sometimes take on an almost Klemperer- or perhaps Churchill-like roughness ('May I say, Charles, how absolutely delighted I am we've got rid of that bloody cow,' he muttered to me when a particularly tiresome female novelist resigned from the Arts Council's Literature Panel); but he more usually dealt in sunnier dismissals. At a meeting of the board of the Poetry Book Society when he was its Chairman, he responded to a member's comment that there was a case to be made for having more non-poets on the board by observing in an aside to me: 'There's a case to be made for having more non-poets in the world generally.'

Philip's inscriptions to me on copies of his books are, for the most part, affectionate. An ambiguous exception, I thought, was 'To Charles, the Smiler with the Knife.' I did not recognize the allusion, and when I asked him he wrote back: 'The smiler with the knife comes in "The Knight's Tale", line 1141. He isn't anyone in particular, just a general nasty idea. Kind regards, Philip.'

Over lunch one day, Philip suddenly asked me, 'Who's the biggest shit you've ever encountered in your life?' We were soon flinging names of candidates about with gay abandon.

At the Arts Council I was forever bullying Philip into serving on committees. For a time he chaired a committee which advised on the acquisition of poets' manuscript material. In theory Philip was in favour of such material being collected, and its purchase by libraries being subsidized by the Arts Council, but in practice he didn't like, as he put it, 'licking the arse of some young thug I'd rather kick'. And he mentioned several good examples.

He allowed me, in 1975, to mount a Larkin poetry reading, on the understanding that he was not expected to be present. I engaged Harold Pinter and Ian Hamilton to read, and I called it 'An Evening Without Philip Larkin'. ('It sounds just what I need,' said Philip.) Later, when I reported to him on the success of the occasion, he wrote, 'I'm sorry I didn't hear the "Evening". That bearded figure with the long overcoat and the middle-

Europe accent that you turned away with rather more force than was necessary was me, I suppose you realize.'

When I was Secretary of the Poetry Book Society, I once received a cheque from a would-be member, accompanied by the following letter, written in a hand which matched the style and spelling:

> Dear Mr Ozborn,
> I am fond of potery and love to join the
> Poultry Book Society. I hop that yuo publish Patent Storng, she is my faverit, next to Ted Huge of course.
> Yours respectfully,
> P. A. Larkin (Mrs.)

When my volume of Collected Poems was published, Philip wrote to say that he especially liked 'Song of Nothing', 'The Aged Actor Speaks', 'and the more atrabilious ones.' His letter continued:

> Glad to see a boot for [Auberon] Waugh's arse. He has started jeering at me after I said his dad was a bit of a tuft hunter, or he thought I did. Wouldn't you like to write a book called Talentless Sons of Famous Fathers? I can think of several: Randolph Churchill, Richard Hutton, Philip Toynbee. And others!
>
> Are you really leaving the Arts Council? You were the last bastion of civilization against the nitwitted hordes. But it must have been hell for you.

A note from Philip in 1981 reads: 'Congratulations on your photograph in *The Times* this morning. So far from abolishing the Literature Department, I should think they will put you in charge of all the others. I am delighted to hear of Ms Forster's resignation.'

In 1984 I mounted another Larkin poetry reading, and again, of course, in the poet's absence. This was not an Arts Council-sponsored affair, but one of the Gallery Poets series of readings at the Odette Gilbert Gallery in Mayfair, organized and paid for by Josephine Hart. These were delightful occasions, which always ended with the performers and friends being taken to supper by the amiable Maurice Saatchi, Josephine's husband. For the Larkin evening, Alan Bates and I were the performers. Alan read most of the poems, while I read a few and provided the linking commentary. This was after the death of John Betjeman but before the announcement of a new Poet Laureate had been made, and Philip Larkin knew that the Arts

Council had been consulted on the appointment. 'I am delighted,' he wrote, 'to hear that the evening was a success – how could it be otherwise with such superstar performers? . . . All this is one more alarming symptom of my growing notoriety. I hope you have told Mrs Thatcher that, while ten years ago I was indisputably the best poet in England, I am now a back number, and should be quite unable to sustain the showbiz side of laureateship. Suggest a West Indian, a Liverpudlian – anything but me.'

I received my last letter from Philip in November, 1985. Thinking that I had already left the Arts Council, he ended: 'I envisage you in some garret with a single candle, punching away at a 1926 Remington. I hope things aren't as bad as that. I have spent this week having influenza, which has been quite nice really, though adds to the general weakness that is leading me inexorably into the Valley.'

I replied: 'Far from dripping grease from my candle onto a 1926 Remington, I have recently purchased (albeit reluctantly) a word processor-computer. So things are even worse than you fear. I hope you are now over your influenza, and that you'll soon be able to travel. I am leaving the Arts Council at Christmas, and I must wait another two years before I qualify for cheap rail travel to Hull to see you.'

But I was to travel to Hull only two weeks later, for Philip's funeral. The service was held in the church of St Mary the Virgin, at Cottingham, where Philip, who was not a Christian believer, used to go to sing the hymns. On 9 December we sang his favourites, among them 'Lead, kindly light amid the encircling gloom', which pleased me, for those were the words which had come into my mind when I was told Philip had died. He always contrived to be both kindly light and the encircling gloom. We sang the hymn again some weeks later at Philip's memorial service in Westminster Abbey, but he would not have enjoyed it, for this time it was to a non-kosher tune. 'I hate it when they invent these bloody awful new tunes for the hymns I know.'

LEE, Jennie (Baroness Lee of Asheridge). At a dinner party in his flat one evening in 1966, Lord Goodman said to me, *à propos* Public Lending Right, 'We must rouse Miss Lee to the cause. She'll make all the difference.' 'Isn't she too nice?'' I asked. He looked at me reprovingly. 'Miss Lee, when roused, makes the Medusa appear a tame and gentle creature,' he assured me.

Later, when he and I and the Secretary-General of the Arts Council faced her across a conference table at the Department of Education and Science, Arnold Goodman said to Jennie, 'For a very small amount of money, one and a quarter million pounds, you can gain a large amount of popularity.' Jennie Lee's response was immediate: 'To descend to your crude level, how many votes?'

LEGGE, Walter. My happiest memory of him is at a supper party in a restaurant in the hills outside Salzburg. Our hosts were Nicolai and Stacey Gedda. Nicolai had given a superb recital in the Grosses Festspielhaus, and we were all excited and happy. The other guests included Helmut Storjohann, Nicolai's German record producer, and the superb baritone George London. Walter was in good form (his wife, Elisabeth Schwarzkopf, was not with us: she was hiking somewhere in the vicinity), and told splendidly indiscreet stories about conductors and singers. He also told us of the time Sir Thomas Beecham sent him to Germany to find a decent Brünnhilde. Finding one, Walter wired her name to Beecham: 'MARTA FUCHS'. He received a reply from Sir Thomas: 'DELIGHTED YOU'RE ENJOYING YOURSELF, BUT CAN THE LADY SING?'

LEHMANN, Lotte. I was a child when I first met her in Brisbane in 1938, and I kept in touch with her until 1976, the year of her death. I never saw her in opera, but I often think that I did, because her master classes in London in the late fifties remain so vividly in my memory, and even more so do the few days in 1962 at the old Metropolitan Opera, at Broadway and 39th Street, when she invited me to attend rehearsals of *Der Rosenkavalier*, in which she directed Régine Crespin (singing her first Marschallin), Anneliese Rothenberger (Sophie) and Herta Töpper (Octavian).

Lehmann coached Elisabeth Schwarzkopf when Schwarzkopf first sang the Marschallin. 'But it was very difficult,' she said. 'Her husband, Walter Legge, always insisted on being present. He would sit by the piano, puffing at a horrid cigar and blowing the smoke in her face. I think there was something sexual about it.'

She took me to the opera many times in Vienna and Salzburg, and we met for the last time at her eighty-fifth birthday party.

LENYA, Lotte. I never knew Kurt Weill, the composer of so many musicals I have enjoyed in the theatre, from *Der Dreigroschenoper* and *Happy End* to *Street Scene* and *Lady in the Dark.* It was in 1955, five years after Weill's death, that I first met his widow, the Viennese-born dancer, actress and singer, Lotte Lenya. A compelling performer of her husband's music, she was also a superb raconteur, and she told me many stories of their Berlin days before they were forced to flee from Germany in 1933. Artur Schnabel once said to her, of another pianist, 'I don't like him, he has such a noisy spiritual life.' Georg Kaiser had a hatred of press reviews. 'I remember,' said Lenya, 'that if somebody in ignorance brought a paper to the house to show him, he would pick it up with the tongs and put it into the fire as if it were contagious.'

LEVIN, Bernard. He said recently, to a friend of mine, 'Auberon Waugh is like Aids. It exists in the world, and one just has to live with the incurable fact.'

Levin is surely the most distinguished journalist we have. I frequently find myself disagreeing with him, but it's a pleasure to disagree with someone who writes with such elegance and wit. I do not disagree with his estimate of my recent book on Schubert, which he reviewed favourably, though I would rather he hadn't called me the 'Dracula of the Arts Council'.

LEVY, Benn. At a conference on Obscenity, organized by the Arts Council at the Wigmore Hall, the usual people said the usual things. Mary Whitehouse was, of course, the most vociferous member of the censorship faction. At one point in the proceedings, bored with the long-windedness of it all, I rose and said, 'What it amounts to is this: Mrs Whitehouse insists on shouting, "I don't like this, therefore you shall not read it," whereas all she has a right to shout is, "I don't like this, therefore *I* shall not read it." '

This brought me, the following day, a brief note from Benn Levy. 'Dear Charles,' he wrote. 'Congratulations on what was certainly the shortest and probably the best speech of the Conference. I only wish you hadn't chosen a moment when Mrs Whitehouse was out of the hall!' I hadn't noticed that the wretched woman had gone to the loo.

LIFAR, Serge. Years ago, before World War II, when they were both young, Sidney Nolan designed the decor in Sydney for a new ballet, *Icare*, by Serge Lifar. Sidney recalls trying to steal the limelight from Lifar at the curtain-calls, only to be defeated by the dancer who, under the guise of kissing him, muttered angrily, *'Allez, allez!'*

This bears a relation to the well-documented story of Puccini, simulating shyness and reluctance as he was dragged onstage by his prima donna, to whom he was muttering, '*Tirami, tirami.*' (Pull me, pull me.)

LOWELL, Robert. I could never see the point of Robert Lowell, though I was almost won over by Ian Hamilton's superb biography. I suppose he couldn't be blamed for being a part-time nut-case, but he could be blamed, certainly, for his insensitivity to the poetry of others.

At a Poetry International performance, shortly before I was about to go onstage with the Russian poet Joseph Brodsky, Lowell (who had read his own poems in the first half of the programme) took me aside. He was such a great admirer of Brodsky's poetry, he said, that he would dearly love to read the English translations of Brodsky which would precede Brodsky's Russian, and which I had intended to read.

'Well, all right,' I said, 'if you're sure you can read them coherently at sight. Have you looked at them?'

He assured me he would not have any problem with them, and foolishly I let him go on. But he read the translations abominably, stumbling over every line, fluffing every few seconds and, monstrously, breaking off now and then in mid-poem to reminisce or to comment on Brodsky's work. Afterwards he appeared not to understand why I was angry.

I once confessed to Philip Larkin that I was allergic both to Lowell and to his poetry. 'I don't know what all the fuss is about,' Philip said. 'He's just an American Heath-Stubbs.'

There had to be something wrong with a man happy to go through life being called by his friends 'Cal' (after Caligula). I began to feel some sympathy for him only when I read Ian Hamilton's biography, which is absorbing in the way it charts Lowell's dives into and out of madness.

MACKENZIE, Sir Compton. When I was asked by the BBC to interview Compton Mackenzie for the World Service on the occasion of his eightieth birthday, I prepared myself by dipping into a few of those forty novels and thirty non-fiction books, the majority of which I had never read. I made out a list of questions relating not only to literature and politics but also to music, and especially music on record, for Sir Compton had been the founder and first editor of the monthly magazine, *Gramophone*.

We met in a studio in Bush House, and chatted easily enough until the technicians were ready for us. The red light went on. 'Sir Compton,' I began, 'you say in the first volume of your autobiography, *My Life and Times*, that –'

He interrupted me, and began to speak of his life and times. Thirty minutes later, when the red light went off, he was still talking and I had not uttered another word.

MAHLER, Anna. Gustav Mahler is one of the four great composers who most deeply affect me. (The others are Mozart, Verdi and Schubert.) So, when I met his only child, Anna, at one of John Calder's dinner parties about twenty years ago, I felt I was not simply meeting a sixty-year-old sculptress but was somehow forging a link between myself and the composer, who had died in 1911. I drove Anna Mahler home afterwards to her flat in

Kinnerton Street, near Hyde Park Corner, and as I drove on to my own flat I kept saying to myself, 'Mahler's daughter was in this car.' When I got home I took a book down from my shelves and stared for some minutes at a photograph of Mahler on a ship crossing the Atlantic in 1910, with his little girl, Anna, in his arms.

MASEFIELD, John. On 11 May 1966, John Masefield's nephew rang me to say that the old man was dying, and would the Arts Council help to get his ashes placed in Poets' Corner in Westminster Abbey. I consulted a senior colleague at the Arts Council, who said, 'This is in the nature of a political appointment. You'd better talk to Downing Street.' So I rang the Prime Minister's Office at Number 10, and spoke to his private secretary, John Hewitt, who said, 'We'll make an approach to Eric Abbott.' 'Who the hell's Eric Abbott?' I asked, irritably. 'The Dean of Westminster,' was the answer.

Two days later, John Masefield, the Poet Laureate, died, and the Press Association rang me to ask for a tribute, and for a guess as to who would be his successor. His ashes were placed in Westminster Abbey.

MELBA, Dame Nellie. No, I did not know her. She died when I was three. But fifteen years after her death I lodged in Melbourne for a few weeks with a retired Scottish nurse, a Sister Hopkinson, who had come to Australia as nurse-companion to Dame Nellie. The arrangement, Sister Hopkinson told me, had been that, after one year's service, if she wished to leave Melba's employ her fare back to Europe would be paid by the diva.

After a year, Sister Hopkinson could stand no more of her employer's tantrums, and gave Melba notice of her intention to quit. When the time came for her to leave, Dame Nellie handed her an envelope containing one week's wages. 'Where's my fare back to England?' Sister Hopkinson asked. 'Jesus Christ walked on the fucking water, and so can you,' replied Melba. That was why, more than fifteen years later, Sister Hopkinson was still in Melbourne, taking in lodgers in Dandenong Road.

MILLER, Jonathan. Once upon a time, many years ago, Jonathan Miller and I lunched together, and he, knowing of my love of opera, told me at some length what an absurd art-form he thought it was. We argued amiably, and I failed to dislodge Jonathan from his firmly held anti-opera views. As we were parting, however, he asked, 'If I wanted to direct opera, where would be the best place for me to offer myself?' Within months his career as a director of opera had begun.

In 1976, Jonathan and I were in Australia at the same time. He was in Melbourne, directing a production of Janáček's *The Cunning Little Vixen*, while I was a few hundred miles away in Adelaide, participating in the Adelaide Festival. One of the major events in Adelaide was to be a lecture by Tennessee Williams in the Town Hall, which had been sold out for several months in advance. Alas, two days before the date of the lecture, Tennessee sent a wire from the United States informing the Festival's organizers that he would not be coming to Australia.

The Festival people were frantic. I was consulted, and advised them to try to get Jonathan Miller to talk to the audience, which was expecting Tennessee. 'But who is Jonathan Miller?' I was asked. 'No one in Adelaide will have heard of him.' 'Perhaps not,' I said, 'but he's a brilliant speaker.' 'On what subject?' 'On any subject.'

And so it proved to be. I rang Jonathan in Melbourne, he flew to Adelaide, was met and driven to the Town Hall, and talked to a packed house about theatre, life, religion, psychology, opera, politics and one or two other topics. He was greeted cautiously, but at the end he received a prolonged ovation which he thoroughly deserved.

I note that Jonathan shares my disenchanted view of what passes nowadays as creativity. In a recent interview, he said: 'There just aren't many modern works that are any good, that aren't obsessed with the sort of propagandist messages that would be laughed out of a first-year seminar. We live in an age of graffiti, aerosol merchants rather than writers.'

MONROE, Marilyn. I met her once, while she was married to Arthur Miller, but there were hordes of other people present and I exchanged only a few words with her. A friend in California, a retired actor-director who once coached her, tells me that she was, early in her career, 'a sweet kid', though clearly too stupid not to be ruined in the process of being turned into a movie star.

Marilyn's name appears above simply to catch your attention. This entry ought really to be headed 'Famous Graves'. I do not travel the world seeking the graves of the famous, but I do seem to have made my way to the graves of many of the dead whom I most admire. I visited Marilyn, whose ashes are in a wall at the Westwood Presbyterian Church, only because Ken Thomson, who was with me in Hollywood, wanted to make a pilgrimage to Monroe. But I actively sought out Nelson Eddy in the Hollywood Memorial Cemetery, Mahler in Grinzing, most of the other Viennese composers in the Zentral Friedhof in Vienna, Wilde at Père Lachaise, Verdi in his Casa di Riposo in Milan, Wagner in the garden of his villa at Bayreuth, Shakespeare in the church at Stratford, and Richard Tauber in the Old Brompton Road.

Some I have stumbled across almost by accident, among them Stravinsky and Diaghilev on their island in the Venice lagoon, Boris Godunov at Zagorsk, and several notorious characters at various places in the American Wild West. Pasternak I was led to by Yevtushenko, as I have already described.

NEWBY, P. H. Mr Newby is a novelist who for some years worked for the BBC as Controller of the Third Programme (which is what Radio 3 was called in his day). He has not the kind of personality which immediately imprints itself upon one's memory, hence this story. I first met him at a BBC party shortly after I began broadcasting regularly on the Third Programme. Some months later, at another party, a producer attempted to introduce us to each other again. 'Do you two know each other?' I said 'No' as Newby was saying 'Yes'. I had simply not remembered him.

Alas, the same thing happened again, weeks afterwards, at an early evening party given by the publishers Barrie & Rockliff. This time Mr Newby was quite understandably annoyed. 'Really, Mr Osborne,' he said, 'this *is* the third time we've met.' I apologized, and we conversed somewhat awkwardly for a few minutes. I left the party at seven, as I had to be in a BBC studio at eight, for a live broadcast on the Third Programme. Outside the publishers' office I saw a taxi, parked a few yards from a public lavatory. The driver was not in the taxi, so I waited. Some seconds later, a man emerged from the lavatory and approached the taxi. 'Broadcasting House, please,' I said to him, my hand on the door handle. 'Mr Osborne, I am *not* the driver of this taxi,' replied P. H. Newby, 'but I am willing to share it with you since I, too, am going to Broadcasting House.'

Surprisingly, I continued to be engaged to broadcast on the Third Programme for some years. Much later, when I was working for the Arts Council, I tried to make amends with P. N. Newby by inviting him, together with Francis Wyndham, to judge an Arts Council prize for the best new novelist of whatever year it was. I had chosen Newby and Wyndham because they were regular fiction reviewers and could be expected already to have read most of the serious contenders.

Francis Wyndham said immediately, 'The best first novel of the year was *At the Jerusalem* by Paul Bailey.' P. H. Newby didn't want to know what his fellow-judge thought. He insisted on being provided with a copy of every first novel published during the relevant period. He then, in due course, produced a short list of titles which he thought Francis Wyndham should read.

I showed the short list to Francis, who was not interested in it. '*At the Jerusalem*,' he said. And so it went on. Eventually Newby narrowed his choice down to three. Would Francis at least read or re-read these three? No. '*At the Jerusalem*.'

I rang Newby. 'Francis Wyndham thinks –' I began.

'I don't wish to be influenced by what he thinks,' Newby interrupted. 'I would award the prize to *At the Jerusalem* by Paul Bailey.'

NICOLSON, Harold. I was told by a boy who was being kept by Harold Nicolson that when he first went to bed with Harold, he was disturbed to find a note on the bed-side table, which read: 'In case I suffer a heart attack during sexual intercourse, the phone number of my doctor is . . .' I told this to Colin Spencer, who wickedly attempted to use it in a novel in which H.N., thinly disguised, was a character. Colin showed me the novel in typescript, and I think I persuaded him to delete the reference.

NOLAN, Sir Sidney. We have been friends for nearly forty years. I have written about him on several occasions, and once chose the paintings for a retrospective exhibition when Sidney was out of the country and unable to make the choice himself. He has, in the volume *Swansong*, illustrated my poems most beautifully. If there exists an Australian mafia in Great Britain, then we are its only two members, and Sidney is definitely the *capo*. For years we used to meet regularly over lunch to gossip and plan, or destroy a few ill-deserved reputations.

Sidney occasionally asks my advice on operatic matters. I dissuaded him from designing a *Don Giovanni* to be produced by Peter Brook ('To hell with the Ashanti, he's a madman, Sidney'), and I hope I have encouraged him as far as the next Royal Opera House *Ring* is concerned.

When Patrick White's memoirs, *Flaws in the Glass* (popularly referred to in Australia as *Claws in the Arse*), appeared in paperback, Sidney went into Hatchard's bookshop in Piccadilly and bought their entire stock of twelve copies. Emerging from the shop, he walked to the nearest receptacle for rubbish and threw them in. (For an explanation of why he might have done so, see under Patrick White.)

Sidney once told me of the time when he had taken Patrick White to meet Benjamin Britten, in the hope that Britten might be persuaded to compose an opera to a libretto by Patrick. Britten was polite and urbane. He would, of course, like to write an opera with Patrick, but the question was 'When?' He and Peter Pears were about to embark upon a tour of America, after which he had to conduct various performances of his works, and then he would have to go to Paris to record a concert of his music. He continued to list his commitments, until Patrick interrupted him. 'Have you no control over your own life?' he asked in his most *grande dame* manner.

That story is really part of the saga of the great unwritten Australian opera. I was brought into it by Sidney Nolan, and first heard of it some time after the abortive Britten–White encounter, which Sidney had the tact not to tell me about until much later. 'Charles,' he said, 'you know that the Sydney Opera House, which is only a few years behind schedule, will be completed in four or five years' time. I have been asked to design the opening opera. Would you be interested in writing the libretto?'

'Of course I'd be interested, Sidney. Who is the composer?'

'Well, that's the point. The committee dealing with this in Sydney don't have any ideas about that. They decided to start with me, as the artist who'd design it. I thought of you, naturally, and hoped you'd have some ideas about a possible composer.'

'What a typically Antipodean way to go about it. All right, let's think. You and I are Australians, so I suppose they want the composer to be Australian, as well?'

'Not necessarily,' said Sidney. 'They were wondering about Stravinsky.'

'Not a good idea,' I replied. 'They'd get a marvellous piece of music but it would last about forty-five seconds.'

'I think they have something longer in mind,' Sidney murmured.

'What about Copland?' The name of Aaron Copland was put forward, but either the Aussies hadn't heard of him, or weren't impressed. I was asked to think again.

'The more I consider this,' I said to Sidney, 'the more convinced I am that the composer should be an Australian. The best of the young Australian composers is Peter Sculthorpe. It doesn't matter that he's unknown. After all, they've got the most famous living Australian artist to do the décor.'

Sculthorpe was commissioned. The subject was, at Sidney's suggestion, the story of Mrs Fraser, who had been shipwrecked off the Queensland coast in the nineteenth century, and captured by aborigines. He had done a series of Mrs Fraser paintings. Somewhere along the line I dropped out of the enterprise, to be replaced first by Patrick White and, when Patrick withdrew, by Alan Moorehead. Sculthorpe, who was teaching at an American university, began to compose the music. The eager Australians had already engaged a producer for the opera, Sir Robert Helpmann, and Helpmann visited Sculthorpe in the United States, where he heard some of the music.

'Fantastic,' he exclaimed. 'This is far too good to be wasted on an opera. You must turn it into music for a ballet, and I shall do the choreography!'

The Sculthorpe-Helpmann ballet was, in due course, performed in Australia, but the Sydney Opera House opened with Prokofiev's *War and Peace*.

I surprised Sidney by writing a poem for his fiftieth birthday, and giving it to Jack Lambert to publish in the *Sunday Times* on the actual birthday. Sidney's wife, Cynthia, accused me of having published prematurely a poem which, because it was written in the past tense, she was convinced I had intended for Sidney's obituary ('No, Cynthia, it's in the past tense because it's about memory,' I told her in vain). Fortunately, the artist himself was pleased by it:

> You painted landscape, people, skies
> and distant prospects, tenderly:
> dark men walked naked from the sea
> for you, who painted memory.
>
> Sun-dancing beaches, outback pubs,
> sad oval faces, all conspired
> to tempt you into knowing them.
> Square-headed outlaws used to ride
>
> Through bush. But that was long ago,
> and in another country too,
> where fifty suns blaze in the sky,
> and birds fly upside down for you.

OLIVIER, Lord. I have, so far, been fortunate in not quite achieving the ambitions I confessed to in an issue of *The Australian Women's Weekly* when, for a reason I have mercifully forgotten, I was chosen as their 'Teenager of the Week' some time in 1945, was photographed and interviewed. I said I wanted to have left Australia by the time I was twenty-one (I was twenty-five before I managed this); publish my first book while I was still in my twenties (I didn't do this until I was thirty-five); and act in a film or play with Laurence Olivier (in due course I got into a film with Redgrave and on to a stage with Gielgud, but I never acted with Olivier). I prefer not to achieve ambitions, for fear that, having achieved them, one might find that one's life had then become a permanent anti-climax.

I did rub shoulders with Olivier, however, on three occasions. The first was when he and Vivien Leigh came to Australia in 1948 with an Old Vic company, to play *School for Scandal*, *Richard III*, and Thornton Wilder's *The Skin of Our Teeth*. When they came to Brisbane, where they appeared at Her Majesty's Theatre (now demolished), I was a few hundred yards away at the Guild Café Theatre (also demolished), giving (as they used to say) my Marchbanks in *Candida*. Olivier gave me his autograph on a copy of my *Candida* programme, which I still possess. (What did I say to him, I wonder: 'As one actor to another, Larry . . .'?)

The second time was nearly ten years later when I was filming at Pinewood Studios in *Geordie* with Bill Travers, Virginia McKenna and Alastair Sim. I was a newspaperman who photographs Bill Travers behaving heroically in an accident in a Melbourne street. On the set next door, Olivier was filming his *Richard III*, and whenever we had a break in shooting I would rush next door to catch a glimpse of the great man at work. On one occasion, I found him in his Richard costume and make-up, staring gloomily at a group of actors as a scene was being set up. He looked as though he were in the depths of despair.

The third occasion was in 1966, at a reception at the Arts Council when we were still at 4 St James's Square. My right arm was in a sling, after a motor accident, and I was standing by a window of the big first-floor reception room when Olivier approached me. 'What have you done to yourself?' he asked.

I told him, he made sympathetic noises, and offered advice about physiotherapy. 'I have a great deal of experience of this sort of thing,' he said, directing an almost scornful glance at my arm. 'I'm always breaking an arm or a wrist or an ankle or something. It's because I'm such a physical actor.'

'You certainly are,' I murmured fatuously.

He looked reflectively at me and beyond me, with that Mahlerian *Weltschmerz* I recognized from his Heathcliff, his D'Arcy, his Hamlet. 'I would like, really, to be a cerebral actor, but I haven't got the equipment,' he said.

To my exasperation and relief, someone came up to us at that moment and led Olivier away.

I had occasion, once, to send a script to Olivier. Having just been reading about Cocteau addressing an envelope to Proust in verse (Cent-deux Boulevard Haussman, Oust!/Tirez, facteur, chez Marcel Proust) I thought I'd trying something similar. The Oliviers were living in Eaton Square (number 90, I think), so I addressed my package thus:

Oh postman deliver this parcel, I pray,
To the Eaton Square flat of Olivier.

You'll find him there, or if not he,
Please hand it instead to Miss Vivien Leigh.

It was delivered.

Years later, I was walking down Charing Cross Road in the direction of Trafalgar Square when I saw an evening newspaper's poster, something about Olivier undergoing an emergency operation. I was approaching the church of St Martin in the Fields, and on an impulse I popped into the church, sat in a pew and offered up a prayer for his recovery. It's not the kind of thing I'd have done on my own behalf, but I saw no reason why our greatest actor should be deprived of a prayer simply because *I* happen to be an agnostic. As I walked out again into the square, the church bells began to peal. A good omen, I thought, and so it turned out to be.

ORWELL, Sonia. Though she liked to make a great fuss about being the widow of George Orwell (she was his wife only briefly), she was occasionally capable of ironic detachment, and laughed when I introduced her to a French diplomat as *'une veuve distinguée'*. Basically, however, she was a tiresome creature. It's unfair, I suppose, that aggressive women should seem so much worse than aggressive men; but they do, and Sonia was essentially a bully. She must have been attractive as a young woman: she went through a large number of literary men like a dose of salts. She was a sort of literary groupie. Romain Gary's memoirs contain an amusing description of her, without mentioning her by name. Not realizing this, I asked Sonia to review the volume for *The London Magazine*. Her negative reply was very colourfully worded.

OSBORNE, John. No, we are not related. I first became aware of his existence a year or so before *Look Back in Anger* made him famous in 1956. At that time he and I were both struggling young actors, grabbing jobs in touring companies and provincial repertory theatres. On one occasion, a repertory company with whom I had appeared for one or two 'special weeks' rang *Spotlight*, the central casting agency, in order to engage me again. By mistake they were given John Osborne's telephone number and engaged him, thinking they were getting me. (He, monster of duplicity, must have known he was not the actor they wanted.) I was told later that, though he was even less convincing as an actor than I, he was not quite bad enough to be sacked. He was also several inches taller than I, which they rather liked.

He may well have done me out of more than that one job in those days. If he did, I had my revenge later, and on more than one occasion. The first was in 1957, when I was in Moscow to attend an arts festival, about which I wrote and broadcast upon my return to London. One morning in Moscow, two students turned up at my hotel while I was having breakfast. They had come, they said, to invite me to a seminar on the subject, 'Theatre in the Western World', which was to be held at Moscow University the following week. At least, I thought that was what they said: their English was poor and my Russian non-existent. I accepted the invitation.

On the appointed day they arrived with a car to take me to the University. On the way, merely to make conversation, for we were finding small-talk difficult, I asked, 'What did you say was the subject of the seminar?'

'Is not seminar,' they said. 'Is lecture. Theatre in the West.'

'Ah, I see. And who is giving the lecture?'

They looked surprised. They looked at each other. Then one of them spoke. 'You are,' he said.

Instant panic, which I was careful not to show. There flashed through my mind that scene in Carol Reed's *The Third Man* in which Joseph Cotten thinks he is being kidnapped, and considers leaping out of the car, which is bearing him only to a British Council lecture which he is to give. I wished desperately that, in my case, the reverse was true and I *was* being kidnapped. Should I attempt to escape? No chance. May as well lie back and think of England.

We arrived at the University, and I was led up a flight of steps, greeted at the top by some professor or other, and escorted into a large lecture hall. I walked down the centre aisle, through an audience of several hundred students, and up onto the platform. There was much applause. I was introduced to the audience, again in Russian. Fortunately my introducer concluded by saying, presumably for my benefit, in English, 'Mr Osborne will speak in English, but he will pause after each few sentences, while a précis of what he has said is given in Russian.'

That was what saved me from total disaster. There were no simultaneous translation devices in those days, at least not in Russia, so I was able to begin with a few sentences of sheer waffle, and then, while these were being repeated in Russian by the translator, who stood beside me on the platform, I was able to think of what to say next. Somehow I managed to stay on my feet for an hour (perhaps minus an *akademische Viertelstunde*). I confessed that my knowledge of theatre in the western world was confined mainly to Great Britain, but I asserted that the most interesting recent developments had been in England, rather than on the continent. I talked mostly about the new English Stage Company, which had begun its life the previous year at the Royal Court Theatre in London, and I discussed the new school of playwrights which was beginning to emerge, the so-called 'kitchen sink' dramatists, who were so different in attitude and style from the Cowards and Rattigans. Naturally, I had a great deal to say about *Look Back in Anger*, which I had found most impressive, though I had certain criticisms to make of it, mainly on grounds of technique.

When I finished, there was tremendous and prolonged applause. Then the professorial-looking old character who had introduced me made a speech of thanks. It was only when he repeated some of it in English that panic set in again. 'We must thank Mr Osborne,' he said, 'for giving us so authoritative an address on the new school of playwrights in England, and we must marvel at the modesty and extraordinary objectivity with which he spoke of his own play, *Look Back in Anger*.'

I attempted a smile, and was led through the again applauding audience to where my car was waiting outside. A crowd of students held me up with demands for autographs, which I gave freely and graciously, and a photograph of my doing so appeared the next day in *Pravda*, with a caption informing readers that this was the English playwright, John Osborne.

Five or six years later, in Vienna, Ken Thomson and I were given VIP treatment at the Hotel Sacher because they assumed I was John Osborne. When the *maitre d'hôtel* said he hoped that my presence in Vienna indicated that they could look foward to a new *Theaterstück*, I admitted that I did have a subject in mind but that I expected I would find it difficult to improve upon *Blick Zurück im Zorn*.

Having by now perfected my John Osborne impersonation, I presented it again in Georgia (the Soviet-imprisoned country, not the American state), and gave my opinion of a performance of one of my plays in an ex-church in Tbilisi. (Although I attended the performance, I didn't recognize the play.)

There is a rather pathetic postscript to all this. About five years ago I contributed a piece to a book called *The Anti-Booklist*. Before the book went to press, I received a letter from the publishers, Hodder & Stoughton, enclosing a copy of what they proposed to say about me in the notes on contributors. Would I check it and let them know if there were any errors? It read: 'Charles Osborne is the Literature Director of the Arts Council of Great Britain. His books include *Look Back in Anger*, *The Entertainer*, *Inadmissible Evidence*, and *Luther*.'

I was tempted to let it stand. After all, I'd be proud to have written *Look Back in Anger* and *The Entertainer*. It was the inclusion in the list of *Luther* that made me decide I'd rather be known as the author of my own works.

PASOLINI, Pier Paolo. I had thought him quite a charmer when I first met him in Rome. Was he a talented film-maker who dabbled in poetry, or vice versa, or (more likely) a political animal who used words and images for an impure purpose? And what is a pure purpose?

When we invited him to take part in Poetry International it was because one or two of us who selected the poets were impressed by his lyric style, and I thought his subjects were interesting.

We saw very little of him during his time in London. I think he dashed from the stage of the Royal Festival Hall to the pavements of Piccadilly in search of attractive English youths. Sex may have been more important to him than either poetry or politics. And why not?

PATMORE, Derek. Derek, who died some years ago, was the great-grandson of the Victorian poet, Coventry Patmore. His mother, Brigit Patmore, whom I knew only towards the end of her life, had been the inamorata of several famous literary figures. Ezra Pound described her as 'one of the charming people on this planet'. She was the friend of Pound, of Hemingway, of Yeats, of T. S. Eliot and of D. H. Lawrence, and the lover of Richard Aldington, with whom she lived for ten years. She had wonderful stories to tell of these people, but they are her stories, not mine, and she was persuaded by her son Derek to recount them in a volume of memoirs, *My Friends When Young*, which was published posthumously in 1968, three years after Brigit died.

Derek (to whom I was introduced by Felix Aprahamian) was very kind to me, or at least he intended to be. When I was between engagements as an actor, he employed me to help him sort out and catalogue his literary papers. This turned out to be something of a farce, for his papers consisted mainly of threatening letters from his tailor, his wine merchant and other tradesmen. For three weeks or more, however, I spent a couple of hours each morning in the basement flat in Bayswater in which he and his mother lived, and I shared their frugal lunch, which Brigit prepared. At the end of the three weeks, as I was leaving, Derek pressed into my hand an envelope containing my wages for the entire period. I opened it in the bus going home. I don't know what I had expected for three weeks' work of about ten hours per week, but it must have been something more than the seventeen shillings and sixpence which was the amount of his cheque. On the top of the bus, I burst into laughter. What else could I do? When I thought about it, I realized that Derek must have worked out the amount very carefully. If it had been more than a pound, his cheque would probably have bounced, and he wouldn't have wanted to embarrass us both by having that happen.

Derek tried to be helpful to me in other ways. He introduced me to

Stephen Spender, and also to Somerset Maugham, whose secretary he thought I might become. 'What a team you and Willie would make,' he said. But Maugham and I took an instant dislike to each other, so nothing came of that. I had been, and I still am, an admirer of Maugham as a novelist and playwright, but I thought him an insufferably snide and unpleasant creature, and he clearly thought I was a dreadful little upstart because I did not wag my tail with delight at every nasty remark he made. I think now that my judgment of him was crass, and that beneath the sneering exterior he was a shy, vulnerable and not unpleasant person. But I didn't wait around to find out.

Derek spent his last years conning various countries into inviting him to lecture or attend conferences. 'I'm getting on very well with the Spanish dear,' he would say, or 'I'm afraid the Turks are proving rather recalcitrant.' He was delightful company, rather useless, but completely harmless.

PLATH, Sylvia. The one or two references to me in Edward Butscher's *Sylvia Plath: Method and Madness* convey the impression that I was a closer friend of Sylvia than, in fact, I was. When I first met her, during my *London Magazine* days, she was already married to Ted Hughes. Ray Mathew, an Australian poet and playwright, came with me to visit Ted and Sylvia when they were living in Primrose Hill, in a small flat in Chalcot Square. Vulnerability and tantrums are what I most associate with Sylvia at this time. The poems impressed me despite themselves. They were not the kind of poems I liked, but some of them were remarkable.

Butscher appears to have read a number of letters between Sylvia and myself, written to and from *The London Magazine* office, and subsequently sold with other *London Magazine* material to the Humanities Research Center at the University of Texas. I do not recall these, but they must have been mainly about her poems. Though, as Butscher says, I remained 'sympathetic and supportive' after Sylvia and Ted had ceased to live together, I did not feel the necessity to take sides. Indeed, I felt it very necessary not to do so, for I knew nothing of the intimate details of their relationship. I think it was because Sylvia's lack of mental stability was already apparent to me that I wanted to comfort her. As I had no emotional commitment to her, this was easy enough for me to do.

POWER, Tyrone. When I was twelve, I could not decide whether he (*In Old Chicago, Alexander's Ragtime Band, Jessie James*) or Hedy Lamarr (*Algiers*, messing about with that middle-aged Charles Boyer) was the more attractive.

I did not meet him until I was in my late twenties and he, producing a film in London, was in his early forties. My agent put me forward for a role in the film, *Seven Waves Away*, and this led in due course to my being given tea by Mr Power at Gunters (no longer there). He looked older than I had thought he would. Disconcertingly, almost his first words to me indicated that he thought *I* looked too old for the role he was trying to cast. So why shouldn't we just forget it and talk, he asked. We did. He was charming and friendly, and did not make me feel he was in a hurry to get rid of me. I was too busy attempting to hide my disappointment at not being wanted for the film, and to match his amiability, to remember much of what we talked about, although Shaw, whom he admired as greatly as I did, came into it. Power was either contemplating appearing on stage in *The Devil's Disciple*, or had just done so.

I boasted to a friend, also an actor, that I had had tea with Tyrone Power. So had he, but he didn't get the role either. Power died suddenly on the set of another film, about a year after our brief encounter. Twenty years later I came across his grave in the Hollywood Memorial Park Cemetery on Santa Monica Boulevard. The tombstone is a raised horizontal slab which almost invites one to sit on it.

PRICE, Vincent. The suave Vincent, star of countless horror films but also an actor of wide range in films of the forties before he began to specialize, has a most mellifluous voice and is a superb reader of verse. Of the two or three occasions on which I have shared a platform with him, the one I recall as the most exciting was the 'Poetry of the Macabre'. Vincent read most of the items allotted to him with style and conviction, but we had not rehearsed the two big Edgar Allen Poe poems with which he was to end each half of the programme: 'The Conqueror Worm' before the interval, and 'The Raven' to end the evening. We had not rehearsed them because Vincent had said, casually, that he'd done them before and would rather concentrate, in rehearsal, on the poems that were new to him.

His performances of both poems were electrifying. Sitting behind him during 'The Conqueror Worm' I could see and feel the audience tense with concentration, and the applause after 'The Raven' was tremendous.

In the dressing room before we went on, I had said to Vincent, 'I hope Coral is coming this evening.' I had been unable to persuade his wife, Coral Browne, to take part in the performance.

'Oh, no,' Vincent replied. 'She said we could make fools of ourselves if we wished, but that was no reason why she should have to watch us.'

'That's forthright enough!'

'Well,' Vincent continued, 'at least you know where you are with an old broad like that.'

REDGRAVE, Sir Michael. I have mentioned elsewhere that I played a tiny role in *The Dam Busters*, filmed at Elstree in 1954. The leading roles were played by Michael Redgrave, a great actor, and Richard Todd, a non-actor. When we were filming a scene in which we were being briefed by Todd (as Wing-Commander Guy Gibson) and Redgrave (as Barnes Wallis, inventor of the new type of bomb we were to use), my sympathies were with Todd, for Redgrave behaved so unkindly towards him.

Todd and Redgrave were on a platform, addressing us. Todd stood at a blackboard with a pointer. He had one line to speak. Let's say it was 'And when you reach the southern end of the dam, you are to fly low at one thousand feet until you have dropped the first bomb.' Redgrave, as the bomb's inventor, sat nearby in a chair, with nothing to say. The rest of us, about twenty-five actors and a hundred extras, sat in the main body of the hall. The director, Michael Anderson, called for a first take. Todd began, 'And when you reach the northern end –'

'Cut. Richard, it's "the southern end". Let's do it again. Ready? Camera. Action.'

'And when we reach –'

'Cut. Richard, it's "you", not "we". "When you reach the southern end . . ."'

Every time Todd fluffed and Anderson called 'Cut', Michael Redgrave would take up the book he had been sitting on, and begin to read. I have never seen anyone else read so ostentatiously. Todd became increasingly nervous, and Redgrave increasingly snide. We must have done twenty takes of that simple set-up, Redgrave breathing more heavily with each one until he almost began to groan with over-played exasperation.

Another day on the set, I was sitting in one of those canvas chairs, reading, and waiting to be called. Redgrave paced up and down quite near me. Occasionally I looked up and caught his eye. We had talked to each other more than once, but now he looked away and went on pacing. The Assistant Director walked past, and Redgrave stopped him and said something. The assistant came back to where I was sitting, and said to me, 'I'm afraid that's Mr Redgrave's chair you're sitting on.' I vacated the chair. 'Couldn't he have told me himself?' I asked, loudly enough for Redgrave to hear. That evening, when we had finished filming, Redgrave invited me for a drink. It seemed to be his way of apologizing.

I had seen him give remarkable performances on the stage, and was to see him give many more: Shakespeare's Antony, with Peggy Ashcroft as Cleopatra; a very intellectual Hamlet at Stratford; the 'publishing scoundrel' in his own adaptation of Henry James's *The Aspern Papers*; and, most memorably, the title-role in Chekhov's *Uncle Vanya*, with Olivier as Astrov, the doctor. But even if I had never seen him do anything else, I would have known I was in the presence of a great actor on my first day of filming in *The Dam Busters*. He and Richard Todd had to walk down the centre aisle of the briefing-room while we watched. They stood chatting, just out of camera range, until the director called for action. Then they walked. Richard Todd was just Richard Todd in Air Force uniform, but Michael Redgrave had within seconds, transformed himself into a different character. He *was* Barnes Wallis. He may or may not have looked like the real man, but he was the Barnes Wallis of the script, and he had obliterated all trace of the personality of Michael Redgrave as though by a sudden act of will.

REDGRAVE, Vanessa. On one of the two Aldermaston marches in which I participated, in 1960 and 1961, I marched under the British Theatre banner, alongside Peggy Ashcroft, Vanessa Redgrave, Miles Malleson, Mai Zetterling and many others. 'Good old Alfie,' someone amongst the onlookers shouted as we went past. Vanessa turned to Alfie Bass and remarked sourly, 'You're popular with the mob, aren't you?'

REES, Roger. After we had seen him play Hamlet at Stratford, Roger mentioned over supper that, at a matinée the previous week, he had come on stage and begun the soliloquy, 'To be or not to be', when he heard a woman in the front stalls say, earnestly to her neighbour, 'Yes, that is the question.'

SASSOON, Siegfried. In 1966, the year in which Siegfried Sassoon celebrated his eightieth birthday, a group of his friends and admirers, among them W. H. Auden, John Betjeman, Cecil Day Lewis, Roy Fuller, Robert Graves, Ted Hughes, Philip Larkin, John Lehmann, myself, Herbert Read and Eric Walter White, organized the private publication of a group of eight of his recent poems, under the title, *An Octave*. I supervised the printing of the volume by the Shenval Press, and on 8 September, Sassoon's birthday, Eric White and I drove down to Heytesbury, in Wiltshire, to present the poet with 100 of the 350 copies we had printed. (The remaining copies went to the 250 subscribers we had found no difficulty in assembling.)

It was a fine day. I drove, and Eric provided a picnic lunch, which we enjoyed at Stonehenge. We arrived at Sassoon's large manor house in time for tea. There was a cake, with candles, and there was the poet reclining on a chaise longue, spruce and un-eightyish. He told us amusing stories of Max Beerbohm and others, and recalled that he had written his memoirs, *Siegfried's Journey*, with more than twenty American Army officers occupying the upstairs rooms at Heytesbury, and an armed sentry on duty. When I asked him what he thought of today's younger poets, he said, 'For a time they wrote stuff you couldn't understand, but I believe they've given that up now.'

SAYERS, Dorothy L. In March 1955 she came to a performance of Sophocles' *Philoctetes* in which I and two other actors were the Chorus. It was a freezing winter's night, and the streets were covered in snow. After the performance, Miss Sayers, a large, butch lady, came backstage. With a glance at my costume, a very skimpy loincloth, she said to me, 'I imagine your balls must be freezing.' It was not the kind of remark I expected from the author of the religious play, *The Man Born to be King*, which was to be our next production at the Theatre Centre.

We performed *Philoctetes* in a modern translation by E. F. Watling. On the first night, when I suffered a loss of memory in the middle of one of my speeches, I managed not to reveal this to the audience. Our director, Brian Way, congratulated me: 'That's the first time I've heard an actor successfully improvise for several lines in impeccable blank verse.'

SCHLESINGER, John. The famous film director was once a no more than moderately successful actor at the same time that I was attempting to earn a living in the theatre. John's hobby was photography, and he used to earn money between theatre engagements by taking actors' photographs for their publicity portfolios. His flattering photographs of me, tastefully autographed in pencil by the photographer, got me a number of interviews with casting directors.

SCHWARZKOPF, Elisabeth. When I first heard her sing, in Brisbane in 1950, I was taken backstage to meet her after the performance and found myself roped in to help her patch her music together with Sellotape. In Vienna a few years later I thought her a thrilling Donna Elvira, an enchanting Countess in *Capriccio*, and, in Salzburg, a near-perfect Fiordiligi (with Christa Ludwig as Dorabella). I always attended her *Lieder* recitals, loved her in Strauss, Brahms and Wolf, but thought her far too mannered for Schubert. Towards the end of her career, she kept letting it be understood that her next recital would be her last. Consequently, when she finally did announce her real farewell recital in London, in the old St Pancras Town Hall, it was not well attended. I said at the time that it was because she had cried Wolf too often.

SERKIN, Rudolf. Many years ago, Rudolf Serkin told me how strongly he agreed with me in distrusting the concept of 'interpretation'. He simply played the notes on the page, he said. We went on to talk of another pianist's performance of Schumann's *Carnaval*, and I mentioned how beautifully gentle it was. Serkin murmured, 'I see it as a rather daemonic work.' He played it the following day at the Festival Hall, and daemonic it most assuredly was. I now have a healthy respect for interpretation.

In 1985 I dedicated to him, 'most Schubertian of musicians', my book on Schubert and Vienna, and was rewarded with an affectionate hug. At eighty-three, he is the last of the great classical pianists of his generation, survivors of pre-Second World War Europe. There are pianists and there are musicians. Rudolf Serkin is a musician.

SEXTON, Anne. I did not have good luck with Anne Sexton. When I invited her to share a platform with W. H. Auden at a Poetry International performance, Wystan was rude to her because he found her poems boring ('Who the hell cares about Anne Sexton's grandmother?') and because she read them for about twice as long as we had asked her to. Backstage afterwards, he contrived to reduce her to tears, and left me to console her, which, since I wasn't all that keen on her, was distinctly unkind of him.

In Boston, where she lived, I rang her when I was in town for a few days to give a poetry reading at Harvard, and we arranged to meet for lunch. On the morning of the day on which we were to meet, I read in my newspaper that she had killed herself. I was really so out of sympathy with the lady that I remember thinking it was an extreme measure for her to take simply to avoid a lunch date.

SHAFFER, Peter. I have a reputation, second only to that of my ex-colleague at the Arts Council, Richard Pulford, for walking out of shows well before the interval if I am bored. I think that Richard must now take second place to me, for I surpassed myself at Peter Shaffer's *Yonadab* at the Olivier Theatre. Ever since *Five Finger Exercise*, I have recognized Shaffer for what he is: a women's romantic writer masquerading as an innovative playwright. Under the trappings of technique there lurks the mind of a Georgette Heyer. As I sat waiting for *Yonadab* to begin, staring at the stage set, a huge carton with Hebrew letters all over it like a Jewish Christmas box, I realized I was unlikely to enjoy the play. (I was present only out of duty, as an Arts Council

Director.) As the lights lowered for the play to begin, I whispered to my companion, 'This isn't going to be any fun. Let's go and have a decent supper instead.'

We made our way past a group of four men standing at the back of the stalls. Recognizing one of them as Peter Shaffer, who was looking surprised to see two members of his audience leaving before the performance had begun, I decided not to creep sheepishly past him. Giving the playwright what I hope was a warm, friendly smile, I whispered to him, 'We're escaping early.' It took him a moment or two to find words. As I passed out of the exit door, I heard him murmur, 'So I see.'

SHAW, George Bernard. As a worshipper at the shrine of reason, I admit George Bernard Shaw and a few others to my calendar of saints. Shaw's plays are *sui generis*, not to be compared with what one normally thinks of as plays. Elsewhere, his prose is beautiful, his mind sharp, his music and drama criticism both brilliant and funny. When I was a teenager I wrote to Shaw, in the hope that I would get one of those postcards which I could display proudly on my desk. I did get a reply to some silly question I had asked concerning *Candida*, in which I was about to play Marchbanks. It was kind and understanding; it must have disappeared in a fire which carried off all the papers I left in Australia.

SINDEN, Donald. At the time of writing Donald is a member of the Arts Council, where he has brightened many an otherwise tedious meeting. During a recent discussion in which others got rather carried away with the idea of providing access to our subsidized theatres for the disabled, and suggestions were being made that certain historic theatres should be compelled to modify themselves architecturally, Donald exclaimed, 'The Eiffel Tower presents certain difficulties for those suffering from vertigo.' Common sense was immediately, if temporarily, restored.

SITWELL, Dame Edith. One day in 1960 she told me how pleased she was that I had a novel about to appear. 'But I haven't,' I informed her. 'You have, I've read the opening chapters in an Australian magazine,' she said. I was forced to admit that, when asked by Australian magazines for short stories, I found it convenient to describe anything I sent them as 'the opening of a novel in progress', because I found it difficult to bring my stories to a conclusion, and that way I could keep my options open.

Edith had a penchant for unusual pets. When I told her I had acquired a female tortoise, she insisted I call it Edith. When later I was given a male, I named it Osbert without asking permission of either her or Sir Osbert.

SPENCE, Sir Basil. The architect of that housing-estate church, Coventry Cathedral, Sir Basil Spence drove me back to London after the first performance of Britten's *War Requiem* on the occasion of the cathedral's consecration. I did not know Sir Basil or Lady Spence: it was Cynthia Nolan who cajoled them into giving me a lift back to London. The Spences seemed a pleasant and friendly couple, he easily overawed by others ('That was a very distinguished gathering,' he said of the party we had just left), and both of them ignorant of and not at all interested in music. Spence told me pleasant stories about sitting for Epstein, and recounted a story Epstein had told him of Shaw sitting for the sculptor, and taking all his clothes off. 'Put your clothes on, man,' Epstein had ordered the playwright. 'You're far too skinny.'

SPENDER, Stephen. We first met in 1954 when Stephen was co-editor of *Encounter.* Derek Patmore had shown him some of my poems and Stephen had expressed an interest in meeting me. I made an appointment to see him in his *Encounter* office, which was then in Panton Street, a few yards from the Haymarket. I was a shy young poet, about to meet one of the most famous of living poets. He had been one of that select group whose work I read voraciously at school. The others were Eliot, Auden, Day Lewis and MacNeice. In time I was to know them all personally, but Stephen was the first, and I really did feel very nervous as I was shown into his office.

He rose from behind his desk to shake hands with me. Goodness, how tall. But what a limp handshake. Oh well, he's English. We sat. I waited for him to speak. He waited for me to speak. The silence was not electric. Eventually, since someone was going to have to say something, I stammered, 'It was very good of you to see me.'

'Oh, not at all.' He *could* speak, then. His voice was soft, pleasant. He was looking at me expectantly, but I didn't know what he expected. The silence returned. Again, when it seemed clear that he did not intend any further utterance, I said, 'Derek Patmore tells me you liked my poems.' I felt like a desperate prompter with a completely dried-up actor.

'Yes, I did,' Stephen replied.

Another pause. The admission was not about to be amplified. The thought occurred to me that perhaps he considered me brash to be talking about my poems – perhaps I should have been speaking of something else. The plight of the author in modern society? It was too late. I found myself continuing what must have seemed to him like a relentless cross-examination. 'Which did you like best?' I asked.

'Oh, I liked all of them.'

I gave up, and offered a re-statement of my opening theme: 'It was very good of you to see me.'

He smiled. I stood up. He remained seated at his desk, his look still expectant. I made my way to the door. As I was fumbling with the handle, he got up and loped to the door, where he stood, looming over me. The limp hand was extended again. 'I've so enjoyed meeting you,' said the distinguished poet and editor.

Over the years we have come to know each other a little better. Stephen severed his links with *Encounter* when it became publicly known that the magazine had been receiving subsidy from the CIA. Almost everyone I knew had for years assumed this to be the case, but Stephen declared in angry letters to the press that he had not been told, and that he considered he had been manipulated by his co-editor, Melvin Lasky.

In 1970, when Gerald Hamilton died, I found myself phoning his friends and acquaintances to ask them to help me pay for his funeral. I think that Christopher Isherwood, John Lehmann and one or two others contributed £20 each. When I rang Stephen and asked him for £20, he said it was a bad month for him, he was short of cash, of course he would try to help if I couldn't raise the money elsewhere, but at the moment . . . I said I understood, and was about to hang up when Stephen added, 'Charles, if it had been for Melvin Lasky I'd have willingly paid a hundred pounds.'

STEINER, George. I've never met him, but he's fun to tease. I first got under his skin when *Encounter* published, in June 1982, the following self-explanatory letter by me:

> In his article on George Steiner's morally obnoxious, intellectually spurious and aesthetically poor Hitler novella [*The Portage to San Cristobal of A.H.*] (*Encounter*, May), Hyam Macoby refers to Steiner as 'the accomplished linguist, the scholarly semanticist, the connoisseur of literary styles'.
>
> The first of these Steiner may well be, but certainly neither the second nor the third. A semanticist and stylist would, surely, be aware of the difference in meaning between 'infer' and 'imply'. 'I am not, God knows, inferring any comparison between such precedents and my small novel': quote from Steiner.

In March 1984, I attended the PEN Writers' Day lectures on the South Bank. In the morning, Angus Wilson spoke on Angus Wilson, and George

Steiner's subject was 'The Home Ground Under Siege'. After lunch, there was a discussion of the morning's lectures, in the course of which I felt moved to comment on, indeed to deplore, Steiner's reference to Philip Larkin. Steiner had castigated Philip for having admitted his ignorance of Borges, an ignorance which Steiner thought quite shocking in its provincialism. I tried to explain to him that, though it was no doubt important for us readers to be aware of, for example, Borges, it was crass and philistine of Steiner to imagine that it was important for a major poet to be aware of anything which he did not feel would contribute to his own poetic development. It was more 'important', I said, for Philip Larkin to write like Philip Larkin than to satisfy Steiner by dutifully swotting up on all the right names in world literature.

I invited Steiner to discuss this, but he seemed unable to grasp the issue, evaded my point, and merely spluttered something abusive: 'Mr Osborne can't have been listening. His mind is no doubt on more important matters. As in so much of his published work, he is beside the point.' It was oddly ferocious, and not, to put it mildly, one of the good Doctor's more impressive or articulate performances.

Stephen Spender, who had been sitting next to me, missed most of this. As Steiner rose to speak, Stephen had muttered, 'Here's the cut-rate Isaiah Berlin,' and fled. A letter Stephen wrote me some weeks later began: 'It was nice seeing you at the luncheon, intoxicated by the fumes of George Steiner.'

STOCKWOOD, Mervyn, Bishop of Southwark. At a party at the *Observer*, he assured me that, as Bishop of Southwark, he was authorized to ordain other bishops. As I was living in Battersea at the time, I asked if he would ordain me Bishop of Battersea, and this he obligingly agreed to do. I am not sure if the ordination was supposed to 'take' on the spot, but in the absence of evidence to the contrary I consider myself still to be the Bishop of Battersea.

SUTHERLAND, Dame Joan. Joan and Richard Bonynge are both old friends, and artists for whom I have the greatest admiration. Joan's voice, given by the good Lord or whomever, and helped by Richard to acquire its technique, is a phenomenon, but Joan is much more than a good-natured woman with a phenomenal voice. She is a musician of acute intuitive intelligence, and her interpretations (all achieved and conveyed through the voice) of Donizetti, Bellini and Verdi are high on my list of things that make life worth living.

Acting in opera is an art which not a great many people understand.

It is very different from acting in the non-musical theatre, for it relies much more on the voice and comparatively less on the *plastique du rôle*. Most people would have considered Maria Callas a better actress than Joan Sutherland, and indeed Callas's Violetta in *La traviata* was very intelligently acted. But it was, to me, completely unmoving. Joan Sutherland, on the other hand, by virtue of standing still and singing the part so beautifully, moved me to tears. Whose, then, was the more effective performance?

TAUBER, Richard. He was one of the idols of my boyhood and youth, a great *Lieder* singer, a superb Mozartian, and the possessor of an immediately identifiable voice whose timbre could both excite and console. I was a child when I first heard him sing Schubert, Schumann and Grieg in recitals when he toured Australia; I was hitch-hiking from Brisbane to Melbourne when I heard the news of his death on 8 January 1948 in a London hospital; and amongst my Tauber memorabilia there is, hanging above my desk, a portrait of Franz Lehár which the composer presented to his favourite tenor. The inscription, in Lehár's hand, reads: '*Zigeunerliebe, Frasquita, Paganini, Zarewitsch, Friederike, Land des Lächelns, und was noch folgen wird – alles ist Dir gewidmet, mein lieber einziger Richard!* Berlin 10/10, 1929. Franz.' ('*Gypsy Love, Frasquita, Paganini, Zarewitch, Frederica, Land of Smiles*, and what is to follow them – all are dedicated to you, my dear unique Richard!')

THESIGER, Ernest. Ernest complained to Somerset Maugham, 'Willie, you used to write lovely roles for me in your plays, and now you've stopped doing so.' 'Not at all, Ernest, dear,' Maugham replied. 'I still write them for you, but Gladys Cooper plays them.'

TYNAN, Kenneth. One Sunday evening in 1957 I went with Colin Wilson to the Royal Court Theatre to see the only performance of a play, *The Tenth Chance*, by his chum Stuart Holroyd. Before the show, we had a drink at the pub next door, where Colin introduced me to John Osborne, who thought he'd met me before (disingenuous creature). I have now totally forgotten the play, which was generally agreed at the time to be a load of old rubbish, but I remember the extra-theatrical events of the evening. The first was that, during the interval, I avoided shaking hands with Sir Oswald Mosley, whom Stuart had invited to the performance. The other events are interconnected. During a particularly turgid scene in the second half of the play, a rather gravelly voice in the stalls shouted 'Rubbish'. I thought for a moment that the play had begun to improve, with the author refuting his own arguments from the stalls, but then a female voice called out, 'Get out of this theatre, Christopher Logue.'

Somehow the play limped to its conclusion. Colin, his girl-friend and I then made our way back to the pub next door, whither practically the entire audience had preceded us. As he entered Colin caught sight of Christopher Logue, who was sitting at a table drinking with Ken Tynan. Colin went across to him, and I followed. (*'Que diable est-ce que je fais dans cette galère?'* I wondered). To my horror Colin took a swipe at Logue, knocking him off his chair. I attempted to drag Colin off Christopher, whereupon everyone suddenly wanted to join in the act. While I was still trying to separate Colin and Christopher, Ken Tynan tapped me angrily on the shoulder. 'Leave him alone, you fascist bully,' he shouted. Meanwhile, John Osborne had retreated to the bar, on which he sat, gaily uncommitted, dangling his long legs, sipping his gin and calling out, 'Carry on, chaps.' An excitable little Cockney playwright called Michael Hastings jumped onto a table, shouting 'Get fucked, you bastards,' to nobody in particular.

The *Daily Express* next morning splashed the story across its front page, under the heading, 'Angry Young Men fight it out in bar.'

VAIZEY, Lord. To the best of my knowledge I never met John Vaizey, though I used to encounter his wife Marina at Arts Council meetings. The noble Lord himself came to my attention when I was informed by other members of a Garrick Club membership committee on which Vaizey sat that, when my name came up for consideration, he had blackballed me. I ought, I suppose, to have been grateful to him, for, essentially unclubbable, I had never really wanted to join the Garrick or any other club, but had allowed my name to go forward in order to avoid offending the friends who wanted to sponsor me. (The last club people tried to persuade me to join was the Groucho, but you would have to be a masochist to join a club where you were likely all the time to run into Carmen Callil, one of its founder-members.) Oddly, however, I felt little gratitude to Vaizey, which is, I suppose, why I took the opportunity, when it afforded itself some time later, to tease him.

The opportunity arose as I was sitting in a reading room on the first floor of the Garrick, awaiting a member with whom I was to have lunch. I picked up a copy of *The Illustrated London News*, carried it to my armchair, and was about to browse through it when my attention was caught by a piece of paper stapled to the magazine. On the paper was a typed message from the Club Secretary: 'Will the member who habitually removes this periodical from the premises kindly refrain from doing so in future.' Some angry and frustrated member had scrawled an addition: 'Or resign!'

Taking out my biro, I malevolently added a note of my own. 'This person,' I wrote, 'has now been identified as Lord Vaizey.'

VAUGHAN, Keith. I first met Keith in the late 1950s, through John Lehmann. I used occasionally to dine with him and his friend Ramsay McClure at their flat in Belsize Park, and to meet Keith at parties. In 1977 Keith killed himself to avoid a more painful and prolonged dying from cancer.

Many years after his death, excerpts from Keith's journals were published in *The London Magazine.* In the entry for Wednesday, 20 March 1973, I read:

> Reading in the Gide-Valéry correspondence. They met in 1890 both about 21. Rimbaud died the next year. Cézanne and Picasso were painting. What an age to be alive in. Of course there may be circles of similar quality of intelligence today, but if so I do not know them. The nearest I get is a dinner party with John Lehmann, Roy Fuller and Charles Osborne – which is not very near.

WESKER, Arnold. We were on a public platform, somewhere, debating burning issues of the day with an audience. Arnold began to hold forth about the terrible unfairness of drama critics reviewing a play on its very first public performance, before it had a chance of running itself in smoothly. 'The first night of a play,' he declared, 'should be much later, towards the end of the run.'

'In your case, Arnold, it almost invariably is,' I said.

WHITE, Patrick. I hope I have made it clear elsewhere in these pages that I regard Patrick as a great novelist. In my view he has no equal among living writers. *Voss* is generally thought to be his masterpiece, but I think that *Riders in the Chariot*, though flawed, is an even more impressive achievement. He has also written some extremely literate and entertaining plays. So one must allow him, I suppose, to be a pretty impossible character. He has quarrelled with friends across the years. Sidney Nolan and I remained close to him longer than most, but when Patrick wrote foully about Sidney in his memoirs, *Flaws in the Glass*, in 1981, that was the end of his friendship with Nolan and, I suppose, with me.

I reviewed *Flaws in the Glass* for the *Financial Times* (and was interviewed about the book by the BBC's World Service), and could not avoid commenting on Patrick's ill-considered paragraphs on Nolan.

I realized that my long-standing friendship with Patrick might not survive what I wrote and broadcast about his memoirs. 'Under the style of the great novelist,' I said, 'there lurks the soul of a New South Wales grazier.' I regretted deeply that I was probably losing Patrick as a friend. But, in loyalty to Sidney, whose friendship has endured for forty years, I could not do otherwise. I must consider myself fortunate (and rare) to have known Patrick for as long as I did without quarrelling with him. It took great self-control on my part not to fight with him during the week I was his house-guest in Sydney in 1973, for I found him very provocative.

It was in the autumn of 1973 that Patrick was awarded the Nobel Prize for Literature. He did not want to travel from Australia to Stockholm, so he was grateful when Sidney offered to attend the Nobel ceremony in Stockholm and accept the prize on his behalf. After the ceremony, Sidney phoned Patrick. I understand the conversation went something like this:

Nolan: Patrick, I'm calling you from Stockholm. It's very cold, and everything is covered with snow.
White: It sounds awful.
Nolan: I attended the ceremony, and was presented to the King of Sweden –
White: I'm an anti-monarchist now, I think those people are outmoded and irrelevant.
Nolan: There were speeches about you by –
White: How ghastly.
Nolan: No, the occasion was actually rather splendid. In fact –
White: I can't stand all that stuff.

Finally a defeated and depressed Nolan hung up.

I used to review Patrick's novels for English newspapers and magazines, the *Sunday Times*, the *Times Literary Supplement* and the like. My reviews were always favourable, but there were, of course, occasions when I felt the need to be critical of something or other. I used to sweat over those passages in my reviews. For Patrick, praise had to be total and unqualified. When Paul Bailey give him a less than completely favourable review in the *Observer*, Patrick wrote to me as though I bore some responsibility for it: 'What about your little friend Pearl Bailey in the *Observer?* His use of one word in particular made me guess that Clive James had a finger in it. I expect the *Observer* will have cast me out for the duration of the ubiquitous Clive's reign. *Tant pis!* He will bite the dust.'

Months later he was still going on about the *Observer*: 'At last I have seen a photograph of Clive James – he's a mandrill, not a man. I am now investigating other members of the entourage such as Christopher Wordsworth and Russell Davies.'

Patrick was forever threatening to leave Australia with his Greek friend Manoly ('but not until the dogs are dead') and settle in England. On the other hand, whenever he was in London he professed to prefer Sydney. *'Dort,'* as the minor German romantic poet wrote, *'wo du nicht bist, dort ist das Glück'* ('Where you are not, there is happiness').

WILLIAMS, Kenneth. When I interviewed him in front of an audience on the South Bank, Kenneth thought it would make an amusing change if, instead of my introducing him to the audience, he went on first, alone, and introduced me. I agreed, and he walked onto the stage while I lurked in the wings. When he was greeted with applause, he responded by telling funny stories, and I feared I would spend the entire hour and a half sulking off-stage. But at last I heard Kenneth exhorting the audience to 'give a warm welcome to the world's greatest authority on Verdi, Mr Charles Osborne'. I walked on, and got a laugh by thanking Kenneth for being such an excellent warm-up man. Later I asked him if the story was true that, when she was invited to appear in a play with him, Dame Edith Evans had replied, in her inimitably idiosyncratic tones, 'But I couldn't possibly act with Kenneth Williams – he has such an extraordinary voice.' It was true.

WILLIAMS, Tennessee. We met in 1958, during my *London Magazine* days. Tennessee, who had just given us a new story for the magazine, was staying at Claridge's. He was finishing a play, *Sweet Bird of Youth*, and asked me if I could recommend someone to type a final draft. He needed it done in a hurry, so I volunteered to type it myself, which is how I came to find myself holed-up with Tennessee in his very small room at the back of the hotel, for two or three mornings. Usually, I typed while Tennessee strode about in his polka-dot underpants, snatching each page from me as I typed it, and making immediate alterations. I made some suggestions too, and can claim to have written, or at least to have contributed to, three or four of Chance's lines.

Tennessee wanted to pay me for my typing, but I said I preferred him to owe me a favour. When the time came, I'd remind him. He liked the idea of this, and agreed. But he also took me to dinner and gave me an inscribed copy of his recently published poems, *In the Winter of Cities.*

Nearly twelve years passed before I had occasion to remind him of the favour he owed me. I wrote to him, asking him to come and read his poems at the 1970 *Poetry International* for a fee of £50. He rang me from Key West, touched that I should have remembered his poems. 'No one else does,' he said. 'Do you really want me to come?' He came, and was the star of the show. However, he took some looking after, from the moment he rang me from Ireland, having got off the plane at Shannon by mistake, to his departure a couple of weeks later for, as he put it, 'sun and debauchery' in the Mediterranean.

WORTH, Irene. One day, many years ago, Irene invited me to lunch, saying she had a favour to ask of me. Towards the end of an agreeable meal in which we had gossiped about a number of mutual friends and acquaintances in the theatre, Irene revealed the nature of the help she sought from me. She had been invited to play Hedda Gabler in Canada, the following year, and she was dissatisfied with the existing English translations of the play. She wanted a young writer or poet to produce a new version for her, and so she had thought immediately of me.

'I'm flattered, of course, Irene,' I said immediately, 'but I must tell you right away that I'd have to say no. I'm somewhat behind with the book I'm writing at present, and my publishers are leaning on me. And I have another book already contracted, which I must begin to write as soon as –'

Irene looked appalled. 'Oh, I don't expect *you* to do it,' she interrupted. 'I want you to recommend a *young* writer.'

YEVTUSHENKO, Yevgeny. We meet occasionally in London, where he is usually on his best behaviour. I cannot say the same for him in the Soviet Union. When I took him to a party in Moscow, given by the British cultural attaché, Zhenia made me help him steal four bottles of wine, which we smuggled out through the kitchen. We drove out into the country. When we were stopped, somewhere in the suburbs, by a policeman who claimed we had violated a traffic regulation, Zhenia thrust his head out of the window and was recognized by the policeman, who saluted us on our way. 'See,' exclaimed Zhenia, 'they all love me!' (I had to admit I couldn't see Ted Hughes getting away with that on the M4.) That was the night we later found ourselves drinking on the grave of Pasternak.

5

LEAVING FOR THE NEXT WORLD

□ □ □

EXTRACT FROM *THE TIMES*, 10 December 2010.

At a memorial luncheon at the Caprice Restaurant, held yesterday to celebrate the life of Charles Osborne, who died last week at the age of eighty-three, a number of his friends and former colleagues paid tribute to the writer and ex-Arts Council Director, and to the contribution he made to cultural life in Britain over a period of more than half a century.

Among those present were Lord Bragg (Chairman of the BBC, and one of Charles Osborne's oldest friends); Lord Sinden (Chairman of the Arts Council of Great Britain); Dame Pamela Ayres (Poet Laureate); Lord O'Mara, Publisher by Royal Appointment to King Charles and Queen Diana, and a lifelong friend and publisher of Mr Osborne (Lady O'Mara was abroad, selling translation rights in O'Mara books to a number of African nations); and Sir Kenneth Thomson, Head of the Independent Broadcasting Authority, and lifelong close friend and companion of Mr Osborne.

Dame Joan Sutherland, Mr Nicolai Gedda and Sir Richard Bonynge performed songs and arias by Verdi, Schubert and Lehár (the eighty-four-year-old diva, and the even older tenor, revealing themselves to be still in firm and youthful voice); and a message of sympathy was received from Her Majesty Queen Edna I of Australia (the former Dame Edna Everage), who was unable to be present, due to the constitutional crisis in her country, consequent upon the recent revelation, made by Lord Patterson, Prime Minister of Australia, that Dame Edna had, in fact, been a love child of King George VI of England.

The Prime Minister of Great Britain, Mr Tariq Ali, spoke movingly of his long friendship with Charles Osborne, who, he recalled, used years ago, during the rebellious 1960s to refer to him jocularly as 'The Chocolate Soldier'.

The Archbishop of Canterbury, Dame Iris Murdoch, recited by heart several poems by the Australian 19th-century bush poet, A. B. ('Banjo') Paterson.

Mr Auberon Waugh's attempt to escape from protective custody, in order to attend the memorial luncheon, unfortunately failed. Mr Frank Delaney tried to send his apologies, but had difficulty with the spelling and punctuation.

INDEX

□ □ □

Charles Osborne is referred to as CO. The entry under his name is divided into paragraphs: Life; Acting; Broadcasting; Music; Travels; Writing

Numbers in *italics* refer to illustrations

p. 199 – Auden & on poetry & politics.